Restoring *the* Vocation
of a Christian College

Restoring *the* Vocation *of a* Christian College

A Framework for Holistic Christian Education in a Post-Christian World

edited by
BRAD PARDUE
&
ANDREW T. BOLGER

WIPF & STOCK · Eugene, Oregon

RESTORING THE VOCATION OF A CHRISTIAN COLLEGE
A Framework for Holistic Christian Education in a Post-Christian World

Copyright © 2022 Wipf and Stock Publishers. All rights reserved. Except for brief quotations in critical publications or reviews, no part of this book may be reproduced in any manner without prior written permission from the publisher. Write: Permissions, Wipf and Stock Publishers, 199 W. 8th Ave., Suite 3, Eugene, OR 97401.

Wipf & Stock
An Imprint of Wipf and Stock Publishers
199 W. 8th Ave., Suite 3
Eugene, OR 97401

www.wipfandstock.com

PAPERBACK ISBN: 978-1-7252-9810-1
HARDCOVER ISBN: 978-1-7252-9811-8
EBOOK ISBN: 978-1-7252-9812-5

MAY 13, 2022 1:38 PM

Scripture quotations are from the ESV® Bible (The Holy Bible, English Standard Version®), copyright © 2001 by Crossway, a publishing ministry of Good News Publishers. Used by permission. All rights reserved.

Scripture quotations taken from the (NASB®) New American Standard Bible®, Copyright © 1960, 1971, 1977 1995, 2020 by The Lockman Foundation. Used by permission. All rights reserved. www.lockman.org.

Scripture quoted by permission. Quotations designated (NET) are from the NET Bible® copyright ©1996, 2019 by Biblical Studies Press, L.L.C. http://netbible.com. All rights reserved.

Scriptures taken from the Holy Bible, New International Version®, NIV®. Copyright © 1973, 1978, 1984, 2011 by Biblica, Inc.™ Used by permission of Zondervan. All rights reserved worldwide. www.zondervan.com The "NIV" and "New International Version" are trademarks registered in the United States Patent and Trademark Office by Biblica, Inc.™

Scripture taken from the New King James Version®. Copyright © 1982 by Thomas Nelson. Used by permission. All rights reserved.

Contents

Contributors | ix

Preface | xi
    Eric Bolger

Faithful Education: Christian Worldview, Character Formation, and Vocation | 1
    Brad Pardue

PART ONE
Faithful Education and the Christian College

1.   Faithful Administration | 27
    Eric W. Bolger

2.   Faithful, Narrative Student Development: Vocation and Virtue | 42
    Andrew T. Bolger

3.   Faithful Assessment | 53
    David Parrish

4.   A Portrait of the Faithful Professor | 67
    James M. Todd III

5.   Faithful Education and Healthy Community: Some Thoughts on Education for a Kingdom Perspective | 89
    Daniel Chinn

PART TWO
FAITHFUL EDUCATION ACROSS THE DISCIPLINES

Faithful Education in the Humanities

6   A Faithful Literary Education: *Mythos* and the "Theory of Everything" | 109
   DAVID PEDERSEN

7   Historical Thinking and Vocation | 125
   JOSEPH WESTERN

8   Faithful Foreign Language Instruction | 139
   WELLINGTON ESPINOSA

Faithful Education in the Social Sciences

9   A Faithful Attempt at Integrating Psychology and Christianity | 151
   JEFF ELLIOTT

10   Christian Worldview and the Helping Profession: Answering the Question of *Telos* and *Praxis* | 164
   TRACY J. BELL

11   A Faith-Filled Accounting Education | 184
   STEVEN FOWLER

Faithful Education in Mathematics and the Natural Sciences

12   Faithful Education in the Discipline of Human Biology | 199
   GABRIELA GALEY

13   Faithful Education in Mathematics | 215
   CRAIG L. HAILE

14   Faithful Science Education | 230
   BARBARA FENNELL

Faithful Education in the Creative Arts

15 Living Worship: How God's Revealed Story
    of Humanity Informs an Approach to
    Teaching in the Academic Disciplines | 247
    RICHARD W. CUMMINGS

16 Assuming a Posture of Care:
    The Role of Composition in Christian Formation | 263
    PAIGE A. RAY

17 The Study of Music and the Faithful Educator | 285
    CLARA CHRISTIAN

Faithful Education in the Professional Disciplines

18 The Teleology of Argument | 303
    GARY C. HIEBSCH

19 Faithful Education in Engineering | 321
    GEOFF AKERS

Afterword
    Show Me: The Way We Learn Forms the Way We Live | 335
    STEVEN GARBER

Appendix
    Thrive Pathway | 341

Contributors

Geoffrey Akers (Ph.D., P.E.), Professor of Engineering at College of the Ozarks.

Tracy Bell (M.S.W., L.C.S.W.), Assistant Professor of Family Studies and Social Services at College of the Ozarks.

Andrew T. Bolger (Ph.D.), Director of the Keeter Center for Character Education at College of the Ozarks.

Eric Bolger (Ph.D.), Vice President for Academic Affairs and Dean of the College & Professor of Biblical and Theological Studies at College of the Ozarks.

Daniel Chinn (D.Min.), Associate Professor of Biblical and Theological Studies at College of the Ozarks.

Clara Christian (D.M.A.), Associate Professor of Music at College of the Ozarks.

Richard Cummings (M.A.F.A, D.W.S.), Professor of Art at College of the Ozarks.

Jeff Elliott (Ph.D.), Professor of Psychology at College of the Ozarks.

Wellington Espinosa (M.S.), Associate Professor of Foreign Language at College of the Ozarks.

Barbara Fennell (Ed.D.), Associate Professor of Physics at College of the Ozarks.

Steven Fowler (M.S., C.P.A.), Assistant Professor of Accounting at College of the Ozarks.

Gabriela Galey (M.D.), Associate Professor of Biology at College of the Ozarks.

Craig Haile (Ph.D.), Director of Institutional Effectiveness and Professor of Mathematics at Avila University.

Gary Hiebsch (Ph.D.), Professor of Communication Arts at College of the Ozarks.

Brad Pardue (Ph.D.), Associate Professor of History at College of the Ozarks.

David Parrish (Ph.D.), Associate Professor of Humanities at College of the Ozarks.

David Pedersen (Ph.D.), Assistant Professor of Humanities at College of the Ozarks.

Paige Ray (M.A.T.), Associate Professor of English at College of the Ozarks.

James M. Todd III (Ph.D.), Associate Professor of Biblical and Theological Studies at College of the Ozarks.

Joseph Western (Ph.D.), Assistant Professor of History at College of the Ozarks.

Preface

Eric Bolger

THE QUESTION OF VOCATION is especially germane for a college that calls itself Christian. The institution that produced this book, College of the Ozarks, is a case in point. The College was founded in 1906 by a Presbyterian missionary. He founded what was then a high school to provide a tuition-free and distinctively Christian education for students in the impoverished Ozarks region of southern Missouri and northern Arkansas.[1] Students were expected to work on campus to help cover the cost of their education.

The College is now a four-year bachelor's degree-granting institution with a K-12 lab school, but the focus remains the same: providing a tuition-free Christian education for students who are willing to work. The mandatory work program makes the College distinctive but not unique—there are a handful of other work colleges in the United States. While the work program has remained central to the College's operation and mission, its commitment to a Christian education has been renewed over the past decade.

In 2012, the Dean of the College office began an effort to encourage faculty to wrestle with what it means to pursue their discipline in light of their (and *the*) Christian faith. To avoid some of the problems with "integration" language (i.e., the so-called "integration of faith and learning"), we chose a broader, more flexible term: *faithful education*. Newly-hired faculty would be required to read relevant materials and then write an

---

1. The stated mission of College of the Ozarks is "to provide the advantages of a Christian education for youth of both sexes, especially those found worthy, but who are without sufficient means to procure such training."

essay answering the question, "How can I faithfully educate students in my discipline?" These faculty members would receive a teaching course load reduction their first year. By August 1 after their first year of teaching, they would submit a Faithful Education Project (FEP) for review. They would also give a ten-minute presentation on their FEP to other faculty members.

After a few years, veteran faculty were tasked with preparing an FEP as part of their regular six-year professional review. Faculty members at the College have submitted well over one hundred FEPs over the past ten years. The current volume includes examples of new faculty and veteran faculty FEPs. Those included in this volume were chosen to provide the reader with examples of reflection on faithful education in a wide range of disciplines. These essays are arranged by the broader disciplinary perspective they embody: humanities, social sciences, math and natural science, creative arts, and professional studies. Most of the authors are current members of the faculty of College of the Ozarks.

Since faithful education extends beyond the classroom, we have also included essays on various topics relevant to higher education. These include faithful administration, faithful student development, faithful assessment of student learning, faithful professorship, and the relevance of community to the task of faithful education. Each of these essays is written by a practitioner. For example, the person who wrote the chapter on faithful assessment of student learning serves as the director of academic assessment at the College. The person who wrote about faithful student development is responsible for the College's character development initiative, called THRIVE.

While faculty members have benefited greatly from the FEPs, the broader goal is to faithfully educate students. To reach this goal, the College's general education program offers Christian worldview classes that bookend the core curriculum. Students take the first as freshmen and the second as seniors. The senior-level class requires students to write an essay on the true, good, and beautiful in their chosen field of study. Students writing this essay are encouraged to ask their professors about how they understand faithful education. Faculty members are encouraged to faithfully educate students throughout the College's curricula. The next frontier, so to speak, is to extend this emphasis on faithful education to the College's mandatory Work Education Program, which uses faculty and non-faculty supervisors. This frontier is described in the College's 2022–27 strategic plan.

It is our hope and prayer that this book will provide a resource for faculty, administration, and students at other Christian institutions. It is noteworthy that College of the Ozarks is not denominational or focused on a particular theological perspective. It is broadly Protestant and Evangelical, with some Roman Catholic faculty members. This breadth is reflected in the essays contained within this volume.

Faithful Education
Christian Worldview, Character Formation, and Vocation

BRAD PARDUE

SINCE ITS ESTABLISHMENT IN 1906, College of the Ozarks has centered its mission on providing students "an intentionally Christian education."[1] Although the College has avoided the gradual process of secularization that has steadily eroded the religious identity of many historically-Christian American institutions of higher learning, our efforts to provide a robust Christian education have still played out in the midst of what Charles Taylor has called "a secular age."[2] Taylor's work demonstrates that the very "conditions of belief" in Western society have changed as we have moved from "a society where belief in God is unchallenged and indeed unproblematic, to one in which it is understood to be one option among others, and frequently not the easiest to embrace."[3] These developments have profound consequences for both us as faculty and for our students.

---

1. College of the Ozarks, *2020–2021 College Catalog*, 6. The institution was founded as School of the Ozarks, a residential high school, by the Reverend James Forsythe and the Missouri Synod of the Presbyterian Church in 1906. It became a junior college in 1956 and then received accreditation as a four-year, liberal arts college in 1971. In 1990, the Board of Trustees approved a resolution changing the institution's name to College of the Ozarks. For more on the history of the College, see Davis, *Miracle in the Ozarks*, and Godsey and Godsey, *Flight of the Phoenix*.

2. For further discussion of some of these long-term trends, see Ringenberg, *Christian College*. Charles Taylor's magnum opus is *A Secular Age*.

3. Taylor, *Secular Age*, 3. For more on Taylor and his ideas and influence, see Smith, *How (Not) To Be Secular*, and Hanson, *Secular Age*.

Fortunately, several generations of educators and scholars have worked tirelessly to think through what authentic Christian higher education should look like, both in theory and practice, in our current cultural context. From Arthur Holmes's *The Idea of a Christian College*, first published more than forty years ago, to David Smith's recent *On Christian Teaching*, an ever-growing literature is available to inform our work at Christian colleges and universities.[4] Despite the challenges that we face, there are many reasons for confidence that Christian educators and institutions can fulfill their missions.[5] Indeed, Perry Glanzer, Nathan Alleman, and Todd Ream have argued that Christian colleges and universities can counteract the fragmentation of the modern multiversity by remaining grounded in "an overarching identity and story with a substantive vision of the good, the true, and the beautiful" and perhaps they can even "save the university's soul."[6]

The various essays included in this volume—representing the experiences and perspectives of college administrators, cocurricular staff, and faculty from across the disciplines—explore the ways in which College of the Ozarks has sought to preserve its institutional "soul" and provide a well-rounded Christian education to its students, what we here at the College call "faithful education."[7] Steven Garber has written about the importance of helping students become people who "are connecting what they believe with the way they live in and through their vocations."[8] This statement concisely conveys three emphases that have emerged in College of the Ozarks' approach and which will serve as the primary lenses for framing the chapters that follow: Christian worldview, character formation, and vocation.

All three of these lenses are reflected in the language of the *Educational Philosophy* of the College. In terms of worldview, we affirm that "In Jesus Christ all knowledge is integrated and whole—there are not many

---

4 Holmes, *Idea of a Christian College*; Smith, *Christian Teaching*.

5. Joeckel and Chesnes, *Christian College Phenomenon*; Schmalzbaur and Mahoney, *Resilience of Religion in American Higher Education*.

6. Glanzer et al., *Restoring the Soul of the University*, 6, 10.

7. Like Glanzer, Alleman, and Ream, I am using "the term 'soul' as merely shorthand for a university's core identity, story, and mission" (Glanzer et al., *Restoring the Soul of the University*, 13). The earliest use of the word "faithful" to describe Christian education of which I am aware is in an essay by Nicholas Wolterstorff entitled "The Christian College and Christian Learning" from 1987, republished in Wolterstorff, *Educating for Shalom*, 106.

8. Garber, *Visions of Vocation*, 28.

disconnected disciplines but one God-created reality through which the one God reveals himself consistently in many places and ways."[9] We also recognize that education is about more than just knowledge and content, it is also about character formation—"faithful education shapes the hands and heart as well as the head" and "at the center of the educational experience [is] the formation of each student's heart."[10] Finally, we believe that Christian education is about preparing students "to be effective in whatever vocation God calls them to . . . good citizens, spouses, parents, workers, and community members."[11]

Although this language and these themes are in many ways the product of organic developments in the history of our own institution, they are probably familiar to those working at other colleges and universities and they also intersect with and embody ideas and insights in the growing literature on Christian education noted above, such as Steven Garber's categories of "convictions, character, and community."[12] The rest of this introduction will survey some of the most significant recent work on worldview, character formation, and vocation, and the profound connections between these essential aspects of faithful Christian education. The chapters that follow will then apply these concepts in specific academic spheres and disciplinary contexts. Although we certainly do not claim to have all the answers, we hope that readers will discover valuable resources and practical models as they learn more about the work we are doing here at College of the Ozarks to faithfully educate our students.

---

9. College of the Ozarks, *2020–2021 College Catalog*, 58.
10. College of the Ozarks, *2020–2021 College Catalog*, 58–59.
11. College of the Ozarks, *2020–2021 College Catalog*, 59.
12. Garber, *Fabric of Faithfulness*, 51. Garber elaborates, "Convictions: they were taught a worldview which was sufficient for the questions and crises of the next twenty years, particularly the challenges of modern and postmodern consciousness with its implicit secularization and pluralization. Character: They met a teacher who incarnated the worldview which they were coming to consciously identity as their own, and in and through that relationship they saw that it was possible to reside within that worldview themselves. Community: They made choices over the years to live out their worldview in the company of mutually committed folk who provided a framework of stimulation and support which showed that the ideas could be coherent across the whole of life" (Garber, *Fabric of Faithfulness*, 51–52).

CHRISTIAN WORLDVIEW

In what has become a classic text on the nature and purpose of Christian education, Arthur Holmes argued in *The Idea of a Christian College* for "the basic conviction that Christian perspectives can generate a worldview large enough to give meaning to all the disciplines and delights of life and to the whole of a liberal arts education."[13] Like many other evangelical institutions and educators in the more than forty years since Holmes first penned those words, we here at College of the Ozarks have found the concept of "Christian worldview" extremely fruitful. At the end of their first year at the College, all new faculty members craft and submit an essay reflecting on what it means to teach their discipline through the lens of a Christian worldview.[14] Likewise, our General Education Program is framed by two Christian Worldview courses, which provide the essential context in which students experience the rest of the GE curriculum.[15]

So, what is a worldview? James Sire provides the following helpful definition: "a worldview is a commitment, a fundamental orientation of the heart, that can be expressed as a story or in a set of propositions (assumptions which may be true, partially true or entirely false) which we hold (consciously or subconsciously, consistently or inconsistently) about the basic constitution of reality, and that provides the foundation on which we live and move and have our being."[16] By keeping in mind the nuances of Sire's definition we can avoid some of the potential shortcomings of less robust conceptions of worldview, but more on that in a moment.

The term worldview is derived from the German *Weltanschauung*, originating in the works of nineteenth-century philosophers such as Immanuel Kant, "who argued that human perception is shaped by

---

13. Holmes, *Idea of a Christian College*, 10.

14. These Faithful Education Projects (FEPs) were the genesis for many of the chapters that follow in this volume.

15. BTS 103 Christian Worldview I provides, "An introduction to the concept of worldview, with a special focus on understanding and practicing a Christian worldview rooted in the overarching biblical narrative of Creation, Sin, and Restoration, and the development of Christ-like character," while BTS 4003 Christian Worldview II focuses on, "A continuing examination of the concept of worldview, with comparative analysis of a Christian worldview and other prevalent worldviews . . ." (College of the Ozarks, *2020–2021 College Catalog*, 216, 219).

16. Sire, *Naming the Elephant*, 122.

preexisting mental categories."[17] Søren Kierkegaard would use the concept in his writings to refer to "the fundamental perspective that undergirds a person's self-understanding and gave unity to thought and action."[18] It would be Reformed thinkers in the late nineteenth and early twentieth centuries, particularly the Dutch Calvinist theologian and statesman Abraham Kuyper, who would appropriate the term and systematically describe the basic assumptions of a Christian worldview in contrast to other worldviews.[19] Francis Schaeffer's writings in the 1960s further popularized the concept, particularly among evangelicals.[20]

Gene Edward Veith has pointed out that the notion of *Weltanschauung* also continues to play a central role in many modern secular intellectual trends, even when the term worldview is not used explicitly. In his words, "The Weltanschauung of the philosophers was taken over by the cultural anthropologists, who became more and more interested in describing and analyzing cultural worldviews. Historians of science, such as Thomas Kuhn, pointed out how scientific progress consists of the construction of explanatory paradigms, and how those paradigms keep shifting. Postmodernists began insisting that perception, knowledge, and truth itself is culturally conditioned."[21] In the midst of this intellectual landscape, Christians can confidently affirm, "Neutrality on matters of belief and value is humanly impossible. Objectivity consists rather in acknowledging and scrutinizing one's point of view and testing presuppositions."[22]

Susan VanZanten distinguishes between two different ways of approaching the concept of worldview, the "foundational" and the "narrative." The former emphasizes "the cognitive, intellectual, propositional nature of one's perspective on life."[23] Advocates of this approach

17. Veith, "Reading and Writing Worldviews," 119.

18. Ryken, *Christian Worldview*, 24. For more on Kierkegaard, see Backhouse, *Kierkegaard*.

19. See, for example, Kuyper's *Christianity: A Total World and Life System*, based on his 1898 L.P. Stone Lectures. For more on Kuyper's life and thought, refer to Mouw, *Abraham Kuyper*.

20. Noll, *Scandal of the Evangelical Mind*, 223.

21. Veith, "Reading and Writing Worldviews," 121. For a classic example of how cultural historians have engaged the concept of worldview, see Darnton, *Great Cat Massacre*, 37, 261.

22. Holmes, *Idea of a Christian College*, 71. This insight is developed even further in Smith, *Who's Afraid of Postmodernism?*

23. VanZanten, *Joining the Mission*, 115.

often compare a Christian worldview with other worldviews, religions, or philosophies. This is the organizing principle, for example, of Mary Poplin's *Is Reality Secular?: Testing the Assumptions of Four Global Worldviews*.[24] Several of the essays in this volume explore the ways in which the underlying assumptions of various academic fields are often grounded in worldviews at odds with the beliefs that Christians affirm.

Meanwhile, the latter approach "defines worldview not in propositional but in narrative terms" arising directly "from the basic dramatic plot of Scripture: creation, fall, redemption."[25] In the words of Timothy Keller and Katherine Alsdorf, "Narratives are actually so foundational to how we think that they determine how we understand and live life itself. The term 'worldview' . . . means the comprehensive perspective from which we interpret all of reality. But a worldview is not merely a set of philosophical bullet points. It is essentially a master narrative, a fundamental story about (a) what human life in the world should be like, (b) what has knocked it off balance, and (c) what can be done to make it right."[26] Again, several of this volume's contributors introduce their disciplines to students with reference to the master narrative at the heart of the Christian worldview.

Recently, several prominent Christian educators have raised questions about the continuing value and even validity of the concept of worldview as a tool for approaching Christian education. Nicholas Wolterstorff, for example, has asserted that worldview can put "too much emphasis on a 'view,' that is, on what we have called cognition. To be identified with the people of God and to share in its works does indeed require that one have a system of belief. But it also requires more than that. It requires the Christian way of life. Christian education is education aimed at training for the Christian life, not just education aimed at inculcating the Christian world[view]."[27] Susan VanZanten, having also noted that worldview approaches can overemphasize the cognitive and propositional aspects of the Christian life, concludes, "I have little hope that either integration or worldview are recoverable terms, despite the

---

24. Poplin, *Is Reality Secular?* Poplin compares and contrasts the basic assumptions of naturalism, secular humanism, pantheism, and monotheism.

25. VanZanten, *Joining the Mission*, 117. For an example of this approach, see Colson and Pearcy, *How Now Shall We Live?*, which is organized around the themes of creation, fall, redemption, and restoration.

26. Keller and Alsdorf, *Every Good Endeavor*, 157.

27. Quoted in Wilhoit et al., "Soul Projects," 192.

strengths and possibilities of each."[28] Instead, she proposes "a new model for Christian education: faithful learning within God's story."[29] Likewise, James K. A. Smith suggests in *Desiring the Kingdom* that "we consider a (temporary) moratorium on the notion of 'worldview.'"[30] Like VanZanten, Smith is concerned that the concept of worldview as it is often used is not sufficiently broad to capture the lived experience of Christians and the affective and formative role of liturgies, whether religious or secular.

It is interesting that both VanZanten and Smith point to the writings of Charles Taylor as providing possible alternatives to the language of worldview. Smith explicitly argues for the adoption of Taylor's concept of "the social imaginary."[31] Smith continues, "Taylor describes this as an imaginary in order to refer to 'the way ordinary people imagine their social surroundings,' which is 'not expressed in theoretical terms, but is carried in images, stories, and legends.'"[32] VanZanten also quotes from Taylor's *Sources of the Self*, "Our lives exist [in a] space of questions, which only a coherent narrative can answer. In order to have a sense of who we are we have to have a notion of how we have become, and of where we are going."[33]

I agree with Smith and VanZanten that Charles Taylor's reflections on social imaginaries, particularly the modern social imaginary, are helpful in *enriching* the concept of worldview. In *A Secular Age*, Taylor explains social imaginaries as "the ways in which they [people] imagine their social existence, how they fit together with others, how things go on between them and their fellows, the expectations which are normally met, and the deeper normative notions and images which underlie these expectations. . . . [It is] that common understanding which makes possible common practices, and a widely shared sense of legitimacy."[34] Taylor's comment that when it comes to the ways in which social imaginaries shape the lives of actual people—"If the understanding makes the practice possible, it is also true that it is the practice which largely carries the

---

28. VanZanten, *Joining the Mission*, 121.
29. VanZanten, *Joining the Mission*, 121.
30. Smith, *Desiring the Kingdom*, 65.
31. Smith, *Desiring the Kingdom*, 65.
32. Smith, *Desiring the Kingdom*, 65.
33. VanZanten, *Joining the Mission*, 118. See Taylor, *Sources of the Self*.
34. Taylor, *Secular Age*, 171–72. See also Taylor, *Modern Social Imaginaries*.

understanding"—particularly resonates with ideas developed by James K. A. Smith in his Cultural Liturgies series.[35]

However, ultimately I think that Philip Ryken is correct when he asserts, "We can learn from these and other criticisms without jettisoning the vital project of articulating a Christian view of the world. Worldview thinking should be rejuvenated, not rejected."[36] The most robust definitions and articulations of worldview already address the concerns of these critics. For example, James Sire's definition, which I quoted earlier, identifies a worldview as "a commitment, a fundamental orientation of the heart," language fully compatible with Smith's emphasis on the liturgies that "shape and constitute our identities by forming our most fundamental desires and our most basic attunement to the world."[37] Likewise, Sire's acknowledgment that we can inhabit our worldviews "consciously or subconsciously, consistently or inconsistently" corresponds to the pretheoretical nature of Taylor's social imaginaries.[38]

One of the most fully-developed models of worldview that I have encountered is that presented by N.T. Wright in *The New Testament and the People of God*. Wright is worth quoting at length:

> There are four things which worldviews characteristically do, in each of which the entire worldview can be glimpsed. First . . . worldviews provide the *stories* through which human beings view reality. Narrative is the most characteristic expression of worldview. . . . Second, from these stories one can in principle discover how to answer the basic *questions* that determine human existence: who are we, where are we, what is wrong, and what is the solution? . . . Third, the stories that express the worldview, and the answers which it provides to the questions of identity, environment, evil and eschatology, are expressed . . . in cultural *symbols*. These can be both artifacts and events. . . . Fourth, worldviews include a *praxis*, a way-of-being-in-the-world. The implied eschatology of the fourth question ('what is the solution?') necessarily entails action. Conversely, the real shape of someone's worldview can often be seen in the

---

35. Taylor, *Secular Age*, 173.
36. Ryken, *Christian Worldview*, 27–28.
37. Sire, *Naming the Elephant*, 122; Smith, *Desiring the Kingdom*, 25.
38. Sire, *Naming the Elephant*, 122. Taylor writes, "Humans operated with a social imaginary well before they ever got into the business of theorizing about themselves" (Taylor, *Secular Age*, 173).

sort of actions they perform, particularly if the actions are so instinctive or habitual as to be taken for granted.[39]

If we keep all four of these elements in play—stories, questions, symbols, and praxis—worldview remains a powerful, flexible, and relevant concept.

As will become evident in the chapters that follow, many of the contributors to this volume continue to find the concept of Christian worldview (both foundational and narrative) extremely helpful as they wrestle with what it means to engage, practice, and teach their disciplines faithfully. Worldview is also a concept that seems to be highly accessible for students, even for those encountering it for the first time.[40] It should also be pointed out that by engaging students in worldview analysis, we are developing in them the higher-order thinking skills described in Bloom's Taxonomy.[41] In the following sections of this introduction we will turn to two other concepts or lenses for understanding the nature of well-rounded Christian education, character formation and vocation. Both can be understood as elements of worldview thinking but have also given rise to extensive literatures in their own right.

CHARACTER FORMATION

Steven Garber argues in *The Fabric of Faithfulness*, "True education is always about learning to connect knowing with doing, belief with behavior; and yet that connection is incredibly difficult to make for students in the modern university."[42] Some of this difficulty arises from the extremely pragmatic approach of many students to a college education. Yuval Levin has recently observed that there are "three [competing] understandings of the purpose of the university as an institution, all of which have been part of the American university from its earliest days."[43] The first view is

---

39. Wright, *New Testament and the People of God*, 123–4.

40. Many of those who have put forward recent criticisms of worldview are themselves products of the Reformed tradition that first popularized worldview as a category of analysis. I wonder how much they are suffering from a concept fatigue that those less immersed in the secondary scholarship do not experience.

41. Bloom, *Taxonomy of Educational Objectives*; Anderson and Krathwohl, *Taxonomy for Learning, Teaching, and Assessing*.

42. Garber, *Fabric of Faithfulness*, 57. Framing the same issue in slightly different terms, Garber also asks, "Do you have a *telos* sufficient, personally and publicly, to orient your *praxis* over the course of life" (Garber, *Fabric of Faithfulness*, 56)?

43. Levin, *Time to Build*, 92.

that institutions of higher education exist to give students the knowledge and skills they need for employment in the modern economy. The second focuses on giving students "a consciousness of the moral demands of a just society."[44] The third emphasizes the transmission of tradition and engagement with the liberal arts.

The first understanding, which focuses on marketable skills, is probably the most widespread, particularly among students. As evidence of this, Levin points out that the most popular undergraduate majors in America in 2018 were business, nursing, psychology, biology, and engineering, "all of which suggest a fundamentally professional orientation among students."[45] At least in the current cultural landscape, moral activism as the guiding principle of higher education is most often associated with progressive forms of social justice, while advocates of the traditional liberal arts are often on the conservative end of the ideological spectrum. However, Christian approaches to education can and should incorporate all three of the purposes that Levin identifies.

In his defense of the Christian liberal arts, Arthur Holmes encourages us when students ask, "What can I do with all this stuff anyway?" to push them to consider instead, "What will all this stuff do to me?"[46] Holmes then asks faculty to reflect on "[w]hat sort of men and women will they become by wrestling with this material in the way I present it? And what sorts of materials and methods could I develop to help them become more fully the people they are capable of being?"[47] These questions draw on ancient traditions, both classical and Christian, which see education as a process of formation.

The idea that colleges and universities ought to be involved in the business of formation, particularly character formation, has recently come under attack in some quarters.[48] In his book *Save the World on Your Own Time*, Stanley Fish argues, "Teachers cannot, except for a serendipity that by definition cannot be counted on, fashion moral character, or inculcate

---

44. Levin, *Time to Build*, 92.

45. Levin, *Time to Build*, 93. In the next section, we will explore how a fuller Christian understanding of vocation can enrich and even redeem our students' pursuit of and engagement in these careers.

46. Holmes, *Idea of a Christian College*, 24.

47. Holmes, *Idea of a Christian College*, 24.

48. For a discussion of the broader context of these developments, see Hunter, *Death of Character*.

respect for others, or produce citizens of a certain type."[49] This critique, if true, would invalidate the claims that most institutions of higher learning, both religious and secular, make in their mission statements and promotional materials. It is also at odds with how most college educators view their roles. Tim Clydesdale reports that "60 percent to 80 percent of faculty nationally agree that 'help[ing] students develop personal values,' 'develop[ing] moral character,' [and] 'instill[ing] in students a commitment to community service'... are 'very important' or 'essential' goals for undergraduate education."[50]

The reality is that we can't help but form our students. Levin observes, "[I]nstitutions are by their nature formative. They structure our perceptions and our interactions, and as a result they structure us. They form our habits, our expectations, and ultimately our character."[51] This is true of all institutions, but particularly of educational institutions filled with young men and women navigating the formative years of emerging adulthood.[52] In the words of Mark Schwehn, "the question for educators is not *whether* to form character but, rather, *what kind of character* they should strive to form. And the question for students is not only what kind of knowledge they wish to obtain, but also what kind of human being they wish to become."[53] These are questions related to the proper *telos* of education, the answers to which always reflect one's underlying worldview.

Although our focus for much of this section will be on character formation, it is worth pointing out that even if we could set questions of morality aside, successful education always requires the development of certain intellectual virtues and dispositions such as inquisitiveness, attentiveness, objectivity, self-awareness, creativity, and determination, all of which are prominent in recent pedagogical literature.[54] Jason Baehr explains, "Intellectual character virtues... are cultivated traits. They are

---

49. Quoted in Schwehn, "Good Teaching: Character Formation and Vocational Discernment," in Cunningham, *Vocation across the Academy*, 297. Glanzer and Alleman have recently compared and contrasted Fish's position to that of Parker Palmer. See Glanzer and Alleman, *Outrageous Idea of Christian Teaching*, 610.

50. Clydesdale, *Purposeful Graduate*, 63.

51. Levin, *Time to Build*, 20.

52. For more on emerging adulthood, see Smith, *Souls in Transition*, and Smith, *Lost in Transition*.

53. Schwehn, "Good Teaching," 313.

54. See, for example, Cavanagh, *Spark of Learning* and Duckworth, *Grit*.

settled states of character that come about by way of repeated choice or action."[55] Such intellectual virtues have an affective component, which James K. A. Smith also emphasizes in his discussion of character formation. Likewise, "intellectual virtue concepts and language provide an apt description of some of the proper *aims* and *goals* of education . . . [and] a plausible way of 'fleshing out' or 'thickening' certain familiar, worthy, but nebulous educational goals, like a 'love of learning,' 'lifelong learning,' and 'critical thinking.'"[56]

As Christian educators, our goal is not merely to cultivate intellectual virtues in our students, as important as such virtues are and as obviously compatible with and even grounded in a Christian worldview as they might be. We are also called to cultivate the moral character of our students. N.T. Wright has defined character as "the transforming, shaping, and marking of a life and its habits."[57] Wright's analysis of character draws heavily on Aristotle's thought in the *Nicomachean Ethics*, in which Aristotle argues that virtue consists in developing habits directed towards the goal of *eudaimonia* or human flourishing.[58] However, for the Christian, character is actually another way of describing the process of sanctification as we anticipate the full coming of God's kingdom and the restoration of creation. This links character both to the central narrative of the Christian worldview and informs the Christian understanding of vocation and calling.

In many of his writings, James K. A. Smith has explored the intimate connections between formation and education. In *Desiring the Kingdom*, for example, he makes the case that "every liturgy is an education" and "behind ever pedagogy is a philosophical anthropology."[59] Much of his critique of a worldview approach to Christian education is grounded in his conviction that in focusing too much on the propositional content of the Christian faith, we ignore the ways in which the liturgies in which we participate, "whether 'sacred' or 'secular' . . . shape and constitute our

55. Baehr, *Inquiring Mind*, 22.
56. Baehr, *Intellectual Virtues and Education*, 4.
57. Wright, *After You Believe*, 7.
58. Wright, *After You Believe*, 33. Wright explains, "Virtue . . . is what happens when someone has made a thousand small choices, requiring effort and concentration, to do something which is good and right but which doesn't 'come naturally'—and then, on the thousand and first time, when it really matters, they find they do what's required 'automatically'" (Wright, *After You Believe*, 20).
59. Smith, *Desiring the Kingdom*, 25, 27.

identities by forming our most fundamental desires and our most basic attunement to the world."[60] He concludes, "I think Christian colleges, universities, and schools have unwittingly bought into a stunted picture of the human person and a somewhat domesticated construal of Christian faith."[61]

Smith's discussion of liturgies fits in with a broader literature on practices, a terminology that may be more accessible to many educators.[62] In their edited volume, *Teaching and Christian Practices*, James K. A. Smith and David I. Smith, drawing on the insights of Alasdair MacIntyre, explain that "a practice is social, communal, and inherited: it is a complex of routines and rituals that is handed down from others."[63] It is obvious that this definition provides a helpful way of thinking about education, both in terms of content and pedagogy. Again, Smith and Smith affirm, "any education worth the name has to be formative, and that formation happens only through practices which inscribe a *habitus*—an orientation and inclination towards the world, aimed as a specific *telos*.[64]

Craig Dykstra has observed, "The practice of Christian faith is a lot more physical than we usually recognize or let on. It is body faith—an embodied faith—that involves gestures, moves, going certain places ... and doing certain things."[65] Much of the recent literature on pedagogy has also emphasized that all learning is a lot more physical than we used to believe. This is reflected in the emphasis on active rather than passive learning, on experiential learning, and even our understanding of how memory consolidation works.[66] Christian educators could benefit immensely from immersing themselves in this recent scholarship on teaching and learning, but we here at College of the Ozarks also believe

---

60. Smith, *Desiring the Kingdom*, 25.

61. Smith, *Desiring the Kingdom*, 217.

62. Dykstra, *Growing in the Life of Faith*; Smith and Smith, *Teaching and Christian Practices*; Wilhoit et al., "Soul Projects: Class-Related Spiritual Practices," in Balzer and Reed, *Building a Culture of Faith*; Pardue, "Incorporating Christian Practices into the Study of Church History," 53–59; Osborne, "Liturgies of Learning," 27–30.

63. Smith and Smith, *Teaching and Christians Practices*, 8.

64. Smith and Smith, *Teaching and Christians Practices*, 9. Chapter 3 of this volume will explore how consideration of the *telos* of education must inform both curriculum and assessment.

65. Dykstra, *Growing in the Life of Faith*, 71.

66. See, for example, "Chapter 4: Authenticity" in Eyler, *How Humans Learn*, 149–70. Other important recent works include Ambrose et al., *How Learning Works*; Brown et al., *Make it Stick*; and Lang, *Small Teaching*.

that Christian faculty have something constructive to contribute to these conversations.

The full implications of these ideas on character formation, liturgies, and practices, and how best to apply them in Christian institutions of higher education are still being worked out. David Smith has recently asked, "is there such a thing as *teaching* Christianly, teaching in such a way that faith somehow informs the processes, the moves, the practices, the pedagogy, and not just the ideas that are conveyed or the spirit in which they are offered?"[67] Through our Thrive Initiative at College of the Ozarks (discussed in chapter 2), we have attempted to build structures, processes, and experiences across both the cocurricular and curricular elements of the student experience that are formative. We are also wrestling with how both the content and pedagogical methods in our classrooms can faithfully shape our students, bridging the gaps between knowing and doing, belief and behavior.

VOCATION

The final lens through which I would like to consider the nature of Christian education is the concept of vocation. Garber observes, "The word *vocation* is a rich one, having to address the whole of life, the range of relationships and responsibilities. Work, yes, but also families, and neighbors, and citizenship, locally and globally—all of this and more is seen as vocation, that to which I am called as a human being, living my life before the face of God."[68] Likewise, Holmes asserts, "The human vocation is far larger than the scope of any job a person may hold because we are human persons created in God's image, to honor and serve God and other people in all we do, not just in the way we earn a living."[69]

---

67. Smith, *Christian Teaching*, vii. He continues, "An account of Christian education that focuses only on the truth of what is taught, and fails to address the meanings molded through *how* it is taught and learned is at best incomplete" (Smith, *On Christian Teaching*, 4). Glanzer and Alleman report that while 79% of the Christian faculty they surveyed said their theology influenced the "Foundations, worldview, or narrative" guiding their courses, only 40% said it influenced their "Teaching methods" (Glanzer and Alleman, *Outrageous Idea of Christian Teaching*, 41, 82).

68. Garber, *Visions of Vocation*, 11.

69. Holmes, *Idea of a Christian College*, 25. Indeed, Holmes devoted an entire chapter to "Liberal Arts as Career Preparation," arguing that "Liberal arts education is the education of responsible agents for the vocation of life itself, life in all its parts and as a whole" (Holmes, *Idea of a Christian College*, 38). For reflections on the vocation of

The topic of vocation is experiencing a massive resurgence of interest in American higher education and the scholarship on vocation is rapidly expanding.[70] Tim Clydesdale's recent book, *The Purposeful Graduate: Why Colleges Must Talk to Students about Vocation*, is "an account of what happens when colleges and universities infuse undergraduate education with exploration of meaning and purpose.... to resist marketplace pressures, return to the big questions of life, and recapture the historic role that universities used to play in society."[71] More specifically, Clydesdale offers an assessment of "one of the largest curricular and cocurricular undertakings in American higher education history," which began in 1999 when the Lilly Endowment launched its Programs for the Theological Exploration of Vocation (PTEV).[72]

Lilly awarded grants, in some cases of more than two million dollars, to eighty-eight colleges and universities to develop initiatives focused on helping their students explore the idea of vocation. From this initial program grew the on-going Network for Vocation in Undergraduate Education (NetVUE), administered by the Council of Independent Colleges (CIC), which has two hundred and seventy-one institutional members as of July 2021. Colleges and universities of all sizes and types have found the language of vocation a powerful tool for considering their institutional missions and for students transitioning into adulthood.

The concept of vocation has a long and rich history within the Christian tradition. In the introduction to his anthology, *Callings: Twenty Centuries of Christian Wisdom on Vocation*, William Placher offers a helpful survey of the various meanings and association of the language of calling over the course of the last two thousand years.[73] More specifically,

---

the educator, see Hughes, *Vocation of a Christian Scholar*.

70. In addition to other works cited throughout the notes of this section, see the three recent volumes on vocation edited by Cunningham, *At This Time and In This Place*, *Vocation across the Academy*, and *Hearing Vocation Differently*, as well as the following anthologies: Placher, *Callings*, and Schwehn and Bass, *Leading Lives that Matter*. For a defense of engagement in the manual trades, see Crawford, *Shop Class as Soulcraft*.

71. Clydesdale, *Purposeful Graduate*, 2.

72. Clydesdale, *Purposeful Graduate*, 3, 42–44.

73. Placher, *Callings*. Our word "vocation" has as its root the Latin *vocare/vacatio* (to call, calling). The Greek equivalent is *kaleo* (to call), which appears in such passages as Eph 4:1, in which Paul writes, "[L]ead a life worthy of your calling, for you have been called by God" (NLT). *Kaleo* is also one component of the Greek term *ekklesia*, which is translated as "church" in English New Testaments. The church is thus "ones called

he identifies four major historical periods. During the first period, that of the early church from the first through the fourth centuries, vocation meant primarily the call to salvation. Placher writes:

> For the first several hundred years of Christianity, Christians were a minority, rapidly growing in size but often at risk. Many Christians joined the church as adults, and their decision often meant a break from family and previous way of life.... Thus the fundamental vocational questions for Christians or potential Christians were initially, first, should I be a Christian? and, second, how public should I be about my Christian faith?[74]

This is still a form of calling that all Christians experience, and we must still answer those same two questions. It is also important to note that while God's call to salvation is directed at individuals, the rampant individualism of our western culture can obscure the corporate nature of the call to membership in God's family and kingdom.[75]

Placher's second period corresponds to the portion of European history often called the Middle Ages, after Christianity became the official religion of Western Europe. He explains:

> For roughly a thousand years in the Middle Ages, by contrast to the situation in the early church, the vast majority of Christians grew up in the church, surrounded by other Christians. Whether to be a Christian was scarcely a real issue for them. But what kind of Christian should they be? Some felt called to be priests, monks, nuns, or friars. Indeed, for medieval Christians 'having a vocation' (in Latin, *vocatio*) meant almost exclusively joining the priesthood or some monastic order.[76]

Many Christians today, particularly in the American Bible Belt, may also have grown up in an environment where Christianity seemed pervasive, a part of the culture that was taken for granted (although this is now quickly changing as our society becomes more secular). And, even though the Protestant Reformation would challenge the Catholic idea that vocation meant primarily a call to the priesthood or the monastery,

---

out" (Keller and Alsdorf, *Every Good Endeavor*, 65). For another survey of Christian views on vocation, see the third chapter of Ray, *Working*.

74. Placher, *Callings*, 6.

75. This insight has been at the heart of much of N.T. Wright's writing over the last thirty years. See, for example, Wright, *After You Believe*, 67–71.

76. Placher, *Callings*, 6.

many Protestants today still think that only those who go into full-time Christian ministry—pastors and missionaries—have a special calling from God.

The Reformation of the sixteenth century led to significant developments in the way in which vocation was understood. Martin Luther's writings were particularly important in the Protestant reassessment of vocation.[77] Placher says of this period:

> Around 1500 . . . many European ideas about vocation began to change. . . . Martin Luther proclaimed 'the priesthood of all believers'[78] and, like most other Protestant pastors, got married. Thus among Protestants, everyone was a priest, and pastors increasingly lived more like everyone else. One could be called to a life of preaching, but alternatively to government, commerce, crafts, farming, or anything else.[79]

In his German translation of the Bible, Luther translated the Greek word for calling using the term *Beruf*, which was the ordinary German word for an occupation. For Luther, and for many other Protestants who followed him, being a farmer or a shoemaker was just as much a God-given calling as being a priest or a pastor, although it is important to keep in mind that at the time most people did not get to choose their occupations. However, our contemporary association of callings with jobs and careers is definitely a legacy of the Reformation era.

Finally, Placher discusses what he calls "Vocations in a Post-Christian Age," a period that began for many people in the late nineteenth century. He writes:

> In the last two centuries, patterns of thinking about Christian vocation have continued to change . . . In more economically advanced countries, at least, most people have lots of choices of job or career. . . . New options in work and family life offer great freedom, but they also impose significant burdens. 'What does God want me to do with my life?' becomes an even harder

---

77. See Wingren, *Christian's Calling*.

78. Luther argued in his *Appeal to the Ruling Class of the German Nation* (1520), "To call popes, bishops, priests, monks, and nuns, the religious class, is a specious devise . . . all Christians whatsoever really and truly belong to the religious class, and there is no difference among them except in so far as they do different work" (Dillenberger, *Luther*, 407).

79. Placher, *Callings*, 7.

question. Moreover, many people grow more nervous about identifying 'vocation' with 'job' or 'career.'[80]

This "Post-Christian age" is the one in which we now find ourselves, where both we and our students must wrestle with questions of vocation. Vocation and calling mean different things to different people, and these different meanings introduce profound tensions into our lives, ironically more so as we take the idea of calling seriously.

As Placher's historical survey makes clear, while the language of vocation has its roots in the Christian tradition, it also has powerful resonances for secular people as well.[81] David Cunningham argues that the concept of vocation is so useful because it is capacious, dynamic, and elastic. Capacious in that, "even for those students whose career trajectories seem fairly straightforward, engaging in serious reflection on vocation can help them focus on larger questions about the direction and purpose of their lives."[82] Dynamic in that it "recognizes the shifting contexts in which human beings live."[83] And elastic, "allowing it to be adopted by a wide variety of academic institutions, departments, and programs."[84]

Even for many Christian students, the primary association of vocation will continue to be the career that they hope to pursue. Insofar as we can help them to understand their job in light of a Christian worldview, and to recognize that their careers do not exhaust the callings on their lives, this is absolutely fine. Already, more than a century ago, Walter

---

80. Placher, *Callings*, 8. Placher further observes, "Many of us today also live much of our lives after retiring from our 'job.' We are apt these days to be more aware of the severely disabled and others who cannot hold a job at all. Does anyone without a job not have a calling and thus not have a meaningful life? At a different extreme, some careers seem so to dominate people's lives as to leave us worrying if the idea of job as vocation is not a danger to our roles as spouses, parents, free creatures of God. Should our jobs consume our whole lives?" (Placher, *Callings*, 9). For more reflections on choice, particularly as it relates to vocation, see Schwartz, *Paradox of Choice*, and Badcock, *Way of Life*, 134–42.

81. Although, given that a "calling" implies a "caller," secular people will account for the experience of calling differently than those who approach the concept from a religious worldview. For further discussion of this point, see Cunningham's "'Who's There?,'" in Cunningham, *At This Time and In This Place*, 143–64; and Sayers's "Story of Me," in Cunningham, *Hearing Vocation Differently*, 175–94.

82. Cunningham, *Vocation across the Academy*, 11.

83. Cunningham, *Vocation across the Academy*, 11.

84. Cunningham, *Vocation across the Academy*, 12.

Rauschenbusch recognized that Christians could further God's kingdom through a huge range of occupations. He wrote, "If now we could have faith enough to believe that all human life can be with divine purpose; that God saves not only the soul, but the whole of human life; that anything which serves to make men healthy, intelligent, happy, and good is a service to the Father of men; that the kingdom of God is not bounded by the Church, but includes all human relations—then all professions would be hallowed and receive religious dignity."[85]

More recent authors have continued to reflect on how Christians ought to approach their jobs in the midst of a rapidly shifting cultural landscape. In a chapter entitled "Called, Not Employed," Gabe Lyons has argued that Christians can, and indeed must, pursue work in what he calls the "Seven Channels of Cultural Influence": media, arts and entertainment, government, education, business, the social sector, and the church.[86] He applauds the fact that "as a natural by-product of God's plan for his Kingdom . . . Christians are being dispersed as restorers through all channels of culture. They are carrying the message of Jesus—bringing restoration, renewal, and healing; fighting injustice; telling the truth; affirming goodness; and celebrating beauty—in their places of service."[87] More pessimistically, Rod Dreher warns that as a result of rapid secularization within American society, "we are on the brink of entire areas of commercial and professional life being off-limits to believers whose consciences will not allow them to burn incense to the gods of our age."[88] It is our responsibility as educators to help our students prepare to navigate both the opportunities and the challenges that they will face as they walk out their vocations in their professional lives.

It is also important that we help our students to realize that their callings are more than just their jobs.[89] Perhaps most broadly, Margaret

---

85. Quoted in Placher, *Callings*, 384. Rauschenbusch also noted that Christianity should exclude believers from some careers and circumscribe how they engaged in others. He declared, "As soon as religion will set the kingdom of God before it as the all-inclusive aim, and will define it so as to include all rightful relations among men, the awakened conscience will begin to turn its searchlight on the industrial and commercial life in detail, and will insist on eliminating all professions which harm instead of helping, and on coordinating all productive activities to secure a maximum of service" (Placher, *Callings*, 384).

86. Lyons, *Next Christians*, 116.

87. Lyons, *Next Christians*, 115–17.

88. Dreher, *Benedict Option*, 179.

89. This is particularly important, as they wrestle with the inevitable setbacks that

Mohrmann encourages us to think of our various vocations in terms of responsibility.[90] Mohrmann writes, "Responsibility is the ability to be responsive—to other people, to situations, and to the world."[91] This echoes Luther's insight back in the sixteenth century that marriage and parenthood are important vocations to which many of us are called. Our students should also see their studies as a vocation. In the words of Arthur Holmes, "the student must realize that education is a Christian vocation, one's prime calling from God for these years, that education must be an act of love, of worship, of stewardship, a wholehearted response to God."[92] Even friendship can be understood as a form of vocation.[93]

All college students wrestle with questions of vocation, as will most people over the course of their lifetimes. However, the concept of vocation is particularly resonant here at College of the Ozarks. A vocational goal, "To promote a strong work ethic, encouraging the development of good character and values," is one key piece of our institutional five-fold mission.[94] This goal is reflected most obviously in our unique work college model, in which all of our students work fifteen hours per week on campus to help defray the cost of their education and do not pay tuition. In recent years, administrators, faculty, and staff have sought diligently to better undergird the work program with a more robust theology of

---

they will encounter in both their professional and personal lives. See Robert Wuthnow, "Changing Nature of Work," originally published in *The Cresset* Vol. 67 No. 1 (Michaelmas 2003) 5–13, and republished in Schwehn and Bass, *Leading Lives That Matter*, 255–63.

90. She quotes Dietrich Bonhoeffer, "Vocation is responsibility, and responsibility is a total response of the whole human being to the whole of reality" (Mohrmann, "Vocation Is Responsibility," in Cunningham, *Vocation across the Academy*, 21).

91. Cunningham, *Vocation across the Academy*, 21. Mohrmann points out that "responsibility" comes from the Latin *responsus* and "its root (*-spons*) refers to a promise or pledge, as can be detected in other English derivations (such as *sponsor* and *spouse*)" (Cunningham, *Vocation across the Academy*, 21).

92. Holmes, *Idea of a Christian College*, 49. For more on this theme, see C.S. Lewis's classic essay "Learning in Wartime," in Lewis, *The Weight of Glory*, 55–63.

93. See Meilaender, "Friendship and Vocation," in Schwehn and Bass, *Leading Lives That Matter*.

94. "The mission of College of the Ozarks is to provide the advantages of a Christian education for youth of both sexes, especially those found worthy, but who are without sufficient means to precure such training." Tied to this mission are clearly articulated academic, vocational, Christian, patriotic, and cultural goals (College of the Ozarks, *2020-2021 College Catalog*, 7).

vocation.[95] We have also engaged students explicitly in discussions of this topic through two one-hour, vocation-themed Big Questions courses ("What Are Our Callings" and "Vocation & The Future of Work").[96]

STRUCTURE OF THE VOLUME

This book builds on themes and insights from the ever-growing literature on Christian higher education, some of which we have just surveyed, and explores the vocation of College of the Ozarks (and of other Christian colleges and universities)—to faithfully educate students—and how individual faculty and staff can contribute to that mission.[97] Through individual essays by College of the Ozarks administrators, cocurricular staff, and faculty from a wide range of disciplines, it provides both thoughtful reflection and concrete application of the concepts discussed in this introduction—insights that speak to specific institutional settings and the actual classroom experience.

Part One, "Faithful Education and the Christian College," will focus on what faithful education means at the institutional level, with chapters on college administration, the cocurricular, assessment, faculty, and community.[98] Part Two, "Faithful Education Across the Disciplines," includes sections devoted to the humanities, the social sciences, mathematics and natural sciences, creative arts, and the professional disciplines, fourteen essays in all, in which faculty explore what it means to faithfully educate students in their disciplines, engage with the growing literature on faith integration in their fields, and discuss the concrete steps they have taken to provide a robust Christian education to their students and fulfill the Christian mission of College of the Ozarks. We hope and pray

---

95. See, for example, volume 1 of the College's journal, *Faithful Lives: Christian Reflection on the World—Faithful Work* (Fall 2016). We also successfully applied for a faculty development grant from NetVUE, which funded a three-semester faculty and staff reading group exploring recent resources on vocation.

96. Students in BTS 4003 Christian Worldview II, the capstone course in our GE curriculum, also write an essay reflecting on what it means to pursue their chosen fields in light of a Christian worldview.

97. See Cunningham's essay "Colleges Have Callings, Too," in Cunningham, *Vocation across the Academy*, 249–71.

98. These are all areas of concern identified by Glanzer et al. in *Restoring the Soul of the University*, particularly in Part II of their book, "The Fragmentation of the Multiversity."

that you will find resources and examples in these pages that will help you to faithfully educate your students as well.

BIBLIOGRAPHY

Ambrose, Susan, et al. *How Learning Works: 7 Research-Based Principles for Smart Teaching*. Hoboken, NJ: Jossey-Bass, 2010.

Anderson, Lorin and David Krathwohl, eds. *Taxonomy for Learning, Teaching, and Assessing: A Revision of Bloom's Taxonomy of Educational Objectives*. London: Pearson, 2000.

Babcock, Gary. *The Way of Life: A Theology of Christian Vocation*. Grand Rapids: Eerdmans, 1998.

Backhouse, Stephen. *Kierkegaard: A Single Life*. Grand Rapids: Zondervan, 2016.

Balzer, Cary and Rod Reed, eds. *Building a Culture of Faith: University-Wide Partnerships for Spiritual Formation*. Abilene, TX: Abilene Christian University Press, 2012.

Baehr, Jason, ed. *Intellectual Virtues and Education: Essays in Applied Virtue Epistemology*. New York: Routledge, 2016.

———. *The Inquiring Mind: On Intellectual Virtues and Virtue Epistemology*. Oxford: Oxford University Press, 2012.

Bloom, Benjamin, ed. *Taxonomy of Educational Objectives: The Classification of Education Goals by a Committee of College and University Examiners*. New York: Longmans, 1956.

Brown, Peter, et al. *Make it Stick: The Science of Successful Learning*. Cambridge: Belknap, 2014.

Cavanagh, Sarah Rose. *The Spark of Learning: Energizing the College Classroom with the Science of Emotion*. Morgantown: West Virginia University Press, 2016.

Clydesdale, Tim. *The Purposeful Graduate: Why Colleges Must Talk to Students about Vocation*. Chicago: University of Chicago Press, 2015.

Colson, Charles and Nancy Pearcy. *How Now Shall We Live?* Carol Stream, IL: Tyndale House, 2004.

Crawford, Matthew. *Shop Class as Soulcraft: An Inquiry into the Value of Work*. New York: Penguin, 2009.

Cunningham, David, ed. *At This Time and In This Place: Vocation and Higher Education*. Oxford: Oxford University Press, 2016.

———. *Hearing Vocation Differently: Meaning, Purpose, and Identity in the Multi-Faith Academy*. Oxford: Oxford University Press, 2019.

———. *Vocation across the Academy: A New Vocabulary for Higher Education*. Oxford: Oxford University Press, 2017.

Darnton, Robert. *The Great Cat Massacre and Other Episodes in French Cultural History*. New York: Basic Books, 1984.

Davis, Jerry C. *Miracle in the Ozarks: The Inspiring Story of Faith, Hope, and Hard Work U*. Point Lookout, MO: College of the Ozarks Press, 2007.

Dillenberger, John, ed. *Martin Luther: Selections from His Writings*. New York: Anchor Books, 1962.

Dreher, Rod. *The Benedict Option: A Strategy for Christians in a Post-Christian Nation*. New York: Sentinel, 2017.

Duckworth, Angela. *Grit: The Power of Passion and Perseverance.* New York: Scribner, 2018.

Dykstra, Craig. *Growing in the Life of Faith: Education and Christian Practices.* Louisville: Westminster John Knox, 1998.

Eyler, Joshua. *How Humans Learn: The Science and Stories Behind Effective College Teaching.* Morgantown, WV: West Virginia University Press, 2018.

Garber, Steven. *The Fabric of Faithfulness: Weaving Together Belief and Behavior.* Downers Grove, IL: IVP, 1996.

———. *Visions of Vocation: Common Grace for the Common Good.* Downers Grove, IL: IVP, 2014.

Glanzer, Perry and Nathan Alleman. *The Outrageous Idea of Christian Teaching.* Oxford: Oxford University Press, 2019.

Glanzer, Perry L., et al. *Restoring the Soul of the University: Unifying Christian Higher Education in a Fragmented Age.* Downers Grove, IL: IVP Academic, 2017.

Godsey, Helen and Townsend Godsey. *Flight of the Phoenix: A Biography of the School of the Ozarks.* Point Lookout, MO: School of the Ozarks Press, 1984.

Hanson, Collin, ed. *Our Secular Age: Ten Years of Reading and Applying Charles Taylor.* Deerfield: Gospel Coalition, 2017.

Holmes, Arthur. *The Idea of a Christian College.* Grand Rapids: Eerdmans, 1987.

Hughes, Richard. *The Vocation of a Christian Scholar: How Christian Faith Can Sustain the Life of the Mind.* Grand Rapids: Eerdmans, 2005.

Hunter, James Davison. *The Death of Character: Moral Education in an Age Without Good or Evil.* New York: Basic, 2000.

Joeckel, Samuel and Thomas Chesnes, eds. *The Christian College Phenomenon: Inside America's Fastest Growing Institutions of Higher Learning.* Abilene, TX: Abilene Christian University Press, 2012.

Keller, Timothy and Katherine Alsdorf. *Every Good Endeavor: Connecting Your Work to God's Work.* New York: Penguin, 2012.

Lang, James. *Small Teaching: Everyday Lessons from the Science of Learning.* Hoboken, NJ: Jossey-Bass, 2016.

Levin, Yuval. *A Time to Build: From Family and Community to Congress and the Campus, How Recommitting to our Institutions can Revive the American Dream.* New York: Basic, 2020.

Lewis, C.S. *The Weight of Glory.* New York: HarperCollins, 2001.

Lyons, Gabe. *The Next Christians: The Good News About the End of Christian America.* New York: Doubleday, 2010.

Mouw, Richard. *Abraham Kuyper: A Short Introduction.* Grand Rapids: Eerdmans, 2011.

Noll, Mark. *The Scandal of the Evangelical Mind.* Grand Rapids: Eerdmans, 1994.

Osborne, William. "Liturgies of Learning: Shaping Our Classes for Christian Formation." *DidaktikosJournal.com* (February 2021): 27–30.

Pardue, Brad. "Incorporating Christian Practices into the Study of Church History." *Fides et Historia* 50.2 (Summer/Fall 2019): 53–59.

Placher, William, ed. *Callings: Twenty Centuries of Christian Wisdom on Vocation.* Grand Rapids: Eerdmans, 2005.

Poplin, Mary. *Is Reality Secular? Testing the Assumptions of Four Global Worldviews.* Downers Grove, IL: InterVarsity, 2014.

Ray, Darby. *Working.* Minneapolis: Fortress, 2011.

Ringenberg, William. *The Christian College: A History of Protestant Higher Education in America*. Grand Rapids: Baker Academic, 2006.

Ryken, Leland, ed. *The Christian Imagination*. Colorado Springs, CO: Waterbrook, 2002.

Ryken, Philip. *Christian Worldview: A Student's Guide*. Wheaton, IL: Crossway, 2013.

Schmalzbaur, John and Kathleen A. Mahoney. *The Resilience of Religion in American Higher Education*. Waco, TX: Baylor University Press, 2018.

Schwartz, Barry. *The Paradox of Choice: Why More Is Less*. New York: Harper Perennial, 2005.

Schwehn, Mark and Dorothy Bass, eds. *Leading Lives that Matter: What We Should Do and Who We Should Be*. Grand Rapids: Eerdmans, 2006.

Sire, James. *Naming the Elephant: Worldview as a Concept*. Downers Grove, IL: InterVarsity, 2004.

Smith, Christian. *Lost in Transition: The Dark Side of Emerging Adulthood*. Oxford: Oxford University Press, 2011.

———. *Souls in Transition: The Religious and Spiritual Lives of Emerging Adults*. Oxford: Oxford University Press, 2009.

Smith, David I. *On Christian Teaching: Practicing Faith in the Classroom*. Grand Rapids: Eerdmans, 2018.

Smith, David I. and James K. A. Smith. *Teaching and Christian Practices: Reshaping Faith and Learning*. Grand Rapids: Eerdmans, 2011.

Smith, James K. A. *Desiring the Kingdom: Worship, Worldview, and Cultural Formation*. Grand Rapids: Baker Academic, 2009.

———. *How (Not) To Be Secular: Reading Charles Taylor*. Grand Rapids: Eerdmans, 2014.

———. *Who's Afraid of Postmodernism?: Taking Derrida, Lyotard, and Foucault to Church*. Grand Rapids: Baker Academic, 2006.

Taylor, Charles. *Modern Social Imaginaries*. Durham: Duke University Press, 2003.

———. *A Secular Age*. Cambridge: Belknap, 2007.

———. *Sources of the Self: The Making of the Modern Identity*. Cambridge: Cambridge University Press, 1989.

VanZanten, Susan. *Joining the Mission: A Guide for (Mainly) New College Faculty*. Grand Rapids: Eerdmans, 2011.

Wingren, Gustaf. *The Christian's Calling: Luther on Vocation*. London: Oliver and Boyd, 1958.

Wolterstorff, Nicholas. *Educating for Shalom: Essays on Christian Higher Education*. Grand Rapids: Eerdmans, 2004.

Wright, N.T. *After You Believe: Why Christian Character Matters*. New York: HarperOne, 2010.

———. *The New Testament and the People of God*. Minneapolis: Fortress, 1992.

Part One

Faithful Education
and the Christian College

1

Faithful Administration

Eric W. Bolger

INTRODUCTION

THE GOAL OF THIS chapter is to explore what it means to be a faithful college administrator and, more broadly, what faithful college administration looks like. By faithful, I mean both "full of faith" in the Christian God and consistent with the gospel of Jesus Christ. I will argue that Christian institutions of higher education can develop a faithful identity that includes "slow wisdom"[1] through the implementation of distinctively Christian practices.[2]

BACKGROUND

In August 1992, I stepped into my first classroom as a full-time college professor. I had been trained well in my discipline, which was biblical theology and exegesis. I had done some teaching of both graduates and undergraduates as an adjunct professor. But this was my first experience of teaching as my full-time vocation.

---

1. Using a term coined by Walter Brueggemann, see Glanzer et al., *Restoring the Soul of the University*, 299.

2. On the topic of Christian practices, see, for example, Smith, *Desiring the Kingdom*; Smith and Smith, *Teaching and Christian Practices*; Pohl, *Living in Community*; and Dykstra, *Growing In The Life Of Faith*.

I remember being impressed that my students were arriving early to my 8 a.m. New Testament class. When I arrived at 7:55 a.m. that first day, the students were already seated and waiting for instructions on how the class would run. They were polite and encouraging, and my entry into the life of college professor went smoothly for the most part. I spent the next ten years of my life teaching full-time.

In 2002, I was asked to take on the role of division chair for the humanities division. This request was an honor and I agreed to the role with a reduction in teaching load. But my center of gravity was still in the classroom, where I was able to develop relationships with students and extend my knowledge into additional areas of study within biblical theology. The rhythm of teaching suited my personality well. I loved the reflective nature of teaching; first, reflecting on the content so that I understood it well, and then reflecting on the sharing of that content with students.[3] The reflective rhythm of teaching supported me in other responsibilities, too, for example in preparing to give Sunday morning sermons on a regular basis at my church.

Being asked to step into a full-time administrative role in 2010 changed the rhythm of my life. The rhythm of academic administration is not naturally reflective. Instead, it is a rhythm of responsivity to a continuous rush of responsibilities and requests: addressing financial issues; dealing with faculty hiring, training, and evaluation; ensuring assessment of student learning; managing committees; preparing materials for accreditation; and working with students, from registration to academic awards to transfer course requests to discipline, etc. Academic administrative work also necessitates integration into the broader administrative activities of the institution, including enrollment, finances, student life, and, in the case of my institution, a mandatory work education program for full-time students.[4] Each day brought many unexpected challenges, even those days that seemed at first to offer the promise of unfettered time for reading and research.

While teaching in the classroom offers obvious opportunities for developing a Christian approach to content and practice, the concept of Christian administration seemed vague to me. Did it mean being nice to people? What about when I had to make difficult decisions, saying

---

3. David I. Smith writes of a "process of faith-informed reflection on how we teach"(Smith, *Christian Teaching*, 129).

4. Full-time students at College of the Ozarks work fifteen hours per week and two forty-hour work weeks per academic year and pay no tuition.

no to financial requests or addressing a faculty member's struggles in the classroom or disciplining a student for academic dishonesty? How would what I do look different than the activities of an administrator at a secular institution, if at all? Did being a Christian administrator simply mean that I would pray for my colleagues and students and perhaps open meetings with prayer?

THE CHRISTIAN COLLEGE[5]

In their book *Restoring the Soul of the University*, Perry L. Glanzer, Nathan F. Alleman, and Todd C. Ream point us toward a Christian understanding of academic leadership. They argue that distinctively Christian colleges and universities are in a unique position to help restore the soul of the university: "Freed from the burden of tending the cultural majority, Christians are now able to focus on life as a faithful, alternative, and perhaps even radical presence in a post-Christendom age."[6] They urge academic leaders to "make sense of the times" rather than looking to the past as a means of restoring the university's soul. This requires recognition of a new set of tools (rooted in an old set of tools) that can help to locate our institutions in the current cultural moment and to learn to pursue faithfulness in the midst of this moment.[7]

   5. In this chapter, for simplicity's sake, I will use the term "college" and not "university." The context in which I work is a college, not a university, though what is said might certainly apply to those teaching in university contexts.
   6. Glanzer et al., *Restoring the Soul of the University*, 297. See also James Davison Hunter, who writes of Protestant Fundamentalists and Evangelicals that "their proprietarian relationship to American culture has obligated them to preserve the nation as well as preserve their faith" (Hunter, *Change the World*, 214). He describes the three "paradigms of cultural engagement" of Christians with contemporary culture as "Defensive Against," "Relevance To," and "Purity From," aligning these respectively with, for example, conservative Protestants, progressive Evangelicals, and neo-Anabaptists.
   7. "The practice of faithful presence, then, generates relationships and institutions that are fundamentally covenantal in character, the ends of which are the fostering of meaning, purpose, truth, beauty, belonging, and fairness – not just for Christians but for everyone" (Hunter, *Change the World*, 263). Hunter raises questions about what it means to be faithfully present in late modern culture: How can one be authentically Christian in circumstances that, by their very nature, undermine the credibility and coherence of faith? What is an authentically biblical way of existing within a pluralistic world in which Christianity will never be anything other than one culture among others? How should the Christian think about the "other"? How is faithfulness that gives full expression of the gifts of the entire body of Christ for the benefit of the church and the common good possible? What does it mean for the believer to be faithful in this

The authors rely on work by Old Testament scholar Walter Brueggemann.[8] Brueggemann's reflection on higher education, rooted in the prophet Jeremiah's prophecies to Jerusalem before the Babylonian exile of Israel, points to a need to critique the forces that are forming higher education today and a visionary reimagining of the identity and purpose of higher education.[9] Based on Jer 9:23–24, he identifies what he terms a "triad of fidelity" (love, justice, righteousness) and a "triad of control" (might, wisdom, wealth) with which colleges can intentionally or unintentionally engage. Engagement with the former yields "slow wisdom," while engagement with the latter yields "fast wisdom."[10] The university has benefitted greatly from engagement with the triad of control, and thus fast wisdom, as has society at large in the West, but the Christian college can become a prophetic example by embracing slow wisdom. Brueggemann concludes that "the 'slow' mystery of God requires a relational integrity that appears as steadfast love, justice, and righteousness," that "slow wisdom calls us to sustain and evoke relational identity for the common good," and that Jeremiah's prophetic poetry is clearly relevant to the contemporary situation.[11]

In contrast to many voices proclaiming the end of higher education as we know it, Brueggemann posits the frames "late," "very late," and "too late" based on Jeremiah's prophecy and Israel's historical context on the verge of the Babylonian exile. Administrators interviewed by the authors generally confirmed the presence of fast wisdom (rooted in the triad of control: might, wealth, and wisdom) in higher education and in their institutions.[12] Examples offered "emphasized wealth in some combination

---

generation? (Hunter, *Change the World*, 224).

8. "Slow Wisdom as a Sub-version of Reality" (lecture, Baylor University, October 28, 2011). A slightly modified version of the talk was published in Davis, *Educating for Wisdom*.

9. One example of this reimagining is David Cunningham's chapter entitled "Colleges Have Callings, Too," in Cunningham, *Vocation Across the Academy*, 249–71. As the title implies, Cunningham argues for a shift from mission statements, which imply being sent for a purpose, to vocational statements, which imply being called to a purpose.

10. Slow wisdom, according to Brueggemann, includes body, neighborhood, pain, dreams, imagination, vocation, and commandments (Torah), while fast wisdom includes abstraction, the club, numbness, present possession, explanation, career, and gold/honey.

11. Glanzer et al., *Restoring the Soul of the University*, 299.

12. The authors admit it is puzzling to include wisdom in this triad, since the term

with might and wisdom."[13] Respondents expressed "[c]oncerns about the commodification of higher education as a market good and related educational implications."[14] Some specific "late" issues identified were a focus on debt and income, employee pay disparity, the student debt, tuition, and aid model, and complicity in supporting student careerism and consumerism and even modeling this behavior for students.[15] All these issues and others suggest the interplay of wealth and power that characterizes the triad of control.

Other respondents identified the times as "very late" for higher education. In this view, the surrounding culture has successfully coopted the discussion of the value of higher education. The problem is viewed as increasingly impossible to solve, as one respondent described the situation of being caught within the system as being "deep."[16] Some also responded that the times may be "too late" for higher education to extract itself from its predicament. One participant put it this way: "The university is in danger of losing its creative redemptive role in society by giving in too much to the power elite structures of its day and really becoming a tool that kind of supports those ongoing structures rather than challenging those."[17] The authors then reflect on what "late" meant in the time of King Josiah of Israel, when God had already said the exile to Babylon was inevitable; they use this observation to transition to a brief excursus on what it means for Christian higher education to be living in exile.[18]

Regarding living in exile, the authors sketch two paths to follow.[19] The first is "separation." This countercultural approach aims to move away from the prevailing cultural narrative of might, wisdom, and wealth. It allows Christian higher education to establish itself uniquely and as an

---

usually and biblically has positive connotations.

13. Glanzer et al., *Restoring the Soul of the University*, 301.

14. Glanzer et al., *Restoring the Soul of the University*, 301.

15. For a brief summary of these types of issues, see Clydesdale, *Purposeful Graduate*, xv-xxiii.

16. Glanzer et al., *Restoring the Soul of the University*, 302.

17. Glanzer et al., *Restoring the Soul of the University*, 303.

18. On living in exile, see Hunter, *Change the World*, 27-69.

19. On this topic, see Hunter and his emphasis on "faithful presence": "[F]aithfulness works itself out in the context of complex social, political, economic, and cultural forces that prevail at a particular time and place" (Hunter, *Change the World*, 197). He describes the different cultural challenges assessed by theological conservatives, theological progressives, and neo-Anabaptists.

alternative model, rooted in the triad of fidelity (love, justice, and righteousness). This approach, however, may not be realistic considering all the ways Christian colleges are intertwined with the broader academy (e.g., through accreditation relationships, professional associations, etc.). The second path, then, is "cooperative subversion." A biblical model for this path is the prophet Daniel in exile in Babylon. As Brueggemann states, Daniel's story demonstrates that "one can live amid the regime of might, wisdom and wealth but still be a practitioner of love, justice, and righteousness."[20] Like Daniel, administrators today live in a culture where might, wisdom, and wealth are "culturally and functionally normative."[21] They are also, thereby, freed from the responsibility to manage the cultural narrative and able to explore what slow wisdom looks like in their own institutions. Within cooperative subversion are the redemptive approach, wherein Christian administrators and institutions seek to live within the triad of fidelity and influence for the good of the broader educational community that lives in the triad of control, and prophetic margin, which places emphasis on the development of identity within institutions and students so they can live faithfully within unfaithful cultural structures. The authors summarize:

> However much we prefer the vision of living in the Promised Land, the Christian experience in early twenty-first-century American is more accurately reflected in the analogy of Israel in exile. Christian cultural influence has waned and is waning. Unbelief has become normative and secularity prevalent . . . Embracing exilic life means accepting that the rules of the higher-education game are set largely outside of the control of Christian higher education. Consequently demonstrating competence if not excellence will mean jumping through the hoops of accreditation, federal policy, and marketplace credibility that are required to establish legitimacy."[22]

Citing Brueggemann once again, though from a different source,[23] they list three elements of response, rooted in Israel's captivity in Egypt: a critique of the dominant ideology, public processing of pain, and the release of a new social imagination. In the critique of dominant ideology, Israel (and so Christian higher education) can live and speak in a way that

20. Cited in Glanzer et al., *Restoring the Soul of the University*, 308.
21. Glanzer et al., *Restoring the Soul of the University*, 308.
22. Glanzer et al., *Restoring the Soul of the University*, 315.
23. Brueggemann, *Hope within History*.

delegitimizes the reigning system, in the present case one of secularism and unbelief. For academic administrators this critique may take implicit (e.g., hiring and personnel policies) or explicit (e.g., faculty training) form in programs and structures. Public processing of pain allows the institution to cry out to the Lord regarding the pressures faced.[24] The release of a new social imagination "heralds the possibility of an order not yet realized."[25] This can be done by an appropriate communication of the broader goals of the institution and their coherence, and by recognizing that administrators of Christian institutions will spend the bulk of their time doing the same things colleagues at other institutions do. The question, therefore, is what they will do with the remaining time. Since students will naturally come to college with expectations set by the surrounding culture, it is vital for Christian institutions to develop the value of love, justice, and righteousness and help students to distinguish their functioning in the culture from their kingdom identity.

Glanzer, Alleman, and Ream are helpful in identifying the natural tensions in Christian academic leadership. Due to the waning of Christian influence on society, Christian higher educational institutions are increasingly at odds with the culture and with their secular counterparts. Pursuing the triad of fidelity (love, righteousness, and justice) allows the Christian administrator to be faithful to the biblical understanding of reality and to position his or her institution as a prophetic critique of the reigning narrative of higher education. This pursuit includes willingness to make public the cries of pain and to develop a new social imagination for what is a truly Christian education.

This analysis raises practical questions for the Christian academic administrator. How can one move from a focus on wealth and power to the narrative of love, righteousness, and justice? How can one live within the tension of accreditation expectations and the call to fidelity? How ought the administration at a Christian college look different than that at a secular school? We turn now to a consideration of Christian social practices as a way of addressing these questions.

---

24. While Glanzer, Alleman, and Ream take this public processing of pain to be confession of wrongdoing or struggle by the administration, in Brueggemann's understanding it is the cry of people as a result of their oppression (e.g., Israel publicly processing its pain over its onerous enslavement in Egypt).

25. Glanzer et al., *Restoring the Soul of the University*, 317.

CHRISTIAN SOCIAL PRACTICES

On the topic of social practices in general, and Christian practices in particular, David I. Smith and James K. A. Smith have provided an excellent summary.[26] The authors begin with a description of Alasdair MacIntyre's work, *After Virtue*.[27] In contrast to Enlightenment thinkers who dismissed the concept of a moral goal or *telos* for humans, MacIntyre argues for the significant role of communities of practice that help form persons towards virtue. This virtue formation requires an understanding of a *telos*, that is, what is "good." Virtue is the combination of habits and dispositions that incline one towards the "good." What is good is communicated to persons in a community by the stories in which they find their identity. Virtue is not natural in the sense of being something people are born with, but rather constitutes a second nature that is formed in persons through participation in the practices of a particular community, including imitating those held up as examples by the community. Education in this understanding is about more than the passing on of information to students; it is formative of student character. The question before us is, how could participation in an administrative community of practice help form the character of students, faculty, and other administrators? More broadly, how could it help an institution develop slow wisdom rooted in the triad of fidelity?

Smith and Smith summarize MacIntyre's understanding of practices as "a complex of routines and rituals that is handed down from others," with "goals that can be achieved *only* by engaging in the practice," with "relevant standards of excellence" established by the community.[28] Practices help form in persons a *habitus* or "orientation and inclination toward the world, aimed at a specific *telos*."[29]

From the educational literature, Smith and Smith explicate the work of Etienne Wenger, which focuses on "communities of practice."[30] They summarize:

---

26. Smith and Smith, *Teaching and Christian Practices*, 123.
27. MacIntyre, *After Virtue*.
28. Smith and Smith, *Teaching and Christian Practices*, 89 (emphasis theirs).
29. Smith and Smith, *Teaching and Christian Practices*, 9. The authors also describe the work of Pierre Bourdieu, who, like MacIntyre, describes the development through practices of a *habitus*, "internalized as a second nature" (Smith and Smith, *Teaching and Christian Practices*, 10). See Bourdieu, *Logic of Practice*.
30. Smith and Smith, *Teaching and Christian Practices*, 1114. See Wenger, *Communities of Practice*.

> People come together on a regular basis and do things together in certain ways in pursuit of certain shared goals, and in doing so, they become a community that is defined and held together by shared practices (rather than, for example, family ties or affectionate attachments).[31]

The authors cite three aspects that constitute communities of practice. The first is *participation* by members of the community of practice, which varies according to the community and the member. The second is *reification*, in which ideas within the group are expressed through physical acts or objects. In the teaching context, Smith and Smith use "chairs, desks, textbooks, grades, syllabi, tests, gestures" as examples of reification.[32] The types and arrangements of these things impact the functioning of the classroom community and thus group member participation. The third aspect of community practice is *repertoire*, which is "a set of behaviors having particular meaning for [the] group."[33] These patterns of behavior define the life of the group and provide boundaries that distinguish one community of practice from another. Also impacting the function and identity of the group, according to Wenger, is a shared imagination, which defines "what goods [the group] is pursuing and why."[34] This imagination is made visible for the community in its repertoire, consisting of what the group says and does.

When applied by scholars to Christian education, an understanding of a community of practice implies that such education is not simply an intellectual activity passing on information. Rather, it is a formative activity in which "something is done to us."[35] Understood in terms of Christian theology, however, this formative activity is ascribed to the Holy Spirit, through whom the triune God shapes us into God's image. This shaping extends beyond the spiritual aspects of our lives to include how we as persons engage the world with our whole person. That is, this character-shaping activity is wholistic and impacts all of life.[36]

---

31. Smith and Smith, *Teaching and Christian Practices*, 12.
32. Smith and Smith, *Teaching and Christian Practices*, 13.
33. Smith and Smith, *Teaching and Christian Practices*, 13.
34. Smith and Smith, *Teaching and Christian Practices*, 14.
35. Smith and Smith, *Teaching and Christian Practices*, 15, quoting Dykstra, *Growing in the Life of Faith*, 67.
36. On the formative importance of embodied activities, see Smith, *Desiring the Kingdom*.

A question can be raised as to what constitutes a Christian practice. Smith and Smith are again helpful here, distinguishing between a narrower view of worship practices (e.g., baptism, communion, confession) and a broader view of spiritual disciplines (e.g., hospitality, Sabbath-keeping, testimony, simplicity, etc.).[37] Christian practices are "things Christian people do together over time in response to and in the light of God's active presence for the life of the world."[38] The goal of Smith and Smith is to apply scholarship on practices, particularly on Christian practices, to the higher education classroom. They argue Christian higher education must be formative, and that the Christian tradition provides many historically tested practices that may serve as resources for the professor at a Christian college or university.

Smith and Smith make clear that communities of practice can and do have a significant impact on the development of virtue. Applied to our question, we may say that academic administration can include intentional practices designed to form a community of virtue, that is, of slow wisdom and the triad of fidelity. The Christian tradition is rich with such practices, of which we will now consider a few, including hospitality, Sabbath-keeping, and testimony.

TOWARDS A FAITHFUL ACADEMIC ADMINISTRATION

As noted above, academic administration does not lend itself to reflection. It is, in fact, a profession characterized by significant short term and long-term problem solving, financial and relational challenges, a constant stream of matters perceived as urgent by others, and emotional and political pressures. For this reason, the cultivation of slow wisdom and the triad of fidelity must be intentional and ultimately sustainable. The implementation of Christian practices in communities of practice, as described by Smith and Smith, provides a means to achieve this goal.

In my academic administrative setting, there are a variety of possible communities of practice. One is fellow administrators, all vice presidents (the President's cabinet), who each oversee one of the five primary goals of the College (academic, vocational, Christian, patriotic, and cultural growth). This group currently meets at least twice weekly, once in person

---

37. Smith and Smith, *Teaching and Christian Practices*, 16.

38. Dykstra and Bass, "Times of Yearning, Practices of Faith," 5, quoted in Smith and Smith, *Teaching and Christian Practices*, 16.

and once virtually. In addition, there are frequent interactions among members of the cabinet during each week. A second potential community of practice is the academic division chairs. This group of six faculty administrators meets weekly with me, with informal meetings among individuals on a regular basis. Third, there is the office of the Dean of the College, which includes an assistant to the dean, a registrar, an assistant registrar, and eight student workers. This office serves the broader faculty and student populations at the institution. Finally, there is the full-time faculty that numbers just under one hundred at my institution.

As an example of a Christian practice that could help one or more of these communities develop slow wisdom, let us take the practice of hospitality.[39] In a higher education culture in which treatment of students is naturally motivated by the desire to retain students and thereby maintain tuition revenue, a financial survival motive, the Christian administrator has a qualitatively different motivation: to incarnate the love of God to one's students and colleagues and to guests.[40] Under this motivation, the value of students and others is not linked primarily to their economic potential, but rather to their creation in the image of God (*imago Dei*).[41]

As the lead academic officer, my decision-making on student and faculty requests provides a primary opportunity to practice hospitality. How will I receive students and faculty? How will I respond to their requests and perceived needs? My office staff and students likewise have an opportunity to receive faculty and students, as well as staff and guests, with hospitality, i.e., by recognizing them first and foremost as persons created in the image of God. To do so requires time and energy, which can be in short supply in a hectic office. Nonetheless, an office can practice hospitality by treating students and other guests with honor, considering their backgrounds before making decisions, and (especially in the case of students) remembering their developmental stage. As one means of

---

39. On hospitality as a Christian practice, see Pohl, *Making Room*.

40. Regarding guests, one may recall the exhortation by the author of Hebrews, "Do not neglect to show hospitality to strangers, for thereby some have entertained angels unawares" (Heb 13:2, ESV).

41. "In all, the practice of faithful presence generates relationships and institutions that are covenantal. These create space that fosters meaning, purpose, and belonging and by so doing, these relationships and institutions resist an instrumentalization endemic to the modern world that tends to reduce the value of people and the worth of creation to mere utility, whether utility is oriented toward market efficiency, expanding power, or personal fulfillment" (Hunter, *Change the World*, 266).

practicing hospitality, my office has an "open door" policy, which makes me generally accessible to faculty, students, and staff.

As a second example, we can take the Christian practice of Sabbath-keeping.[42] This practice is especially notable at an institution that has vocational growth as one of its five primary goals, has for all full-time students a mandatory work study program, promotes the development of a strong work ethic, and which the Wall Street Journal nicknamed "Hard Work U®" in 1973.

Despite sometimes legalistic associations, the biblical practice of Sabbath-keeping is for the benefit of humans.[43] Participation in Sabbath rest is a means of aligning the rhythm of one's life with God's creative[44] and redemptive[45] activity. It is significant that the biblical work week was six days, with a day of rest on the seventh, i.e., this practice was not a way to avoid hard work or a long work week. It was, instead, a way to take one day out of seven intentionally to slow down and recognize the Lord as ultimately in control of one's life and well-being. It is obvious how this slowing down aligns with the cultivation of what Brueggemann terms "slow wisdom." For the Christian academic administrator, the practice of Sabbath rest must be given precedence, both personally and professionally. To set aside weekly times of rest, of freedom from the need to be productive and to be doing work, is central to this practice. The administrator can encourage others in the office, faculty members, and even students to practice Sabbath rest, for example, by avoiding scheduling major projects and assessments on Mondays, since Sunday is often understood as the Sabbath day in Christian practice. Like hospitality, encouragement towards Sabbath rest can also be given to administrative colleagues who are under pressures like those of the academic administration.

The academic calendar fortunately lends itself to times of rest beyond the weekly level, if planned for accordingly. At College of the Ozarks the administration typically and graciously gives faculty and staff the entire week of Thanksgiving as a holiday and does the same with the week of Christmas Day. Spring break can, likewise, be a time of rest not only for students but also for faculty members. The College offers only a handful of summer classes, typically in person, and teaching these

---

42. On Sabbath-keeping as a Christian practice, see Dawn, *Keeping the Sabbath Wholly*, and Meador, *Search of the Common Good*.

43. Mark 2:27.

44. Exod 20:11.

45. Deut 5:15.

intensive classes is voluntary. The academic administrator can encourage faculty members and students to make rest a priority during these breaks from academic study.

The practice of testimony is about speaking truth, and historically can refer to the making known of one's experience of God, even in the midst of everyday life.[46] While testimony can and should function as prophetic critique, it is also a means of proclaiming the Christian narrative in a way that forms and informs the community of practice.

One way the College has practiced testimony with faculty is the Faithful Education Project (FEP). This project is required of all new faculty members after their first year of service and completed by current faculty members the year after their six-year review. The focus of the project, which includes recommended readings, is for the faculty member to write an essay about how one can educate faithfully in their discipline (math, agriculture, psychology, etc.). In addition to writing a three thousand word essay, faculty members also give a ten minute presentation on their project to other faculty members. The FEP requires additional work for each faculty member, and new faculty members receive a course load reduction to recognize this fact. The opportunity for faculty members to give testimony of their reflection on Christian faith and their discipline has been a source of encouragement for the faculty at College of the Ozarks. The oral presentations offer a rare opportunity for faculty members to hear someone from outside their area of expertise speak about how their Christian faith impacts the way they teach and engage with their discipline. The College also provides opportunity for testimony through its new faculty orientation process, which is a year-long sequence of meetings using Susan VanZanten's book *Joining the Mission* as a focal point.[47]

How can testimony function in the life of a busy administrative office? One way is through the related discipline of listening, that is, allowing others in the community of practice to share their experiences. Much like the practice of hospitality, this discipline honors the one speaking by treating as important what they say because they are created in the image of God. It is a challenge to pursue the discipline of listening as an administrator, but this discipline can open the door for others to share what God is doing in their lives.

---

46. See Smith and Smith, *Teaching and Christian Practices*, 69–71.
47. VanZanten, *Joining the Mission*.

CONCLUSION

Christian higher education is increasingly in exile from the broader culture of higher education. Learning to live as exiles frees Christian college administrators from the weight of being the moral guardians of society and allows them to focus on developing what Brueggemann calls slow wisdom. This wisdom offers a prophetic critique of the prevailing culture, and forms those who participate in Christian higher education. Christian practices such as hospitality, Sabbath-keeping, and testimony, and the recognition of communities of practice, can help academic administrators cultivate slow wisdom in themselves, their colleagues, and their students. These practices, engaged in with intentionality, distinguish the Christian college administrator and administration from others in the higher education community, and create an environment in which love, justice, and righteousness can flourish.

BIBLIOGRAPHY

Bass, Dorothy C. *Practicing Our Faith*. San Francisco: Jossey-Bass, 1997.

Bourdieu, Pierre. *The Logic of Practice*. Translated by Richard Nice. Stanford: Stanford University Press, 1990.

Brueggemann, Walter. *Hope within History*. Atlanta: John Knox, 1987.

Clydesdale, Tim. *The Purposeful Graduate: Why Colleges Must Talk to Students about Vocation*. Chicago: University of Chicago Press, 2015.

Cunningham, David. *Vocation across the Academy: A New Vocabulary for Higher Education*. Oxford: Oxford University Press, 2017.

Davis, Darin H., ed. *Educating for Wisdom in the Twenty-First Century*. South Bend, IN: St. Augustine's, 2019.

Dawn, Marva J. *Keeping the Sabbath Wholly: Ceasing, Resting, Embracing, Feasting*. Grand Rapids: Eerdmans, 1989.

Dykstra, Craig. *Growing in the Life of Faith: Education and Christian Practices*, 2nd ed. Louisville: Westminster John Knox Press, 2005.

Glanzer, Perry L., et al. *Restoring the Soul of the University: Unifying Christian Higher Education in a Fragmented Age*. Downers Grove, IL: IVP Academic, 2017.

Hunter, James Davison. *To Change the World: The Irony, Tragedy, and Possibility of Christianity in the Late Modern World*. Oxford: Oxford University Press, 2010.

MacIntyre, Alasdair. *After Virtue: A Study in Moral Theory*, 3rd ed. Notre Dame: University of Notre Dame Press, 2007.

Meador, Jake. *In Search of the Common Good: Christian Fidelity in a Fractured World*. Downers Grove, IL: InterVarsity, 2019.

Pohl, Christine D. *Living in Community: Cultivating Practices that Sustain Us*. Grand Rapids: Eerdmans, 2012.

———. *Making Room: Recovering Hospitality as a Christian Tradition*. Grand Rapids: Eerdmans, 1999.

Smith, David I. *On Christian Teaching: Practicing Faith in the Classroom*. Grand Rapids: Eerdmans, 2018.

Smith, David I. and James K. A. Smith. *Teaching and Christian Practices: Reshaping Faith and Learning*. Grand Rapids: Eerdmans, 2011.

Smith, James K. A. *Desiring the Kingdom: Worship, Worldview, and Cultural Formation*. Grand Rapids: Baker Academic, 2009.

VanZanten, Susan. *Joining the Mission: A Guide for (Mainly) New College Faculty*. Grand Rapids: Eerdmans, 2011.

Wenger, Etienne. *Communities of Practice: Learning, Meaning, and Identity*. Cambridge: Cambridge University Press, 1999.

2

Faithful, Narrative Student Development
Vocation and Virtue

Andrew T. Bolger

This chapter explores the intersection of vocation and virtue development as a paradigm for faithful education in a post-Christian world. In education, especially higher education, the focus of institutions is often on content mastery more than character mastery. Yet, content has little effect without the practice of its right moral application. I am reminded of Edmund Burke's famous quote as he considered civic education and America's future:

> But what is liberty without wisdom, and without virtue? It is the greatest of all possible evils; for it is folly, vice, and madness, without tuition or restraint. Those who know what virtuous liberty is, cannot bear to see it disgraced by incapable heads, on account of their having high-sounding words in their mouths.[1]

This understanding of embodied life as one of right action, right thought, and right emotion is not new. Aristotle rehearsed this famous refrain multiple times in his *Nicomachean Ethics*. Nonetheless, those of us in education often forget that this refrain is not merely content that needs to be mastered, but praxis that needs to be applied.

---

1. Burke, *Burke Select Works*, 290–1.

But how can content be mastered and applied in transformative ways within our society? Many books with millions of words have been dedicated to this intellectual inquiry. Each deserves reflection. However, at our small, liberal-arts-based work college, we developed a system that works for our community by incorporating the reflections of the ancients with an awareness of the present moment.

In the next several sections of this chapter, I will explore the theoretical framework of this system and how we express it in our context. The center of this developmental system revolves around the commitment that virtue and vocation are not separate endeavors, but rather complementary, mutually beneficial pursuits. Vocation directs the shape and goal of our lives, and virtue strengthens this pursuit.

Before I engage this philosophical—and formational—endeavor, let me lay the groundwork with some institutional context and commitments that shaped our paradigm and programs.

COLLEGE OF THE OZARKS: MISSION, VISION, AND A BRIEF HISTORY

In a letter to the Missouri Synod of the Presbyterian Church in 1905, James P. Forsythe, the Presbyterian missionary who founded the College, expressed his dream of establishing a school for "boys and girls from the Ozarks . . . who were unable to secure an education above the free school."[2] He further stated the purpose of the school should be to become a "self-sustaining 'family' by requiring all students to spend a portion of their time in the various duties assigned to them in the classroom building or on the campus and farm, such as kitchen, dining room, and laundry work, or in securing fuel and provisions, improving property, etc."[3] Forsythe's vision became a reality a year later, in 1906, when School of the Ozarks, now College of the Ozarks, was commissioned to provide through a work education model a "Christian education for youth of both sexes, especially those found worthy but who are without sufficient means to procure such training."[4]

A commitment to virtue development paralleled the College's commitment to vocational development. At the original cornerstone

---

2. College of the Ozarks, "Unique College."
3. College of the Ozarks, "Unique College."
4. College of the Ozarks, "Unique College."

dedication in 1906, a local pastor, Reverend Abbott, anticipated in a prophetic prayer that "youth entering the long, hard road of life" might pause at the institution to be,

> shod for the journey—lingering a little while to put on the full armour [sic] of Christian education; we see men standing in legislative halls, ministering as physicians, preaching the gospel, tilling the soil and living in peace and purity beneath their vine and fig tree, all of whom received inspiration and equipment within these sacred walls.[5]

This commitment to a *Christian education* continues today. Despite many institutional changes, the College has maintained its original mission and commitment to virtue and vocational development. These commitments are best expressed in the College's mission and vision statement. The mission statement hearkens back to James P. Forsythe's day, emphasizing the College's audacious goal "to provide the advantages of a Christian education for youth of both sexes, especially those found worthy, but who are without sufficient means to procure such training" in the rural—and perceived as backward—Ozarks mountains.[6]

Comparatively, the vision statement of the College echoes Reverend Abbott's prophetic prayer, illuminating the distinct Christian citizenship and callings graduates from the College would undertake. Simply put, the vision of the College "is to develop citizens of Christ-like character who are well-educated, hard-working, and patriotic."[7] This vision integrates the five goals of the College, also known as the "five-fold mission," into a concise statement that serves as the primary student learning outcome of the College. The five goals of the College are listed as follows:

1. Academic goal: To provide a sound education, based on the liberal arts.

2. Vocational goal: To promote a strong work ethic, encouraging the development of good character and values.

3. Christian goal: To foster the Christian faith through the integration of faith with learning, living, and service.

4. Patriotic goal: To encourage an understanding of American heritage, civic responsibilities, love of country, and willingness to defend it.

5. Godsey and Godsey, *Flight of the Phoenix*, 98.
6. College of the Ozarks, "Unique College."
7. College of the Ozarks, "Unique College."

5. Cultural goal: To cultivate an appreciation of the fine arts, an understanding of the world, and adherence to high personal standards.[8]

These goals provide structure and consistently emphasize the College's mission and vision across all programs and departments. Beyond their operational impact, the goals emphasize the College's commitment to cultivating students' callings and character. This commitment is intentionally holistic, multifaceted, and directional—it concludes with students strengthened through virtue and a robust understanding of vocation in their lives.

THE KEETER CENTER FOR CHARACTER EDUCATION

In 2007, the College's leadership developed a center, The Keeter Center for Character Education, devoted to strengthening existing character development programs and synthesizing the College's five goals into a coherent expression that could energize the College's vision "to create citizens of Christ-like character."

In so doing, the Center reflects the principle upon which College of the Ozarks was established: character in young people is best developed by means of an education that includes the head, the heart, and the hands, through its five-fold commitment to the following goals:

- To reflect the College's five-fold mission emphasizing academic, Christian, vocational, cultural, and patriotic growth and to provide society with productive, responsible citizens.
- To promote basic Judeo-Christian values such as honesty, respect for and service to others, good citizenship, generosity, honor, courage, wise use of time and talents, and work ethic.
- To serve as a resource for administrators, teachers, and parents as they seek to fulfill their responsibilities as partners in the character-building process.
- To publicize information on character education.
- To serve as a model for those throughout the country who have the desire to establish similar centers or programs.[9]

---

8. College of the Ozarks, "Unique College."
9. College of the Ozarks, "Keeter Center."

As a part of a larger institutional initiative and The Keeter Center for Character Education, THRIVE, a co-curricular framework and series of programs, emerged. THRIVE synthesized the College's commitment to virtue and vocation, as expressed in its mission, vision, and goals, into a more accessible and student-focused expression. Before I describe the THRIVE framework for faithful curricular and co-curricular education, it is important to establish the philosophical and theoretical basis for THRIVE's development.

FOUR FUNDAMENTAL PHENOMENA FOR FAITHFUL FORMATION

N.T. Wright has argued persuasively that humans rely on four phenomena to construct meaning in their lives: symbols, questions, stories (meta-narrative), and practices.[10] These phenomena illuminate a presuppositional understanding of a person's view of the world and, when excavated, yield deeply held views and affections of reality. They also provide a robust framework for consciousness-building that undergirds so much of virtue and vocational development.

Scaffolding university programs with these four phenomena encourages vocational and virtue reflection for students, as well as other adults. At the presuppositional level, Wright's fourfold framework examines whether coherence exists between one's personal and communal vision of life (vocation) and the practices that support this life. Wright's model is also suggestive of the Aristotelian framework for virtue development that it echoes, specifically that virtue, as a vocation, is formed "through action and reaction."[11] In these ways, virtue and vocation complement each other's development by encouraging humans to live in a holistic, embodied form, what Christians often refer to as an incarnational life.

Incarnational living also has a communal context. This communal context provides the *telos* for vocation and virtue development.[12] For instance, the vocation and virtue of a public servant, as in Aristotle's framework, contributed to the flourishing of a city-state. As public servants practiced their vocation—virtuous public service—the city-state

---

10. Wright, *New Testament and the People of God*, 123–4.

11. Kristjansson, *Virtues and Vices*, 52.

12. See Sanderse, *Character Education*; MacIntyre, *After Virtue*; Meilaender, *Theory and Practice of Virtue*.

flourished.[13] Thus, Hauerwas is right to evaluate any community by its politics: "The truest politics, therefore, is that concerned with the development of virtue."[14] Corporate expressions of virtue and vocation empower individuals and sustain communities.[15]

Wright also advocates that virtue and vocation—holistic, embodied life—are best formed in the community through fundamental institutions of life, whether they be family, neighborhood, church, university, or nation.[16] This occurs because virtue and vocation require life-long incarnational conversations, "dialectic" in Wright's language. In this sense, the pursuit of vocation and virtue development is a mutual endeavor that requires persistent question-asking and answering with seasoned women and men, who have undertaken a similar journey. This is the model of ancient myths, epics, and sacred writings. The pursuit of thriving is a whole, not partial, life endeavor.

Each of these phenomena also helps solidify and synthesize one's sense of calling, community, and character as they are shared in a community.[17] Thus, narrative—the storytelling, person-making, reflective venture—is necessary to virtuous development because it allows humans to relive previous episodes of their story and identify the relationships, practices, symbols, questions, and stories that support their endeavor.[18] Undertaken in community, these individual pursuits are galvanized and tested by more seasoned individuals, as they continue the dialectical act of virtue and vocation with the young people in their care.

Epochs, sagas, and myths reminded ancient audiences of the dramatic unfolding of virtue and vocation in human life.[19] This practice of narration through vocational reflection remains paramount for embodied virtue as people consider, discover, and live into their vocations.

---

13. For further discussion, see Wadell, *Happiness and the Christian Moral Life*, and Wadell, "Itinerary of Hope," in Cunningham, *At This Time*.

14. Hauerwas, *Community of Character*, 10.

15. Hauerwas, *Community of Character*.

16. Wright, *New Testament and the People of God*; Kristjansson, *Virtues and Vices*, 197.

17. Annas, *Intelligent Virtue*.

18. See LaReau, *Getting a Life*; Hauerwas and Burrell, "System to Story," in Hauerwas and Jones, *Truthfulness and Tragedy*.

19. MacIntyre, *After Virtue*; Hauerwas and Burrell, "System to Story," in Hauerwas and Jones, *Truthfulness and Tragedy*.

CHALLENGES TO BUILDING TESTED VIRTUE DEVELOPMENT

Yet, building meaningful paradigms that produce practiced virtue remains challenging in higher education settings.[20] There are many reasons for this reality; however, this often occurs because virtue and vocational reflection are abstracted and separated from each other.[21] As students connect their vocation with virtue, a rich and textured environment for growth emerges.[22] One helpful mechanism for engaging questions of virtue and vocation involves identifying, evaluating, and realigning the fundamental phenomena humans use to construct meaning in their lives.

THRIVE—A STUDENT-FOCUSED VISION OF CHARACTER

THRIVE was developed to help students at College of the Ozarks understand the process of virtue development through a story-based lens, connecting virtue and vocation development and directing them towards a common outcome: *thriving*.

Early on, we used Wright's framework to structure a cohesive vocation and virtue development pathway for students. As a Christian work college, we recognized a common meta-narrative, the Christian story, and a set of common practices—learning, worship, and work. With these established practices and a common meta-narrative, we focused our energy on developing and branding developmental symbols and questions.

Rather than focusing on specific character qualities, we built our developmental symbols and questions to reflect the Apostle Paul's process of virtue development as described in Rom 5:3–5: "suffering produces endurance, and endurance produces character, and character produces hope."[23] Focusing on process, rather than character qualities, proved especially effective for us because it gave us a narrative way to describe the consistent challenge of virtue and vocation development that can

---

20. Schwehn and Bass, *Leading Lives that Matter*.
21. See Schnell, "Commitment and Community," in Cunningham, *At This Time*.
22. Wadell, "Itinerary of Hope," in Cunningham, *At This Time*.
23. Rom 5:3–4 (ESV).

inform all of life, while also building for common practices that would shape character and calling in our community.

This commitment to practices taps into Wright's fourfold pattern for holistic Christian formation, while also illustrating the engine of character development. James K. A. Smith describes this engine in *You Are What You Love: The Spiritual Power of Habit*.[24] As Christians in a postmodern world, "learning virtue" by reinforcing the *activity*, as opposed to the *passivity*, of virtue development may be one of our most powerful tools for faithful education, because virtue and vocation development parallel other forms of faithful, embodied education. In this same book, Smith illustrates the importance of practices for character development by describing the importance of embodied forms of faithful education:

> Learning virtue is more like practicing scales on the piano than learning music theory: the goal is, in a sense, for your fingers to learn the scales so they can then play "naturally," as it were. Learning here isn't just information acquisition; it's more like inscribing something into the very fiber of your being.[25]

For our institutions, the scale we want our students to practice until it becomes second nature is a virtue/vocational development process that parallels Rom 5:3–5.

- Till (suffering) encourages us to embrace struggle and suffering.
- Root (endurance) encourages us to seek a greater understanding of our God-given identity.
- Grow (character) encourages us to consider the constellation of relationships we need to continue to mature throughout our whole lives.
- Fruit (hope) encourages us to give back out of what we've received.

We believe this organic process, which draws on many of Jesus' metaphors in the gospels, provides a paradigm that can be repeated throughout life. We believe, as suggested in the title of our program, this framework promotes the *thriving* life referenced by the psalmist in Ps 1—the virtuous person is like a tree planted by streams of living water, whose fruit is always in season.[26]

24. Smith, *You Are What You Love*.
25. Smith, *You Are What You Love*, 18.
26. Ps 1:3.

Equally important to our paradigm and programs is the role of questions. Questions reframe the educational *telos* of our institution, reorienting students to a holistic personal development, not just academic or work goals. Questions also require response. They are dialectical by nature. In this way, question-asking at significant markers in the educational endeavor provides a strategic place for university staff and faculty to promote reflection, collaborate with students in synthesis, and incarnationally offer their distinct life experiences of the *tilling, rooting, growing,* and *fruiting* that we hope occurs for our whole community, not just our students.

At a program level, we built a structured opportunity where students who participate in the THRIVE Pathway at the College meet with a faculty or staff person of their choice—a faculty/staff guide—and discuss a question for each year of their college experience. For their first year (Till), the question is foundational but sets the course for the rest of their college experience. It is simply, "Is it (a rigorous work college) experience worth it?" This question is, once again, contextual to our environment. Despite this reality, it echoes a common aspect of *tilling* that can occur in any context, community, or relationship in life. Given that we live on this side of the fall, every relationship, community, institution, and culture is broken. There is no perfect expression of humans relating to each other, whether at a personal, corporate, or civic level. Choosing to stay in relationships and communities that are flawed, despite their brokenness, remains one of the most incarnational expressions of faithful education that we can practice as Christians.

During the first year, the College's programs intentionally challenge students to embrace the struggle of *tilling*, whether that means they are working in the dish pit of our cafeteria, milking dairy cows at 4 a.m., struggling through an academically rigorous composition sequence, or simply learning to balance the expectations of our community in terms of worship, learning, and working. This question promotes *ownership* by challenging students to evaluate their commitment, discern if it is worthwhile, and commit themselves to others despite the imperfection of our institution, community, and the relationships that form them. Through this dialectic, we have seen students explore the challenges they face, their struggle to make sense of these challenges, and, despite these challenges, a more durable commitment to our community amidst its brokenness and flaws. This process of ownership is a fundamental outcome of the faithful education we seek to cultivate at the College.

Similarly, each successive year builds on the question from the previous year, building consciousness, a sense of vocation, and a challenge to practice new cadences of thinking, reflecting, and being. Although each of these questions has its distinct outcomes for second-year (Root), third-year (Grow), and fourth-year (Fruit) students, I will not spend time elaborating on these qualities here; however, I will offer the four questions we use (these questions are reflexive and are intended to be asked by the student):

- Till: Is it, a rigorous work college education, worth it?
- Root: Who am I?
- Grow: What relationships and community do I need to continue to *grow* and *thrive*?
- Fruit: How can I give back to my family, community, nation, and world out of who I've become?

Once again, these questions reinforce our communal practices (*tilling, rooting, growing,* and *fruiting*), the icons for each of these movements, and our common meta-narrative, the Christian story. Together they build consciousness, encourage choice and character development, and help students construct a faithful sense of virtue and vocation as they consider the direction of their lives and the challenges they may face.

CONCLUSION

A narrative approach to student development can strengthen faithful education, especially in co-curricular programs on university campuses. At our institution, we have seen at individual and institutional levels the coherence and consciousness that Wright's framework of symbols, questions, practices, and meta-narrative brings to faithful education, virtue development, and vocational discernment. Our students are considering their callings and character development in new and more sustainable ways. This engagement empowers them and encourages staff and faculty on our campus.

BIBLIOGRAPHY

Annas, Julia. *Intelligent Virtue*. Oxford: Oxford University Press, 2011.

Aristotle. *Nicomachean Ethics*. Translated by D. Ross. Oxford: Oxford University Press, 2009.

Burke, Edmund. *Burke Select Works, Vol. II: Reflections on the Revolution in France*. Edited by E.J. Payne. Oxford: Clarendon, 2005.

College of the Ozarks. "A Unique College." *2021–2022 College Catalogue*. https://catalog.cofo.edu/content.php?catoid=16&navoid=735.

———. "The Keeter Center for Character Education." https://www.cofo.edu/Goals/Cultural/Character-Education.

Cunningham, David, ed. *At This Time and In This Place: Vocation and Higher Education*. Oxford: Oxford University Press, 2016.

Godsey, Helen and Townsend Godsey. *Flight of the Phoenix: A Biography of the School of the Ozarks*. Point Lookout, MO: School of the Ozarks Press, 1984.

Hauerwas, Stanley. *A Community of Character: Toward a Constructive Christian Social Ethic*. Notre Dame: Notre Dame University Press, 1991.

Hauerwas, Stanley and L. G. Jones, eds. *Truthfulness and Tragedy: Further Investigations in Christian Ethics*. Eugene, OR: Wipf and Stock, 1997.

Kristjansson, Kristjan. *Virtues and Vices in Positive Psychology: A Philosophical Critique*. New York: Cambridge University Press, 2013.

LaReau, Renee. M. *Getting a Life: How to Find Your True Vocation*. Maryknoll: Orbis, 2003.

McCabe, Herbert. *The Good Life: Ethics and the Pursuit of Happiness*. New York: Continuum, 2005.

Meilaender, Gilbert C. *The Theory and Practice of Virtue*. Notre Dame: Notre Dame University Press, 1984.

Sanderse, Wouter. *Character Education: A Neo-Aristotelian Approach to the Philosophy, Psychology, and Education of Virtue*. Delft: Eburon Academic, 2012.

Schwehn, Mark and Dorothy Bass, eds. *Leading Lives that Matter: What We Should Do And Who We Should Be*. Grand Rapids: Eerdmans, 2006.

Smith, James K. A. *You Are What You Love: The Spiritual Power of Habit*. Grand Rapids: Brazos, 2016.

Wadell, Paul. *Happiness and the Christian Moral Life*. Lanham, MD: Rowman & Littlefield, 2012.

Wright, N.T. *The New Testament and the People of God*. Minneapolis: Fortress, 1992.

3

Faithful Assessment

David Parrish

As the introduction to this volume makes clear, there is an abundance of excellent scholarship addressing the idea of Christian education. Over the past forty years, Christian educators have brought clarity to the purpose and vision of Christian higher education.[1] But as David Smith and James Smith noted as recently as 2011, much of this work on Christian education has addressed larger theoretical concerns such as worldview, epistemology, and content, and, despite this abundance of scholarship on worldview and/or the integration of faith and learning, few, especially within traditionally Protestant spheres, have specifically addressed the idea of Christian pedagogy.[2] Since 2011, Christian scholars have sought to fill this critical gap, articulating and implementing specific Christian practices as part of a larger movement to imagine a distinctly Christian pedagogy.[3]

Although scholars have begun exploring the contours and practices of a Christian pedagogy, few have addressed how best practices identified in the scholarship of teaching and learning not only fit comfortably within a framework of Christian education, but actually substantiate

---

1. See, for example, Holmes, *Idea of a Christian College*; Dockery, *Renewing Minds*; Wolterstorff, *Educating for Shalom*; and VanZanten, *Joining the Mission*.

2. Smith and Smith, *Teaching and Christian Practices*, 123.

3. Smith and Smith, *Teaching and Christian Practices*; Smith, *Christian Teaching*; Brad Pardue, "Incorporating Christian Practices," 53–59.

claims made by proponents of Christian education and Christian pedagogy. As this chapter will argue, assessment is not simply compatible with Christian education and Christian pedagogy; it is, in fact, a necessary component of both.

Two recent works at the forefront of Christian pedagogy are David Smith's *On Christian Teaching* and Perry Glanzer and Nathan Alleman's *The Outrageous Idea of Christian Teaching*.[4] What is striking about these otherwise excellent books is the absence of sustained discussions of assessment. However, implicit in their arguments is the assumption that good teaching is reflective teaching. Assessment is that reflective process. It is, in the words of Peggy Maki, "curiosity about what and how well our students learn."[5] While for many this curiosity about what students are learning might focus primarily on academic ideas or "informational teaching," this chapter seeks to bridge the gap between assessment and Christian pedagogy and contribute to a fuller discussion of "transformational teaching."[6] By reimagining and resituating the practice and process of assessment within the larger, often disconnected, literatures of teaching and learning, Christian education, and Christian pedagogy, Christian educators are equipped to understand the importance *and* utility of assessment. Assessment has of course become associated with accreditation, but when done well, such reflective pedagogy is a necessary component of faithful education.

It has become a truism that many faculty members shudder when they hear the term "assessment." Susan VanZanten has even referred to it, tongue-in-cheek, as the academic scarlet letter.[7] Visions of unrewarded busy work, diminished faculty autonomy, standardized classes, or of syllabus templates generate a sense of dread, resignation, or outright hostility. Faculty manifest their displeasure in numerous ways. For instance, delaying tactics such as endless questions about the philosophy of assessment rarely seem to have been asked in good faith. Similarly, faculty might turn in assessment reports in a less-than-timely manner, refuse to revise poorly written outcomes, or engage in a studied refusal to analyze the data in meaningful ways. The worst thing about this is, I *understand* the

---

4. Smith, *Christian Teaching*; Glanzer and Alleman, *Outrageous Idea of Christian Teaching*.

5. Maki, *Assessment for Student Learning*, 3.

6. Rosebrough and Leverett, "Faith and Transformational Teaching," in Dockery, *Faith and Learning*, 475–98.

7. VanZanten, *Joining the Mission*, 175.

opposition. The stated reason for assessment, that of measuring student learning, often seems redundant, prompting questions about the sufficiency of grades, and faculty who are teaching heavy course loads may not often have time to engage in the extensive literature on the subject. Equally problematic is that even when faculty are invited to participate, assessment is perceived as another example of the bureaucratization of the university occurring at the expense of those tasked with teaching; it is service, or in other words, additional responsibility without additional compensation.[8] Though often the lived reality, this perception needlessly diminishes the value of academic assessment.

Attempts to overcome faculty recalcitrance generally focus on ways in which faculty can be rewarded for their participation or ways in which engagement with the assessment process might feature into promotion or tenure decisions. Rewards can range from the all-to-infrequent larger perks like monetary stipends or course reductions, to smaller incentives like snacks or thank-you notes.[9] While not entirely unsuccessful, these minor manipulations often fail to communicate the true value of assessment. They buy short-term compliance but not long-term understanding, and such extrinsic motivators do not necessarily create intrinsic desire.

This problem is compounded by the lack of clarity regarding the purpose of assessment. At its most basic, assessment is the collection and interpretation of data useful for measuring what a student knows and can do.[10] This is often necessitated by accreditation requirements, but to view it only in terms of accreditation is misguided. Assessment is, by its very nature, teleological, and carefully considering the nature of this *telos* is vital. Recent scholarship primarily promotes the process as a means of measuring student learning.[11] As Trudy Banta and Christine Palomba explain, the "overriding purpose of outcomes assessment is to understand how educational programs are working and to determine whether they are contributing to student growth and development." Such statements posit that the goal of measuring student learning is to evaluate the strengths and weaknesses of courses, programs, or institutions.[12] Strengths and weaknesses or the concept of improvement, however, only

---

8. Banta and Palomba, *Assessment Essentials*, 52–54.

9. Smith and Gordon, "How are Faculty Rewarded and Recognized for Assessment Work?," 65–77; Banta and Palomba, *Assessment Essentials*, 46–48.

10. Banta and Palomba, *Assessment Essentials*, 1.

11. Suskie, *Assessing Student Learning*.

12. Banta and Palomba, *Assessment Essentials*, 2.

make sense in light of a teleological framework, but in many institutions, not to mention higher education as a whole, there is little agreement about what this guiding purpose is or should be.

Perhaps the most useful definition of assessment, which I mentioned above, is "intellectual curiosity about what and how well our students learn," but if anything, discussion of assessment immediately raises the issue of meaning, requiring an answer to the question, "What is the purpose of learning?"[13] Answers to this question abound, ranging from securing employment in the field of study to making a large salary. For instance, Linda Suskie argues that what students most need to learn today are transferable skills, but the evidence she points to is survey data from potential employers. This tacitly concedes that the objective of learning is to secure employment and assumes that the most important constituency for determining the purpose of learning is potential employers, a concept rejected by many educators.[14] Moreover, different constituencies including donors, employers, parents, administrators, faculty, and students might answer this question differently, thereby preventing any shared sense of meaning and precipitating a war that "tears the purpose, or the soul, of the university into pieces."[15] This fractured purpose means that "education today is rootless," lacking a coherent outcome and therefore lacking "unifying educational goals."[16] This is not intended to disparage the aforementioned goals, which, as we will see, are good when rightly ordered. On the contrary, the intent is to help faculty and students situate them more appropriately.

Many faculty feel acutely the consequences of facile answers that focus on employment or financial return on investment. The evisceration of humanities departments and the endless debates about the utility, or lack thereof, of general education programs has exacerbated the fracturing of the university into competing vocational interests.[17] This vocational parochiality diminishes the importance of liberal learning and transformational teaching and sees higher education as a "skills-training venture, where we produce cogs in the machine, but those cogs have

---

13. Maki, *Assessment for Student Learning*, 3.
14. Suskie, *Assessing Student Learning*, 46.
15. Glanzer et al., *Restoring the Soul of the University*, 3.
16. Holmes, *Idea of a Christian College*, 9.
17. Glanzer et al., *Restoring the Soul of the University*, 96–109. For more on general education, see Wells, *Realizing General Education*.

more polish."[18] Polishing cogs is not terribly inspiring (unless you are an engineer or economist) and such a *telos* is likely to promote a cynical disengagement among faculty who already see themselves as participating in transformational teaching at the class level, but who, because of this fractured educational environment, feel disconnected from larger, more holistic institutional learning goals.

Disconnection has arguably become more pronounced over the past hundred years or so as the mission and purpose of higher education has continued to change.[19] Engagement with the "what" and the "how" might be the primary focus of the day-to-day classroom experience, yet many imagine that teaching has a more transcendent meaning. As one recent book has argued, teaching is more than career preparation; it is a radical act of hope or an "assertion of faith in a better future in an increasingly uncertain and fraught present. It is a commitment to that future even if we can't clearly discern its shape."[20] This hope is rooted not in a conviction that students will be wealthy. Instead it is rooted in a hope that students will live lives filled with some combination of justice, joy, peace, kindness, generosity, and informed civic engagement. This is not a uniquely Christian view, but Christians are uniquely positioned to develop and pursue a more holistic and constructive education and therefore more holistic ways of imagining or measuring what constitutes learning.[21]

For Christian faculty, there is a very clear vision of what this hope entails. Christian educators have long argued that the aspiration of academic education is to lead us outside ourselves and to a greater, loftier vision of human flourishing or *shalom*.[22] Careers, relationships, and happiness are merely byproducts of the pursuit of *shalom*, which is "universal flourishing, wholeness and delight—a rich state of affairs in which natural needs are satisfied and natural gifts fruitfully employed."[23]

---

18. Holmes, *Idea of a Christian College*, 37–43; Gannon, *Radical Hope*, 22.

19. Both Hunter, *Death of Character*, and Glanzer et al., *Restoring the Soul of the University*, outline the long history of this transformation.

20. Gannon, *Radical Hope*, 15.

21. Critical pedagogy, for example, stresses the need for transformational teaching and the expression of what that transformation entails possesses significant overlap with a Christian critique of the modern university's focus on job skills and employability, but much less overlap with a constructive understanding of education for *shalom*.

22. Holmes, *Idea of a Christian College*; Fea, *Why Study History?*

23. Plantinga, *Not the Way it's Supposed to Be*, 10; see also, Wolterstorff, *Educating*

It is the working out of our right relationship with God and his creation. The beauty of this description is that it encompasses all fields of inquiry and practice and provides space for disparate interpretations of how this might be implemented in the classroom. An engineer, a social worker, a biologist, or an artist should all participate uniquely in the pursuit of universal flourishing.[24] As is the case at many Christian institutions of higher education, at College of the Ozarks academic programs are teaching more than narrow content in a specific subject field. Instead, there is a commitment to a distinct educational philosophy that recognizes Jesus, the creator and sustainer of the universe, as the fount of all knowledge and wisdom. Engaging students with content knowledge is a means by which they come to know more about Christ and his kingdom while laying a foundation for the exercise of Christ-like character in particular vocational contexts. As the College of the Ozarks educational philosophy states, we seek to develop students who are both "holy and wholly-educated."[25] Academic programs are key components of our vision to develop "citizens of Christ-like character who are well-educated, hardworking, and patriotic."[26]

Education equips us to wrestle with meaning, to struggle for *shalom* and to find joy in the struggle, and educators are equipping students with the skills and knowledge necessary to pursue this greater goal.[27] In other words, "Liberal education is an open invitation to join the human race and become more fully human."[28] Perhaps most importantly for the purposes of this essay, this notion of *shalom* provides an overarching vision that fits comfortably with the argument made by Glanzer, Alleman, and Ream that "to order one's identities and loves, one needs an overarching identity and story with a substantive vision of the good, the true, and the beautiful that allows one to prioritize multiple, competing purposes."[29] The resurgence of interest in the language of calling

---

for Shalom.

24. VanZanten, *Joining the Mission*, 121–8.

25. College of the Ozarks, *2020-2021 College Catalog*, 58.

26. College of the Ozarks, *2020-2021 College Catalog*, 6.

27. Wolterstorff, *Educating for Shalom*. See, also, Spears and Loomis, *Education for Human Flourishing*.

28. Holmes, *Idea of a Christian College*, 35.

29. Glanzer et al., *Restoring the Soul of the University*, 6.

and vocation highlights this larger trend toward recapturing a unifying purpose.[30]

This awesome calling and responsibility should be both inspiring and daunting. It also raises the question of how this is to be achieved. As mentioned earlier, there is an abundance of scholarship examining what this means at the theoretical level for institutions and specific disciplines. But while many scholars have discussed this, even to the level of assignment or discussion questions, answers for how best to instantiate this at an institutional level or how to transform this into a practical ethos are not always apparent.

Assessment at all levels, ranging from the institution to the classroom assignment, serves three vital functions. First, it makes meaning explicit. Learning is a "multidimensional process of making meaning," but without clear vision or objectives that meaning making is individualistic, unstructured, and directionless.[31] Academic assessment at the broadest levels requires conversations about institutional mission, meaning, and direction, which must result in the transposition of abstract goals into concrete mission and/or vision statements. It also entails metacognitive engagement with the meaning and function of various program, whether general education (GE) or majors, a purpose that must be made manifest in the form of courses and assignments. Second, appropriate reflection reorients us toward our goals of transformational teaching and education as the pursuit of *shalom*, but this is an ongoing process during which we re-narrate our meaning. Finally, academic assessment helps us to identify whether or not we are properly equipping students for the struggle for *shalom*, thus enabling us to identify areas of strength and weakness and alter our practice in order to promote transformational student development.

MEANING-MAKING

Assessment necessitates structured reflection, individually and corporately, on vision and meaning, and this structured reflection must involve administration, faculty, and students. Mission statements, objectives, and course learning outcomes are all expressions of purpose communicated

---

30. Cunningham, *Vocation Across the Academy*.
31. Maki, *Assessing for Learning*, 2.

to different audiences, that are bound together by a consistent goal.[32] Discussions of institutional mission are especially important at mission-driven colleges and universities, of which Christian colleges make up a large percentage, because they force a clear articulation of what institutional mission is and how it is to be realized.[33] This, in turn, enables faculty and administrators to imagine, construct, and narrate program structures and objectives—whether GE, major, minor, or extracurricular—in ways that serve this larger goal. Such discussions raise questions about the ways the training and equipping of students is successful or not by forcing conversations about what is deemed success or failure. These conversations are a necessary part of creating what Arthur Holmes called a climate of learning.[34]

For example, the mission of College of the Ozarks is "to provide the advantages of a Christian education for youth of both sexes, especially those found worthy, but who are without sufficient means to procure such training." The vision statement is "to develop citizens of Christ-like character who are well-educated, hard-working, and patriotic."[35] This vision statement is further fleshed out into five goals: academic, Christian, vocational, cultural, and patriotic. Like many Christian institutions of higher education, the mission, vision, and goals of the College are broad, general, and multi-faceted. But as Holmes noted, "Generalizations of this sort can readily be translated into objectives for different disciplines."[36] It is through this process of translation from broad generalization to discipline-specific expressions of those goals that faculty can begin to more fully unite their areas of learning into a more coherent whole, while also retaining an appropriate level of subjective narrativity regarding how each discipline fits into this more coherent whole.

At College of the Ozarks, for instance, each academic program, GE and departmental, was required to develop objectives directly connected to the five-fold goals of the College. Certain goals were, of course, easier for some disciplines. Others proved more difficult. What about biology

---

32. Some have called for institutions to move beyond mission and toward vocation. See Cunningham, "Colleges Have Callings, Too," in Cunningham, *Vocation across the Academy*, 249–71.

33. VanZanten, *Joining the Mission*, 111.

34. Holmes, *Idea of a Christian College*, 82.

35. Both of these can be found on the homepage of the College's public website, cofo.edu.

36. Holmes, *Idea of a Christian College*, 35.

or music is patriotic? Even if these conversations were, at times, difficult, it was the process of wrestling with these questions that united faculty in a shared enterprise. This is not a unique problem. Many universities have something resembling a patriotic goal, though it might be couched in very different terms, such as civic engagement, community service, or improving the lives of people in the community, nation, and world. Thus, a biology program could easily identify knowledgeable and responsible consumption of scientific news as an important civic responsibility. In doing so, what is achieved is a broader vision of education that breaks out of parochial disciplinary boundaries and envisions disciplines within a more holistic and even transformational framework.

Once objectives have been drafted, they can easily be transformed into outcomes, and these outcomes "translate learning into actions, behaviors and other texts from which observers can draw inferences about the depth and breadth of student learning."[37] More importantly, outcomes are both promises and invitations. They are promises insofar as they communicate what students will be able to do or be able to do better as a result of the course.[38] The act of connecting course outcomes to program and institutional outcomes transforms them into invitations. As such, they invite students into both a specific learning process and also a teleological narrative framing that learning process. Building on the example above, if the program objective was knowledgeable and responsible consumption of scientific news, the outcome could be that students will be able to analyze the reliability of stories in major news outlets. This could easily be translated into an assignment that requires students to identify strengths and weaknesses of articles in a popular newspaper or magazine.

At this point, one might object and argue that the danger in outcomes-based learning is that it reduces learning to a set of discrete, overly practical outcomes, thereby undermining the goal of transformational teaching. While this might be a possibility, it needlessly discounts the possibility of identifying and articulating transformative outcomes tied to characteristics or virtues that may seem difficult to assess. Recognizing the tension between transformational teaching and outcome assessment does not diminish the value of information gathered. Assessing transformational teaching might not be grounded in epistemic

---

37. Maki, *Assessing for Learning*, 89.
38. Gannon, *Radical Hope*, 101.

certainty, but instead, such assessment provides valuable information about whether instruction or assignments are contributing to identifiable success.[39] Moreover, if done well, assessment can be a means by which students are invited into a narrative.

Moving beyond academic knowledge or information to include behaviors and reflection may seem impractical or even misguided, but while, of course, we cannot "see into the soul," there are well-developed ways of helping students identify or narrate how certain habits and actions might be illustrative of certain values.[40] For instance, if a business department has a vocational goal identifying professionalism as an outcome, this can be assessed by examining certain behaviors including timeliness, dress, and appropriateness of communications, and by having students analyze those behaviors as examples of care and responsibility for others. Narrating behaviors becomes a fruitful metacognitive practice that knits together knowledge and action, generating opportunities for students to engage in the process of meaning-making.

Resistance to assessing behaviors is compounded when important but abstract outcomes like Christian formation are included. Fear of works-based legalism hampers attempts to develop and assess Christ-like attitudes and actions. If we cannot see into the soul, we can identify dispositions and actions that suggest a lack of Christ-like character, while simultaneously helping students understand that certain behaviors and intellectual virtues suggest Christ-like actions.[41] For example, if a program had an outcome noting that students who complete the course of study will demonstrate Christ-like character in the completion of their assignments, this can be assessed by how well and carefully a student engages with sources (humility and empathy) and also the lack of evidence to the contrary (i.e., plagiarism). This does not guarantee Christ-like attitudes, and there is a danger of misidentification, but through formative assessment processes, it is possible to help students recognize the fullness of Christ-like character as it is expressed in myriad ways. To have developed honesty is not necessarily to have developed an essential aspect of one's being, but it is to have cultivated virtuous habits, and those habits possess formative power.[42] If liberal education is about

39. Kotzee, "Problems of Assessment in Educating for Intellectual Virtue," in Baehr, *Intellectual Virtues and Education*, 142–60.
40. Suskie, *Assessing Student Learning*, 273–84.
41. For more on intellectual virtues, see Baehr, *Intellectual Virtues and Education*.
42. Wright, *After You Believe*.

transcending the provincialism of discipline or career, that is "seeing life whole rather than fragmented," then the assessment process can be an important part of this by connecting specific knowledge or behaviors to larger, less discipline-specific goals and more proactively to character development.[43]

What is especially fascinating about this process of meaning-making within Christian education is the ways in which it anticipates or complements recent research on both assessment and teaching and learning. For instance, in his recent book titled *The Missing Course*, David Gooblar noted that students tend to engage, self-regulate, and succeed in the learning process when the learning and material is connected to a self-transcendent purpose.[44] Similarly, James Lang has argued that "the most powerful forms of purposefulness arise when students see the ability of their learning to make the world a better place."[45] This invocation of purpose can be communicated in institutional mission, in program learning outcomes, in course learning outcomes, and even at the level of specific assignments. Christian institutions with clear missions and a pronounced vision of a transcendent *telos* or a vision of *shalom* are uniquely positioned to provide students this transcendent *telos* at all levels. Assessment then is the process by which faculty, administration, and students corporately engage in a curricular metacognition or meaning-making and translate this meaning into specific program and course outcomes.

REFLECTION, REORIENTATION, AND PRACTICE

Assessment should be a recurring and structured process; not a one-time discussion of meaning, but a regular reflection on shared meaning. The fact that assessment is an ongoing, annual process can be a source of frustration. But it is possible to conceive of assessment in a more positive light as a corporate habit or ritual. As James Smith has shown, these habits shape us more than we might think.[46] Appropriate and habitual corporate reflection, either among colleagues or among faculty and their

---

43. Holmes, *Idea of a Christian College*, 36.

44. Gooblar, *Missing Course*, 49. This fits, too, with other recent books on teaching and learning, such as Cavanagh, *Spark of Learning*.

45. Lang, *Small Teaching*, 175.

46. Smith, *Desiring the Kingdom*.

students, reorients everyone toward the goal of education as the pursuit of *shalom*. During a busy semester, it is all too easy to begin thinking of classes in terms of the next lecture or the next assignment, at which point the purpose of the lecture or assignment might be forgotten. A course or program with clear outcomes driven by the pursuit of *shalom*, and regularly and corporately re-narrated as such, helps combat fatigue and reconnects students and faculty to one another and an overarching *telos*. The vocal and explicit connection of assignments, discussions, outcomes, and meaning, fosters a re-narration of individual and corporate stories in light of the gospel of Christ reconciling all things to and through himself.[47] "Restoring the soul" of the university requires a sustained engagement, and assessment is a key means of and structure sustaining that engagement.

These habitual practices can also diagnose discontinuities in our teaching practices. If habits associated with assessment can facilitate appropriate re-narration, pedagogical practices, however "normal" they seem, might also unwittingly undermine stated goals. In fact, engagement, or lack thereof, with assessment processes inhibits diagnostic practices that might reveal more about our understanding of teaching than we realize. If, for example, an instructor habitually assigns only objective exams, this communicates to the students that learning is rote memorization. It might not matter how much the instructor imagines they are participating in transformational teaching, their assignments are communicating a very different message.[48] Similarly, if a course has an outcome that students will be able to analyze the complex relationship between politics and religion, but only assigns a true/false quiz, this signals a lack of concern for the outcome, and therefore, the larger *telos* toward which this outcome is directed. Assessment, therefore, is a possible way that faculty members can model the importance of habits and reflection for students, while simultaneously engaging students in the corporate narration of meaning and *telos*.

Finally, when done well, academic assessment shapes our praxis. Sustained reflection on shared meaning and learning outcomes should alter the ways we teach, but critique and hope-filled narration are the easy parts. Kevin Gannon's discussion of Universal Design for Learning is applicable here. Gannon notes that "it's easy to get wrapped up in the

---

47. For more on the idea of re-narrating, see Smith, *You Are What You Love*, 83–110, 158–63.

48. See Smith, *On Christian Teaching*.

language of critique and simply remain in that space."[49] Construction of praxis rooted in new habits and directed toward transformational teaching is *hard*. But assessment helps us identify how well students are equipped to participate in the struggle for *shalom* in specific vocational contexts. As mentioned above, this necessarily involves both content knowledge and the practical skills necessary to practice that knowledge in a specific career, community, and/or family. This might require substantial changes to expectations, assignments, and classrooms. A holistic and purposeful assessment of our academic programs is a means by which we measure how well we are preparing students for a life of flourishing. But perhaps more importantly, assessment can help identify ways that we can be and are being molded, individually and corporately into people, departments, programs, and institutions that are inching toward transformational teaching that recognizes our awesome responsibility to train effective and winsome disciples of the kingdom of God.

But for this to happen, for this meta-cognitive and narrative experience to occur, faculty must actively engage in the process. It is not enough to engage at the level of ticking boxes. We must recognize the potential formative power that, at its best, assessment possesses, and reclaim assessment through intentional, corporate discussion and participation.

BIBLIOGRAPHY

Baehr, Jason, ed. *Intellectual Virtues and Education: Essays in Applied Virtue Epistemology*. New York: Routledge, 2016.
Banta, Trudy and Catherine Palomba. *Assessment Essentials: Planning, Implementing, and Improving Assessment in Higher Education*. Hoboken, NJ: Jossey-Bass, 2014.
Cavanagh, Sarah Rose. *The Spark of Learning: Energizing the College Classroom with the Science of Emotion*. Morgantown, WV: West Virginia University Press, 2016.
Clydesdale, Tim. *The Purposeful Graduate: Why Colleges Must Talk to Students about Vocation*. Chicago: University of Chicago Press, 2015.
Cunningham, David. *Vocation across the Academy: A New Vocabulary for Higher Education*. Oxford: Oxford University Press, 2017.
Dockery, David. S. *Faith and Learning: A Handbook for Christian Higher Education*. Nashville: B&H Academic, 2012.
———. *Renewing Minds: Serving Church and Society through Christian Higher Education*. rev ed. Nashville: B&H Academic, 2008.
Fea, John. *Why Study History? Reflecting on the Importance of the Past*. Grand Rapids: Baker, 2013.
Gannon, Kevin. *Radical Hope: A Teaching Manifesto*. Morgantown, WV: West Virginia University Press, 2020.

49. Gannon, *Radical Hope*, 74–81.

Glanzer, Perry and Nathan Alleman. *The Outrageous Idea of Christian Teaching.* Oxford: Oxford University Press, 2019.

Glanzer, Perry L., et al. *Restoring the Soul of the University: Unifying Christian Higher Education in a Fragmented Age.* Downers Grove, IL: IVP Academic, 2017.

Gooblar, David. *The Missing Course: Everything They Never Taught You about College Teaching.* Cambridge: Harvard University Press, 2019.

Holmes, Arthur. *The Idea of a Christian College.* Grand Rapids: Eerdmans, 1987.

Hunter, James Davison. *The Death of Character: Moral Education in an Age Without Good or Evil.* New York: Basic Books, 2000.

Lang, James. *Small Teaching: Everyday Lessons from the Science of Learning.* Hoboken, NJ: Jossey-Bass, 2016.

Maki, Peggy. *Assessment for Student Learning: Building a Sustainable Commitment Across the Institution*, 2nd ed. Sterling: Stylus, 2010.

Pardue, Brad. "Incorporating Christian Practices into the Study of Church History." *Fides et Historia* 50.2 (Summer/Fall 2019): 53–59.

Plantinga, Cornelius. *Not the Way it's Supposed to Be: A Breviary of Sin.* Grand Rapids: Eerdmans, 1995.

Smith, David I. *On Christian Teaching: Practicing Faith in the Classroom.* Grand Rapids: Eerdmans, 2018.

Smith, David I. and James K. A. Smith. *Teaching and Christian Practices: Reshaping Faith and Learning.* Grand Rapids: Eerdmans, 2011.

Smith, Elizabeth and Sarah Gordon. "How are Faculty Rewarded and Recognized for Assessment Work Outside the Classroom?" *Research and Practice in Assessment* 14 (2019): 65–77.

Smith, James K. A. *Desiring the Kingdom: Worship, Worldview, and Cultural Formation.* Grand Rapids: Baker Academic, 2009.

———. *You Are What You Love: The Spiritual Power of Habit.* Grand Rapids: Brazos, 2016.

Spears, Paul D. and Steven R. Loomis. *Education for Human Flourishing: A Christian Perspective.* Downers Grove, IL: InterVarsity, 2009.

Suskie, Linda. *Assessing Student Learning: A Common Sense Guide*, 3rd ed. Hoboken: Wiley, 2018.

VanZanten, Susan. *Joining the Mission: A Guide for (Mainly) New College Faculty.* Grand Rapids: Eerdmans, 2011.

Wells, Cynthia. *Realizing General Education: Reconsidering Conceptions and Renewing Practice.* Hoboken, NJ: Wiley Periodicals, 2016.

Wolterstorff, Nicholas. *Educating for Shalom: Essays on Christian Higher Education.* Grand Rapids: Eerdmans, 2004.

Wright, N.T. *After You Believe: Why Christian Character Matters.* New York: HarperOne, 2010.

4

A Portrait of The Faithful Professor

James M. Todd III

As COLLEGE PROFESSORS, we have been entrusted with the important task of educating the next generation. Although the impact we make on the students who sit in our classrooms and walk into our offices varies from student to student, our role as professors ensures we will influence many students, whether for good or bad. We should not take such a responsibility lightly and thus must think deeply and clearly about our teaching.

As Christian professors, our teaching is not merely a job but a calling from God, a vocation.[1] Although we should affirm that non-Christians professors also have a vocation, our awareness of our role in God's redemptive plan should make us better professors, but does it? While exploring such a question, Elton Trueblood argues that when all things are equal, "the Christian scholar is likely to be a better scholar because of the nature of his motivation."[2] Trueblood's claim should challenge those

---

1. The idea of Christian vocation will be discussed in more detail below.
2. Trueblood, *Idea of a College*, 19. Arthur Holmes clarifies Trueblood's statement in the following manner: "The comparison is not between the Christian and non-Christian scholar, because there are other variables involved when you compare two people, but between the one individual as Christian and the same person as non-Christian" (Holmes, *Idea of a Christian College*, 48).

of us who teach at Christian institutions to ponder if we indeed are better professors because of our Christian faith.

One question that might arise out of such consideration is: how does the Christian faith make one a better professor? To put it another way, how does the Christian faith impact how we approach our vocation of teaching? In what follows, I will sketch a portrait of the faithful professor[3] and show how this portrait flows out of the Christian worldview.[4] In order to sketch this portrait, I have divided this chapter into three major sections. After providing the theological foundations upon which a Christian professor should build his educational philosophy, I will discuss the faithful professor's character and curriculum.

THEOLOGICAL FOUNDATIONS FOR THE FAITHFUL PROFESSOR

How a person approaches his vocation hinges on what he identifies as the purpose of his vocation. Olympic athletes put themselves through a rigorous training process because they have identified an Olympic gold medal as their goal. Numerous businessmen and women work endless hours with little to no rest because they have made wealth accumulation their goal in life. From a Christian perspective, numerous believers have laid down their lives through the centuries because they knew they had a reward greater than their own lives.

In like manner, Christian faculty must begin with the "why" question, since the answer to this question significantly impacts how we fulfill our calling before God. The more robust our understanding of the "why" question, the more thoughtful and enriching our teaching practices will become. As the Reformers emphasized, the purpose of our vocation is to

---

3. I am using the term "faithful professor" in order to cohere with College of the Ozarks' emphasis on "faithful learning." Susan VanZanten also uses both these terms throughout her work (VanZanten, *Joining the Mission*).

4. This is not to say these qualities will not be present in non-Christian professors, but these qualities are necessary for Christian professors if they are living consistently with their professed worldview. As will become evident, some of the qualities discussed in this chapter will no doubt be present in non-Christian professors, but others will only appear in a Christian context. In his discussion of Christian virtue, N.T. Wright makes a similar point regarding the overlap "of other human visions of virtue" with Christianity. He also states that there "are points at which Christianity issues quite different demands and offers quite different help in meeting them" (Wright, *After You Believe*, 25).

love and serve others,[5] but more specifically as college professors, our loving service toward others looks different than that of other vocations, so we must identify specific foundational beliefs that serve as the impetus for the specific practices of the faithful professor. In what follows, I will identify and briefly discuss four theological foundations upon which we should build our teaching philosophy.

God as the Creator of All Things

God's creation of the universe marks the starting point for a proper understanding of our tasks as faithful professors. From beginning to end, Scripture repeatedly affirms God as the creator of all things.[6] The apostle John aptly summarizes this starting point when he states concerning the incarnate Son of God, "All things were made through him, and without him was not any thing made that was made."[7] Like a masterful artist, our triune God has left his fingerprints all over his creation. His creation—the object of our studies—reflects his beauty, glory, orderliness, and love, reminding us that our teaching must begin and end with our sovereign King. As Paul writes, "For from him and through him and to him are all things. To him be glory forever. Amen."[8]

Since all things find their origin in the one true God, all academic disciplines are interconnected and non-contradictory. In other words, we confess a unity of knowledge. Like the branches of a tree grow out from the trunk, so all academic disciplines stem from God's creation of the world. Therefore, the church through the centuries has affirmed "all truth is God's truth." Whether discovered under the microscope, in the mind of a master mathematician, in a classic novel, or in a theology textbook, all truth finds its origin in the God of truth.[9]

---

5. Veith, *God at Work*, 44.

6. Gen 1:1; Ps 136:49; Prov 8:22–31; Isa 42:5; 45:18; Col 1:15–20; Heb 1:2; Rev 4:11.

7. John 1:3 (ESV).

8. Rom 11:36 (ESV).

9. Ps 31:5; John 14:6.

Humans as Fallen Image-Bearers

In his creation of the cosmos, God set apart humanity by creating them in his image. Setting aside the perpetual debate over the exact nature of the *imago Dei*,[10] we should focus on the two explicit emphases of the biblical text regarding the image of God in humanity. According to Scripture, the *imago Dei* gives human beings dignity and dominion.[11] Human beings possess inherent worth because we are made in God's image, and human beings rule over the rest of the created order because God has made us his vice-regents.

Unfortunately, Adam and Eve failed to exercise their dominion over creation in the garden and, ultimately, believed the serpent's lie and rebelled against their King. As a result of their rebellion, we too participate in their rebellion, both as those represented by Adam in the garden[12] and as those who willingly follow the rebellious path of our original parents.[13] Our rebellious inclinations influence our actions, motivations, feelings, and thoughts.[14] Even as those who have experienced Christ's redeeming work, we still battle against the flesh and its evil desires,[15] and this battle will not subside until Christ returns and restores his creation fully.[16]

Christ's Supremacy Over All Things

As the agent of creation and redemption, Christ came into this world to ransom a people for himself to declare his praises in all the world, yet Christ's reconciling work did not stop there; his redemptive work also includes his reconciliation of all things.[17] As those who live in the tension between Christ's first and second coming, we acknowledge Christ's exaltation over all things at the right hand of the Father[18] and

---

10. For a discussion of "several aspects of our existence that show us to be more like God than all the rest or creation," see Grudem, *Systematic Theology*, 445–49.
11. Gen 1:26–28; 9:17; Jas 3:9.
12. Rom 5:12.
13. Rom 3:9.
14. Eph 4:17–19.
15. Gal 5:16–26.
16. Rev 21.
17. Col 1:19–20.
18. Ps 110:1.

await the day when the Father will put all things under his feet.[19] Living in a secular culture, we are regularly tempted to leave Christ out of the picture, yet as faithful professors, we must fight against this temptation and regularly remind ourselves and our students—through our actions and our words—that Christ reigns as Lord over all, even our academic disciplines.

The Mind's Centrality in Character Formation

Because of Christ's redemptive work on our behalf, we have been called to a life continually transformed by the Holy Spirit as we submit ourselves to God's Word. Both faithful professors and their students find themselves on the same journey of transformation, albeit hopefully, the professors are a little further down the road than their students. Theologians refer to this journey of transformation as sanctification, and the Bible places the mind at the center of this process.[20] In this sense, the mind serves as a control tower governing our attitudes, actions, and will, which are all also important parts of sanctification.[21] Such an affirmation—as countercultural as it may be in our feeling-driven cultural context—underscores the need for Christians to renew their minds daily through regular meditation on the truths of Scripture.

THE CHARACTER OF THE FAITHFUL PROFESSOR

Education as a journey serves as a common and helpful metaphor.[22] As professors, we play a role in our student's educational journey by serving as guides along the way. To serve as a guide, one must be familiar with various aspects of the journey and thus have visited the sites before taking our students. Because we, as Christian professors, desire to see

---

19. 1 Cor 15:20–28.

20. Rom 12:12; 2 Cor 10:46; Eph 4:20–24. See J. P. Moreland's chapter entitled "The Mind's Role in Spiritual Transformation" in Moreland, *Love Your God*, 63–82.

21. An emphasis on the centrality of the mind should not result in a neglect of the heart; instead, our transformed minds must direct our hearts' affections in virtuous directions. VanZanten notes, "Both head and heart . . . are integral aspects of education . . . Faithful learning is a comprehensive act in which all aspects of the learner—intellect, spirituality, imagination, emotion, memory, practice, and sociability—are involved" (VanZanten, *Joining the Mission*, 123).

22. Smith and Felch, *Teaching and Christian Imagination*.

our students transformed into the image of Christ, we must model what this looks like. We cannot ask our students to be or to become what we are not, thus our character and lives as professors matter. In what follows, I will highlight three qualities we should pursue so that our lives might display Christ's supremacy before our students.

Virtuous Living

Often, businesses and organizations emphasize the importance of various virtues such as honesty, kindness, diligence, etc. Sometimes this emphasis is genuine, but in many cases, an organization's emphasis on virtue has a pragmatic purpose such as customer satisfaction, revenue increase, etc. In Christian higher education, virtue must not serve as an afterthought, a marketing strategy, or a recruiting tool; instead, Christian institutions must affirm the inherent relationship between virtuous living and our identity as image bearers. When we ground our understanding of virtue on the foundation of God's character, living a virtuous life provides others with a more accurate picture of our triune God who exists in perfect holiness.

The best place to begin thinking about how a Christian professor might model virtue before her students in the classroom is the intellectual virtues. Just as one might compile a seemingly endless list of moral virtues, so we could list numerous intellectual virtues. James Sire offers a helpful organizational scheme for the intellectual virtues by dividing them into four categories: (1) acquisition virtues: passion for the truth; (2) application virtues: passion for holiness; (3) maintenance virtues: passion for consistency; and (4) communication virtues: compassion for others.[23] Sire could have added humility as a fifth virtue since he lists it under all four categories.

A detailed discussion of even one of Sire's categories is beyond the scope of this chapter, but a faithful professor must consistently grow and thereby model humility, compassion, and a passion for truth, holiness, and consistency in her classroom. For instance, interacting with opposing viewpoints—whether from students or other scholars—provides one of the greatest tests of our intellectual virtue and a great opportunity

---

23. Sire, *Habits of the Mind*, 109–10. Sire builds on the work of Wood, *Epistemology*. See also Moreland, *Love Your God*, 106–11, and Page, "Developing the Characteristics of a Christian Mind," in Downey and Porter, *Christian Worldview and the Academic Disciplines*, 35–52.

to model these virtues before our students. Not only should we give an accurate reflection of opposing views, but when critiquing these same views, we should critique the central argument and not some peripheral issue. Furthermore, we have the responsibility to give opposing views an honest evaluation even if doing so involves admitting weaknesses in our own viewpoint. Stanley Porter asserts, "positions held in ignorance are not positions honestly held."[24] If we cling tightly to a view and intentionally avoid interacting with opposing views, we misrepresent our God and do both ourselves and our students a grave injustice.

The faithful professor also displays intellectual virtue when she lives her life with an insatiable thirst for learning. Professors who love learning and applying what they learn become a wellspring of wisdom for their students and all those around them. Mark Noll says it well when he writes, "if what we claim about Jesus Christ is true, then evangelicals should be among the most active, most serious, and most open-minded advocates of general human learning."[25] Furthermore, we as Christian professors must be committed to lifelong learning in order to faithfully fulfill our vocation. Learning and teaching are so closely related that Hendricks states, "If you stop growing today, you stop teaching tomorrow . . . as a teacher, [I] am primarily a learner, a student among students."[26] It would be the high point of hypocrisy for us to push our students to learn while we no longer actively pursue learning.

Naturally, our responsibility to continue learning includes our academic discipline, but for the faithful professor, it extends into two other areas: the Christian faith and general learning. As Christians, the primary shaping influence of our lives and thinking is the Bible. As we spend time in the scriptures, we learn how to think God's thoughts, and we are transformed into a reflection of Christ.[27] In fact, our ability to become the professor of character outlined in this chapter is contingent on our devotion to the study of Scripture. Furthermore, our knowledge and proper understanding of the Bible directly impacts our ability to integrate our Christian faith into our academic disciplines. Thus, the entire faculty at an institute of Christian higher education should be people of the Book, not just the biblical and theological studies faculty.

---

24. Porter, "Christian Perspective on Biblical Studies," in Downey and Porter, *Christian Worldview and the Academic Disciplines*, 90.

25. Noll, *Scandal of the Evangelical Mind*, x.

26. Hendricks, *Teaching to Change Lives*, 17.

27. 2 Tim 3:16–17.

Another area of learning for professors is the liberal arts.[28] For many, arguing that a college professor should study the liberal arts may sound strange ("Are not the liberal arts something you study when you are an undergraduate student?"), but if we have an appropriate understanding of the purpose of the liberal arts, their value cannot be denied. So, what is the purpose of the liberal arts? Arthur Holmes identifies the "task of liberal education" in the following manner: "To form the mind, to stretch the understanding, to sharpen one's intellectual powers, to enlarge the vision, to cultivate the imagination and impart a sense of the whole."[29] As educators at a Christian liberal arts college, we without a doubt would like to see these things in our students. Yet we will never see these qualities in our students if we do not first model them in our own lives. As Holmes so eloquently states, the purpose of liberal learning is the shaping of a person.[30] Our development as a person does not stop when we finish our undergraduate education or even graduate school; our development as a person continues throughout our life. Therefore, we must give attention to the study of theology, philosophy, history, literature, art, and various other academic disciplines outside of our specific field. We will never be able to master each of these fields, but as we delve into other disciplines we will "sharpen" our "intellectual powers" to the glory of God.

Closely related to the intellectual virtues are the moral virtues.[31] Faithful professors cannot expect to fulfill their calling by only pursuing intellectual virtue; they must live a virtuous life empowered by the Holy Spirit.[32] Duplicity is the enemy of faithful education. Students can often spot a professor at a Christian institution who simply plays the game of Christianity and does not have a vibrant faith characterized by the fruit of the Spirit. Such a pursuit does not mean a faithful professor is a perfect professor; it means the ethos of the professor's life and teaching consistently conveys a Christ-centered, kingdom-first purpose.

---

28. For a good introductory discussion of the liberal arts, see Fant, *Liberal Arts*.

29. Holmes, *Idea of a Christian College*, 30.

30. Holmes, *Idea of a Christian College*, 29.

31. For a good discussion of the relationship between the intellectual and moral virtues, see Baehr, *Inquiring Mind*, 206–22. For a good discussion of Christian virtue, see Wright, *After You Believe*. For a sample list of Christian virtues, see 1 Cor 13:48a and Gal 5:22–23.

32. Glanzer et al., *Restoring the Soul of the University*, 117–20, discusses how the professionalization and specialization of the disciplines led to professors "no longer be[ing] expected to serve as moral guides who could help students live the good life."

Outside of the classroom, a virtuous life plays itself out in myriad ways, yet a virtuous life also comes out in the classroom in a few specific ways. First, a virtuous professor does not ask his students to do what he himself is unwilling to do. This might include classroom rules such as tardiness, use of technology, submission of late work, etc. Professors who expect their students to arrive at class on time or submit assignments on time must not exempt themselves from such standards. Second and closely related, a virtuous professor must show due diligence to credit sources properly in lectures, visual aids, and class handouts. We cannot demand academic honesty from our students unless we are willing to model academic honesty before them in the classroom. Finally, Christian professors should be willing to own their mistakes before their students even when they have not been caught.[33] A professor's willingness to admit mistakes reveals humility and allows the students the opportunity to extend grace. Such actions also remind students that the professors are still on the journey and have not arrived.

Caring for Students

In his book *God at Work*, Gene Veith argues that "God works through means"[34] and thus providentially provides for the needs of humans through various vocations.[35] Each person has the responsibility to use her vocation(s) for the purpose of loving and serving her neighbor.[36] If we agree with Veith about God's providential work through vocations, it follows that the primary people we love and serve through our vocation of teaching are our students. So, how do Christian professors best love and serve their students? By framing this question in the context of love and service, we are framing it in the context of the great commandments[37] and the greatest Christian virtue. Our teaching therefore is an opportunity for us to demonstrate our love for God by loving our students.

The students whom God places under our tutelage are human beings who have been made in the image of God and thus possess inherent

---

33. Mark Noll states, "Knowing Christ, in other words, means learning humility" (Noll, *Jesus Christ and the Life of the Mind*, 62).
34. Veith, *God at Work*, 28.
35. Veith, *God at Work*, 33.
36. Veith, *God at Work*, 40.
37. Matt 22:35–40.

value and worth; therefore, we have an obligation to care for them not only academically, but also as persons. Many students in our naturalistic culture have never had anyone genuinely care for them. As Christian professors, we have the privilege of demonstrating to our students just how valuable they are in the eyes of their Maker.

One of the most important ways we care for our students is by showing a genuine concern that they walk away from college with more than just a degree. Our ultimate concern must be "the holistic development of persons."[38] In exploring what it means to develop persons, Holmes identifies three features of a person and contends these features must translate into the following essential areas of focus for those in Christian higher education: (1) intellectual development, (2) value development, and (3) the shaping of responsible agents.[39] For Holmes, the combination of the first two produces the third. Thus, truly caring for our students consists of igniting their inquisitiveness, teaching them to ground their values on the foundation of a Christian worldview, and conveying to them that they are "accountable ultimately to God."[40]

If we truly desire the "holistic development of our students," then setting and demanding high standards for our students becomes essential. We must help our students see their academic work as an opportunity to display the excellence and beauty of God. However, like us, our students often need encouragement in this area, and many students aim at the expectations we set for them. If we communicate to our students—implicitly or explicitly—that we will accept sloppy work (and even reward it through inflated grades), then we will receive just that: sloppy work. A genuine concern for students often looks like "tough love," but in the end, we must make our goal student development, not student comfort.

Our high standards for our students must extend to their character formation. Most certainly this would mean that we set high standards for academic honesty in our classes and implement consequences for academic dishonesty, which convey to our students the seriousness of such deceit. Yet, our encouragement towards integrity must go deeper than this. First and foremost, we are responsible to help our students build a foundation for virtue. Then, we must help them understand the importance of virtue in every area of life, not simply their academics.

---

38. Dockery, *Renewing Minds*, 25.
39. Holmes, *Idea of a Christian College*, 29–34.
40. Holmes, *Idea of a Christian College*, 30–32.

A second way we show care for our students is by getting to know them. How much influence we have in our students' lives often relates directly to how much we demonstrate concern for them and the things taking place in their lives. Hendricks proposes that one of the key components of being teachers of impact is knowing our students.[41] Getting to know students is not something that takes place only in the classroom. In fact, great effort must be made to be involved in students' lives outside the classroom. This is not easy work, but as Hendricks states, "Good teaching has a price tag: You've got to be willing to pour out your life."[42] If our goal is to have a long-term impact on our students, then we must be committed to devoting the time and energy required to get involved in our students' lives.

Mentorship—an avenue of involvement in the lives of *some* students—provides one of the most deep and profound examples of caring for our students. In preparation for his work *The Fabric of Faithfulness*, Steven Garber interviewed a group of people whom he describes as those "who still believe that the gospel of the kingdom makes sense of the whole of life—twenty years after their university experience."[43] As he discussed their college experiences, one of the things he noticed was that each of them found a mentor during their college years who embodied the ideals they were learning in the classroom.[44] Garber concludes, "[F]or those who learn the deepest lessons—ones in which visions of one's world and of one's place in it are transformed—there is always a teacher whose purposes and passions ignite a student's moral imagination."[45] In my own experience during my college years, I longed to see a genuine Christian home and how it operated. Thankfully, I found such in several of my college professors' families. Getting a glimpse into their lives gave me hope that I too could replicate that in my own home one day. My own personal experience simply underscores Garber's contention that we must allow our students to get close enough to us that they can see us live out our "purposes and passions."

Finally, the most important way we demonstrate care for our students (and that which should serve as an umbrella over all the others)

41. Hendricks, *Teaching to Change Lives*, 82.
42. Hendricks, *Teaching to Change Lives*, 89.
43. Garber, *Fabric of Faithfulness*, 124.
44. Although this mentor was not always a faculty member, in many instances he or she was a faculty member.
45. Garber, *Fabric of Faithfulness*, 155.

is by helping them cultivate a deeper devotion to Christ. Opportunities to challenge our students in their love for Christ and for others abound. It is incumbent upon us to take advantage of these opportunities, both inside and outside the classroom. Our students' ultimate (and only true) success in life is directly related to their depth of devotion to Christ.

The Pursuit of Excellence

At the end of his masterful work of creation in Gen 1, God looks at everything he made and pronounces it "very good."[46] Though on a much smaller scale, the Christian professor should pursue a similar goal in his teaching: excellent work. As we pursue excellence, both inside and outside the classroom, we are offering our students, colleagues, and the watching world an accurate reflection of our God who acts with excellence in all things. Trueblood is correct when he writes, "[t]he Christian faith, when it understands itself, is the sworn enemy of all intellectual dishonesty and shoddiness."[47] On too many occasions, Christians have been guilty of presenting good work that could easily have been excellent work with a little more time, attention, and effort. Such "getting-by" is not an accurate reflection of the truths we confess and fails to understand that as Christians our "motivation to excellence is . . . a desire to do all things for God's glory because he cares about the quality of work and wants to be involved and reflected in everything."[48] So, how do we become teachers of excellence? In what follows, we will look at two prerequisite qualities for attaining excellence in our work: diligence and evaluation.

In practice, diligence and excellence are often closely related. In fact, the two usually go hand in hand. If one does not put much effort into his work, then the result is usually subpar. It is a very real temptation for us to coast through our courses, but the Christian faith demands our rejection of such a temptation and our diligent pursuit of our subject matter as well as the minds and hearts of our students. We must be diligent to make sure our pedagogical practices produce students whose lives align with our goal of transformation. As we grow in our careers, this effort might be

---

[46]. Gen 1:31 (ESV). Brown et al., *Brown-Briver-Briggs Hebrew and English Lexicon*, 374, translates Gen 1:31 in the following manner, "God saw all that he had made, and behold it was very excellent."

[47]. Trueblood, *Idea of a College*, 19.

[48]. Dockery, *Renewing Minds*, 25.

small tweaks to course content and assignments, but as we have seen in the last twenty years, technological advances have forced institutions and their faculty to make some major changes in teaching. Change does not always equal excellence, and this truth leads us to the second component of pursuing excellence as a professor: evaluation.

None of us have arrived in our teaching, but we will never move further along in the journey toward excellence unless we are willing to critically evaluate our practices.[49] In his discussion of self-evaluation, Hendricks writes, "[E]xperience does not necessarily make you better; in fact it tends to make you worse, unless it's *evaluated* experience [italics original]. The good teacher's greatest threat is satisfaction—the failure to keep asking, 'How can I improve?'"[50] This final question is the question that separates good teaching from excellent teaching. Every lecture, classroom discussion, and dialogue with students must be characterized by excellence, and excellence only comes through the laborious work of self-evaluation.

Yet the appraisal of our teaching does not stop with our own assessment; we need consistent feedback from others. Evidence for such a need can be found in two key assertions of a Christian worldview. First of all, humans have limited knowledge and abilities (i.e., we are not God). Thus, all of us have "blind spots" in our teaching that may prevent us from reaching our full potential. Second, as humans we were not made to live in isolation, but in community with others.[51] On the basis of these affirmations, we can conclude that teaching with excellence requires us to solicit input from both our peers and our students. Such critique should be viewed as a welcome blessing by those who desire to rise above the fray of mediocrity.

---

49. Rebecca DeYoung discusses the importance of making students practice *and* reflect on their practices in our classrooms (DeYoung, "Pedagogical Rhythms," in Smith and Smith, *Teaching and Christian Practices*, 25–42). Such an emphasis on reflection should also be extended to a professor's pedagogical practices.

50. Hendricks, *Teaching to Change Lives*, 33.

51. Bartholomew and Goheen write, "The truly human life is lived in relationship not only with God but also with other human beings" (Bartholomew and Goheen, *Living at the Crossroads*, 43).

THE CURRICULUM OF A FAITHFUL PROFESSOR

As important as a faithful professor's character is, a faithful professor's calling necessitates a consideration of more than just his character qualities. Much of the impact a professor has on his students relates directly to what and how he teaches. As Christian professors, we must think deeply and consistently about how our teaching forms our students. A faithful professor who teaches with excellence focuses on both his character *and* his curriculum. In what follows, I will discuss two characteristics of the faithful professor's curriculum.

Christian Worldview Integration

Our students find themselves in a culture devoid of a connected system of ideas by which they may interpret the world and live a wholesome life. Garber, in speaking of this "sense of disconnectedness," notes that "[i]n every major center of culture-forming power, the possibility of coherence across the concerns of life is discouraged."[52] Such a lack of coherence presents challenges for those of us who are involved in Christian higher education, but at the same time, it provides us an opportunity to offer our students an answer to our culture's dilemma. The answer to that dilemma is to offer our students a robust portrait of the Christian worldview.

As Christian educators, we have the obligation to teach our students that a coherent picture of life and the world is possible and can be found in the Christian faith. Dockery states it best when he writes, "A Christian worldview becomes a driving force in life, giving us a sense of God's plan and purpose for this world. Our identity is shaped by this worldview."[53] Such a formative nature of worldview education was confirmed in Garber's survey of those whose lives reflect a connection between belief and behavior. One of the common themes he noticed in his interviews was that each of them embraced worldview formation during their college years. In Garber's words, each of them had "formed a worldview sufficient for the challenges of the modern world."[54] How do we help our students both form a Christian worldview and then live lives consistent with their professed worldview?

---

52. Garber, *Fabric of Faithfulness*, 67.
53. Dockery, *Renewing Minds*, 43.
54. Garber, *Fabric of Faithfulness*, 124.

Helping college students form a robust vision of the Christian faith takes the work of an entire college campus, but a Christian college's curriculum should include specific classes targeted at building this foundation in students. These foundational classes should train students in biblical theology, systematic theology, and competing worldviews. As students grow in their knowledge of the biblical story and the basic tenets of orthodox Christian theology, they will better understand the points of contrast between the Christian faith and other worldviews in their culture.

Although some faculty will teach worldview-specific courses, all faculty must teach *from* a Christian worldview[55] and thereby reinforce and build upon the foundational knowledge students attain in worldview and theology classes. A faithful professor must resist turning discipline-specific classes into a worldview class; instead, a faithful professor helps her students understand the value of her discipline by integrating a Christian worldview into her subject matter.

The integration of the Christian worldview in one's teaching begins with the faithful professor showing her students how her discipline relates to the Christian worldview.[56] Regardless of the specificity of one's discipline, every Christian professor should articulate the relationship of their academic discipline to the Christian worldview. Most often, grounding one's academic discipline in the Christian worldview involves connecting one's academic discipline to the creation story. For example, professors in the humanities can highlight how the study of literature and history provides a glimpse into both the *imago Dei* and the sinfulness of humanity. Faculty who teach in the natural sciences can show students how the study of God's creation points to his power, wisdom, and beauty. Those who teach in the fine arts can connect the artistic desires and talents of their students to the *imago Dei*. These few examples demonstrate the need for faithful professors to develop the ability to articulate the Christian worldview. Without an understanding of the basic storyline of Scripture and the basic tenets of Christian theology, faculty are at a serious disadvantage in their ability to help students "connect the dots" between their academic discipline and God's grand narrative.

---

55. I borrowed this phraseology from my colleague Dan Kline.

56. VanZanten proposes the questions: "Why should a Christian study X?" and "How does X fit into the larger picture of God's good creation?" (VanZanten, *Joining the Mission*, 125).

Since we live in a fallen and corrupt world, evil and falsehoods have invaded every area of study, some to a larger extent than others. Consequently, another key component of worldview education is worldview critique. Faithful professors should not only train their students to identify what is good in their discipline, but also the evil and lies in the discipline.[57] In my own field of biblical studies, a strong anti-supernatural bias pervades mainstream scholarship. As a professor, I must teach my students the worldview presuppositions driving such an approach to the biblical text and train them to identify how such an approach works itself out in the details of biblical exegesis. Whether it be postmodernism's infiltration of the humanities or naturalism's impact on the sciences, other worldviews and our culture's moral paradigms impact all our disciplines. Our ability to identify these falsehoods and perversions hinges on our knowledge of the worldviews that impact our respective disciplines.

Because we are at our core worshipping beings,[58] we can help students critique their academic disciplines by training them to identify cultural idols and these idols' pervasive influence on their fields of study and future vocations. Brian Walsh and J. Richard Middleton identify the idols of scientism, technicism, and economism as the dominant "gods" of the modern age.[59] Our students are not only exposed to these idols in their daily interactions, but they will also be exposed to these idols in their future vocations. Helping them understand the cultural power of these idols and how they can resist their pervasive influence through the power of the Spirit prepares our students to live Christ-centered lives in a culture that worships these other "gods."

Not every academic discipline must approach worldview integration and critique in the same way or at the same level. Some disciplines

---

57. Warren Smith and John Stonestreet offer four questions to ask regarding our culture: (1) "What is good in our culture that we can promote, protect, and celebrate?"; (2) "What is missing in our culture that we can creatively contribute?"; (3) "What is evil in our culture that we can stop?"; and (4) "What is broken in our culture that we can restore?" (Smith and Stonestreet, *Restoring All Things*, 25–26). At College of the Ozarks, we have taken these questions and substituted "field of study" for "culture." We use these questions as guiding questions for the students when they write a capstone paper during their senior year. For sample critiques of specific disciplines, see Bartholomew and Goheen, *Living at the Crossroads*, 146–73, and Moreland, *Love Your God*, 18–23.

58. Smith, *Desiring the Kingdom*, 46.

59. Walsh and Middleton, *Transforming Vision*, 131–46. See Postman, *Technopoly*, for a proposal on how education might combat the rule of technology over our lives.

deal much less in the realm of worldview ideas than others, and in these disciplines, competing worldviews exert far less influence. For example, a professor who teaches College Algebra will deal far less with worldview issues than a professor who teaches Psychology, a discipline that regularly interacts with ideas driven by worldview presuppositions. J.P. Moreland offers a helpful principle regarding the integration of the Christian worldview and various academic fields:

> The more a field is composed of ideas about the nature of ultimate reality, what and how we know things, moral values and virtues, the nature and origin of human beings, and other issues central to mere Christianity, the more crucial it will be to think carefully about how a Christian should integrate his discipleship unto Jesus with the ideas and practices in that field.[60]

A faithful professor knows his field and the Christian worldview well enough to identify the common ground and points of contrast between the two, and he trains his students to do the same and to understand how false beliefs and evil practices have impacted their field in negative ways.[61]

Character Formation

Filling our students' heads with knowledge is, to use the words of the Preacher, a "vanity of vanities"[62] unless we teach them to apply that knowledge to their lives so they may become wise and virtuous persons. Just like worldview integration, a teaching aimed at character formation looks different for the various academic disciplines, so my purpose in this section is to outline some broad categories for character formation in the classroom.

Unfortunately, many of our students have embraced the common false dichotomy between the sacred and the secular, thus viewing their academic life as an activity divorced from their faith. Faithful professors consistently remind students of their obligation to bring all of life under

---

60. Moreland, *Love Your God*, 181.

61. For extensive treatments of various academic disciplines, see Downey and Porter, *Christian Worldview and the Academic Disciplines*; Crossway's "Reclaiming the Christian Intellectual Tradition" series; and IVP's "Christian Worldview Integration" series, as well as many of the chapters that follow in Part Two of this volume.

62. Eccl 1:2 (*ESV*).

the lordship of Christ. What they do in the classroom reflects and impacts their walk with Christ and their service in his church. By emphasizing academic life as a form of worship, Christian professors provide students with a robust picture of the Christian faith and help their students view their learning as an integral part of their discipleship.

Many students who attend Christian colleges and universities have embraced the culture's emphasis on feelings and emotions as the proper guide for living. The Christianized version of this belief produces a strong anti-intellectual current[63] that sweeps our students into a shallow faith "tossed to and fro by the waves and carried about by every wind of doctrine."[64] Christian professors must help students recognize the life of the mind as "part of the very essence of discipleship unto the Lord Jesus."[65] We best help our students understand the importance of the mind in discipleship by three classroom goals.

First, we should find specific avenues through which to teach our students intellectual virtues. Because intellectual virtue has to do with how our students approach thinking and learning, professors in every academic discipline can highlight various virtues in their class assignments. For example, reading assignments may require some reflection on the process of reading in light of the virtue of humility. Science classes may emphasize the pursuit of truth as it connects to the scientific method. Research papers provide a great opportunity to challenge students to have compassion on their readers by using proper grammar and organization. Countless opportunities exist in the college classroom to highlight an intellectual virtue and push our students to ground the why and how of the respective intellectual virtue in the biblical faith.

A second and closely related goal is to produce students who are good thinkers. Dockery asserts that "[t]he concern of a Christian liberal arts education, then, is . . . for preparing all students to think—to think Christianly, to think critically, to think imaginatively—preparing them for leadership and preparing them for life."[66] Teaching our students to think critically and imaginatively takes the same type of thinking on our part. We must be good thinkers before our students can ever become such. Additionally, simply teaching students to parrot the course material

---

63. See Noll, *Scandal of the Evangelical Mind*, 327.

64. Eph 4:14 (ESV).

65. Moreland, *Love Your God*, 43. See also, Cosgrove, *Foundations for Christian Thought*, 43–53.

66. Dockery, *Renewing Minds*, 20.

is not teaching students to think. Hendricks challenges teachers in this regard when he writes, "Your task as a teacher is to stretch the human mind."[67] Good teaching does not always give students the answers; instead, good teaching equips students to find the answers on their own and kindles in them the curiosity to do so.

Third, a faithful professor's classroom experience should ignite an inquisitiveness in students that extends beyond a specific class or academic discipline. If our goal as Christian educators is to produce wise men and women who live faithful lives, then we must help them understand the role of learning in becoming wise, living faithfully, and loving Christ. Faithful professors build this quality into students by showing students how other disciplines connect with their academic discipline, thus offering their students a picture of the coherence of reality in God's world.

Although an important component of our discipleship, the mind is not the only aspect of our lives involved in discipleship. Our teaching must also aim at our students' hearts and fan the flame of their love for Christ and those around them. James K. A. Smith has highlighted the role of desire in our formation and argues that Christian education must focus on the heart as well as the mind.[68] Worldview training devoid of a focus on the heart's desires only produces smart students, not virtuous students. We must train our students not only how to think, but also how to love God and others.

Training students in moral virtues does not mean our classes have to be a formal worship service each class period. The community of the classroom provides a fertile soil for helping students recognize ways they can love Christ by loving each other. Higher education often provides an environment that fosters pride and self-promotion. Sadly, Paul's maxim "Knowledge puffs up . . ." often finds more expression in Christian higher education than his contrasting statement, "but love builds up."[69] As we facilitate interaction between students in our classroom, we must remind them that the goal of their learning isn't their self-improvement, a better job, or more money; instead, the goal of their education is a deeper love for

---

67. Hendricks, *Teaching to Change Lives*, 41.

68. James K. A. Smith calls for "a 'hearts and minds' . . . pedagogy that trains us . . . by our immersion in the material practices of Christin worship" (Smith, *Desiring the Kingdom*, 33).

69. 1 Cor 8:1 (ESV). Paul uses this proverb in the context of his discussion of meat sacrificed to idols.

God and others. How would our classrooms look different if we created an environment where students were taught to serve other students in the classroom in various ways? What might our classrooms look like if our students were driven by love for one another rather than competition and self-improvement? What would our classrooms look like if our students understood worship as the end goal of their education?

The limited time we have with students in our classrooms means much of their discipleship and character formation takes place outside the classroom, but such a truth does not prevent us from making our classrooms a catalyst for their formation. A few simple practices in our classroom can help remind students of the bigger picture of their education.[70] Some small practices include opening or closing class with prayer, Scripture reading or a short devotional at the beginning of class, singing the doxology or other songs, or various classroom community-building practices. These practices alone do not mean a professor is faithfully educating students, but when coupled with worldview integration, these practices train students to place their studies in the context of worship.

Our culture's influence on our students is strong and consistent; therefore, our students' faith must be strong and vibrant if they are going to allow God's Spirit to transform their lives into Christ's image. Although a Christian institution and the faculty and staff that make up the institution can serve as strong and consistent encouragers for our students during their college years, we must also encourage our students to develop spiritual disciplines that will last a lifetime. One of the most important spiritual disciplines for faithful professors and students alike is involvement in the life of the local church. As James K. A. Smith has argued, a truly Christian education must view itself as an extension of the church.[71] For Smith, this means "drawing on and incorporating the range of Christian practices that form desire and fuel the imagination,"[72] but he also highlights how the "ecclesial university will extend and amplify the formation that begins and continues in Christian worship."[73] The

---

70. The examples I have listed could apply to every classroom. For ideas of discipline-specific practices, see Smith and Smith, *Teaching and Christian Practices*, and Smith, *Desiring the Kingdom*, 228–30.

71. Smith, *Desiring the Kingdom*, 220. Smith proposes the term "ecclesial colleges" and "ecclesial universities" to highlight this significant connection.

72. Smith, *Desiring the Kingdom*, 222.

73. Smith, *Desiring the Kingdom*, 222.

Christian college cannot replace the local church, and faithful professors must remind students of the primacy of the church for their formation.[74]

CONCLUSION

Without a doubt, I could have discussed other qualities of faithful professors, but what we have surveyed briefly in this chapter is a good starting point for thinking about how the Christian faith impacts our vocation of teaching. An institution filled with professors who embody these qualities will produce students who will faithfully serve the church and their communities for Christ's glory.

To be such a professor takes much work, discipline, time, and numerous other sacrifices. In fact, the challenge can be overwhelming. Such a feeling of deep responsibility is a good thing when it drives us to complete dependence on the greatest teacher of all time: Jesus Christ. For those of us who profess Christ, it comes as a great comfort to know we do not have to complete this task alone. In fact, we *cannot* complete it alone. We must allow the Spirit of God to empower us daily as we approach the challenges of our profession. As we do so, we are being faithful professors in every sense of the word.

BIBLIOGRAPHY

Baehr, Jason. *The Inquiring Mind: On Intellectual Virtues and Virtue Epistemology.* Oxford: Oxford University Press, 2012.
Bartholomew, Craig and Michael Goheen. *Living at the Crossroads: An Introduction to Christian Worldview.* Grand Rapids: Baker, 2008.
Brown, Francis, et al. *The Brown-Briver-Briggs Hebrew and English Lexicon.* Peabody, MA: Hendrickson, 2003.
Cosgrove, Mark. *Foundations of Christian Thought: Faith, Learning, and the Christian Worldview.* Grand Rapids: Kregel Academic, 2006.
Dockery, David. *Renewing Minds: Serving Church and Society through Christian Higher Education.* Nashville: B&H Academic, 2008.
Downey, Deane and Stanley Porter, eds. *Christian Worldview and the Academic Disciplines: Crossing the Academy.* Eugene, OR: Pickwick, 2009.
Fant, Gene C. *The Liberal Arts: A Student's Guide.* Wheaton, IL: Crossway, 2012.
Garber, Steven. *The Fabric of Faithfulness: Weaving Together Belief and Behavior.* Downers Grove, IL: IVP, 2007.

---

74. Smith uses the illustration of "a chapel connected to the nave of the cathedral" to explain the relationship between the Christian college and the church (Smith, *Desiring the Kingdom*, 222).

Glanzer, Perry, et al. *Restoring the Soul of the University: Unifying Christian Higher Education in a Fragmented Age.* Downers Grove, IL: IVP Academic, 2017.

Grudem, Wayne. *Systematic Theology: An Introduction to Biblical Doctrine.* Grand Rapids: Zondervan Academic, 1994.

Hendricks, Howard. *Teaching to Change Lives: Seven Proven Ways to Make Your Teaching Come Alive.* Colorado Springs, CO: Multnomah, 2003.

Holmes, Arthur. *The Idea of a Christian College.* Grand Rapids: Eerdmans, 1987.

Moreland, J.P. *Love Your God with All Your Mind: The Role of Reason in the Life of the Soul.* Colorado Springs, CO: NavPress, 1997.

Noll, Mark. *Jesus Christ and the Life of the Mind.* Grand Rapids: Eerdmans, 2011.

———. *The Scandal of the Evangelical Mind.* Grand Rapids: Eerdmans, 1994.

Postman, Neil. *Technopoly: The Surrender of Culture to Technology.* New York: Vintage, 1993.

Sire, James W. *Habits of the Mind: Intellectual Life as a Christian Calling.* Downers Grove, IL: IVP, 2000.

Smith, David I. and Susan M. Felch. *Teaching and Christian Imagination.* Grand Rapids: Eerdmans, 2016.

Smith, David I. and James K. A. Smith, eds. *Teaching and Christian Practices: Reshaping Faith and Learning.* Grand Rapids: Eerdmans, 2011.

Smith, James K. A. *Desiring the Kingdom: Worship, Worldview, and Cultural Formation.* Grand Rapids: Baker Academic, 2009.

Smith, Warren Cole and John Stonestreet. *Restoring All Things: God's Audacious Plan to Change the World through Everyday People.* Ada: Baker, 2015.

Trueblood, Elton. *The Idea of a College.* New York: Harper and Brothers, 1959.

VanZanten, Susan. *Joining the Mission: A Guide for (Mainly) New College Faculty.* Grand Rapids, Eerdmans, 2011.

Veith, Gene Edward, Jr. *God at Work: Your Christian Vocation in All of Life.* Wheaton, IL: Crossway, 2002.

Walsh, Brian and J. Richard Middleton. *The Transforming Vision: Shaping a Christian World View.* Downers Grove, IL: IVP Academic, 1984.

Wood, W. Jay. *Epistemology: Becoming Intellectually Virtuous.* Downers Grove, IL: IVP, 1998.

Wright, N.T. *After You Believe: Why Christian Character Matters.* New York: HarperOne, 2010.

5

Faithful Education and Healthy Community

Some Thoughts on Education for a Kingdom Perspective

DANIEL CHINN

THE YEAR WAS 1997 and I was attempting to pass a required algebra class in the fall semester of my senior year at Oklahoma Wesleyan University in Bartlesville, Oklahoma. Math is not a strong suit for me, and so I had delayed taking this class until the final hour of my college career; it was the course I had to pass in order to graduate. In the end, I and four other classmates failed the final exam and therefore the course. From failure, God brought great good.

My professor, Dr. Roest, modeled something for me that changed my life and launched me into a life-long pursuit to understand what he understood. What he understood and modelled for me was faithful education in the context of a healthy community—in the most unlikely of disciplines, algebra. On a Saturday after the final, he provided for us, as a community of learners, a community in which to learn enough algebra to pass the final and the class. Merely passing the course was my hope. What God had prepared for me through this class, in the end, proved to be much more.

Dr. Roest modeled a healthy community in the classroom. His model held three aspects: mutuality, responsibility, and affection. He understood that mutually we were all in this thing together; and he stayed until we got enough of the problems correct to pass. He took responsibility for helping us succeed by being there and working with us. So, too, we took responsibility to work hard and learn enough algebra to pass. Obviously, Dr. Roest loved us. He cared enough for us to devote his Saturday morning to help us along our academic journey. His affection for us was on display. In other words, he was thinking about community from a kingdom perspective.

Though Dr. Roest's approach that Saturday helped me and positively impacted my future as a professor, I want to offer a suggestion that could help all professors cultivate authentic community in the classroom. It seems that the Saturday should have been more than a one-time event. The four students and I who failed the final exam struggled throughout the semester, not merely at the end. If multiple Saturdays (or other opportunities, as well as introducing meals around which the community could gather) had been provided all along, we would have grasped more clearly the aspects of community (mutuality, responsibility, and affection) as well as algebra.

Meals and food may seem like an odd thing to mention in this context, but if you think about it, it's not odd at all. Casting our minds back to the garden with Adam and Eve (the first human community), gathering to enjoy the fruit of all the trees (except one) was the intended normal practice of God's communal people as they learned together about God their Creator and the world he had created. And though Adam and Eve stepped away from that blessed invitation to learn, eat, and worship the Creator, doing so did not alter God's intention for his people to gather as learners throughout the coming redemptive ages. Think of the manna in Exodus; the Passover meal observed by God's covenant people throughout the Old Testament; the bread in the Tabernacle. And then right into the New Testament, where, as his disciples assembled to learn, Jesus gathered them around a meal; eventually transitioning that Passover meal into what we now call the Lord's Supper or Communion. Jesus declares himself *to be* the Bread come down from heaven around which the covenant people gather to learn and worship.[1]
And it seems, as learners even throughout eternity, we will gather around

---

1. John 6 (ESV).

a meal known as the Supper of the Lamb.[2] So, it stands to reason that as Christian educators gathering students to learn about God and his world, food/meals could conceivably be part of our pedagogical approach. At least Walton and Walters think so in their essay "Eat This Class: Breaking Bread in the Undergraduate Classroom."[3] We'll return to their ideas and approach later in this essay.

My suggestion leans toward modeling a healthy classroom community all along the journey. We should structure our class time so that students understand, from day one, what healthy community involves: mutual commitment to each other, mutual responsibility for the class, and mutual affection or love that binds the community together. I help my students understand healthy community and how it relates to faithful learning on the first day of class. I offer a lecture/discussion called "The Learning Community," which lays out three things: one, that they see what constitutes healthy community; two, that they understand what is true about themselves as learners (they are God's image bearers; they make a unique contribution to healthy community; they can learn; learning can be difficult yet rewarding; and class time is set apart as a safe, healthy time for community-building and learning); and three, that if they struggle in the class, help is available outside the classroom. It is here my suggestion comes into play: providing multiple experiences of healthy community for faithful learning the entire semester, especially if they struggle with the material. Dr. Roest did provide a meaningful learning community, but as I look back, I see that he could have provided it over the course of the semester.

Dr. Roest modeled a healthy community in the classroom resulting in faithful learning; and it changed my life. Now I'm the professor with the opportunity to model the same approach for my students in the unique context of a Christian college and its emphasis on faithful education. This chapter, therefore, seeks to weave together a fuller understanding of what constitutes a healthy community and how the communal context can enable faithful education, so ably modeled by Dr. Roest. How did he know that a healthy community holds the three aspects of mutuality, responsibility, and affection? And how did he know that such a learning environment most readily lends itself to faithful learning? As

---

2. Rev 19:9 (ESV).

3. Walton and Walters, "Eat This Class," in Smith and Smith, *Teaching and Christian Practices*.

every faithful, Christian educator should, Dr. Roest knew that the God of Scripture is a God in community.

UNDERSTANDING HEALTHY COMMUNITY—GOD IS OUR MODEL

God speaks to the topic of community in Scripture. The word "community" is used eighty-three times in the Old and New Testaments. The word "fellowship/*koinonia*" is used ninety-six times. The capacity for communal relationships is found not merely in humankind, but in man's creator first. "In the beginning, God created . . ." and he was not alone. God said, "Let us make man in our image, after our likeness."[4] Scripture does not provide a comprehensive explanation of the community enjoyed by the Trinity. The word "trinity" is not used in Scripture to *describe* the triune God, but the Bible does reveal some of the interactive relationship between the Father, Son, and Holy Spirit to help us understand their communality. The self-chosen names of God indicate the communal, familial relationships of the Trinity, i.e., father/son. God, as one God existing and revealed in three persons, existing in a cohesive, mutual community, is simply one of the aspects or attributes of God's character.

Theologian John Frame further helps us understand the communal nature of the persons of the Trinity by highlighting that the concurrence of the three persons of the Trinity in all they do is a profound indication of their unity. There is no conflict in the Trinity. The three persons are perfectly agreed on what they should do and how their plan should be executed. They support one another, assist one another, and promote one another's purposes. This intra-Trinitarian "deference, this disposability" of each to the others, may be called "mutual glorification."[5]

We find, then, three characteristics occurring in the trinitarian community: mutuality, responsibility, and affection (love).[6] Mutuality is the idea that the persons of the Trinity belong to each other. In other words, they are "in this thing together." Each person of the Trinity possesses characteristics that are expressly his alone, i.e., the differing roles each

---

4. Gen 1:26 (ESV).
5. Frame, *Doctrine of God*, 621.
6. Though modeled early on for me by Dr. Roest, I am indebted to Dr. Steve Garber for a fuller understanding of these three relational aspects, as well as Wendell Berry, though responsibility for any flaws in the presentation is my own.

person possesses; but mutuality means they share things in common for the overall good and benefit of the trinitarian community. Responsibility in the Trinity means each person is accountable to the others. The Father is not free or able to "do his own thing." The Son cannot act in his own regard without consideration for the other persons. The Holy Spirit cannot disregard the will or love or mutuality of the Father and Son. Affection speaks of the emotional regard each person of the Trinity has for the others. As mentioned, love is the fundamental characterization of God: thus, their trinitarian love is self-love, but also love that is given away as expressions of affection, devotion, care for, and love one to the others. Summarily, since the persons of the Trinity are in community together (mutuality), they are, of necessity, accountable to one another (responsibility), and they, of necessity, love one another (affection).

GOD'S COMMUNAL PEOPLE—
A BRIEF HISTORICAL SURVEY

This love expresses itself, then, in a cohesive, responsible community. Cohesive community has been defined by novelist Wendell Berry as,

> The mental and spiritual condition of knowing that the place is shared, and that the people who share the place define and limit the possibilities of each other's lives. It is the knowledge that people have of each other, their concern for each other, their trust in each other, the freedom with which they come and go among themselves.[7]

For Berry, community clearly includes the spiritual and a common understanding of belonging to each other and to a place; it is an arrangement involving mutuality, responsibility, and affection for all in the community—human and non-human. A community cannot be made or preserved apart from the loyalty and affection of its members and the respect and goodwill of the people.[8] Community life, insists Berry, is by definition a life of cooperation and responsibility.[9] And to speak of the health of an isolated individual is a contradiction in terms.[10] Berry, we

---

7. Berry, *Long-Legged House*, 61.
8. Berry, *Sex, Economy, Freedom, and Community*, 14.
9. Berry, *Sex, Economy, Freedom, and Community*, 121.
10. Berry, *Another Turn of the Crank*, 91.

need to note, always thinks of healthy community in terms that include nutritious food, sustainable farming, and meals shared together.

The kind of community described by Berry is what God desires for his people to learn and flourish in the context of this kind of healthy community. A brief historical survey of God's dealing with his people reveals his desire for us to reflect his communal nature in the way we learn and live the lives that we are given to live.

Beginning with Adam, God said, "It is not good that man should be alone."[11] And so, God created a wife for Adam, and they flourished in community with each other and with their Creator, who himself lives in community. When God rescued Noah from the destruction of the flood waters, he placed seven others in the ark with him, lest he be alone.[12] Abraham was told by God that he would make him a great nation.[13] The very design of the Old Testament tabernacle[14] spoke of God's desire for his people to live in community with him at the very heart of his people, the God who draws near.[15] Many of the Psalms speak of the communal nature of God's relationship with his people and their relationship with one another.[16]

Entering the New Testament, the very name God gives his Son, Immanuel ("God with us"), speaks of God's continuing desire to be with his people.[17] When Jesus is baptized by John, as Jesus comes out of the Jordan waters, the other two members of the Trinity appear, again reminding the people of the communal nature of their God.[18] As Jesus moved from that event, the Holy Spirit accompanied him as he launched his teaching ministry, thus highlighting the need for a healthy community for faithful learning.[19] As Jesus' teaching ministry grew, he surrounds himself with twelve men whom he sends out in pairs to teach, emphasizing again the need for community for learning.[20] At Jesus' ascension, he promises the Holy Spirit to indwell and empower his people to carry

---

11. Gen 2:18 (ESV).
12. Gen 7:13 (ESV).
13. Gen 17:5 (ESV).
14. Num 14:14 (ESV).
15. Welch, *Created to Draw Near*, 21.
16. Pss 46:5; 116:19 (ESV).
17. Matt 1:23 (ESV).
18. Mark 1:10–11 (ESV).
19. Luke 3:23; 4:1 (ESV).
20. Luke 5:1 (ESV).

on and expand the Church of which he is head. He calls his followers the *ecclesia*, assembled ones, those experiencing *koinonia* (fellowship, togetherness, oneness, mutuality).[21] Finally, at the end of all things, the book of Revelation depicts the triune God as making his dwelling among the assembled men and women who are the Bride of Christ, all gathered as one in worship of the Father, Son, and Holy Spirit.[22] Surely, from this brief survey of redemptive history, we see that God is community and desires his people to learn, live, and flourish in that same communal context.

HEALTHY COMMUNITY—
TAKING IT TO THE CLASSROOM

How does knowing that God is community and desires his people to learn and flourish in community touch our teaching and classroom experience in the Christian learning context? How did Dr. Roest relate his understanding of mutuality, responsibility, and affection to my learning so many years ago? To unpack these questions, let me mention three considerations.

One, we are *Christian* educators. This maxim seems painfully obvious, but consider its weight. Are we truly *Christian* educators? May God spare us the misery of teaching at a Christian college or university whose focus is "faithful education," but which does not possess the Christ of the vision or the Christian faith upon which the idea of "faithful education" is founded. Also, consider those who are in fact Christian but who see little or no connection between their faith and their teaching or their students' learning. They are Christians doing education, but they do not really participate in Christian education. May God spare us that fate as well. Functioning as Christian educators in our university context, we take our cues, as did Dr. Roest, from Scripture both for understanding healthy community and how that relates to faithful education in the classroom culture. We are serious about education and educating from God's point of view. Thinking comprehensively (across all disciplines), professor emeritus of philosophy at Wheaton College, Arthur Holmes, in the attentive chapter "College as Community" from his book *The Idea of a Christian College*, helps educators, specifically those teaching

---

21. Acts 1:1; Col 1:18 (ESV).
22. Rev 22:1–5 (ESV).

in the context of Christian colleges and universities, understand that the "Christian college, moreover, is largely a community of Christians whose intellectual and social and cultural life is influenced by Christian values, so that the learning situation is life as a whole approached from a Christian point of view. It is a situation calculated to teach young people to relate everything to their faith."[23]

Two, we desire to see our students succeed and flourish. This Dr. Roest understood as essential to learning. He took responsibility to see us flourish—not merely to pass the final and the class—but to learn something about the aspects of communal learning (mutuality, responsibility, and affection). We, too, desire to see our students grow in convictions and character. Steve Garber reminds us that community is the context for growth in convictions and character.[24] In his helpful book *Fabric of Faithfulness*, where he asks and answers the question, "How can we weave a fabric of faithfulness between what we believe and how we live?" he also reminds us that, "from the most sophisticated cultural critiques to the street-level despair of the 'dissed' generation, the evidence seems conclusive; for individuals to flourish they need to be part of a community of character, one which has a reason for being that can provide meaning and coherence between the personal and public worlds."[25] Garber, who travels the world helping people think about education in faithful ways so as to help their students weave a faithful fabric between a worldview and a way of life, is concerned about helping students (and their teachers) answer the big questions in life: "Do I have a telos (purpose) that is sufficient to meaningfully orient my praxis (practice) over the course of life? Or in the language of the street, and therefore, a bit more playful: why do I get up in the morning?"[26] Believing, as Christian educators (regardless of our discipline), that we are interested in helping our students ask and hopefully answer those same questions, it seems to me that Garber is spot on in his insistence that the best (and perhaps only) context in which to accomplish this worthy goal is that of healthy community.

Three, we desire Christian *formation*, not merely Christian *information*. At our respective places, we are eager and certain that our students learn the right information (knowledge that accords to the reality of God

23. Holmes, *Idea of a Christian College*, 77.

24. See also Spears and Loomis, *Education for Human Flourishing*, 191–217, for an in-depth consideration of character and its indispensable link to education.

25. Garber, *Fabric of Faithfulness*, 159.

26. Garber, *Fabric of Faithfulness*, 22.

and his created order). Dr. Roest wanted (required!) us to learn and know the facts about working an algebra problem, but he desired more than passing along mere information. By creating a learning environment, he created the opportunity to pass along *in-formation* with a purpose. Through the experience of learning the information communally, he also created the opportunity for Christian formation—one of the basic goals of Christian education. Most of our vision statements proclaim clearly the kind of formation we target: formation into Christ-likeness. Our desire is to create learning environments wherein our students are enabled to grasp the information, and through that often difficult process, we also provide the context in which our students may encounter the living God, who through the task of learning communally, transforms them more and more into loving and flourishing like Christ as they weave fabrics of faithfulness.

COMMUNAL HOSPITALITY AND LEARNING

An essential aspect of learning environments for Christian formation is hospitality, an intentional effort on the part of Christian educators to carve out a space wherein students feel welcomed, valued, and respected. Hospitality is concerned with creating a space where we weave together our private and public lives. Hospitality is largely about knowing and being known. As Christian educators, we possess a strong desire to know our students and (with appropriate and wise boundaries) be known by them. Carving out a space, i.e., our classroom, in which to cultivate the desirability of knowing and being known "requires both personal and communal commitments, and settings which combine aspects of public and private life."[27] To grow in conviction, character, and community, our students need a place where they feel safe to be known and to develop beyond their own sense of self to reach out and know others. Too often, hospitality is relegated to the private sphere, the home; but Christian hospitality is seen as both private and public, intentionally bringing together elements that create an environment where our students feel welcome, safe, and perhaps even refreshed. Here I pick up again the idea that hospitality in our classrooms could involve food or meals around which to gather our students so as to help them feel welcome, safe, and refreshed. "The Christian practice of the shared meal seemed a practical way to foster

---

27. Pohl, *Making Room*, 151.

these reconciling virtues through student-student and student-faculty relationships, because meals have the potential to turn strangers, perhaps even competitors, into friends."[28] "In such environments," insists Pohl, "weary and lonely persons can be restored to life."[29] Pohl continues, "But if hospitality is important to human flourishing, we may want to consider the concerns it embodies and suggest some alternate ways of shaping work places.[30] This may help us to think of our classroom as a workplace that needs, perhaps, fresh perspectives that offer characteristics that lend themselves to integrated, faithful education. And if conceivably possible, perhaps even orient some of the class time and space to offer a restorative meal, or at least a snack food that communicates, "Welcome. You are safe. We are fellow learners. We're glad you're here. We're in this together." Such education creates spaces that offer comfort, safety, care, shelter, stability, rest, space for human brokenness, comfortable furnishing, and inviting lighting, etc.[31] Could not food or a meal be part of this educational setting? With perhaps a bit of imagination, I think so. These and other physical and metaphysical characteristics help create an environment in which students may weave the three strands of conviction, character, and community into a life-shaping tapestry; a tapestry whose contours look more and more like the environment provided by Jesus. In Jesus' teaching model, he often gathered learners around the table to share a meal together. Imagine food, human flourishing, and learning all woven together for pedagogical purposes.

This possibility is why we may need to revise our pedagogical approach to the content and convention in the classroom. Hospitality necessarily implies a two-way conversation. As noted by David Gooblar in *The Missing Course*, "Such revision is necessarily an active process; when all we ask of students in class is to sit and listen to us lecture, we make this revision far less likely to occur."[32] If we are to revise our approach to both the content of a class and the environment of the class, authentic hospitality forces us to reconsider our balance between lecture, where the content is primarily about the professor, and conversation, where the content revolves around both the professor and our students.

28. Walton and Walters, "Eat This Class," in Smith and Smith, *Teaching and Christian Practices*, 82.
29. Pohl, *Making Room*, 151.
30. Pohl, *Making Room*, 153.
31. Pohl, *Making Room*, 168.
32. Gooblar, *Missing Course*, 14.

COMMUNAL FAITHFUL EDUCATION ON THE STREET

What is the *telos* (the end goal) of Christian education? Summarily, it is to witness to God's truth and flourish while doing it. This is the very reason Jesus says he came into the world: "For this reason I came into the world, to bear witness to the truth."[33] He then commissions his people (the church) to the same task in the Great Commission: "Go . . . make disciples . . . in the name of the Father, and of the Son, and of the Holy Spirit, teaching them to observe all that I have commanded you."[34] The purpose of Jesus teaching his people is that they may give faithful witness to the person and work of Christ to all nations. The same purpose (witness), it seems to me, belongs to our purpose for contemporary education: to enable our students to be citizens who are well-educated so that they can give consistent, persuasive, winsome, truthful witness to God's story, centered on Jesus Christ, in all areas of life. This task is best accomplished in the context of community. Bartholomew and Goheen provide a substantive list of authors' attempts to answer the question of the purpose of Christian education: responsive discipleship, freedom, responsible action, shalom, commitment, etc.[35] "Education," they then argue, "is for the purpose of equipping students to witness faithfully to the gospel in the whole of their lives . . . authentic Christian education is *for* witness."[36]

Of course, God's larger purpose in our witnessing (educating/teaching) is that humanity (individually and collectively) will flourish in a life of shalom. In the words of Bartholomew and Goheen, "A world of shalom is characterized by justice, love, thankfulness, and joy . . . shalom, in other words, is the way things ought to be . . . in a shalmic state each entity would have its own integrity and structures of wholeness, and each would also possess many edifying relationships to other entities."[37] From God's nature described simply, though with intense profundity, as "love," we begin to grasp why community matters to us as Christian educators and the students we care for. And part of that love is holding students responsible for class expectations.

As we cultivate relationships with our students, we can also cultivate the same mentorship/flourishing in relationships with our colleagues.

33. John 18:37 (ESV).
34. Matt 28:19, 20 (ESV).
35. Bartholomew and Goheen, *Living at the Crossroads*, 45.
36. Bartholomew and Goheen, *Living at the Crossroads*, 170.
37. Bartholomew and Goheen, *Living at the Crossroads*, 170.

This goal could include asking a colleague to visit your classroom as a guest lecturer on an area of his or her expertise. It may look as simple as inviting a colleague to join you for lunch in the cafeteria. A mentoring relationship between colleagues may provide an opportunity to cultivate deeper relationships. Passing relevant information wisely between each other and students could help make educating for faithful learning more meaningful and perhaps less difficult. Most tasks are easier to accomplish with relevant and helpful information. Wisdom, of course, is the key here: wise exchange of information between colleagues and students; not gossip or rumors, or information that should not be shared.

CONVICTIONS, CHARACTER, AND COMMUNITY

Such communication produces trust and a reason to develop faith. Our students learn of God's truth and world and love best in healthy community. In the words of Garber, "But the young adult is still in formation, still engaged in the activity of composing a self, world and 'God' adequate to ground the responsibilities and commitments of full adulthood. The young adult is searching for a worthy faith."[38] Might we say also that the young adults under our tutelage are looking for a community of students, faculty, and administration with which to develop their convictions, character, and community? The young adults in our care are searching, not only for a worthy faith, but a love worthy enough to orient their *telos* (purpose) and *praxis* (practice) over the course of a life-time of learning.

"So, the formative nature of Christian education may be in need of renewed attention."[39] So asserts Walton and Walters in their essay on creating a broader understanding of healthy community by introducing a meal as part of the class gathering. If Garber is correct and our students are looking for a love worthy of their faith and practice, might we not give some renewed attention to broadening our understanding of community to include the most basic elements such as food. Which is what they did. To broaden both their concept of community and that of their students, they structured one of their classes around a mid-point break where the students and professors enjoyed a meal together. They conclude by reminding us that, "If our teaching and learning has erred on the side of

---

38. Garber, *Fabric of Faithfulness*, 96.

39. Walton and Walters, "Eat This Class," in Smith and Smith, *Teaching and Christian Practices*, 84.

information gluttony, creating shallow learning with a tenuous understanding, then this is not a nutritious way to learn."[40] And to keep the concept of a learning community broad, they offer for our consideration the following acronym: MEALS—mindfulness, expectancy, acceptance, love, and sharing.[41]

Thinking again of the three aspects of healthy community (mutuality, responsibility, and affection), Walton and Walters suggest that, "Practices in the classroom, those sustained, cooperative actions that produce mutuality and cohesive community for the development of deep understanding, are essential to student engagement and the learning project."[42] To think most broadly about the idea of healthy community and learning, we must think as broadly as Christ's kingdom. It seems to me that any Christian philosophy of education must flow from a thirty-thousand-foot perspective—a kingdom perspective—wherein all educational aspirations, conventions, spaces, and approaches must exist for the advancement of the kingdom and helping our students understand how their story connects to the larger story of the kingdom of Jesus, as well as helping them understand how their story is used to advance healthy community (*shalom*) in the broadest terms. This broad approach "represents the deeper reality of the Christian whose life is lived in Christ, that is, one always feasts at the table of the kingdom."[43]

Dr. Roest never gathered us around a meal and he knew I would never learn the finer points of the mathematical world; but he also knew that by modeling healthy community, creating an environment of hospitality in which he positioned himself mutually, responsibly, and affectionately, I could and would learn; and by learning, I would experience growth in convictions, community, and formation in Christ-likeness. He was right! Algebra remains Greek to me. But, my experience in that little community of learners launched me into a life-long pursuit to understand more deeply what constitutes a healthy community and how healthy community contributes to faithful education. And I love Jesus more, too, because of algebra!

40. Walton and Walters, "Eat This Class," in Smith and Smith, *Teaching and Christian Practices*, 87.

41. Walton and Walters, "Eat This Class," in Smith and Smith, *Teaching and Christian Practices*, 84.

42. Walton and Walters, "Eat This Class," in Smith and Smith, *Teaching and Christian Practices*, 88.

43. Oden, *Welcomed Me*, 146.

Let us hope that, as professors at Christian colleges and universities, we are eager to help our institutions fulfill their vision of developing citizens of Christ-like character through faithful education. We, hopefully, are eager to experience life lived in healthy community inside and outside the classroom so that our students and we are transformed into Jesus in the struggle of learning and flourishing as we seek healthy community and faithful education—even in the most unlikely of places, like algebra! And MEALS, it seems, might find a place at our educational table too.

BIBLIOGRAPHY

Allitt, Patrick. *The Art of Teaching: Best Practices of a Master Teacher*. Chantilly, VA: The Great Courses, 2010.

Bain, Ken. *What the Best Teachers Do*. Cambridge, MA: Harvard University Press, 2004.

Bartholomew, Craig. *Where Mortals Dwell: A Christian View of Place for Today*. Grand Rapids: Baker, 2011.

Bartholomew, Craig and Michael Goheen. *Living at the Crossroads: An Introduction to Christian Worldview*. Grand Rapids: Baker, 2008.

Berry, Wendell. *Another Turn of the Crank: Essays*. Washington, DC: Counterpoint, 1995.

———. *The Long-Legged House*. New York: Harcourt, 1969.

———. *Sex, Economy, Freedom, and Community: Eight Essays*. New York: Pantheon, 1993.

Block, Peter. *Community: The Structure of Belonging*. San Francisco: Berrett-Koehler, 2009.

Forster, E. M. *Howard's End*. London: Edward Arnold, 1910.

Frame, John. *The Doctrine of God: A Theology of Lordship*. Phillipsburg, NJ: Presbyterian and Reformed Publishing, 2002.

Garber, Steve. *Fabric of Faithfulness: Weaving Together Belief and Behavior*. Downers Grove, IL: Intervarsity, 2007.

Gooblar, David. *The Missing Course: Everything They Never Taught You About College Teaching*. Cambridge, MA: Harvard University Press, 2019.

Holmes, Arthur. *The Idea of a Christian College*. Grand Rapids: Eerdmans, 1987.

Lane, Timothy and Paul Tripp. *How People Change*. Winston-Salem, NC: Punch, 2006.

———. *Relationships: A Mess Worth Making*. Winston-Salem, NC: Punch, 2008.

McGrath, Alister. *Theology: The Basics*. Malden, MA: Blackwell. 2012.

Nisbet, Robert. *The Quest for Community*. Wilmington, DE: Intercollegiate Studies Institute, 1981.

Oden, Amy. *And You Welcomed Me: A Sourcebook on Hospitality in Early Christianity*. Nashville: Abingdon, 2001.

Pohl, Christine. *Making Room: Rediscovering Hospitality as a Christian Tradition*. Grand Rapids: Eerdmans, 1999.

Smith, David I. and James K. A. Smith. *Teaching and Christian Practices: Reshaping Faith and Learning*. Grand Rapids: Eerdmans, 2011.

Spears, Paul and Steven Loomis. *Education for Human Flourishing: A Christian Perspective*. Downers Grove, IL: Intervarsity, 2007.
Wadell, Paul. *Happiness and the Christian Moral Life: An Introduction to Christian Ethics*. Boulder, CO: Rowman and Littlefield, 2012.
Welch, Edward. *Created to Draw Near: Our Lives as God's Royal Priests*. Wheaton, IL: Crossway, 2020.

Part Two

Faithful Education
across the **Disciplines**

Faithful Education in the Humanities

6

A Faithful Literary Education
Mythos and the "Theory of Everything"

David Pedersen

It is no secret that the formal study of literature is not highly regarded at present in the West. Since the Enlightenment and the Industrial Revolution, the prioritization of utility (narrowly defined) and technological advancement has left little room for the "ingenious nonsense" of literary expression.[1] As I will explain below, amidst the increasing awareness of the mechanics of the natural world, and their predictability and manipulability, the study of literature has become little more than a training ground for snobby baristas (as a fellow regular at a local coffee shop informed me upon learning my profession). In this view, the study of English might at best produce a starry-eyed romantic who feels the knowledge and understanding she has acquired will allow her to negotiate the human condition in the interest of some abstract "common good." At worst, she will focus on the knowledge itself, looking down her nose at those who cannot draw upon the theories of Strauss and Derrida or follow her effortless allusions to Iago and the Pequod. Either way, she will lack the skills to pay the bills, or to produce anything of worth to our (post)modern culture.

While there are many astute and varied responses to this accusation, defending the practical value of literature in both secular and Christian

---

1. Sir Isaac Newton quoting Isaac Barrow, taken here from Gallagher and Lundin, *Literature through the Eyes of Faith*, xiv.

contexts,[2] I believe that literary study also provides a much more fundamental service than either of these contexts can articulate. The study of literature does indeed impart the skills of critical analysis and synthesis, and it certainly provides extensive training in research and problem solving. And, if one accepts the fact that every person bears the *imago* of a creative *dei*, then the study of literature is a study of humankind's expression of its created image.[3] But when we apologize for literature only on these grounds we are making the tacit assumption that the cultural contexts that we have constructed for ourselves are the correct contexts for assigning value to any endeavor. And such an assumption neglects the contingency of all human knowledge and understanding.[4] Thus, I would like in the present chapter to defend the study of literature by considering its relationship to another much maligned subject in the present age: the mythic. For through its connection to *mythos*, literature has the power to remind us that, try as we might, we simply cannot construct our own meaning and purpose. We, along with all our knowledge, exist "under the sun," and, as Solomon reminds us, all here is vanity if it is not imbued with some other value by something beyond the sun. And this is a reminder that our modern age desperately needs.

MYTHOS: REDEFINITION

I use the term *mythos* in this essay very deliberately, but with extreme caution. For in a travesty of human understanding, the term "myth" has become a euphemism for "lie." During the Enlightenment and the Industrial Revolution, application of the humanistic, inductive methods of ancient Greek philosophers made the West increasingly aware of

---

2. Written in the fourth century BC, Aristotle's *Poetics* was essentially a defense of the value of poetry in response to Plato's banishment of lying poets from his Republic. Since the Early Modern Period, various poets and literary critics have added countless defenses of poetry and literary invention. See, for example, Sidney, *Defense of Poetry*; Shelley, "Defence of Poetry;" Arnold, "Literature and Science;" Lewis, "On Stories;" Tolkien, "On Fairy Stories;" Ungar, "7 Major Misperceptions About the Liberal Arts;" and Gallagher and Lundin, *Literature through the Eyes of Faith*.

3. Anonby, "Christian Perspective on English Literature," in Downey and Porter, *Christian Worldview and the Academic Disciplines*, 233. This argument is explored in greater detail in Sayers, *Mind of the Maker*, 21–22, and Tolkien, "On Fairy Stories."

4. Weibe, "Christian Perspective on Philosophy," in Downey and Porter, *Christian Worldview and the Academic Disciplines*, 350–63, where he compares the Christian and secular responses to this contingency.

the ways that religion, which we might consider an applied mythology, was used to manipulate individuals and enforce orthopraxy. This focus on induction and the capability of human inquiry led to an increasing emphasis on fact—that which is done or proved (from *facere*—to do).[5] Somewhere along the way, this became our standard for truth, and myth, with its focus on that which is beyond full human comprehension, which cannot be tested or proved, came to mean untruth.

Thus, the conflation of "myth" and "lie" stems from our refusal to indict the positivist methods for assigning value that we have come to prioritize in the West. Unable to shake off the uncritical dichotomy between fact and lie, mythologists working in the wake of the Enlightenment interpreted mythology as a sort of proto-science, a way of explaining natural phenomena.[6] Pointing to literary and anthropological evidence of ritualistic efforts to participate in these natural phenomena, these mythologists maintained that myths were interpreted literally by ancient civilizations, and that these interpretations were enforced dogmatically through religious rites and observances. Of course, myths were uncritical, for they grew up in societies that lacked the means of inductive inquiry to perform necessary tests to establish them as "fact" by post-Enlightenment standards. In other words, these mythologists believed that primitive cultures were doing badly what natural philosophers after the Enlightenment were learning to do well.

But, as Christians know all too well, it is rarely sufficient to judge an ideal by its practitioners. The enforcement of proto-scientific rituals based upon myths is the fault of people who read mythic narratives and applied them dogmatically, not of the narratives themselves. And such application was far from universal. In the literature of primitive "mythic" cultures, we see very little of the hubristic feeling of control over ourselves and our environment that modern scientific inquiry has given us today. Indeed, the responses to cosmic deities depicted in the enduring texts of the ancients scream to us the contingency of our experience and the ineffectuality of our efforts. This is the realization of Gilgamesh—"[Enlil has decreed that] the heroes, the wise men, like the new moon have their

---

5. See Key, "Metaphors of Meaning," in Mosteller and Anacker, *Contemporary Perspectives on C.S. Lewis*, 157.

6. While this view has been asserted countless times, it is most often associated with the Victorian anthropologist Edward Tylor. See Segal, *Theorizing about Myth*, 7–18.

waxing and waning"[7]—of Hector—"At last the gods have called me down to death ... And now death, grim death is looming up beside me ... this was their pleasure long ago—Zeus and the son of Zeus, the distant deadly Archer" (22.351–357)[8]—and of Job—"where were you [Job] when I [God] laid the earth's foundations?"[9] It seems these cultures were far more concerned with what rituals could not accomplish in response to natural phenomena than with what they could.

The common response to the accusation that myths are proto-scientific lies is that myths are metaphors. To call a myth a lie is to condemn the geometrician who tells her student that a dot made with a pencil on a page is a point.[10] Insofar as a dot is distinct from a segment, a line, a plane, etc., it is sufficient to represent the concept of a geometric "point." Yet, insofar as it has an area, however small, the dot is, by definition, not a point. Before the student of geometry can get far in her studies, she must learn to negotiate this paradox, and it is a poor geometrician indeed who cannot understand the dot metaphorically. Similarly, the student of mythological literature must learn to understand that he might be lured away from studying the night before an exam by a beautiful, scantily-clad, rain-soaked Carthaginian queen while at the same time knowing that this beauty might be "clad" in a hard black casing and go by the name of Xbox. Those who look only for a literal Dido, and who coerce others into looking for her as well, have certainly been in a sense "lied to," but only by their own limited understanding. The fault here is in the practitioner, not the myth.

Of course, the metaphor that the Dido episode represents is not the kind of metaphor that is in danger of being branded a malicious lie; I know of no ancient rites performed ostensibly at Dido's behest. This is because Dido's symbolic significance in *The Aeneid* belongs to a particular type of metaphorical myth that we call allegory—that is a metaphor whose tenor (in this case, distraction) is easy enough to identify in terms we can understand. But the metaphorical vehicles that myths employ often refer to tenors that are not so close to the realm of human experience. An ancient sailor, for example, whose life depended on the favor of the sea had no means of processing why a life-threatening gale might appear out

---

7. *Epic of Gilgamesh*, 118.
8. Homer, *Iliad* (parenthetical citation refers to the book and line numbers).
9. Job 38:4 (NASB).
10. Frye, *Anatomy of Criticism*, 351.

of nowhere. Staring into the face of possible annihilation—for what is death but the annihilation of what we know "under the sun" as it were?—he felt a sense of dread at the contingency of his existence. Northrop Frye notes that this "sense of alienation, or 'thrownness,' from nature" brings humanity face to face with the terrifying possibility that "the fact of human existence [and, by extension, the cessation of this existence] is an arbitrary fact."[11] Seeking purpose or meaning in the face of death, the sailor is met with a gaping unknown, and so he gives this unknown a name and a personality: "Poseidon is angry." Poseidon both is and is not the sea in the same way that a dot both is and is not a point, and, just as the student of geometry needs the dot to introduce and discuss the concept of the point, humanity needs Poseidon (or some other metaphorical vehicle) to introduce the concept of whatever controls the sea.

In "peopling" the natural world with personalities that can be understood, myths present "a world of implicit metaphorical identity."[12] Because the thing to which "Poseidon" refers is beyond our ability to encounter or comprehend (which in itself undermines the conflation of myth with "lie"[13]), we have nothing to which we can relate but the metaphor itself, and we are forced to confront the fact that it refers to we know not what.[14] It may refer to nothing, but this is not a conclusion that humanity has ever been truly able to accept or practice (more on this below). Indeed, this conclusion would confirm our fear that "the fact of human existence is an arbitrary fact." The only other option with which we are left is that we are characters in someone, or something, else's story.[15] Myth, then, provides us with a *telos*, a purpose, but at the cost of our own agency in creating and defining this purpose. This is the uncomfortable recognition of the heroes of the narratives I noted a moment ago: their lives are not their own, and they cannot be sure of their significance in the *teloi* that give their lives meaning. By extension,

---

11. Frye, *Words with Power*, 35.

12. Frye, *Anatomy*, 136. See also Lewis, "Bluspels and Flalansperes," in *Selected Literary Essays*, 261–63.

13. Sidney, "Defense," 1068–69, famously answered Plato's accusation that poets are liars by noting that creators of poesy make no claim to truth-telling.

14. The inaccessibility of the essential tenor of the universal metaphorical vehicle is an essential tenet of Christian belief. See, for example, McGrath, *Theology*, 23, and Sayers, *Mind*, 22–26.

15. Lewis, "Stories," 19–20, explores the implications of this ultimatum in further detail.

then, we might consider ritualistic religion—or applied mythology—as an attempt to garner what little agency we can within this imposed *telos*.

MYTH AND LITERATURE

When mythic metaphors are organized into a narrative, they become literary.[16] To extend the analogy from geometry further, if mythic metaphors are geometric dots, then literature is the mathematical equation into which the dots (or the values that the dots represent) are inserted—literature is the application of the metaphor for human use. Of course, not all literature is necessarily myth, but all literature is constructed toward a *telos* that has been established by the author.[17] In this way, as N.T. Wright observes, "literature . . . reflects, in the way appropriate to its own area, the basic shape of the problem of knowledge itself."[18] Thus the characters about which we read in literature experience the narrative mythically in much the same way that we experience our own existence mythically.[19] And by relating to these characters, we are able to process the "thrownness" of our essential contingency.

The analogous relationship between our own existential circumstance and the circumstances of the characters about which we read in literature has two important implications for how we define and experience reality. First, the way that we respond to various types of literature draws us constantly back to the mythic nature of our existence. When we read stories merely for entertainment, for example, we essentially express our desire for a *telos*. We relate to a hero or heroine for whose good the story exists, and in so doing we express our own desire to matter, to exist non-arbitrarily. When we read for edification, on the other hand, we confront the inescapability of the fact that we do not know that our existence is meaningful or purposeful; we know only that our existence is not really ours to define.

---

16. This is what I believe N.T. Wright means when he defines literature as "the telling of stories which bring worldviews into articulation" (Wright, *New Testament*, 65).

17. Because of this fact, Frye contends that all literature is derived from myth (Frye, *Words*, 36).

18. Wright, *New Testament*, 31.

19. Anonby addresses the value of literature as analogous to life and the philosophical implications thereof. See Anonby, "Christian Perspective on English Literature," in Downey and Porter, *Christian Worldview and the Academic Disciplines*, 236–38.

Indeed, when stories operate too closely to a *telos* that we might have defined, we hold them in low esteem. At best these kinds of stories are contrived; at worst they are silly. Shakespeare gives us such a story in the first two acts of *Romeo and Juliet*. So common is the image of a scorned pubescent lover who is convinced that, without his love, human existence is merely a "Mis-shapen chaos of well-seeming forms" (1.1.184),[20] that we relegate this kind of image to a type, a cliché. We wait expectantly, trying to keep our eyes from rolling, for this lover's life to take on new meaning the moment his vision alights upon another "well-seeming form":

> Oh she doth teach the torches to burn bright!
> It seems she hangs upon the cheek of night
> Like a rich jewel in an Ethiope's ear;
> Beauty too rich for use, for earth too dear! (1.5.51–54)

And we try to hold down our lunch when, in the throes of requited love, this young couple now has new purpose in this relationship—a new sense of identity:

> O Romeo Romeo, wherefore art thou Romeo?
> Defy thy father and refuse thy name.
> Or, if thou will not, be but sworn my love
> And I'll no longer be a Capulet. (2.2.36–39)

We call this kind of narrative "the stuff of fairy tales," "too perfect" for the real world. When such a narrative actually occurs in real life, we call it "stranger than fiction," by which we mean that it is so closely aligned with a *telos* we might have defined for ourselves that, were we to encounter it in a story, we would judge it to be contrived.

But the very sense that the story is "too perfect" in its alignment with our expectations and desires implies that we are convinced of an ideal level of perfection regarding such an alignment. In other words, we do not believe ourselves to be good custodians of real narratives; we cannot create reality. Thus, at the very moment we are thinking that "this is the sort of thing that only happens in stories" we are also waiting, perhaps even hoping, for Shakespeare not to patronize us with this story that is "too perfect." We almost expect with Romeo the realization of "Some consequence yet hanging in the stars" that "Shall bitterly begin his fearful

---

20. All references to *Romeo and Juliet* are from Peter Holland's edition in Orgel and Braunmuller, *William Shakespeare The Complete Works* (citations are included in text by act, scene, and line numbers).

date with this night's revels" (1.4.114–16).[21] And it is no coincidence indeed that at the very moment the love story stops being "too perfect" for us, when Romeo in a fit of vengeful rage kills his beloved's cousin and seals his banishment from his home and from Juliet, Shakespeare seems to pass the narrative off to a mythic metaphor for the unknown: "O I am Fortune's fool!" (3.1.98; my emphasis). This deferral to a mythic goddess who has purportedly constructed the narrative, this moment of obvious mythic metaphor is, paradoxically, the first moment of the narrative that feels truly "real." Indeed, Romeo is not the darling of the author, who bends the narrative to Romeo's desire. Romeo is like us, contingent.

And this overweening sense of our own contingency brings us to the second implication of the analogy between literature and life. In forcing upon us the awareness that our sense of purpose, identity, and meaning is contingent upon things that are outside of our control, literature provides us with the means of processing and negotiating this contingency. This process and negotiation is entirely emotional as opposed to intellectual, for the awareness of our contingency brings us to the limit of our intellect. We are left only with empathy for the characters we encounter, catharsis from the sense that they are like us, and an awareness that the only way forward is feeling, soul-sense, (dare I say) faith.[22] We are forced to trust that the sense of good and bad that impresses itself upon us in the midst of our "thrownness," the feeling that there is a *telos* in service to which we can, should, indeed must act comes from a kind of truth that lies beyond fact. For, indeed, all we know at this point with epistemological certainty is that we are beyond the realm of fact.

THE INEVITABILITY OF MYTH

Given the ability of literature, and its progenitor myth, to keep us constantly in view of our fundamental contingency as characters of some other entity's story, it is no wonder that the modern age has so often condemned myths as lies and literature as useless. We live today in the

---

21. This expectation is compounded, of course, by the fact that the plot of the play has so penetrated our social consciousness that almost nobody today encounters the play without knowing the trajectory of the denouement. But this sense of the imminent tragic turn derives not merely from prior knowledge, for the very implication that the love story is "too perfect" suggests that the perfection is doomed.

22. In this way, literature ultimately shapes what has been defined as "worldview" in the introduction to this volume.

shadow of Descartes, where only what we can know with epistemological certainty is of any value.[23] Descartes's famous enthymeme "I think; therefore I am" is essentially an assertion of the human intellect's ability to explain itself—a rejection of the mythic nature of our existence.[24] In the nineteenth century we killed God, no longer needing a universal author for a story we had come to believe we control.[25] It is no coincidence that the book that first gave us the maxim "God is dead" is called *Die Fröliche Wissenschaft* (*The Happy Science*), for it is in the name of that which we know (*scientia*) that we have felt emboldened to take the universal story upon ourselves. More recently, the most prolific "prophet" of our scientific age, Stephen Hawking, has made the audacious claim that philosophy, the field of ostensibly inductive inquiry that deals with questions that have not yet entered the realm of *scientia*, or fact, has been killed by physics:

> How can we understand the world in which we find ourselves? How does the universe behave? What is the nature of reality? Where did all of this come from? Did the universe need a creator? . . . Traditionally these are questions for philosophy, but philosophy is dead. Philosophy has not kept up with modern developments in science, particularly physics. Scientists have become the bearers of the torch of discovery in our quest for knowledge.[26]

Indeed, ours is an age that has no use for human contingency.

But excluding the possibility that we are characters in a universal story simply has not worked. In "How the World Lost Its Story," Robert Jenson traces the failure of modernity's "attempt to live in a universal story without a universal storyteller," noting that this failure was inevitable.[27] Nietzsche followed his famous assertion that "God is dead" with the admonition that we must become gods ourselves to be worthy of the deed,[28] and Matthew Arnold's famous nineteenth-century defense of the

---

23. For a discussion of Descartes's influence on subsequent philosophical perspectives, see Smith, *Desiring the Kingdom*, 41–42, and Pate, *Plato to Jesus*, 57–58.

24. Descartes, *Discourses on Method*, 21. This rejection of myth is, I believe, an essential cause of the secularity to which this volume responds.

25. Nietzsche, *Gay Science*, 120.

26. Hawking and Mlodinow, *Grand Design*, 5.

27. Jenson, "How the World Lost Its Story." See also Poplin, *Is Reality Secular?*, 105–11.

28. Nietzsche, *Gay Science*, 120.

study of "humane letters" against scientists' growing accusations of their uselessness essentially equated the study of humanity's *belles lettres* to the theology of the new humanism.[29] But to become gods—that is to say, to take hold of the story of existence—is to admit that a story exists. And to admit that such a universal story exists is to admit that we can no more be its authors than a pot can be its own potter.

Once again we are brought back to the brink of the unknown void of being, desperate to find some way to assuage our fear that we are arbitrary. But having barred ourselves from telling silly, naïve, unscientific lies about this unknown, we have lost the means to confront it.[30] This is what Jenson defines as post-modernity, the rejection of the universal narrative altogether. Our literary and artistic response, as Jenson notes, has been to try to embrace this fear by adding "a new genre of the theater to the classic tragedy and comedy: the absurdist drama that displays precisely an absence of dramatic coherence." Indeed, modern literature, like Camus's *Le Estrange* and Delillo's *White Noise*, presents us with a relentlessly arbitrary world, a world where the narrative meaning by which we can even call a tragedy a tragedy is not present. These works refuse to give the unknown a metaphorical, mythic identity, mocking us for our desire for fundamental meaning and purpose. Yet precisely in their relentless meaninglessness, they betray themselves. Indeed, the meaninglessness is a meaning in the same way that the claim "there are no absolutes" is an absolute. By conveying meaning with their meaninglessness, these stories remind us that we cannot create meaninglessly, that within our frame of reference, a thing cannot be without being meaningful.[31] And so we are prompted to ask once again, "what is our meaning?"

But far more damning than modernist authors' failed attempts to create unmeaningfully is the absolute lack of intellectual integrity of the scientific impulse that has condemned the mythic mode in the modern age. Let us return, for a moment, to Hawking's claim that philosophy is dead. He asserts that physics has the capacity to answer the questions of meaning and purpose that historically fell within the domain of philosophy. Yet, in the same breath he admits that the M Theory of physics, which he offers as the new custodian of philosophical inquiry, cannot be proved without "a Hadron Collider the size of the Milky Way."

---

29. Arnold, "Literature and Science," esp. 90–95.
30. Poplin, *Is Reality Secular?*, 133–35.
31. Gallagher and Lundin, *Literature*, 3.

Hawking is not operating in the realm of scientific inquiry here; he is operating in the realm of *mythos*.[32] He has substituted one "metaphor" for the unknown—God—for another—M Theory. Worse, he has called this "science." Similarly, in his lecture "The Beginning of Time," Hawking excludes the necessity for a universal creator by calling upon the concept of imaginary time.[33] But in his book *The Universe in a Nutshell* he defines imaginary time essentially as a mythic metaphor for something beyond human comprehension:

> One might think this means that imaginary numbers are just a mathematical game having nothing to do with the real world. From the viewpoint of positivist philosophy, however, one cannot determine what is real. All one can do is find which mathematical models describe the universe we live in. It turns out that a mathematical model involving imaginary time predicts not only effects we have already observed but also effects we have not been able to measure yet nevertheless believe in for other reasons. So what is real and what is imaginary? Is the distinction just in our minds?[34]

And Hawking is by no means alone in this charlatanry. Indeed the very field of string theory, the so called "theory of everything," rests on the tenuous foundation that it is the most consistent explanation for why gravity exists.[35] It fills a gap of the unknown; it has no more to recommend its truth than the claim that an intelligent, superhuman entity maintains the spatial relationship between objects with mass; it is mythic.

Indeed, science, the acquisition of natural knowledge, has been a poor custodian of the mythic impulse. It has replaced mythic metaphors with different metaphors and then sought to impose the literality of these new metaphors dogmatically. Of course, as Jenson asserted, this result was inevitable, for as James K. A. Smith has explained, "Whenever science attempts to legitimate itself, it is no longer scientific but narrative, appealing to an orienting myth that is not susceptible to scientific legitimation."[36] When we take upon ourselves the responsibility to define reality, the inevitable end of that road is the kind of nonsense questions

---

32. Poplin, *Is Reality Secular?*, 48 discusses this contradiction in Hawking's and Mlodinow's reasoning.

33. Hawking, "Beginning of Time."

34. Hawking, *Universe in a Nutshell*, 59.

35. See Horgan, "Why String Theory is Still Not Even Wrong."

36. Smith, *Who's Afraid of Postmodernism?*, 68.

that conclude the Hawking quote above: "So what is real and what is imaginary? Is the distinction just in our minds?" And we are terrified that the answer to the latter question is "yes," for this would mean that our very existence is a matter of opinion.

FAITHFUL EDUCATION

As a professing Christian, I admit that I am guilty of something very much akin to the hubristic audacity of those whom I have been criticizing. Just as Hawking or a priest performing a primitive fertility ritual claims to know that his universal metaphors for the unknown (M Theory and the sun-god, respectively) are, in fact, literal, I claim to know that the *mysterium tremendum*,[37] the author of the universal story, is Yahweh, the God of Abraham, Isaac, and Jacob. But I also know that I have come by this knowledge emotionally, feelingly, mythically. If I enforce my awareness of this tenor on others dogmatically, I no more cultivate a comparable awareness than a teacher cultivates a love of learning by threatening homework as a punishment for insubordination. For someone else to accept the truth of God's existence, this truth must resonate with her soul, her questions of meaning and purpose, her mythological wonder, in the same way that it has with mine.[38]

Thus, my work as a Christian educator is very much an expression of my faith. It *has* to be. I have faith that the God I acknowledge is the one true God. I have faith that he is testifying his existence to the hearts of the students he brings me. I have faith that he will meet my students in the sense of terrifying wonder that lies in the gaping epistemological hole of the tenor of the universal mythic metaphor. I have faith that the texts with which I ask my students to engage are creations of creative minds that express the *imago Dei* and that their creations are expressions of this image. All literature, sometimes in spite of itself, points us back to the sense that there is a universal *telos* and an author who is directing us there, and I have faith that this author is God.[39]

---

37. I am taking this term from Campbell, *Thou Art That*, 2.
38. See McGrath, *Theology*, 29.
39. In a sense, then, my role in my student's character formation is to teach them to ask honest questions and then to step back, knowing faithfully that God will answer them.

While my faith is expressed primarily in my motives for teaching my subject, it also has a few measurable effects on my pedagogy. I am careful, for example, to impress upon my students the contingency of human existence. My students in Western Civilization I are often indignant when they encounter Marvin Perry's claim in our standard textbook that Christianity is a mythic religion.[40] They are scandalized when I inform them that I agree with Perry. They assume, as they have been programmed to assume, the conflation of "myth" and "lie," and I relish the opportunity to disabuse them of this faulty assumption. Thus, I make them read the writings of prominent humanist mythographers (like Hawking) alongside the more apparently mythological writings of the ancient Hebrews, Sumerians, and Egyptians. I ask them to compare the methods for describing reality that these different texts apply, and this comparison always results in the awareness that, while all of them reveal human contingency, the ancient texts at least display the intellectual honesty to acknowledge this contingency.

In addition, I expect my students to read widely from a range of creeds and beliefs. If (as I believe) the God of Abraham is the tenor to the universal mythic metaphor, and if (as I also believe) the God of Abraham has imbued humankind with his image and with a desire for the *telos* that this image implies, then it follows that all literature is, in some sense, an expression of this image and reveals a veiled awareness of this *telos*. Thus, I ask my students to look for truth to be found in Christian and non-Christian texts alike. I want my students to see for themselves that Christianity is not just for Christians—that the desire for purpose and the fear that we have none is every bit as ubiquitous as the *imago Dei*.

Finally, I require my students to engage literary expressions of the true myth, God's Word, from a literary and mythic perspective. This is not to say that I discount the value of assuming the sanctity of Scripture as an *a priori* premise, only that I trust that the sanctity of Scripture is capable of impressing itself upon the souls of my students when they engage it from another lens. My application of this lens might be broken into two categories. First, I expect students to consider the literary merits of the various narratives, poems, and philosophical investigations found in Scripture from a critical purview. Most of them have been told, for example, that Ecclesiastes and Job are sacred texts and, therefore, superior to other philosophical treatises and epic narratives.

---

40. Perry, *Western Civilization*, 119.

While this may provide them with a high view of Scripture, the height of the view is in many ways artificial. When they read *Ecclesiastes* alongside Aristotle's *Metaphysics* or Job alongside *The Epic of Gilgamesh*, they have the opportunity to recognize that the questions and concerns raised in texts sacred to the Judeo-Christian tradition are the same questions and concerns raised in texts that lie outside that tradition. In other words, Judeo-Christian values are relevant to all walks of life. Furthermore, reading these texts comparatively impresses upon students the fact that the Judeo-Christian texts "hold water" in an academic context, that they are of at least equal literary and intellectual value as other texts that are often more highly regarded for their literary merit by the academy. And in justifying the comparison, I believe I invite students into their own honest consideration of what might make the texts that they hold sacred superior.

Second, and more importantly, I invite my students to "read" God's interaction with his creation as a story.[41] Take, for example, the genealogy of Christ at the beginning of Matthew. This genealogy participates in a literary genre that was thriving in the Greco-Roman world. Romulus and Remus, the legendary founders of Rome, were the result of a union between the god Mars and a vestal virgin who was, herself, a descendant of Venus through Aeneas. Genealogies like this express a desire to be "like the gods," to collapse the distance between the divine and human. They are, in a sense, a sort of literary Tower of Babel, with the divine at the top and humanity tracing its bloodline back to them. The genealogy in Matthew works in the opposite direction, beginning with a human (Abraham), and ending with the divine (Jesus). From a literary perspective, this can hardly be coincidence: it is a deliberate subversion of the prevailing narrative. This is not a God that humanity must reach; it is a God that has reached humanity.

Of course, this may be "just a story," "too perfect" to be real. But this kind of incredulity is for the *imago Dei* of my students to work out with the Holy Spirit. My job is to introduce them to tension, to the *mysterium tremendum* of the grand mythic metaphor. I believe this mystery, once acknowledged, is a thin veil indeed; and behind it, waiting eagerly, is the face of God.

---

41. Wright, *New Testament*, 116, notes the essential congruity between stories and historical events.

BIBLIOGRAPHY

Aristotle. *Poetics*. Translated by M. Heath. New York: Penguin, 1996.
Arnold, Matthew. "Literature and Science." In *Discourses in America*, 72–137. London: MacMillan, 1912.
Campbell, Joseph. *Thou Art That: Transforming Religious Metaphor*. Novato: New World Library, 2001.
Descartes, René. *Discourses on Method*. Translated by Laurence J. Lafleur. New York: MacMillan, 1956.
Downey, Deane and Stanley Porter, eds. *Christian Worldview and the Academic Disciplines: Crossing the Academy*. Eugene, OR: Pickwick, 2009.
The Epic of Gilgamesh. Translated by N.K. Sandars. New York: Penguin, 1972.
Frye, Northrop. *Anatomy of Criticism: Four Essays*. Princeton: Princeton University Press, 1957.
———. *Words with Power: Being a Second Study of "The Bible and Literature."* Edited by Michael Dolzani. Toronto: University of Toronto Press, 2008.
Gallagher, Susan V. and Roger Lundin. *Literature through the Eyes of Faith*. New York: HarperOne, 1989.
Hawking, Stephen. "The Beginning of Time." *Stephen Hawking: The Official Website* (1996). http://www.hawking.org.uk/the-beginning-of-time.html.
———. *The Universe in a Nutshell*. New York: Bantam Books, 2001.
Hawking, Stephen and Leonard Mlodinow. *The Grand Design*. New York: Bantam, 2010.
Homer. *The Iliad*. Translated by Robert Fagles. New York: Penguin, 1990.
Horgan, John. "Why String Theory is Still Not Even Wrong." *Scientific American* (April 27, 2017). https://blogs.scientificamerican.com/cross-check/why-string-theory-is-still-not-even-wrong/.
Jenson, Robert W. "How the World Lost Its Story." *First Things* (March, 2010). https://www.firstthings.com/article/2010/03/how-the-world-lost-its-story.
Lewis, C.S. "Bluspels and Flalansperes: A Semantic Nightmare." In *Selected Literary Essays*, edited by W. Hooper, 251–65. Cambridge: Cambridge University Press, 1969.
———. "On Stories." In *On Stories and Other Essays on Literature*, 320. New York: Harcourt, 1982.
McGrath, Alister. *Theology: The Basics*, 3rd ed. Oxford: Wiley-Blackwell, 2012.
Mosteller, Tim and Gayne John Anacker, eds. *Contemporary Perspectives on C.S. Lewis' The Abolition of Man*. New York: Bloomsbury, 2017.
Nietzsche, Friedrich. *The Gay Science, With a Prelude of German Rhymes and an Appendix of Songs*. Edited by Bernard Williams. Translated by Josefine Naukhoff and Adrian del Caro. Cambridge: Cambridge University Press, 2001.
Pate, C. Marvin. *From Plato to Jesus: What Does Philosophy Have to do with Theology*. Grand Rapids: Kregel Academic, 2011.
Perry, Marvin. *Western Civilization: A Brief History*. 11th ed. Boston: Cengage, 2016.
Poplin, Mary. *Is Reality Secular? Testing the Assumptions of Four Global Worldviews*. Downers Grove, IL: InterVarsity, 2014.
Sayers, Dorothy. *The Mind of the Maker*. San Francisco: Harper, 1987.
Segal, Robert A. *Theorizing about Myth*. Amherst: University of Massachusetts Press, 1999.

Sidney, Sir Philip. *A Defense of Poetry*. Edited by J. A. Van Dorsten. Oxford: Oxford University Press, 1966.

Shakespeare, William. "Romeo and Juliet." In *William Shakespeare The Complete Works: A New Pelican Text*, edited by Stephen Orgel and A. R. Braunmuller, 1251–94. New York: Penguin, 2002.

Shelley, Percey Bysshe. "A Defence of Poetry." In *Selected Prose Works of Shelley*, edited by Henry S. Salt, 75–118. London: Watts & Co., 1915.

Smith, James K. A. *Desiring the Kingdom*. Grand Rapids: Baker Academic, 2009.

———. *Who's Afraid of Postmodernism? Taking Derrida, Lyotard, and Foucault to Church*. Grand Rapids: Baker Academic, 2006.

Tolkien, J.R.R. *Tolkien on Fairy-Stories*. Edited by Verlyn Flieger and Douglas A. Anderson. New York: HarperCollins, 2014.

Ungar, Sanford J. "7 Major Misperceptions About the Liberal Arts." *The Chronicle of Higher Education* 56.25 (2010): 40-41.

Wright, N.T. *The New Testament and the People of God*. Minneapolis: Fortress, 1992.

7

HISTORICAL THINKING AND VOCATION

JOSEPH WESTERN

"CHRISTIANITY IS A RELIGION of historians," observed the twentieth-century French historian Marc Bloch.[1] Not only do Christians rely on historical books and participate in ritual developed over time, but "the destiny of humankind, placed between the fall and the judgment, appears to its eyes as a long adventure, of which each life, each individual pilgrimage, is in its turn a reflection. It is in time and, therefore, in history that the great drama of Sin and Redemption, the central axis of all Christian thought, is unfolded."[2]

The discipline of history is foundational to the Christian faith. While postmodern approaches to historical study have called into question the ability of historians to know anything firm about the past, "Christianity has always displayed an innate tendency toward historical realism, in large part because it depends upon events that believers—in their creeds, their liturgies, their dogmatics, their preaching, their prayers—assert really happened. Moreover, Christian practice is predicated on the tacit assumption that these past events can be known reliably today and can provide meaning for present life."[3] While much that has happened over the course of time has been lost to the present-day historian, the faithful

---

1. Bloch, *Historian's Craft*, 4.
2. Bloch, *Historian's Craft*, 4.
3. Noll, *Jesus Christ*, 78.

historian asserts that some measure of truth is knowable about the past. When I attempt to learn about the past, I am confronted with many difficulties of evidence, bias, and interpretation, but historical study is a quest for truth.

Time provides the backdrop for the activity of God inside his creation, and it provides a framework in which human beings, the pinnacle of that creation, live out their lives as receivers of that gracious activity. The chronological passage of time is so essential to the human experience that it is right to say that every person is a historian. That is, all people think about things that have happened before the ever-passing present and use that knowledge to shape their interactions with the world around them.

Not only foundational to the understanding and practice of Christianity and basic to the human experience, historical study also has a positive formational effect on its students. In thinking about what it means to faithfully teach students in the discipline of history, I don't wish to reflect on the broader question of what historians do as they practice their discipline. Others have grappled with these questions.[4] On this topic, it will be enough here to note that the study of history encompasses both the framework of the past—the names, dates, and events of historical study—as well as the capacity for making sense of that framework and using that knowledge to inform present day understandings of who we are and where we fit into the world, both spatially and chronologically (and therefore spiritually). The capacity for making sense of that framework is called historical thinking, a basic component of the process of making sense of the world, and it is this aspect of historical study that I believe can enrich a student's understanding of his or her relationship with God and also how to love and serve the people whom God has given us as neighbors.

Historical thinking's ability to enrich each student's relationship with those with whom he or she comes into contact connects it to vocation. While students are called to numerous vocations, Angus Menuge notes that all of these callings have the same purpose. He writes, "Our vocations are means of showing love by giving our neighbor what he really needs. This is accomplished by honest, trustworthy work of high quality, not by shoddy work adorned with superficial piety."[5] This applies

---

4. See, for example, Bloch, *Historian's Craft*; Carr, *What is History?*; Gaddis, *Landscape of History*; Maza, *Thinking About History*.

5. Menuge, "Vocation," in Englebrecht, *Lutheran Difference*, 481. Gene Edward

both to students and the instructor. For the historian, doing high quality work begins with an honest study of history. A historian strives to uphold professional standards developed within the discipline to interpret and communicate the truth of the past clearly and as accurately as possible. While this is somewhat intuitive, understanding how teaching history shows "love by giving our neighbor what he really needs" requires more unpacking. In fact, students often question the relevance of studying history as they are packed into required general education classrooms to take a subject that many see as disconnected from their own personal experiences or the career trajectories that they envision for themselves.

I wish to explore this idea that teaching history gives our neighbor what he really needs by thinking about Christ's commands to love God and to love and serve the neighbor.[6] This works both in terms of how I can serve my students by instructing them, but also how I can equip them to go out into the world and strive towards those twin aims.

Scott Ashmon's reflections on the relationship between faith and learning shed light on the purpose of education in a Christian framework. The relationship between faith and learning is "neither integration for transformation nor avoidance via separation, but the mutual, responsible, and fruitful interaction of faith and learning for service."[7] He continues to say:

> [a Biblical] integration occurs by each discipline having the integrity to pursue the truth in its areas with its own methods and terms . . . Coupled with this integrity is an inseparable complementarity where Christian theology and each discipline are connected and useful to the other. This occurs by Christian theology and each discipline confidently and humbly dialoguing, questioning, critiquing, and informing each other as is appropriate to their spheres of knowledge so that they mutually benefit each other.[8]

Teaching is only faithful insofar as it is done in the faith that receives the creating, forgiving, and sanctifying gifts of God. It cannot be faithful

---

Veith adds, "When God blesses us, He almost always does it through other people" (Veith, *God at Work*, 14).

6. Matt 22:37–39.

7. Ashmon, *Idea and Practice*, 27. For Ashmon's critique of these two views, see pages 21–27. For another perspective on models for understanding the relationship between faith and learning, see chapter 5 of VanZanten, *Joining the Mission*, 97–128.

8. Ashmon, *Idea and Practice*, 27.

on its own merit, nor is there a methodology that an instructor can use to make it holy by saying or doing the right things. It is a gift, both to the instructor and to the students, a good work born of faith and placed into the words and actions of an instructor by the Creator, Redeemer, and Sanctifier of all things. God works to communicate his truth by calling men and women to study and share it with others through their vocations as instructors.

In his critique of educational practice, Thomas Korcok observes that "Individual autonomy—which is characterized by the ability to think critically about the issues that are central to one's life—is the chief aim of liberal education."[9] Much contemporary secular education sees this autonomy as the basic goal of learning. Korcok notes that this should not be its ultimate end, however. A faithful educator recognizes that education, no matter how much it liberates the mind from ignorance, cannot redeem the sinner.[10] Thus the ultimate goal of all education must be to support the proclamation of the gospel, whose gifts do not depend on the amount of knowledge one receives, or the self-construction or imposition of a worldview. Rather it is worked by the Holy Spirit, creating faith in the individual that receives divine gifts, which themselves are tied to a specific historical time and place: the cross. Martin Marty notes, "Only Christian higher education is committed to what Christians mean by *Vocation*. They mean lives that find their coherence in Christ, 'in whom everything holds together.' [Students] learn that each of them is distinctively marked, irreplaceable, in God's scheme of things, and that they are not merely integers among the thrones and principalities and authorities."[11]

While teaching history does not create or sustain faith, it can complement a student's theological formation as it explores the story of the human past. Historians do not have to teach Christian history to accomplish this, or even provide a uniquely Christian interpretation of events.[12] When speaking of the power of story, N.T. Wright notes, "Christians believe that all human life is itself a gift of God and, however much it may be distorted, a reflection of God. Thus even stories written

9. Korcok, *Lutheran Education*, 256.
10. Ashmon, *Idea and Practice*, 16.
11. Marty, "Church," in Henry and Agee, *Faithful Learning*, 60.
12. Arthur Holmes notes that Christian education "shuns tacked-on moralizing and applications, stale and superficial approaches that fail to penetrate the basic intellectual issues" (Holmes, *Idea of a Christian College*, 7).

by writers who are explicitly atheist—indeed, writers whose words were intended to mock or dismiss God—have a strange knack of making crucial points about what it means to be human."[13] If this is true for constructed stories, it must also be true for the lived stories of the human past.

Studying the past aggregates the lived experiences of previous generations. Through this lens, we come to better understand expressions of truth, beauty, goodness, faith, hope, and love. So too do we understand their absence or their opposites: evil, brokenness, disbelief, selfishness, and falsehood. Ronald Wells captures this well when he notes that as we study history, we see confirmation that "every person and society experiences life-as-lived, which is always different—sometimes markedly different—from life-as-hoped for. The 'is' always falls short of the 'ought.' This is part and parcel of the human condition."[14] The stories of lived experiences, even if they are not our own, can exemplify Christian concepts in relatable ways.

LOVING GOD

One of the ways that studying history "gives a student what he really needs" is by enriching the framework that a student needs to understand his or her relationship with God more fully. Ashmon's complementarity between theology and history comes strongly into play here. A person cannot think about God without considering his or her own place in relationship with God. We must, therefore, consider our identity when we consider our theology. We are created by a loving God who breaks into his creation to restore a right relationship with his children, who can't get out of their own way in their rebellion against him. Our theology informs our identity: we are who God describes us to be.

Rod Dreher writes in *The Benedict Option*, "Every educational model presupposes an anthropology: an idea of what a human being is."[15] When we study history, we come to better understand what it means to be human, and as we do so, we come to see the biblical doctrine of human nature played out in specific examples of the shared human experience. As we simultaneously come to deepen our understanding of who we are,

---

13. Wright, *After You Believe*, 265.
14. Wells, *History*, 12.
15. Dreher, *Benedict Option*, 147.

as well as the world around us, our relationship with God, though delineated in God's revelation to us, crystalizes even more clearly. This then prepares us to live lives of repentance, receive forgiveness through Christ, and serve our neighbors in the many places God puts us with humility and empathy.

As we consider this, we naturally find that our identity is shaped both by who we are created to be and by our lived experiences. In this way, each of us is unique from all other people, knit together in our mothers' wombs in a way that is different from anyone else who has ever lived. At the same time, as we live out the lives God has set before us, we find that we do not live in isolation. Our stories weave together with those of others. These other stories both *shape* who we are and give us external perspective that helps us to *understand* who we are. Just as one example, we can consider the ways that our parents have influenced our stories, helping both to shape and to discover our identities. When we project this insight back over even a few generations, we quickly see how the past shapes our contexts. Medieval historian, Marcus Bull, highlights the role of history in identity formation. "That is why amnesia and dementia can strike us as so unsettling: encountering someone suffering from severe memory impairment not only elicits sympathy for the distressing condition, but it prompts reflections on the extent to which personal identity and social interaction hinge on something as apparently banal and taken for granted as the ability to remember."[16] The past shapes who we are and how we understand ourselves.

Living in the physical—and fallen—world shapes how we understand who we are and how we experience our relationship with God. We are not alone in this—we are human. All people share the experience of being created and of living in a physical world. In this sense, being human gives us a common story with others. We can't escape our created-ness or eliminate its ability to shape how we see ourselves. We can only seek to better understand it and live in it so that we come to better appreciate who we are and where we fit in, and in doing so, come to better understand and experience God's loving and merciful work to make us his children.

We thus live in a tension as we understand our own identities. On one hand, we are who God says that we are: his beloved, blood-bought children. Yet on the other hand, we experience this reality in a physical, fallen world in which our stories interact with other people, which shapes

---

16. Bull, *Thinking Medieval*, 99.

how we see ourselves. To dismiss the former is to fail to see the significance of who we are by grounding it in an absolute and cosmic sense. To deny the latter is to fail to ground our created selves in the daily, earthly reality of where God placed us.

This, then, is where historical thinking comes into play. If our identity both comes from who God says we are united to him through Christ, and is shaped by people whom he places in a created world to live in community, and if in this world who we are is influenced both by how we are created and by our interactions with others who shape our identity and give us perspective to understand it, then understanding that world better is a core part of understanding who we are as unique expressions of humanity. This, in turn, helps us to better understand our relationship to our Creator. A knowledge of the world should have as its aim to make us better theologians.

Historical study informs our identity by providing an expanded perspective. Using a vivid metaphor, historian John Lewis Gaddis explains the perspective gained through historical thinking by comparing it to the process of growing up. He writes, "We are born, each of us, with such self-centeredness that only the fact of being babies, and therefore cute, saves us. Growing up is largely a matter of growing out of that condition: we soak in impressions, and as we do so we dethrone ourselves—or at least most of us do—from our original position at the center of the universe."[17] He writes that as people grow up, they face hurdles and challenges that they encounter and overcome. As they do so, they are constantly faced with new ones. It is this tension between mastery and humility that prompts greater understanding of who they are, and who they are not. This principle works throughout time as well, and underlies the capacity of the perspective gained from historical thinking to help individuals curb innate self-centeredness.

Sam Wineburg highlights this same benefit to historical thinking:

> For the narcissist sees the world—both the past and the present—in his own image. Mature historical knowing teaches us to do the opposite: to go beyond our own image, to go beyond our brief life, and to go beyond the fleeting moment in human history into which we have been born. History educates ("leads outward" in the Latin) in the deepest sense. Of the subjects in the secular curriculum, it is the best at teaching those virtues once reserved for theology—humility in the face of limited

---

17. Gaddis, *Landscape of History*, 5–6.

ability to know, and awe in the face of the expanse of human history.[18]

Of course, theology should not abandon this task of teaching such virtues, but rather see historical study as an indispensable companion in this respect. Understanding the past thus helps to develop an understanding of the world that does not have the individual at its center. Rather, it supports the biblical notion that, to use Gaddis's word, "dethrones" the individual from his or her place at the center where sinful human presumption attempts to place its throne. In developing this understanding, people are able to appreciate their standing with their Creator, Redeemer, and Sanctifier more fully.

LOVING AND SERVING THE NEIGHBOR

As the student of history becomes more aware of the human experience across time, not only is he prompted to consider his own humanity and consequent relationship with God, but his awareness is also directed outward towards others. Gaddis provides another metaphor that compares historical thinking with taking off in an airplane. He writes, "Taking off in an airplane makes you feel both large and small at the same time. You can't help but have a sense of mastery as your airline of choice detaches you from the ground, lifts you above the traffic jams surrounding the airport, and reveals vast horizons stretching out beyond it. But as you gain altitude, you also can't help noticing how small you are in relation to the landscape that lies before you."[19] He asserts that historical thinking influences identity by placing a person in the middle of a tension between control of one's life and surroundings and an appreciation for the enormity of the world around them and their spatial and temporal insignificance in comparison. Critically, this insignificance is not one of worth, but rather an appreciation of the vastness of the world. It leads the student of history to a healthy humility in the same way Gaddis's metaphor of growing up illustrates.

Historically-fostered humility prompts empathy for others and a drive to serve them in their various needs. In this way, historical study helps the Christian university to direct:

---

18. Wineburg, *Historical Thinking*, 24.
19. Gaddis, *Landscape of History*, 5–6.

the whole higher education enterprise to the highest end of faith active in love by bringing both aspects of education into a fruitful relationship where students encounter the freedom and joy of learning human, natural, and divine wisdom; develop the ability to think, speak, and act on their own so that they can intelligently and faithfully fulfill their vocations; and become wise, honorable, and cultivated citizens of God's church and society who love their neighbors and nature as little Christs because of Christ.[20]

In addition to this tension between mastery and humility, another tension that historical thinking trains students to embrace is the tension between commonality and alterity, or otherness. Students are often shocked to discover that people in the past were just as complex, dynamic, and "human" as they are. Helping students to see the human connections that they have with people of the past is one of the more exciting aspects of teaching history. As students see these similarities, they recognize the ways in which studying people of the past may be helpful for their present-day lives. However, believing that the past is full of people who thought and acted exactly like us is no more accurate than assuming it is filled with flat caricatures.

Historical thinking places students into a larger context, directing them to consider a very diverse group of people who likely differ from them in numerous ways, including social position, cultural background, and, of course, time. Consequently, the people of the past had different worldviews than the students who study them. When asking my students to consider why historical figures acted the way they did, I challenge them not only to consider the common humanity that they share with their subject of study, but also the differences that make that historical figure very different than them.[21]

As students learn to navigate this tension between the common humanity that they share with the people of the past and the many ways they are different, they more fully come to *understand* the people that they study. This trains them for life as they come into contact with people from different backgrounds and with different worldviews who share a common humanity. This greater understanding prepares them to love the people who they encounter, in spite of any disagreement that they may

20. Ashmon, *Idea and Practice*, 31.
21. Bull, *Thinking Medieval*, 131.

have with them. Importantly, this requires instructors to make the same effort toward their students as well.

The study of history doesn't just *promote* empathy, it *demands* it of the historian. John Fea notes that "people of the past cannot defend themselves. They are at the mercy of the historian" and so faithful historians "must relinquish power and avoid the temptation to use the powerless—those in the past who are at the mercy of us, the interpreters—to serve selfish ends, whether they be religious political, or cultural."[22] He continues, "Doing history will require 'intellectual hospitality' or the willingness to engage the ideas of the people from the past with humility."[23] Una Cadegan notes that this is especially true of historians who study religion. She argues that historians must be cognizant of the relationship of the historian to his or her interpretation of the past, which she calls the "autobiographical connection." "Without conscious reflection, it is too easy to fall into cheerleading on the one hand or score-settling on the other. It is even easier, perhaps, to lapse into self-indulgence."[24]

In these ways, as I train students in responsible and skilled historical study, I do not only build a framework of knowledge that helps my students to understand the world in which they live, but I also aim to cultivate in them the Christian virtues of humility and empathy that lead them to respect the inherent dignity of humanity and to respect others' ideas. In doing so, I attempt to model a passionate love for the responsible pursuit of historical truth so that they see reason and intellect as good gifts from God. Students should utilize them in their engagement with the world "so that they can serve their neighbors and nature, be excellent and faithful leaders in the church and society, and promote temporal peace and life while proclaiming eternal peace and life in Christ."[25]

COLLECTED WISDOM FOR CHRISTIAN LIVING

Students are not alone as they strive to love and serve both God and their neighbors. They are surrounded by a cloud of witnesses whom God gives in order to support and encourage individuals as they embark on these tasks. Historical study reminds us that this cloud of witnesses is

22. Fea, *Why Study History?*, 131.
23. Fea, *Why Study History?*, 131.
24. Cadegan, "Not All Autobiography," in Fea et al., *Confessing History*, 40.
25. Ashmon, *Idea and Practice*, 20.

not limited to the present, but stretches back into the past as well. This includes not only the redeemed gathered around the throne of the Lamb, but *all those* who are accessible to us only through the surviving historical record and who still have wisdom for us to learn.

Historical study gifts us with the collected wisdom of the human experience, and its study serves those in the present. Much popular sentiment on the value of studying history focuses on the goal of avoiding past mistakes. Studying history certainly makes plain the earthly consequences of sin. The past shows those of us in the present much to avoid, "Not, of course, that there is any magic about the past," C.S. Lewis cautions. "People were no cleverer then than they are now; they made as many mistakes as we. But not the same mistakes."[26] That is why he advocates the need "to keep the clean sea-breeze of the centuries blowing through our minds."[27]

However, history has much more of a positive direction to take us. Not only does the past lead us to marvel more deeply at the scriptural truth of God's faithfulness despite human rebellion, it provides us with a record of faithful examples of men and women of faith to emulate. Studying the past contextualizes abstract theological concepts in the human experience of time. We read God's law in Scripture, and then through the study of history we see examples of human striving to keep it so that we may be encouraged. We read about God's gospel, and we see examples of his faithfulness embedded throughout the record of human experience. God's propensity for enfleshing his realities in the human experience stems from his incarnation. The central moment of history brings these tensions of eternal truth and temporal experience into singularity. The incarnation, death, and resurrection of immortal God in Christ acts as the summation of history and the point of departure for making sense of it.

The sixteenth-century reformer Martin Luther notes the practical value to be gained by studying history and other liberal arts. He writes that if children were taught

> the languages, the other arts, and history, they would hear the happenings and the sayings of all the world, and learn how it fared with various cities, estates, kingdoms, princes, men, and women; thus they could in a short time set before themselves,

---

26. Lewis, "Reading Old Books," in Lewis, *God in the Dock*, 220.
27. Lewis, "Reading Old Books," in Lewis, *God in the Dock*, 220.

as in a mirror, the character, life, counsels and purposes, success and failure of the whole world from the beginning. As a result of this knowledge, they could form their own opinions and adapt themselves to the course of this outward life in the fear of God, draw from history the knowledge and understanding of what should be sought and what avoided in this outward life, and become able also by this standard to assist and direct others. But the training which is undertaken at home, apart from such schools, attempts to make us wise through our own experience. Before that comes to pass we shall be dead a hundred times over and shall have acted inconsiderately all our life; for much time is needed to acquire one's own experience.[28]

The aggregated experiences of others thus more quickly helps us to live in love and service towards others and to receive the gifts that God continues to give. This is only helpful, though, if the past that we access is accurate. The job of the history instructor, then, is to help students become better historians. In becoming a better historian, a person hopefully becomes both a better citizen and friend, as well as a better theologian.[29] Because time is inseparable from the human experience, I can accomplish these tasks simply by teaching history well.

Prayerfully, as they consider what it means to be human, students are driven to the cross in repentance, and gather around the means of grace delivered in the Divine Service, where eternal God continues to break into time to deliver his gifts. James K. A. Smith observes that "If something like Christian universities are to exist, they should be configured as extensions of the mission of the church—as chapels that extend and amplify what's happening at the heart of the cathedral, at the altar of Christian worship. In short, the task of Christian education needs to be reconnected to the thick practices of the church."[30] These practices, derived from the reception of God's gifts, then continue that process of identity formation, both on an individual level and on a community level.

---

28. Luther, *Works of Martin Luther*, 91.

29. Garber paraphrases Augustine's response to a student, in which Augustine asks the student about the purpose of his education. "He is asking the young student, 'What is the point of your life? How are your studies of Cicero contributing to your end as a human being, particularly your end as a young Christian?'" (Garber, *Fabric of Faithfulness*, 150). In essence, Augustine is asking how the young man's studies are helping him to be a better theologian.

30. Smith, *Desiring the Kingdom*, 220.

A well-trained, faithful historian is not simply one who is fascinated by old things. Instead, a well-trained, faithful historian is one who cares deeply about his or her relationship with God and who lives to serve others in the present and in the future. The historian Marc Bloch, whose reflections on the historical nature of Christianity began this chapter, remembered a trip he took with the twentieth-century Belgian historian Henri Pirenne:

> I had gone with Henri Pirenne to Stockholm; we had scarcely arrived, when he said to me: "What shall we go to see first? It seems as though there is a new city hall here. Let's start there." Then, as if to ward off my surprise, he added, "If I were an antiquarian, I would have eyes only for old stuff, but I am a historian. Therefore, I love life." This faculty of understanding the living is, in truth, the master quality of the historian.[31]

Seen in each of these ways, all human history broadens and deepens our view of what it means to be human and how each individual life exemplifies that and yet expresses it uniquely. History itself becomes a sermon that convicts us of human sinfulness and prepares us to consider our own individual brokenness. This discovery drives us back to the gospel message and propels us to serve our neighbors. In the end, it is my hope that students might come to better understand that against the vast backdrop of history, filled with many "great" men and women (and even more people that the history books have forgotten), it is a truly miraculous thing to realize that the God who creates all life, governs and sustains it, redeems it with his own precious blood to reconcile it to himself, and creates and sustains faith has chosen to give all that as a free gift to . . . *them.*

BIBLIOGRAPHY

Ashmon, Scott, ed. *The Idea and Practice of a Christian University: A Lutheran Approach.* Saint Louis: Concordia, 2015.
Bloch, Marc. *The Historian's Craft.* Translated by Peter Putnam. Manchester: Manchester University Press, 1992.
Bull, Marcus. *Thinking Medieval: An Introduction to the Study of the Middle Ages.* New York: Palgrave Macmillan, 2007.
Carr, E. H. *What is History?* 2nd ed. New York: Penguin, 1987.
Dreher, Rod. *The Benedict Option: A Strategy for Christians in a Post-Christian Nation.* New York: Sentinel, 2017.

---

31. Bloch, *Historian's Craft*, 36.

Englebrecht, Edward, ed. *The Lutheran Difference: An Explanation and Comparison of Christian Beliefs.* St. Louis: Concordia, 2010.

Fea, John, et al. *Confessing History: Explorations in Christian Faith and the Historian's Vocation.* Notre Dame: University of Notre Dame Press, 2010.

Fea, John. *Why Study History? Reflecting on the Importance of the Past.* Grand Rapids: Baker Academic, 2013.

Gaddis, John Lewis. *The Landscape of History: How Historians Map the Past.* Oxford: Oxford University Press, 2004.

Garber, Steven. *The Fabric of Faithfulness.* Downers Grove, IL: IVP, 1996.

Henry, Douglas V. and Bob R. Agee, eds. *Faithful Learning and the Christian Scholarly Vocation.* Grand Rapids: Eerdmans, 2003.

Holmes, Arthur. *The Idea of a Christian College.* Grand Rapids: Eerdmans, 1987.

Korcok, Thomas. *Lutheran Education: From Wittenberg to the Future.* Saint Louis: Concordia, 2011.

Lewis, C.S. *God in the Dock: Essays on Theology and Ethics.* Edited by Walter Hooper. Grand Rapids: Eerdmans, 1970.

Luther, Martin. *The Works of Martin Luther.* Albany: Books for the Ages, 1997.

Maza, Sarah. *Thinking About History.* Chicago: Chicago University Press, 2017.

Noll, Mark. *Jesus Christ and the Life of the Mind.* Grand Rapids: Eerdmans, 2011.

Smith, James K. A. *Desiring the Kingdom: Worship, Worldview, and Cultural Formation.* Grand Rapids: Baker Academic, 2009.

VanZanten, Susan. *Joining the Mission: A Guide for (Mainly) New College Faculty.* Grand Rapids: Eerdmans, 2011.

Veith, Gene Edward. *God at Work.* Wheaton, IL: Crossway, 2002.

Wells, Ronald A. *History Through the Eyes of Faith.* San Francisco: Harper, 1989.

Wineburg, Sam. *Historical Thinking and Other Unnatural Acts: Charting the Future of Teaching the Past.* Philadelphia: Temple University Press, 2001.

Wright, N.T. *After You Believe: Why Christian Character Matters.* New York: Harper One, 2010.

8

Faithful Foreign Language Instruction

Wellington Espinosa

LANGUAGE IS A BEAUTIFUL gift from the Creator given to humans who were created in his image. Because the members of the Trinity are relational persons, God created humans to be relational as well. As relational beings, humans use language to communicate with each other and believers use language to communicate with God through prayer. Language is an integral part of what makes us humans and distinguishes us from other animals. In fact, God has much to say about language in the Bible, especially in the book of Proverbs. The Lord inspired the human author to write that by "the blessing of the upright a city is exalted, but by the mouth of the wicked it is overthrown."[32] The Spanish compound word *bendecir* (blessing) comes from the Latin *benedicere*, which has the idea of "speaking well or saying good to or about someone." In fact, the Bible reveals that our speech has the potential to nourish our fellow human beings or bring death.[33]

The phrase "and God said"[34] can be found early in the biblical narrative and the same phrase, or variants of it, such as "the Lord said" and "thus says the Lord," are found throughout the Old Testament. In the

---

32. Prov 11:11 (ESV).
33. See Prov 1:21.
34. Gen 1:3 (ESV).

New Testament, "the Word became flesh and dwelt among us, and we have seen his glory, glory as of the only Son from the Father, full of grace and truth."[35] The ability to communicate and comprehend language, either written or spoken, is one of the ways he gives grace, for by hearing and understanding the spoken or written message of the good news of salvation, humans can be granted repentance and faith in Jesus Christ.[36]

IN THE GARDEN

When the Lord created humans in the *imago Dei*, he gave them the ability to communicate through language. When God gave humans the ability to communicate through speech, he made known the stipulations for living in the garden using a language that the newly created Adam and Eve could understand. Adam and Eve received a command to not "eat of the fruit of the tree that is in the midst of the garden."[37] Even though they understood God's command, their disobedience resulted in physical and spiritual death and their expulsion from the garden. Ever since, humans are born dead in sins and trespasses and separated from God without hope. But thanks be to God that he provided a propitiation by sending Jesus as a substitutionary sacrifice on our behalf.

After Adam and Eve sinned, they tried to cover their shame with fig leaves, and Derek Kidner notes that "sin's proper fruit is shame."[38] Later in the story, the Lord comes down to the garden and again uses language to communicate with Adam and Eve. And as Kidner states, the conversation the Lord has with Adam and Eve "has all the marks of grace. It is a question, since to help him He must draw rather than drive him out of hiding."[39] And that is what the gospel does; it draws sinful humans from hiding in the dark to the light that only a gracious and loving God can provide.

The subsequent interaction between God and man shows how language is used in a sinful manner. When God asks a question to draw Adam out of hiding, Adam expresses the first mention of fear in the Bible and hid himself from the face of God because he believed that hiding

---

35. John 1:14 (ESV).
36. See Rom 10:17; 2 Tim 2:25.
37. Gen 3:3 (ESV).
38. Kidner, *Genesis*, 69.
39. Kidner, *Genesis*, 70.

from God was the answer to his sin. Ever since this episode, hiding from God "remains part of our fallen condition."[40] Finally, Adam uses language to confess. However, he does not take responsibility for his disobedience and blames the woman. Thus, man learns to use language in an attempt to hide from the face of God and to make excuses when they sin. But because of his great love, God uses the language of the gospel to draw sinners out of the darkness and into the light of salvation.

THE TOWER OF BABEL

After the flood, the Bible states that there was one language on earth. The pride and arrogance of humans reached such a climax that they wanted to build themselves "a city and a tower with its top in the heavens."[41] As a result of their pride and self-reliance, God confused their languages so that they had to be scattered all over the land. Fast forwarding to the book of Acts in the New Testament, one finds that God used the many languages he created at the Tower of Babel for the spread of the gospel to the nations. The languages God used to bring judgment in Gen 11 on the inhabitants of the land of Shinar are used as a blessing because people heard in their own "tongues the mighty works of God."[42] The final redemption of language is promised in the Old Testament: "For at that time I will change the speech of the peoples to a pure speech, that all of them may call upon the name of the Lord and serve him with one accord."[43]

THE PARABLES

In the incarnation, "the ultimate Word came to live among us and use our basic unit of communication to help us understand more about God and his love for us."[44] Although Jesus used miracles to authenticate his deity, he employed the use of speech and language as the most important way to teach about God. Often, he used language in the form of parables as

40. Kidner, *Genesis*, 70.
41. Gen 11:4 (ESV).
42. Acts 2:11 (ESV).
43. Zeph 3:9 (ESV).
44. Muehlhoff and Lewis, *Authentic Communication*, 67. Also see Eugene Peterson, *Tell it Slant*.

"a powerful method of teaching"[45] during his earthly ministry. In Matt 13:13, Jesus spoke

> In parables to hide the secrets of the kingdom from some and reveal them to others. This does not mean His parables are full of esoteric information that only a select few can grasp with their minds. Christ's enemies often understand exactly what His parables mean; the problem is their refusal to trust His teaching about Himself and God's kingdom. The difficulty the Pharisees have is moral and thus volitional, not intellectual. They choose not to believe our Savior's words.[46]

Jesus' use of words and language to indicate judgment on those who chose not to believe his words in the New Testament echoes how God confused the languages as judgment for man's rebellion at the Tower of Babel. Fortunately, language is also used to bring deliverance from eternal judgment through the words used to preach the gospel.

WORLDVIEW

A worldview is "the lens through which we interpret reality and by which we reason."[47] The main characteristic of all worldviews is that all of them "begin with faith, a metaphysical belief that cannot be verified using scientific methods."[48] As Christians, we see reality through the lens of Scripture and therefore subscribe to a Christian worldview. Essential to a Christian worldview is the belief that an absolute God exists, that mankind is fallen, and that Jesus is the only hope for redemption. In addition, the conviction that the Bible contains the very words of God, that "all truth is God's truth,"[49] and that he is the creator of everything in the universe, including language, is vital for an accurate Christian worldview that is biblically sound.

The Scriptures record the use of language to communicate between God and humans and between humans from cover to cover. It is the responsibility of a foreign language instructor at a Christian college to approach the teaching of a foreign language through the lens of the

---

45. Morris, *Gospel According to Matthew*, 339.
46. Ligonier Ministries "Purpose of the Parables."
47. Poplin, *Is Reality Secular?*, 27.
48. Poplin, *Is Reality Secular?*, 30.
49. Hughes, *Vocation of a Christian Scholar*, 51.

Christian worldview. In that way, the students who do not come from an adequate theological background may understand that something taken for granted daily, such as language, is a gift from a gracious Creator who desired from the foundation of the world, to communicate with the crown jewel of his creation.

Undoubtedly, Darwinian evolution has launched a vicious attack on the Christian worldview with its indoctrination that "humans evolved from lower animals, which began as single-cell organisms that emerged from nonliving matter through an unknown process."[50] In relation to languages, evolution posits that the ability to use speech to communicate evolved because some early hominids needed to communicate to avoid dangers, hunt wild game, attract mates, and "produce advantages for survival."[51] Grunts and unintelligible sounds eventually morphed into a sophisticated system of communication able to express complex ideas after thousands of years. However, the Christian worldview teaches that

> The first humans, Adam and Eve, had the ability to communicate with each other (and God) from the outset, using language. This includes the mental ability (and desire) to communicate, the physical means to produce speech sounds, the ability to hear them, and the mental ability to process the sounds and connect them with the concepts they represent. Since they had no experience of many of the words that God used, much of their vocabulary may have been preprogrammed, rather than acquired.[52]

The Christian belief that there is a God who created a universe that is "obviously brilliant, complex, orderly, exquisitely designed and endlessly fascinating"[53] gives evidence of a thoughtful Creator and is sufficient to explain everything we can ascertain with our senses. In Mary Poplin's words,

> In this metanarrative that has existed for almost six thousand years, there are no gaps; that is, the big bang is explaining God's voice, which explains the appearance of physical and material laws. The gradual appearance of living things and ultimately the creation of man are all part of the intentional and purposive

---

50. Poplin, *Is Reality Secular?*, 68.
51. Poplin, *Is Reality Secular?*, 68.
52. Creation Ministries, "Born to Communicate."
53. Poplin, *Is Reality Secular?*, 98.

actions of God. With each new discovery, we understand more about the mind and heart of God and our own.[54]

In reality, Darwinian evolution and all its branches have one defining doctrine: the rejection of God. Those who reject God do so because if "there were a God, there would be other implications, including moral ones."[55] Advocates of the theory of naturalistic evolution believe that "science's vast accumulation of knowledge is gradually filling in the gaps in our knowledge"[56] in order to understand the created order. The apostle Paul, under the inspiration of the Holy Spirit, wrote to the church in Rome that those who reject Christ claim to be wise, but in reality they have become fools.[57]

How has the advancement and acceptance of Darwinian evolution affected higher education? The genesis of the influence of secularism in the academic realm can be traced to the Enlightenment. During this time, there was a schism between faith and learning "into distinctive areas or parts of life."[58] According to Dockery and George, "The Enlightenment, which blossomed in the eighteen century, was a watershed in the history of Western civilization."[59] The Enlightenment put great emphasis "on the primacy of nature and reason over special revelation."[60] Thus, by the time Darwin's *On the Origin of Species* was published in 1859, the "curse of the Enlightenment that has darkened the Western intellect"[61] had been taking root in the hearts and minds of people.

Today, academic institutions are still very much promoting the views that began during the Enlightenment. These institutions of higher learning promote a secularist view, which emphasizes the "primacy of human reason and science"[62] over the revealed will of God in the Holy Scriptures. However, the toxic worldview upheld by the Enlightenment had not taken a hold of academic institutions during the early days of higher education in America. In fact, the American university was the

---

54. Poplin, *Is Reality Secular?*, 99.
55. Poplin, *Is Reality Secular?*, 98.
56. Poplin, *Is Reality Secular?*, 68.
57. Rom 1:22 (ESV).
58. VanZanten, *Joining the Mission*, 99.
59. Dockery and George, *Great Tradition of Christian Thinking*, 47.
60. Dockery and George, *Great Tradition of Christian Thinking*, 47.
61. Poe, *Christianity in the Academy*, 179.
62. Claerbaut, *Faith and Learning on the Edge*, 28.

result of a Christian "culture that emphasized at least the moral aspects of traditional Christianity."[63] Many of the leaders of the early American universities were theologians. Moreover, one of the most important jobs of those universities was to train men for the ministry. David Claerbaut explains how secularism has changed research, education, and scholarship to the present state of affairs:

> The secularization of the American university continued to accelerate in the 1950s as the term *Christian* gave way to *Judeo-Christian* or *Western*. Religion was no longer integrated into general academic subjects but became a separate area of study, in addition to functioning as an extracurricular activity for students. Over the ensuing decades, religion has continuously become marginalized, even trivialized, in the culture of the academic mainstream and is often regarded as hardly more substantive than a hobby. The behavioral sciences rather than faith were regarded as the vehicle by which humankind could maintain a civilized society. Religious studies themselves no longer focused on the transcendent and uplifting value of faith, but rather on scientific approaches to the study of religion.[64]

DO ALL TO THE GLORY OF GOD

The Holy Scripture teaches that Christians should "do all to the glory of God."[65] Academic endeavors are not excepted from the biblical prescription to bring glory to God in all the different areas of life. In fact, Christians ought to strive to bring glory to God not only with deeds, but also with our thinking. Because Christians understand that all knowledge comes from God, we should "want to respond rightly to this recognition by loving God with all our minds and by promoting intellectual seriousness and intellectual curiosity among our students."[66]

Philip H. Phenix defines worship as "the active response that a person makes to his God. It is the acknowledgement of the ultimate meaning one has found in his life and the renewed determination to fulfill that meaning."[67] How do believers worship God with language?

63. Claerbaut, *Faith and Learning on the Edge*, 28.
64. Claerbaut, *Faith and Learning on the Edge*, 29.
65. 1 Cor 10:31 (ESV).
66. Dockery and George, *Great Tradition of Christian Thinking*, 92.
67. Phenix, *Education and the Worship of God*, 21.

They worship God by hearing and responding to the gospel with confession of sin, and using speech to bless the Lord.[68] Jesus said that those who hear his words and act on them "will be like a wise man who built his house on the rock."[69] Psalm 50:23 says, "The one who offers thanksgiving as his sacrifice glorifies me." Giving praise to God brings glory to him and Christians use their language to express and offer thanksgiving as an active response of worship to God.

Language brings glory to God when Christians lead others to Christ by presenting the gospel in a clear and articulate manner. God is glorified when the power of sin and death is broken, and men and women are loosed from the power of Satan by the words and the language of the message of salvation.

Since education is an act of worship, how can studying a foreign language be an occasion to bring glory to God? First, because God is present everywhere and manifests his presence through creation, then it is logical to say that God's character and attributes are manifested in language. In studying a foreign language, students ought to become aware of the creative power of language. What is more, with language people can produce creative works of art such as songs, poetry, plays, etc., that point to the creative attributes of God. Studying a language and its creative dimensions brings us back to the doctrine of creation.

INTEGRATING FAITH AND LEARNING

The coherent integration of faith and learning is a vital part of an excellent, well-rounded education that would develop citizens of Christ-like character who are well-educated. The integration of faith and learning is more than simply including a Bible verse at the beginning of class or even praying in class. As important as reading the Bible and praying in class are, those activities do not constitute faith and learning integration. According to Suzan VanZanten, authentic integration of faith and learning "incorporates both head and heart, intellect and piety."[70] Faithful teaching and learning begins with the Christian worldview that says that there is a God who created humans to bear his image.

---

68. Jas 3:9–10 (ESV).
69. Matt 7:24 (ESV).
70. VanZanten, *Joining the Mission*, 121.

In a Christian college, the integration of faith and learning means that "the entire range of life and learning"[71] is touched by the instruction given in the classroom because the Christian life encompasses the totality of the individual. Arthur Holmes says that, although there is a place for apologetics in the integration of faith and learning, integration should be more concerned with "the positive contributions of human learning to an understanding of the faith and to the development of a Christian worldview, and with the positive contribution of the Christian faith to all the arts and sciences."[72]

One of the main challenges I face as a foreign language instructor is how to integrate faith and learning in my first and second semester Spanish courses. Because of the limited vocabulary the students possess in the target language, it is difficult to have conversations about Christianity without digressing from the teaching of the Spanish language. According to Susan Carpenter Binkley, foreign language teachers in Christian institutions must find ways "to address the spiritual dimension in a manner that appropriately corresponds to the students' ability to communicate and comprehend."[73]

As explained previously, integration does not have to be a rote activity. If the teacher can communicate to the pupils the greatness and creative power of God in how he made humans able to communicate using language, integration has taken place. When the instructor can impart insights about the implications of missions and evangelism from the studying of a foreign language, integration has occurred. Finally, when the faculty member accomplishes the idea expressed by Philip H. Phenix, integration of faith and learning in the foreign language classroom has occurred. In Phenix's words,

> The aim of learning a language other than one's native tongue is not to be able to think the same thoughts and communicate the same ideas in other words. The goal rather is to enable one to enter into a new world, to categorize existence in novel ways, and to organize experience into fresh modes of understanding ... It is the boundlessness of possible interpretations that make language learning revelatory of the divine. The limitlessness of symbolic formulations is evidence of the infinitude of God, who

---

71. Holmes, *Idea of a Christian College*, 45.
72. Holmes, *Idea of a Christian College*, 46.
73. Binkley, "Integrating Faith and Learning," 430. See also Smith, *Gift of the Stranger*.

is the ground of all being, and who cannot be comprehended within any finite categories.[74]

My desire as an educator is that I would be able to help to develop Christ-like character in the students who sit under my tutelage for one or more semesters. The *Westminster Catechism* asks the question: "What is the chief end of man?" The answer is: "Man's chief end is to glorify God, and to enjoy him forever."[75] I hope that I help my students understand that we can glorify God, even in the studying of a beginning course in Spanish.

BIBLIOGRAPHY

Binkley, Susan Carpenter. "Integrating Faith and Learning in the Foreign Language Classroom." *Christian Higher Education* 6.5 (October 1, 2007): 429–38.
Claerbaut, David, *Faith and Learning on the Edge: A Bold New Look at Religion in Higher Education*. Grand Rapids: Zondervan, 2004.
Creation Ministries International. "Born to Communicate." *Creation.com*. http://creation.com/born-to-communicate.
Dockery, David S., and Timothy George. *The Great Tradition of Christian Thinking: A Student's Guide*. Wheaton, IL: Crossway, 2012.
Holmes, Arthur. *The Idea of a Christian College*. Grand Rapids: Eerdmans, 1987.
Hughes, Richard T. *The Vocation of a Christian Scholar: How Christian Faith Can Sustain the Life of the Mind*. Grand Rapids: Eerdmans, 2005.
Kidner, Derek. *Genesis: An Introduction and Commentary*. Downers Grove, IL: InterVarsity, 1967.
Ligonier. "The Purpose of the Parables." *Ligonier.org*. http://www.ligonier.org/learn/devotionals/purpose-parables/.
Morris, Leon. *The Gospel According to Matthew*. Grand Rapids: Eerdmans, 1992.
Muehlhoff, Tim and Todd V. Lewis. *Authentic Communication*. Downers Grove, IL: InterVarsity, 2010.
Peterson, Eugene. *Tell It Slant: A Conversation on the Language of Jesus in His Stories and Prayers*. Grand Rapids: Eerdmans, 2012.
Phenix, Philip H. *Education and the Worship of God*. Philadelphia: Westminster, 1966.
Poe, Harry L. *Christianity in the Academy: Teaching at the Intersection of Faith and Learning*. Grand Rapids: Baker Academic, 2004.
Poplin, Mary. *Is Reality Secular? Testing the Assumptions of Four Global Worldviews*. Downers Grove, IL: InterVarsity, 2014.
Smith, David I. *The Gift of the Stranger: Faith, Hospitality, and Foreign Language Learning*. Grand Rapids: Eerdmans, 2000.
VanZanten, Susan. *Joining the Mission: A guide for (Mainly) New College Faculty*. Grand Rapids: Eerdmans, 2011.
"Westminster Shorter Catechism." https://prts.edu/wp-content/uploads/2016/12/Shorter_Catechism.pdf.

74. Phenix, *Education and the Worship of God*, 41.
75. "Westminster Shorter Catechism."

Faithful Education in the Social Sciences

9

A Faithful Attempt at Integrating Psychology and Christianity

Jeff Elliott

REFLECTING ON MY PERSONAL worldview and the thoughtful exploration of how it affects my calling as a professor of psychology has furthered my goal of living the intentional Christian life. I have found it rather easy to fall into the routine of existing (performing mindless daily habits of exercise, eating, working, relaxing, and sleeping), rather than intentionally living out my faith in a purposeful way for God's glory. Thinking about the integration of my faith and my vocation and the dialogue between colleagues has awakened within me a renewed passion to engage my students in conversations about what they believe and encourage them to grapple with how their beliefs profoundly impact their lives. As a child of God, follower of Jesus Christ, and his called-out servant, it is my desire to work with the Holy Spirit in clearly presenting the case for a personal relationship with God through the finished work of Christ on the cross. As a Christian, I have been commissioned to make disciples,[1] and a vital piece of this process is the establishment of a Christ-like way of thinking—a Christian worldview.[2] It is my hope to incorporate what I have learned into all facets of my teaching, and to continue to seek out

1. Matt 28:18–20.
2. Rom 12:2; 2 Cor 10:5; Eph 4:23.

opportunities to be more deeply involved in the lives of a few men every semester in a discipleship/mentoring relationship.[3]

In this chapter, I sketch a review of my own personal journey as an emerging adult through the development of a personal spiritual identity that reflected much of what psychology suggests is typical for traditional college-aged students. Then I will identify what many consider the basic tenets of a Christian worldview, while also asserting the primacy of scripture. In the latter part of the chapter, I will review the four major schools of psychological thought through the lens of a Christian worldview. In conclusion, I will suggest why it is important to study psychology from a Christian worldview and how it influences my calling as a professor.

Before discussing where I am on my life journey today, it is important to understand where I have been. During most of my childhood and youth, I attended a conservative, evangelical church with my family, but at times there seemed to be a disconnect between what we believed and how we lived. At the age of twelve, I understood the importance of faith, and that it wasn't enough that my parents believed, but that I needed to place my trust in the substitutionary atonement of Jesus Christ. As Alister McGrath delineates, "saving faith has to do primarily with believing and trusting that Christ was born for us personally, and has accomplished for us the work of salvation."[4] For the next several years, I grew in my knowledge and understanding of God through participating in my own personal Bible study, as well as in small groups. Though I was growing in my understanding of biblical truth, looking back on this time, I don't believe that I saw God or his work as being personally relevant to me or my life-experiences in the "secular" world. I believe I was allowing the dualism so often promoted by the world to divide my thinking into the realms of the sacred and the secular.

Meanwhile, I graduated from public high school in rural Iowa and began college at Iowa State University. In most ways, going off to college really began the developmental "identity crisis" for me.[5] It would be during the next four years that I would actively be challenged to explore what I believed, and why I believed it. As a typical late adolescent, I thought that my experience was somewhat unique, but now after much study in theology, psychology, and education, I know that this exploration of truth and

---

3. 2 Tim 2:1–2.
4. McGrath, *Theology*, 11.
5. See Erikson, *Identity*.

reality, and the cultivation of a coherent and consistent worldview is the normal lot of all emerging adults.[6] While at Iowa State, I was told that my religious beliefs were irrational and childish, and that only through the authority of empirical science could one ever discover truth. For a certain period of time, I thought that maybe having faith in God and his promises required that I sacrifice my intellect and reason. But while my beliefs were being challenged in the classroom, I was privileged to be a part of a dynamic church and an active college-age Bible study. The leaders purposefully took advantage of this important time in our lives, and not only did they share truth through their teaching, they also lived it out in practical ways, and provided a community of like-minded followers of Christ to engender courage and hope.

After reading Garber's *The Fabric of Faithfulness*, I realized that my mentors at that pivotal time in my life had embodied Garber's plan for passing on a Christian worldview.[7] It was also during this time that I learned all people have a worldview and that all worldviews are based on certain fundamental assumptions and/or presuppositions. Naturalism tries to assert that it is value-free, and based only on empirical knowledge, but there is no such thing as neutrality when it comes to worldview.[8] All worldviews begin with statements they must accept as true, before they attempt to offer plausible explanations for reality.

Recently, developmental psychologists have begun researching an age category called "emerging adulthood" that roughly corresponds to the traditional college years, between the ages of eighteen and twenty-five.[9] Erickson originally proposed that adolescents, aged twelve to eighteen, faced the psychosocial crisis of identity versus role confusion, but with a greater number of young adults now attending college, research suggests that this identity crisis is happening more often while students are in college.[10] Based on over twenty years of college teaching, I would agree with this finding. The modern college setting, living among and working with one's peers, provides fertile ground for the exploration of what one believes and why. Unfortunately, I do not think that we, as Christians, have always been involved purposefully and intentionally in

---

6. See Smith and Snell, *Souls in Transition*.
7. Garber, *Fabric of Faithfulness*.
8. Bartholomew and Goheen, *Living at the Crossroads*.
9. Santrock, *Adolescence*.
10. Erikson, *Identity*; Santrock, *Adolescence*.

helping shape a Christian worldview for college students. We may offer a class, or suggest a book, but as Garber asserts, "we learn the deepest lessons looking over the shoulders and through the heart, seeing that a worldview can become a way of life."[11] College students still maintain a high level of idealism, so it is not enough for Christian college professors to espouse the virtues of a Christian worldview; they must live it out, and then provide a nurturing community in which one's hopes and dreams can become reality.[12] At Iowa State, as a freshman and sophomore, I had an upperclassman who invited me into a discipling/mentoring relationship, so that by the time I was finishing college, I was one of the ones mentoring others. My experience was not unique, as many believers could attest to similar results in their lives.

But before continuing on with how a Christian worldview could be intentionally passed on to young adults, and in particular to college students, it is important to map out what is meant by a Christian worldview. McGrath, in *Theology: The Basics*, gives an overview of the fundamental core beliefs of orthodox Christianity as outlined in the Apostles Creed. Using excerpts from McGrath, and scriptural references, I assert that a Christian worldview should include the following essential convictions.

FAITH

The author of Hebrews declares, "Now faith is the assurance of things hoped for, the conviction of things not seen . . . And without faith it is impossible to please him, for whoever would draw near to God must believe that he exists and that he rewards those who seek him."[13] Faith does not mean blindly or ignorantly walking off the cliff of knowledge, but rather is a "motivated belief, based on evidence."[14] Holding to any belief requires an act of faith, so all worldviews have this requirement at their core. Faith in itself has no power, but faith is only as effective as the authority or veracity of its object. For me, I have placed my complete trust in the promises of God, and I am completely sure of his unchanging integrity and the faithfulness of his Word.

11. Garber, *Fabric of Faithfulness*, 19.
12. Santrock, *Adolescence*; Garber, *Fabric of Faithfulness*.
13. Heb 11:1, 6 (ESV).
14. McGrath, *Theology*, 9.

CREATION

McGrath reminds us, "If God is almighty, God must be capable of doing anything. Yet Christian theology insists that God's omnipotence is to be set within the context of God's nature—that of a righteous and faithful God, whose promises are to be trusted."[15] God alone is self-existent, and self-sufficient, dependent on no one else. In contrast, I as his creation am fully dependent on him for every breath and am ultimately accountable to him. In fact, the world depends on God for its existence since it is his creation. Since God created it, he has all the authority over it, and we have been placed here to be good stewards of his creation. Genesis declares, "And God saw everything that he had made, and behold it was very good."[16] The gnostic idea of the evilness of the world contradicts this clear statement.

REDEMPTION

Now, our present world is clearly not perfect. It bears the effects of sin, evil, and death, but a day of complete redemption will someday restore creation. Paul writes to the church in Galatia, "Grace to you and peace from God our Father and the Lord Jesus Christ, who gave himself for our sins to deliver us from the present evil age, according to the will of our God and Father."[17] Only Jesus Christ, the Son of God and the Son of Man, was able to satisfy the Father's holy demands, and he did so on the cross, that focal point of all human history. McGrath points out that Christ brought to fulfillment the three great offices of the Old Testament, "prophet, priest, and king."[18] It was the sin of mankind (past, present, and future) that had separated us from God, yet having been made in God's image, mankind has an inherent need for relationship with God. Mankind has sought to meet that need in many ways, and to some extent, the various worldviews attempt to either fulfill that transcendent purpose or deny its existence. But it can only be satisfied through a vibrant, personal relationship with almighty God by means of the sacrificial atonement of Jesus Christ. Every worldview offers something in the

---

15. McGrath, *Theology*, 37.
16. Gen 1:31 (ESV).
17. Gal 1:3–4 (ESV).
18. McGrath, *Theology*, 98.

future that resembles salvation, or human improvement, but the problem with all other worldviews is that they offer "redemption" to only a portion of life. Only a Christian worldview takes in the redemption of the totality of the person and of the created world, both seen and unseen.[19]

AUTHORITY OF SCRIPTURE

The final conviction necessary for the basis of a Christian worldview would be the place and purpose of scripture; "All scripture is breathed out by God and profitable for teaching, for reproof, for correction, and for training in righteousness, that the man of God may be complete, equipped for every good work."[20] As such, for the Christian, "The first and primary criterion of truth is scripture."[21] The foundational basis for a Christian worldview is the Bible, God's special revelation. The Bible is not a primary source book for religious teaching, but it is God's story, his grand narrative, and in contrast to all other possible stories (worldviews), it proposes to be the real thing, the true story of the world. The Bible begins (Gen 1) and ends (Rev 22) with God's presence and activity in the world, and the entire narrative illustrates God's independence from and sovereignty over all the world as all creation moves toward his ultimate goal.

While scripture claims that God is the author of all truth, it does not claim to provide exhaustive truth.[22] It does not tell the struggling college freshman whether or not he should drop English Composition or Intro to Psychology. Even in spiritual matters, such as our future activities in heaven, there is a lack of clarity and details are sketchy. Nevertheless, the Bible provides true and sufficient information for us to enter into and develop in our relationship to God, and explains how we are to live in this world. In summary, a Christian worldview asserts that the Bible is the first place we go for instruction, and it is the final judge in evaluating truth and right.

19. Col 1:19–20.
20. 2 Tim 3:15–17 (ESV).
21. Wilkens and Sanford, *Hidden Worldviews*, 210.
22. John 14:6; 16:13; 17:17.

A CHRISTIAN WORLDVIEW AND PSYCHOLOGY

Developing a Christian worldview is an ongoing process of examination, evaluation, and purification for believers as we continue on this journey of sanctification. As Goshen and Bartholomew assert, a Christian worldview means "we view life through three lenses: (1) a world created by God; (2) twisted by sin; (3) being redeemed by the work of Christ."[23] Moes and Tellinghuisen suggest the following five themes aid in exploring the relationship between Christian faith and psychological perspectives: humans are (1) relational beings, (2) broken, in need of redemption, (3) embodied, (4) responsible, limited agents (our free will is limited), and (5) meaning seekers.[24] Each of the themes addresses major biblical principles concerning the nature of humankind, as well as many pressing issues in psychology. These themes provide a way to begin understanding psychological concepts through the lens of a Christian worldview.

As a formal field of study, psychology was found in 1879,[25] but humankind has been interested in the study of the soul throughout human history. Throughout the Psalms (13:2, 16:9, 25:17, 38:8, 40:12, 69:20), the psalmist reflected on the inner struggles of humankind, and the early Greek philosophers (Plato, Aristotle) and church fathers (Augustine, Thomas Aquinas) also weighed in with their insights. The historical and philosophical development of psychology is a critical area of study in understanding the nuances of modern psychology.[26] In fact, many of the core issues in understanding the effects of worldview are topics shared with the field of psychology. As Harold Faw highlights in the following statement, it is vital to understand how one's worldview affects one's attempts at making sense of human behavior:

> What is the nature of humankind and the meaning of personhood? And how exactly should we go about studying human experience? It is important to note that these questions, significant though they surely are, cannot be addressed by science acting solely on the basis of empirical evidence. Rather, the answers different people give reflect presuppositions shaped by religious

---

23. Bartholomew and Goheen, *Living at the Crossroads*, 63.
24. Moes and Tellinghuisen, *Exploring Psychology and Christian Faith*.
25. Leahey, *History of Psychology*.
26. Leahey, *History of Psychology*.

and philosophical influences rather than conclusions based on scientific evidence.[27]

Faw's argument is echoed by Poplin, in that every psychological theory that attempts to understand and explain human behavior will have an inherent bias based on its basic presupposition and assumptions.[28]

The four major schools of psychology represent differing secular worldviews. They will each be examined based on how their respective worldview impacts their view of psychology. Sigmund Freud may be the single most recognizable psychologist of all time, and his ideas have had a profound impact on western culture.[29] In many ways, Freud viewed psychoanalysis as a lens (worldview) by which we could understand culture, history, and human behavior. Wilkens and Sanford call Freud's ideas the "salvation by therapy worldview."[30] Freud believed that the internal struggle between the id, ego, and superego was a normal part of the human experience, and "salvation" could only be gained if the proper equilibrium were maintained between the three. He saw the job of psychoanalysts (therapists) as that of a priest who would help clients mediate their inner conflicts. Freud rejected the notion of God and thought religion was a crutch for the psychologically weak to appease their inner struggles.[31]

A second school of psychological thought is humanistic or person-centered psychology. Carl Rogers is its most famous representative, and, as the name suggests, it is the product of a secular humanistic worldview. Rogers espoused the inherent goodness of humankind and believed that people are free to choose and create their own futures. Terms such as self-actualization, self-esteem, and tolerance of others often accompany this psychological viewpoint.[32] When problems do arise in one's experience, Rogers asserted that it was not due to any personal fault, but rather the result of an improper self-concept.[33]

The third and fourth major branches of psychology are behavioral and cognitive psychology. While behavioral and cognitive psychology

27. Faw, *Psychology in Christian Perspective*, 419.
28. Poplin, *Is Reality Secular?*
29. Faw, *Psychology in Christian Perspective*.
30. Wilkens and Sanford, *Hidden Worldviews*, 167.
31. Freud, *Future of an Illusion*.
32. Griggs and Jackson, *Psychology*.
33. Faw, *Psychology in Christian Perspective*.

are very different in how they understand and explain the human experience, I have grouped them together here because they arise from the same scientific naturalism worldview. In this worldview, science became both the source of truth and the method for discovering truth.[34] This Enlightenment creed rejected the idea of the immaterial or spiritual realm and instead insisted that matter was all that mattered. In addition, a specific kind of empiricism developed that placed scientific reasoning as the final arbiter of truth, and only truth claims that could be proven would be accepted in the public realm, while claims that could not be were dismissed or relegated to the private sphere. Both behaviorism and cognitive psychology have increased psychology's body of knowledge and been influential in all educational settings.[35]

As can be seen above, the major schools of modern psychology are either dismissive toward or critical of religion in general, and Christianity in particular. On the other hand, there have been Christians who similarly reject the validity or importance of psychology, because of its foundation on conflicting worldviews.[36] So where does that leave the teaching of psychology at Christ-centered institutions? Is it possible for a Christian professor of psychology to be true to both his academic discipline as well as his Christian faith?

In attempting to answer these questions, it is necessary to see one of the major problems with the current model of modern psychology. One of the greatest difficulties that modern psychology has to overcome is the problem that after one hundred and thirty years, it has yet to come to a unified understanding of the basics of human nature. The previously discussed "theories" of psychology have attempted to explain the complexity of human life, but due to their faulty worldviews, their explanations have been incomplete and fragmented.[37] In contrast, a Christian worldview provides the possibility for a more holistic approach. Based on my Christian worldview, I view people as created by God in his image, yet recognize that all humankind has been profoundly impacted by sin and stand in need of Christ's redemptive work. So how do the ideas of secular psychology fit in a psychology formed from a Christian worldview? According to Faw, "by placing each unique insight in the context

---

34. Bartholomew and Goheen, *Living at the Crossroads*.
35. Griggs and Jackson, *Psychology*.
36. MacArthur, *Sufficiency in Christ*.
37. Faw, *Psychology in Christian Perspective*.

of a larger and better integrated understanding of total humanity, we can arrive at a more correct understanding of the complexities of our experiences."[38] Building a view of psychology from the perspective of a Christian worldview does not mean the wholesale rejection of all the ideas of modern psychology, nor does it mean blind acceptance of these ideas as some contradict direct scriptural teaching.

The key to this integration process is the basis of authority. A Christian worldview accepts the ultimate authority of scripture (God's special revelation) over any understanding of creation or the natural world (God's general revelation). All psychological information must first pass through the filter of Scripture before it can be integrated into a Christian psychology. The Bible does not address every topic in great detail, so there is room for the observation and analysis of psychologists and scientists to fill in the "gaps of understanding," but this cannot replace the foundation of understanding provided through scripture and its interpretation. Psychology is comprised of many specialty areas, and in many of these areas there is little conflict between psychology and Christianity (learning and memory, neuroscience, sensory perception). But in the area of personality and counseling theory, the contrast between a Christian worldview and that of the various secular worldviews is great. The process of developing a uniquely Christian psychology, either with or without any contributions of modern secular psychology is still in its earliest stages.

So, what does this mean for accomplishing the mission of Christian education? And once again, how does it impact the way I teach students? While it is often the mission of Christian education to "provide a sound education, based in the liberal arts" and to "foster the Christian faith through the integration of faith with learning, living, and service,"[39] how do we accomplish them both? After our family moved due to a job change, my wife and I chose to enroll our eight-year-old twin daughters in a Christian school. We were very excited to be able to provide this opportunity for them, but much to our surprise one of them came to us crying. She was very upset and through her tears exclaimed, "But Daddy, I love math and science and history too!" In her thinking, her new Christian school would be eight hours of Sunday School Bible lessons. If the

---

38. Faw, *Psychology in Christian Perspective*, 426.

39. College of the Ozarks, "A Unique College," *2021–2022 College Catalog*, accessible through the College's public website: www.cofo.edu.

mission is to provide the advantages of a Christian education, then it is important that what we do be both "Christian" and "education."

Both today and in the recent past, much of what is called "Christian education" is in reality neither Christian nor education.[40] Many Christians have an anti-intellectual attitude toward academic endeavors and cultural pursuits, but a Christian worldview should foster a positive attitude toward learning because in God's creation all of life and learning may be a worshipful pursuit of his glory and wisdom. On the other hand, other Christians have been lax in allowing their faith and theological beliefs to purposefully and intentionally impact their academic lives and teaching. What I am proposing will necessarily require a greater effort and dedication from both teacher and student, because unlike the secular person, the Christian seeks mastery over the whole realm of knowledge. In other words, unlike the secular professor, the Christian has the freedom to discuss and explore both the supernatural and natural spheres. But again, the danger is for Christians to think that it is enough to be strong in our personal faith, and our light and saltiness will be enough to impact our students as we blindly pass on the information from our secular textbooks. For Christian education to fulfill its mission, it will take more than just having teachers who are professing Christians. It is vital that our goals and objectives, methods and ethics, be Christian as well.[41]

Personally, the process of intentionally reviewing how I faithfully educate students in what many perceive to be a secular field of study has forced me to better understand how I was influenced toward God's calling for my life during a critical developmental period.[42] It also challenged me to be more intentional in how I influence the students God would lead across my path. Even though my life story is unique to me, psychological research suggests that the journey of identity formation is one that all share during late adolescence and young adulthood.[43] Looking back, I now see that I was "taught a worldview sufficient for the questions and crises" of my life.[44] I had mentors and teachers who not only taught a Christian worldview but fleshed it out, and I was welcomed

---

40. Holmes, *Idea of a Christian College*.
41. See Dik, *Redeeming Work*; Dik and Duffy, *Make Your Job a Calling*.
42. Dik, *Redeeming Work*.
43. Santrock, *Adolescence*.
44. Garber, *Fabric of Faithfulness*, 51.

into a community of like-minded pilgrims on the same journey who stimulated and supported my growth.

Not only did this review process affect my personal understanding, but it has also led me to adapt my teaching content and approach, and has further strengthened my commitment to continue mentoring five to ten college men every year. For the past several years, I have begun each of my classes with a section on how worldviews affect the way we understand the class subject matter. I ask all my students to do at least one major writing project where they must evaluate a pertinent psychological idea from the viewpoint of a Christian worldview. Emmons states, "a meaningful life is one that is characterized by a deep sense of purpose, a sense of inner conviction, and assurance that in spite of one's current plight, life has significance."[45] These types of assignments force students to grapple with understanding these psychological concepts and ideas through the lens of their developing Christian worldview. With God's abiding strength and presence, I want to be a godly man of integrity, endeavoring to live out my beliefs and Christian worldview. By intentionally living out the calling God has placed on my life, I find an abiding sense of meaning and peace.[46]

A few years ago, the Lord challenged me to be more intentionally involved in the lives of a few college-aged men who I might disciple/mentor in a deeper way than I was used to doing; to go beyond my interactions with students in my large classes and actually establish and grow meaningful relationships with a few one-on-one. Since that time, God has allowed me the privilege of plugging into several men, including five this past semester. We meet individually on a weekly basis for accountability, growth, challenge, and sharing. Just as God used so many people to influence me in my pursuit of him and my purpose, I want to impact others to embrace a Christian worldview and its importance in successfully completing their callings.

---

45. Emmons, *Psychology of Ultimate Concerns*, 138.
46. Dik and Duffy. *Make Your Job a Calling*.

BIBLIOGRAPHY

Bartholomew, Craig and Michael Goheen. *Living at the Crossroads: An Introduction to Christian Worldview.* Grand Rapids: Baker, 2008.

Dik, Bryan J. *Redeeming Work.* West Conshohocken, PA: Templeton Foundation, 2020.

Dik, Bryan J., and Ryan D. Duffy. *Make Your Job a Calling.* Conshohocken, PA: Templeton Foundation, 2012.

Downey, Deane and Stanley Porter, eds. *Christian Worldview and the Academic Disciplines: Crossing the Academy.* Eugene, OR: Pickwick, 2009.

Emmons, Robert A. *The Psychology of Ultimate Concerns.* New York: Guilford, 2003.

Erikson, Erik H. *Identity: Youth and Crisis.* New York: W.W. Norton & Company, 1968.

Faw, Harold. *Psychology in Christian Perspective.* Grand Rapids: Baker Academic, 1995.

Freud, Sigmund. *The Future of an Illusion.* New York: Liveright, 1955.

Garber, Steven. *Fabric of Faithfulness: Weaving Together Belief and Behavior.* Downers Grove, IL: InterVarsity, 2007.

Griggs, Richard A., and Sherri L. Jackson. *Psychology: A Concise Introduction.* New York: Macmillan Higher Education, 2019.

Holmes, Arthur. *The Idea of a Christian College.* Grand Rapids: Eerdmans, 1987.

Leahey, Thomas Hardy. *A History of Psychology.* 8th ed. New York: Routledge, 2017.

MacArthur, John F. *Our Sufficiency in Christ.* Nashville: Word, 1991.

McGrath, Alister E. *Theology: The Basics.* Hoboken, NJ: Blackwell, 2008.

Moes, Paul, and Donald J. Tellinghuisen. *Exploring Psychology and Christian Faith.* Grand Rapids: Baker Academic, 2014.

Poplin, Mary. *Is Reality Secular? Testing the Assumptions of Four Global Worldviews.* Downers Grove, IL: InterVarsity Press, 2014.

Santrock, John W. *Adolescence.* 14th ed. New York: McGraw-Hill, 2012.

Smith, Christian, and Patricia Snell. *Souls in Transition: The Religious and Spiritual Lives of Emerging Adults.* Oxford: Oxford University Press, 2009.

Wilkens, Steve and Mark L. Sanford. *Hidden Worldviews.* Downers Grove, IL: InterVarsity, 2009.

10

Christian Worldview and the Helping Profession
Answering the Question of Telos and Praxis

Tracy J. Bell

INTRODUCTION: THE QUESTION OF *TELOS* AND *PRAXIS*

As a young professional just out of graduate school, I found myself asking what Steven Garber describes as "the question of *telos* and *praxis*."[1] I studied family life counseling and psychology at a Christian university where the counseling program was housed in the theology department. My graduate degree was through a public university. My faith, to that point in my vocational journey, had gone unchallenged. This changed upon my first encounter with the professor of my first graduate course. This introductory course started with a lecture that explained social work's incompatibility with Christianity. The professor used the first hour to explain her sexual orientation and her disregard for the Christian faith, especially its use within the field of helping. Despite this introduction to the program, I found my way through the two years, due in large part to the foundation I had growing up in a Christian home, as well as my time at Ouachita Baptist University; both environments were rich

---

1 Garber, *Fabric of Faithfulness*, 56.

with safe relationships that cultivated my ability to stay respectfully firm while growing in my faith.

I began to feel my personal and vocational integrity challenged again a few weeks into my first job as a clinical therapist on an acute unit for young children at a psychiatric hospital. It was the first time I was on my own in the world. I had moved away from any financial ties with my family, as well as being independent of daily supervision in my clinical work. This was both exciting and terrifying. The challenge started when what I believed about people and their place within the Creator's redemptive plan began to collide with what I saw and was being asked to practice within the field.

There are stories too numerous to name; however, a client named "James" still has a piece of my heart. James, seven years old, was a tiny child. He had been in and out of foster care since infancy and in more homes than he could remember. Working on an acute unit, the job was to stabilize a child so they could go into weekly outside therapy. I soon found out this meant creating a behavioral modification plan and changing or increasing dosage to medication. James did well (as most kids do) on the unit. He was able to follow the behavioral protocols and at seven years of age was able to explain his list of diagnoses. Each Friday, I would discharge James and send him on his way to the latest foster home or residential facility. Each Monday, upon returning to work, I would hear small feet running to meet me as I came onto the unit. James would throw his arms around my waist, smile widely, and say, "Miss Tracy! I'm back!" James showed pride in his ability to get kicked out of the living situations he had found himself in over the weekends. We would continue this pattern during my time at the hospital. What was happening? Why would this young child continue to desire a psychiatric unit over a home? How could I motivate him and others like him to do well outside of the unit?

Another client, diagnosed as schizophrenic, had also been in and out of the acute unit. He followed the same pattern as James. This child was from inner-city Little Rock and lived with his disabled mother who drew Medicaid, as many of our clients' families did. He was nonverbal and had several sensory-integration issues. When I questioned the psychiatrist if this could be a possible autism case, he confirmed that I was correct; however, he followed the affirmation with: "this is about job security Tracy." This situation, along with the focus on people as a diagnosis, the lack of familial and communal support, and a never-ending pattern of recidivism led to my resignation three months after I began. I was offered more money to stay (tempting at a time in my life where I did not have another financial support system) and I remember wondering if the field I had once viewed as a calling on my life was indeed incompatible with my faith as my graduate professor had argued. How could I work in a system that viewed people, more specifically, vulnerable children, as a means to get ahead? And so, the questions of *telos* and *praxis* and their ability to be integrated became very real for me. Indeed, the tension between what I believe about the world and how my field is usually practiced continues to be challenging as a clinician.

TAKING A CHRISTIAN WORLDVIEW IN THE FIELD OF HELPING

According to Bartholomew and Goheen, "Education is for the purpose of equipping students to witness faithfully to the gospel in the whole of their lives."[2] Being raised as a part of a Reformed tradition, I learned early to answer the Catechism's question: "What is the chief end of man?" Garber explains this in today's terms as, "What is the purpose of my life?"[3] A proper Christian worldview is one that takes seriously the question of purpose and its orientation to our daily actions. Garber quotes Mark Schwehn from *Exiles from Eden: Religion and the Academic Vocation in America* as saying: "Ways of knowing are not morally neutral but morally directive."[4] This moral direction to which Schwehn is referring is embedded in what Bartholomew and Goheen say are, "God's plan for humankind: what it was intended to be when God designed it, how it has been twisted by sin, and how Christ's work in us might redeem our experience of work and direct us in the work that we choose to do."[5] With this knowledge, Christians can look to the biblical narrative as well as to "*all* human discovery," according to Augustine, to give method and direction to how they should think and live within the world.[6]

---

2. Bartholomew and Goheen, *Living at the Crossroads*, 170.
3. Garber, *Fabric of Faithfulness*, 59.
4. Garber, *Fabric of Faithfulness*, 74.
5. Bartholomew and Goheen, *Living at the Crossroads*, 29.
6. Fant, *Liberal Arts*, 36.

Creator

In order to articulate well the ways in which my therapeutic and pedagogical paradigms within the field of helping are upheld by a coherent Christian identity, I will offer a brief conceptual structure to be followed throughout this chapter. The foundation of this framework is creation, or more importantly, the Creator. The authority of Scripture identifies God as Creator in Gen 1 and throughout the Bible, which for the Christian in the helping vocation becomes the overarching means by which we understand clients and their proper relation to the Creator. Relationship must be acknowledged as the major underpinning of this view. Bartholomew and Goheen state, "The doctrine of Creation includes an understanding of the basic relationship between the awesome God and everything else, since everything exists because he has called it into existence."[7] Further, God's creation is sustained throughout the biblical narrative. We see God's people flourishing as healthy images of himself when in proper relationship with the living God, their Creator. The covenant structure seeks to hold this relationship together. Bartholomew and Goheen explain that the covenant structure helps us understand "how sin can cause lives and relationships to disintegrate" and how one's response to God's love will be actualized through trust and obedience.[8] This foundational framework is taught in our Family Studies department as a way of rightly envisioning our students' future work with a hurting clientele.

Another tenet important to the creation theme that has become integral in my personal and pedagogical paradigm of the created, as well as embracing recent discoveries in the field of neuroscience, is what McGrath refers to as the establishment or "imposition" of order.[9] McGrath states, "Creation is not to be understood simply as the forming or shaping of the universe, but in terms of God's mastery of chaos and ordering of the world."[10] Bartholomew and Goheen explain that the first chapter of Genesis is not only about the Creator, but gives great insight into the created world, calling it, "ordered, good and historical."[11] This order becomes essential when binding central themes together within the Family Studies and Social Services department. My goal as a teacher

---

7. Bartholomew and Goheen, *Living at the Crossroads*, 33.
8. Bartholomew and Goheen, *Living at the Crossroads*, 48.
9. McGrath, *Theology*, 37.
10. McGrath, *Theology*, 38.
11. Bartholomew and Goheen, *Living at the Crossroads*, 36.

is for my students to understand that God's created order, at the very basic level of attachment relationships and neurobiology, sets the foundation for macro-level repercussions. When in harmony, we see creation as it was intended. According to Bartholomew and Goheen,

> This harmony should be true also of the range of cultural, social and personal expressions of the life of humankind. Technology and art, schools and businesses, imagination and emotion—all these make their contributing sounds in the symphony of God's creation. Each is good as it conforms to God's creational design, and all are very good as together they serve him in harmony.[12]

Dr. Bruce Perry, a leading neuropsychiatrist in the field of childhood trauma, explains the brain as being organized from bottom to top, with the lower, more primitive parts of the brain being developed first through the infant's attachment relationship and the higher cortical areas entering a final developmental process much later in life.[13] He goes on to say that the brain is a "historical organ."[14] Dr. Perry and others in the field of attachment postulate that a healthy attachment process will produce a trusting individual who interprets their world as safe and predictable. Perry explains that "in order to understand an individual one needs to know his or her history."[15] History becomes important, according to Dr. Dan Siegal, as "experience directly shapes the circuits responsible for such processes as memory, emotion and self-awareness."[16]

When teaching students about what it means to be human, one must begin with the Creator's design for relational attachment and its healthy manifestations throughout life. One cannot explain "mental illness" in a being without first looking to the Creator's intent for that being. Without the knowledge of intent, there would be no basis for explaining the "illness" which one intends to heal. Simply, without understanding what the Creator deems as healthy, one cannot accurately declare someone ill. Psalms 127:1 states, "Unless the Lord builds the house, they labor in vain while they build it; unless the Lord guards the city, the watchman keeps awake in vain."[17] McGrath speaks of the Psalmist's proclamation

---

12. Bartholomew and Goheen, *Living at the Crossroads*, 41.
13. Perry and Hambrick, "Neurosequential Model of Therapeutics," 40.
14. Perry and Szalavitz, *Boy Who Was Raised as a Dog*, 83.
15. Perry and Hambrick, "Neurosequential Model of Therapeutics," 40.
16. Siegel, *Developing Mind*, 4.
17. Ps 127:1 (NASB).

of "purpose, planning and a deliberate intention to create."[18] When attempting to explain human purpose, one does not need to stray far from what we read in Genesis. We were created *through* the experience of relationship, *for* the experience of relationship, and we are *maintained* by experiencing relationship. In McGrath's words, "Humanity is created as a social being and is meant to exist in relation with others."[19] If then, the essence of our very being is relational in its intent, and its very existence hinges upon relationship, would we not suppose that what we refer to as "illness" of the mind could be a direct result of a severance in our key relationships?

The tension I experienced as a young clinician led me to seek answers within my field that would endorse what I already knew as the truth found in creation; that truth being the Creator's intent for human flourishing. My clinical education, along with the majority of my field, exhorted empiricism as the basis for understanding human behavior and experience. However, in my own experience, I found the method lacking in substance. Often clinicians tout what is referred to as "best practices" due to their ability to manipulate behavioral responses. For the Christian practitioner, however, this leaves the totality of healing, redemption, and restoration in question. So, one may be able to show behavioral outcomes in certain contexts, as with the psychiatric hospital; however, the issue of total healing is largely ignored. While empirical methods of science gave rise to the field over one hundred years ago through physiology, physics, and medicine, many today admit these methods need to be used much less rigidly.[20]

Faw states that answers about the nature of humankind "cannot be addressed by science acting solely on the basis of empirical evidence. Rather, the answers different people give reflect presuppositions shaped by religious and philosophical influences rather than conclusions based on scientific evidence."[21] He goes on to outline three major views within the helping profession that have shaped how we go about clinical work: behaviorism, psychoanalysis, and humanism. It is important to note that these psychological models have shaped a paradigm that may be an

18. McGrath, *Theology*, 44.
19. McGrath, *Theology*, 42.
20. Faw, "Christian Perspective on Psychology," in Downey and Porter, *Christian Worldview and the Academic Disciplines*, 419.
21. Faw, "Christian Perspective on Psychology," in Downey and Porter, *Christian Worldview and the Academic Disciplines*, 419.

oversimplification of not only the Genesis account of the created order, but also of neuroscience's advances in the last twenty years.

The apostle Paul declares, "Because that which is known about God is evident within them; for God made it evident to them. For since the creation of the world His invisible attributes, His eternal power and divine nature, have been clearly seen, being understood through what has been made, so that they are without excuse."[22] Fant utilizes this passage from Rom 1:19–21 in order to set the stage for what is called *general revelation*. He states that theologians refer to general revelation as "God revealing himself to persons outside of the scope of scriptural revelation in ways that specifically point to him as Creator and toward Christ as Savior."[23] Fant makes an argument for Christians in their field being mandated to "learn the world's broad secrets as a specific opportunity to learn about its Creator."[24] In the last twenty years, the neurosciences have given much opportunity to not only learn about our Creator and his creation, but have also confirmed truth taught in Scripture.

You may find similar quotes in secular literature like those I have described above from Christian authors. As stated earlier, "Humanity is created as a social being, and is meant to exist in relation with others."[25] Those in the profession of helping will find statements that support this framework by leading neuroscientists and psychiatrists. Bessel Van der Kolk states, "Our capacity to destroy one another is matched by our capacity to heal one another. Restoring relationships and community is central to restoring well-being. We can change social conditions to create environments in which children and adults feel safe and where they can thrive."[26] Bruce Perry has written books on the subject of relationship and mental health, saying, "We are indeed born for love."[27] He also argues, "pleasure and human interactions become inextricably woven together. This interconnection, the association of pleasure with human interaction, is the important neurobiological 'glue' that bonds and creates healthy relationships."[28] Dan Siegel, founder of the field of interpersonal

22. Rom 1:19–21 (NASB).
23. Fant, *Liberal Arts*, 60.
24. Fant, *Liberal Arts*, 60.
25. McGrath, *Theology*, 42.
26. Van Der Kolk, *Body Keeps the Score*, 38.
27. Szalavitz and Perry, *Born to Love*, 5.
28. Perry and Szalavitz, *Boy Who Was Raised as a Dog*, 85.

neurobiology, created a working definition of "the mind" during what has been called "the decade of the brain" in the 1990s. This definition became a way for neuroscientists and those in the field of helping to communicate around the interplay of mind and brain. He states, "A core aspect of the mind is an embodied and relational process that regulates the flow of energy and information."[29]

In teaching students about the helping profession, I have found an easy integration between the sciences and God's created order. The Traumatized Child course concentrates on the themes of an orderly God. Students are taught John Bowlby's Attachment Theory, where we explore the earliest of relational underpinnings for personality and motivation. We go on to study the neurobiological research that has taken place in more recent years to give structure to the theory; the most influential of which is Dr. Bruce Perry's "Neurosequential Model of Therapeutics." This recent model attempts to go beyond the medical model, as well as models based upon philosophical interpretations, in order to map where a child is in their cognitive development. Within this model, one is taught that the attachment process, that is, the primary caregiver's healthy response to an infant's innate behaviors (crying, sucking, clinging, gazing and smiling), directly impact cognitive progression. Therapy based upon this model concentrates on patterned, repetitive relational experiences in order to establish a healthy foundation within brain structure. The premise is that by targeting the primitive brain through sensory-relational experiences and working sequentially upward in an ordered fashion, one can "re-wire" the brain for calm, as this model is based upon "state-dependent functioning." State-dependent functioning promotes the understanding that "people process, store and retrieve information and then respond to the world in a manner that depends upon their current physiological state (in other words, their response is "state-dependent)."[30] State-dependent functioning is another opportunity to integrate faith. Perry explains that we are "wired" through our relational experiences of fear or love. The emotions of fear and love become a running narrative within my classroom as it is within Scripture. It also provides opportunity to move into how the fall has tainted our relational, familial, communal and societal structures.

29. Siegel, *Developing Mind*, 2.
30. Perry and Szalavitz, *Boy Who Was Raised as a Dog*, 429.

The Fall

McGrath states, "An essential component of the Christian doctrine of sin is the recognition that the world has departed from the trajectory upon which God placed it in the work of creation."[31] As we see in attachment theory, confirmed in neuroscience, God has created us as embodied beings with potential to live and work in and out of healthy relationships that point toward his glory. Jones speaks of our humanity as "embodied" in order to convey to the reader that we are, in a very literal sense, part of the earth, that creation is holistic, and that because of this "total depravity means our motivations are intermingled with that which is twisted and evil to varying degrees."[32] God's commanding of obedience in the garden points to his Lordship and order over his creation.[33] While created in his image, in trusting God with our obedience we are reminded of our place in his order. Trust in this "intent" of our humanity being ordered with proper relationship beneath God's lordship would bring us much joy and flourishing. However, due to creation being tarnished by sin, we are now confronted with how to live in depraved relationships within a corrupt, chaotic world.

Yarhouse and Sells explain that this depravity is evident in both condition and behavior. They write, "As a state or condition, it affects all of creation. There are no aspects of the created order that go untouched."[34] Paul explains this in Rom 8:22: "For we know that the whole creation groans and suffers the pain of childbirth together until now.[35]" In order to explain what this looks like within the young clients many of my students will face, I seek to push them beyond genetics and "disorders" in order for them to understand that all behavior makes sense in context, while making sure they recognize that empathy does not contradict accountability. We often discuss the field of epigenetics in order to understand the interactions between genes and environment. This fairly new field of study has done a service to those who fall on the contextual side of the nurture verses nature debate. We are now aware that in order to actualize genetics through what is called "gene expression," they must be nurtured through the appropriate environment. That is, God has created us in

---

31. McGrath, *Theology*, 42–43.
32. Jones and Dockery, *Psychology*, 51.
33. Bartholomew and Goheen, *Living at the Crossroads*, 46.
34. Yarhouse and Sells, *Family Therapies*, 20.
35. Rom 8:22 (NASB).

his image (*imago Dei*) with the capacity for all types of potential. His creation is ordered as well as good. Failure to actualize the potential in perfect harmony is a result of sin.

An infant born today will come into the world with billions of neurons not yet connected. In a sense, their tiny brains are a chaotic mess awaiting mastery. This mastery has been left to the environment into which the baby is introduced. If things go well, the baby will go on to actualize the potentiality of important life skills; one very important skill being empathy found in the frontal lobes of one's brain. If, however, the relational experiences early in life are chaotic, stressful, or traumatic, the child's brain will wire itself for fear, seated in a more primitive area of the brain called the limbic system, disallowing the individual to utilize higher regions of the brain (like the frontal lobes). This fear-state actualizes all the behaviors necessary to protect oneself from harm. These behaviors, while adaptive early in life, tend to produce children and adults who struggle to thrive in daily interactions and often find themselves labeled as defective or "crazy." The nature of our environments is far from what God intended. Eve's distrust in God produced a current of fear and disorder throughout the history of the world. Our fear-state functioning within a disordered world helps maintain the fall and has produced what Perry refers to as "relational poverty." This goes beyond one client or family. The field's narrow focus on behavioral disorders and genetics falls short of dealing with the foundational problems that we now know are systemic in nature. Our communities, society, and world are lacking the empathy that God intends within his creation.

In a longitudinal review of seventy-two studies done between 1979–2009, American college students showed measures of empathy 40% lower than their elders, with the largest drop being after the year 2000.[36] In *Born to Love*, Perry explains sociologist Robert Putnam's work around American social ties and civic engagement. Putnam's research is telling of how far we have strayed from God's original intent for relationship. He demonstrates that in the last five to six decades, America has declined "in virtually every form of social and civic participation from voting rates to church-going to time spent entertaining friends and the proportion of money given to charity."[37] He goes on to write, "On nearly all measures of social life, Americans tend to have fewer and lower-quality interactions

36. O'Brien et al. "Empathic Concern and Perspective Taking."
37. Szalavitz and Perry, *Born to Love*, 228–29.

with one another than our parents and grandparents did."[38] Bartholomew and Goheen explain that the scope of sin "is not simply personal; it also expresses itself communally."[39] To understand the fall properly, one must consider its scope.

Within the field of helping, one can find clinicians and researchers focusing on any one aspect from anthropology to clinical psychiatry. Typically, professionals work in isolation from one another and in isolation from other fields. Siegel writes:

> Neuroscience can inform us about how the brain gives rise to mental processes such as memory and perception. Developmental Psychology offers us a view of how children's minds grow within families across time. Anthropology gives us insights into how patterns within different cultures directly shape the development of the mind. Psychiatry gives us a clinical view of how individuals may suffer from emotional and behavioral disturbances that profoundly alter the course of their lives. Often these disciplines function in isolation from one another.[40]

When teaching a course about the fallen man within a fallen world, I am convicted to do so from what Siegel calls "consilience."[41] This convergence of disciplines plays well into the Family Studies department's focus upon systems theory or a sociological perspective, both of which seek to explain social ills as systemic as well as reciprocal, from the smallest microbe to the larger macro-organism throughout time.

It is not only the disciplines that suffer from this blinding to context; Christian practitioners may also look only to their interpretation of Scripture (as the field of Nouthetics suggests) and avoid general revelation, or may, in daily vocation look at one's part in the redemptive process as isolated from history and the future. When speaking of the redemptive theme as part of a Christian worldview, we must understand the holistic nature of glorification. Revelation 21:5 states, "And He who sits on the throne said, 'Behold I am making all things new.'"[42] Fant explains that "the power of general revelation anticipates the gospel."[43] That is, any

---

38. Szalavitz and Perry, *Born to Love*, 228–29.
39. Bartholomew and Goheen, *Living at the Crossroads*, 49.
40. Siegel, *Developing Mind*, 1.
41. Siegel, *Developing Mind*, 1.
42. Rev 21:5 (NASB).
43. Fant, *Liberal Arts*, 60.

understanding of social ills, whether at an individual level or a societal level, should find clarity through the lens of Christ's redemptive ministry throughout history.

Redemption

In order to understand what the theme of redemption seeks to communicate; we need only look to God's original intent. Many have explained this restoration of humankind and the created world in terms of *shalom*. According to Yarhouse and Sells, "Shalom as a kingdom principle has to do with living in proper relationship with God, with oneself, with others, and with nature or one's physical surroundings."[44] The question for the Christian helping professional becomes, "How are we to be stewards of his creation in vocation?" McGrath states, "The doctrine of creation leads to the idea of human stewardship of the creation, which is to be contrasted with the secular notion of human ownership of the world."[45] Restoration does not call us to save the world, as this would not be restorative to the original intent of creation. Salvation has already been accomplished upon the cross by Jesus' death and resurrection. The original intent of creation and the call upon us in God's redemptive process is to reflect his image and glorify him. We do this by living in shalom with God, which is "to live again under his gracious rule." Augustine of Hippo is quoted as saying, "You made us for yourself, and our hearts are restless until they find their rest in you."[46] How might we reflect a stance of shalom with our clients, our co-workers, our community, and the world? As outlined above, this restorative process is founded upon a safe, responsive relationship that will point to order and goodness, and be comprehensive in nature.

Above I have outlined some of how my pedagogy is expressed around being a steward of God's order in creation. The question of how I might teach "goodness" as well as be "comprehensive" should also be explored. In *Psychology, Theology, and Spirituality in Christian Counseling*, McMinn offers an insightful view of spiritual redemption and interpersonal redemption being complementary. McMinn suggests that as a Christian in vocation, we are more likely to become interested in living out our faith in redemptive relationships with others. He writes, "We are

---

44. Yarhouse and Sells, *Family Therapies*, 24.
45. McGrath, *Theology*, 42.
46. McGrath, *Theology*, 43.

God's hands and feet in a world that needs to be rescued from the pervasive effects of human depravity."[47] He goes on to say, "the redemptive nature of the counseling relationship is a practical way of responding to God's transformative mercy."[48] Relationships with the client, the family, the community and society become the focus for how the Christian in vocation is to connect his or her faith to practice. The theological underpinnings of "goodness" in God's creation must be acknowledged in order for the counselor or social worker to live out this "transformative mercy." Throughout the creation narrative, we read, "God saw that it was good."[49] It has been taught for much of history that good and evil exist in order to make up the nature of the world in which we live.[50] However, Paul explains in 1 Tim 4:4, "For everything God created is good, and nothing is to be rejected if it is received with thanksgiving."[51] Bartholomew and Goheen explain, "In a biblical view, evil is like a stain on the pure fabric of creation: it comes later, it is not essential to the nature of the world, and it may be removed without changing the essential nature of that which is disfigured."[52]

As a helping professional serving to redeem God's creation, one must see the created goodness or potential in the fabric of the world in order to live and work out of relationships that will ultimately be glorifying. Our tendency to focus upon the problem and ignore the created good may certainly skew the redemptive relational opportunity to which we have been called. Yarhouse and Sells ask, "How will what I do and the way I do it reflect delight in relationships with others?"[53] In his book *When Justice and Peace Embrace*, Wolterstorff speaks of shalom as "right harmonious relationships to other human beings and delight in human community."[54] He goes on to speak to how we might "shape the world with our labor and find fulfillment in so doing and delight in the results."[55] Yarhouse and Sells state,

---

47. McMinn, *Psychology, Theology, and Spirituality*, 241.
48. McMinn, *Psychology, Theology, and Spirituality*, 242.
49. Gen 1 (NASB).
50. Bartholomew and Goheen, *Living at the Crossroads*, 40.
51. 1 Tim 4:4 (NASB).
52. Bartholomew and Goheen, *Living at the Crossroads*, 40.
53. Yarhouse and Sells, *Family Therapies*, 25.
54. Wolterstorff, *Until Justice and Peace Embrace*, 70.
55. Wolterstorff, *Until Justice and Peace Embrace*, 70.

> To speak of redemption is to necessarily speak to the created good of human relationships as well as the fallen state in which we live and relate to one another and the future humanity moves toward. When we talk about helping families move in a better direction, we are recognizing that there was some creational intent to how we were to relate in families and that those ways of relating are incomplete and partial after the Fall. But the ways we are to relate also point to something beyond our here-and-now relationships, to transcend reality that is both now and soon to come.[56]

As helping professionals, we create relationships of shalom with our clients and communities through finding pleasure in who they are created to be, thus reflecting pleasure in our Creator. In the words of McMinn, "Ideally the Christian counselor is also a 'healing agent'—one whose spiritual life spills over in interactions with everyone, including clients."[57] Studies have revealed that the effects of counseling cannot be solely attributed to the techniques used by the counselor. In his 1996 book, *Psychology, Theology, and Spirituality in Christian Counseling*, McMinn says, "In a 1993 review of the counseling literature, psychologists Susan Whiston and Thomas Sexton reported that a strong therapeutic relationship is one of the best indicators of success in psychotherapy."[58] The opportunity to create an environment that identifies with what God intended may allow for the wounded to rewire themselves for calm, safety and ultimately his pleasure. This therapeutic-redemptive relationship can be the most healing of factors when working within the helping profession.

Bartholomew and Goheen note, "The first chapter of Genesis describes a creation that is not static but rather moves and develops historically toward a goal. A stable order and historical development do not contradict one another."[59] The comprehensive scope of redemption is important to understand as a helping professional. When speaking of God's original intent for those he created to oversee the earth, Bartholomew and Goheen state,

> All of culture and society, all of human civilization, is in response to this one divine mandate. In the beginning, the creation was like a healthy newborn child. It was "very good" in

---

56. Yarhouse and Sells, *Family Therapies*, 25.
57. McMinn, *Psychology, Theology, and Spirituality*, 13.
58. McMinn, *Psychology, Theology, and Spirituality*, 13.
59. Bartholomew and Goheen, *Living at the Crossroads*, 41.

the sense that there was nothing wrong with it as a newborn; it was complete and healthy in all its parts. But, it must continue to grow and develop. So it is with the creation: God's intention from the beginning was that creation should unfold and develop and move toward a goal.[60]

Cole and Hall speak of the *telos* of transformational psychology being "grounded upon the reality that persons are created for a particular set of ends or goals: the love and glory of God and love of neighbor, by being formed into the image of Christ through union with the filling of the spirit."[61] To work toward redemption in a comprehensive way, one must be committed to the goal of *shalom* in all constructs of the world, throughout time. James Davison Hunter states that we "must be present in the world in ways that work toward the constructive subversion of all frameworks of social life that are incompatible with the shalom for which we were made and to which we were called."[62]

RECIPROCITY: FROM CLASSROOM TO KINGDOM

Looking back, my experiences early in my vocation motivated me to seek out how to employ what I knew to be truth into a secular field often hostile to the Christian faith. While I am thankful for the Lord's leading to seek out how he would have me pursue the call toward redemptive vocation, I am actively seeking ways to teach my students in a manner that is formative and anticipatory of the challenges they will face while staying focused on the created good in which they are called to delight. Garber asks, "How do we help students learn to connect what they believe about the world with how they live in the world?"[63] Going back to earlier tenets within this chapter, I am convicted to follow the same worldview structure in classroom pedagogy as I do in clinical practice. To do this, I must begin with the element of personal integrity prior to challenging my students' growth. Do my students see a professor who is living out what she is teaching? Do they see the elements of empathic character when they get a peek into my social experience? Am I allowing students into my life and making space for safe relationships to occur? It

---

60. Bartholomew and Goheen, *Living at the Crossroads*, 41.
61. Cole and Hall, *Psychology in the Spirit*, 8.
62. Hunter, *Change the World*, 235.
63. Garber, *Fabric of Faithfulness*, 45.

is only out of that same foundational actualization of trust and obedience Bartholomew and Goheen point to that I may challenge students in their own walk and paradigms.

Next, I must challenge the integrity of the students. Within the Integration of the Christian Faith and the Helping Profession course, the students complete a project that for many will begin a habitual process of formative patterns. The class begins by exploring what Elton Trueblood refers to as the "Cut Flower Generation."[64] I've found many students are able to explain Christian worldview tenets, as well as to name values they believe important to this worldview. However, when challenged to apply their personal value base to micro and macro situations in the field, they are frequently surprised at the difficulty they have defending their decision, or in some cases, they find very little reason to apply faith to a problem they view as "work-related." This opens the door for discussion around normative values in the post-modern world and the need for an unchanging interpretive framework.

One student wrote about growing up in a Christian home, knowing the "right worldview" and needing very little convincing when taking courses about Christian worldview. However, when given a project that challenged her to define her value system and apply it to practice, she stated, "I need to start again. My work shows where I go wrong. I place value in the self, over and over again. I ask all the wrong questions. The answers never satisfy." She went on to discuss her desire to create formative liturgies that would connect what was written on her heart with the work of her hands.

While I am only with my students for limited moments of interaction, I believe that the cultivation of trust can be achieved in order to point them toward empathic relationship. Fant states, "Empathy is a critical trait for the wise to possess. Truly Christ-centered education cultivates intellectual empathy, the ability to understand how others think."[65] Family Studies and Social Service majors are taught the importance of Weber's "*Verstehen.*" The concept of "grasping insight" or "placing yourself in someone else's shoes" is taught in repetition throughout the course of the program. This patterned, repetitive learning technique is purposeful. An embodied-integrative learning takes place when my upper-level students no longer look at the individual as being solely responsible for health.

64. Sherwood, "Relationship Between Beliefs and Values," in Hugen and Scales, *Christianity and Social Work*, 12.

65. Fant, *Liberal Arts*, 56.

Over the course of their time with us, each class engages in case studies and experiments that point back to a systemic paradigm. More importantly, our department is cultivating a culture of empathic relationships through experiential means. The mere intellectual understanding of what empathy is does little to promote an empathic individual. My desire is to provide a space for safe attachments with one another and with faculty.

Faithfully educating students through liturgical experiences "shape[s] and constitute[s] identities by forming fundamental desires and basic attunement to the world."[66] This learned attunement or empathy for one's world is what Smith refers to as "pedagogical formation of our imagination."[67] Smith gives a comprehensive analysis of how, being embodied organisms of desire, our hearts and imaginations are being shaped to love cravings that point away from God's kingdom unconsciously. He goes on to state, "If our cultural critique remains captivated by a cognitivist anthropology, then we'll fail to even see the role of practices. This constitutes a massive blind spot in much of the Christian cultural critique that takes place under the banner of worldview thinking."[68] To faithfully educate a student, I must look at the student in a holistic manner with potential to serve redemptively in his or her vocation and life. I am aware lecture and book knowledge may serve their intellect, but I also know that they have formed habits and desires based on cultural liturgies of which they may not be aware. These habits point to where their attunement (love/empathy) is fixated. Thus, the experiences I present in the classroom should bring to light any dichotomy that exist between what they say they believe and how they daily live and practice.

Once the safety of relationship within the classroom and with myself as professor has been established, and the student has been challenged to look at their worldview as formative of how they practice life, I am able to move into the concept of joy and goodness in God's creation and their place within his comprehensive redemptive plan. Vanerwood states:

> To be a social worker is to keep one eye on the hurting person before us, while at the same time keeping the other eye on the big picture. For Christians in social work, the hurting person before us is a fellow human, created in the image of God, declared by him as very good, but unable without God to escape the clutches of sin. The big picture is the grandest story

66. Smith, *Desiring the Kingdom*, 25.
67. Smith, *Desiring the Kingdom*, 26.
68. Smith, *Desiring the Kingdom*, 85.

imaginable, the God-authored drama in which God sees to it that everything eventually turns out well.[69]

I have found challenging students with Middleton and Walsh's analogy of entering a Shakespeare play, in which the second-to-last act is missing, works well to start a dialogue around their place in God's comprehensive drama. We pose questions in the classroom around their response to the missing act, to which they usually find themselves answering with the concept of *order*. Namely, how will they be consistent to the story that has already unfolded and with what they know of the ending?[70] Phillip Eaton asks, "Does the university equip the next generation of leaders with a story of what is true and good and beautiful? Do we bring hope into the world we serve, hope derived from a guiding narrative?"[71] This hope for restoration in God's good creation must be seen throughout our pedagogy. It is within this thinking that I have outlined why I stray from much of my field's focus upon man as a product of genetics. I would like my students to view the client, the community, and society with hope and not bewilderment as they serve redemption through delighting in God's good created order.

CONCLUSION: FAITHFULLY EDUCATING SELF SO OTHERS MAY FLOURISH

I am thankful for the opportunity to work within a college whose *telos* and *praxis* are in alignment. Through the course of my reflection on faithful education, I have been challenged personally, vocationally, and spiritually. My field's focus is not merely to understand human behavior, but to create spaces where humans will flourish. My hope is that this chapter demonstrates how a Christian in the helping profession may create those spaces of flourishing when viewing the world through and in God's redemptive narrative. One final note is that to be faithful in educating students for the field of helping, we must keep "the source of our vision

---

69. Vanderwoerd, "Making Everything New!," in Hugen and Scales, *Christianity and Social Work*, 131.

70. Vanderwoerd, "Making Everything New!," in Hugen and Scales, *Christianity and Social Work*, 131.

71. Eaton, *Engaging the Culture*, 23.

for human flourishing" at the forefront of our pedagogy.⁷² In *To Change the World*, James Davison Hunter states:

> When the word of all flourishing—defined by the love of Christ—becomes flesh in us, in our relations with others, within the tasks we are given, and within our sphere of influence, absence gives way to presence, and the word we speak to each other and to the world becomes authentic and trustworthy. This is the heart of a theology of faithful presence.⁷³

I desire for my students to have opportunities while at College of the Ozarks to experience this authenticity and become embodied projections of God's good creation so that the spaces they fill, whether in vocation, community, or family, will create new spaces and opportunities for others to flourish. In the words of the prophet Jeremiah,

> Build houses and live in them; plant gardens and eat the produce; marry wives and rear families; choose wives for your sons and give your daughters to husbands, so that they may bear sons and daughters. Increase there and do not dwindle away. Seek the welfare of any city to which I have exiled you and pray to the Lord for it; on its welfare your welfare will depend.⁷⁴

BIBLIOGRAPHY

Bartholomew, Craig and Michael Goheen. *Living at the Crossroads: An Introduction to Christian Worldview*. Grand Rapids: Baker, 2008.
Cole, John and Todd Hall. *Psychology in the Spirit: Contours of Transformational Psychology*. Downers Grove, IL: InterVarsity, 2010.
Dockery, David and Timothy George. *The Great Tradition of Christian Thinking: A Student's Guide*. Wheaton, IL: Crossway, 2012.
Downey, Deane and Stanley Porter, eds. *Christian Worldview and the Academic Disciplines: Crossing the Academy*. Eugene, OR: Pickwick, 2009.
Eaton, Philip. *Engaging the Culture, Changing the World: The Christian University in a Post-Christian World*. Downers Grove, IL: InterVarsity, 2011.
Fant, Gene C. *The Liberal Arts: A Student's Guide*. Wheaton, IL: Crossway, 2012.
Fisch, Richard, et al. *The Tactics of Change: Doing Therapy Briefly*. San Francisco: Jossey-Bass, 1982.
Garber, Steven. *The Fabric of Faithfulness*. Downers Grove, IL: InterVarsity, 1996.

---

72. Eaton, *Engaging the Culture*, 195.
73. Hunter, *Change the World*, 252.
74. Jer 29:5–7 (NASB).

Guise, Robert. *Study Guide for the Marriage and Family Therapy National Licensing Examination*. Boston: The Family Solutions Institute, 2009.

Holmes, Arthur. *The Idea of a Christian College*. Grand Rapids: Eerdmans, 1987.

Hugen, Beryl and T. Laine Scales. *Christianity and Social Work: Readings on the Integration of Christian Faith and Social Work Practice*, 3rd ed. Botsford: North American Association of Christian Social Work, 2008.

Hunter, James Davison. *To Change the World: The Irony, Tragedy, & Possibility of Christianity in the Late Modern World*. New York: Oxford University Press, 2010.

Jones, Stanton and David Dockery. *Psychology: A Student's Guide*. Wheaton, IL: Crossway, 2014.

McGrath, Alister. *Theology: The Basics*. Malden, MA: Wiley-Blackwell, 2012.

McMinn, Mark. *Psychology, Theology, and Spirituality in Christian Counseling*. Wheaton, IL: Tyndale House, 1996.

Myers, David and Malcolm Jeeves. *Psychology: Through the Eyes of Faith*. San Francisco: Harper, 2003.

O'Brien, Ed, et al. "Empathic Concern and Perspective Taking: Linear and Quadratic Effects of Age Across the Adult Life Span." *The Journals of Gerontology, Series B; Psychological Sciences and Social Sciences* 68.2 (2013): 168–75.

Perry, Bruce and Erin Hambrick. "The Neurosequential Model of Therapeutics." *Reclaiming Children and Youth* 17.3 (2008): 38–43.

Perry, Bruce and Maia Szalavitz. *The Boy Who Was Raised as a Dog: And Other Stories from a Child Psychiatrist's Notebook*. New York: Basic, 2006.

Siegel, Daniel. *The Developing Mind: How Relationships and the Brain Interact to Shape Who We Are*. New York: Guilford, 2012.

Smith, James K. A. *Desiring the Kingdom: Worship, Worldview, and Cultural Formation*. Grand Rapids: Baker Academic, 2009.

Szalavitz, Maia and Bruce Perry. *Born to Love: Why Empathy is Essential—and Endangered*. New York: William Morrow, 2010.

Van Der Kolk, Bessel. *The Body Keeps the Score: Brain, Mind, and Body in the Healing of Trauma*. New York: Viking, 2014.

Wolterstorff, Nicholas. *Until Justice and Peace Embrace*. Grand Rapids: Eerdmans, 1983.

Yarhouse, Mark and James Sells. *Family Therapies: A Comprehensive Christian Appraisal*. Downers Grove, IL: InterVarsity, 2008.

11

A Faith-Filled Accounting Education

Steven Fowler

INTRODUCTION

THE BIBLE EXPLICITLY WARNS in the book of James that "not many of you should become teachers."[1] James further explains the reason for the warning as well by explaining that those who do become teachers "will be judged more strictly."[2] While this warning is given in the context of someone who wishes to teach the precepts of the Bible and, therefore, does not necessarily apply in all teaching situations, I believe that it does apply to the faculty of Christian colleges. After all, it is the responsibility of faculty to make the classroom experience meaningfully different from that of secular institutions. This alone renders them the most important element in distinguishing Christian colleges from secular institutions, with the primary subject matter of distinction being biblical precepts themselves. Indeed, faculty members of Christian colleges must embrace the gravity of the biblical warning as part of their job description.

This reality became evident to me shortly after I accepted a position as an accounting instructor at College of the Ozarks. As I reflected on this truth, it became clear as to why teachers will be judged more

---

1. James 3:1 (NET).
2. James 3:1 (NET).

strictly. Teachers are entrusted with a responsibility of molding and shaping young minds that are not fully developed. The relationship between teacher and student is comparable to that of a doctor and his patient. A doctor has a fiduciary responsibility to provide proper care for his patient. The doctor holds the patient's health in his hands and the patient trusts that the doctor will administer the best healthcare possible. Students likewise implicitly trust that a teacher will impart appropriate knowledge and skills that will benefit them in their lives. Jesus, in speaking of the dire consequences of negatively influencing children, stated that "if anyone causes one of these little ones who believe in me to sin, it would be better for him to have a huge millstone hung around his neck and to be drowned in the open sea."[3] The Lord takes very seriously the proper handling of influence over young minds. As his disciples, we should take this responsibility seriously as well.

CHRISTIAN WORLDVIEW

A worldview is "an underlying set of beliefs about the world that serves to shape all of our subsequent thinking."[4] Essentially, our worldview acts as a filter. External data that we receive through the senses goes through our filter and what comes out of the filter is our interpretation, which then guides our actions. If our filtering process is guided by biblical precepts, then it can be said that we have a Christian worldview and our actions will be guided by those principles. However, if our filtering process is guided by worldly precepts then our interpretation and subsequent actions will likewise be guided by worldly principles. It is important to note that a person's worldview is seen most clearly in their actions, including their economic activity.

In Luke 12, Jesus teaches the parable of the rich man whose land produced an abundant crop. The rich man's worldview was made clear by his reaction to his good fortune. He was delighted! He pondered how good his life would be with his excessive harvest. His only concern was how to store all that he had so that he could consume it at some later time. His solution was to tear down his barns and build them bigger so that he could eat, drink, relax, and celebrate for many years. He was suddenly in a position to help the poor or needy, but it never crossed his mind. Why

---

3. Matt 18:6 (NET).
4. Bartholomew and Goheen, *Living at the Crossroads*, 13.

would it? Serving others was not part of his worldview. There was no thought of serving a purpose higher than himself.

In contrast, the poor widow whom Jesus praised in Luke 21 put two small coins into the offering box, which was "everything she had to live on."[5] The worldview of the poor widow likewise was portrayed by her actions. While she gave only a small fraction compared to what others gave that day, Jesus said that she gave more than anyone. Why would she give so sacrificially? It was because her treasures were in heaven. She served a purpose higher than herself. Her worldview was revealed by her actions.

Now suppose that the rich man in Jesus' parable and the poor widow both professed to be Christians. Would the rich man be justified if he at least professed a Christian worldview? No! The book of James admonishes its readers to "be sure you live out the message and do not merely listen to it and so deceive yourselves."[6] According to James, the rich man would not be justified. Rather, he would be deceiving himself. This speaks to one of the most difficult problems that all Christians face, that of having consistency between beliefs and deeds. Even the apostle Paul struggled with this saying, "I do not do the good I want, but I do the very evil I do not want!"[7] If the apostle Paul had difficulties connecting his spiritual aspirations to his actions, then most certainly we all do!

Likewise, as difficult as it may be, as instructors we must strive to articulate a Christian worldview in both word and deed. Our worldview must guide our actions both inside and outside the classroom. If our purported worldview is strikingly different from our actions, then it is not in fact our worldview. A Christian worldview, of necessity, requires us to filter our thoughts, words, and actions through the prism of the "Golden Rule." That is, you should treat others as you would want them to treat you. In the context of the teacher and student relationship, often that means practicing patience and understanding. At other times, it might require a harsh rebuke. Jesus displayed great mercy to an adulterous woman in John 8. He calmed a mob by piercing their conscience with the words, "whoever among you is guiltless may be the first to throw a stone at her."[8] He then gently admonished her by saying, "go, and from

---

5. Luke 21:4 (NET).
6. Jas 1:22 (NET).
7. Rom 7:19 (NET).
8. John 8:7 (NET).

now do not sin anymore."[9] On the other hand, Jesus strongly rebuked Peter by stating, "Get behind me, Satan! You are a stumbling block to me, because you are not setting your mind on God's interests, but on man's."[10] It takes great wisdom to know when to use each approach. It is my belief that if an instructor will first exhibit godly love to his students, then when the time comes to issue a rebuke the student will know that the purpose of the rebuke is for their own benefit (whether or not they will admit it, of course, is a different story).

Essential to the attributes of an effective instructor are the virtues of credibility and integrity. An instructor who lives by the unstated principle of "do as I say, not as I do" has neither. In his book *The Fabric of Faithfulness*, Steven Garber articulates this principle by stating, "true education is always about learning to connect knowing with doing, belief with behavior."[11] Without integrity, an instructor will never connect belief with behavior in their own lives, much less the lives of their students, and where integrity is lacking so is credibility. Jesus, upon Phillip's request to "show us the Father," replied, "the person who has seen me has seen the Father!"[12] Christ could make this claim with boldness, having both integrity and credibility, because his words and actions were in unison. While in agony on the cross, he lovingly stated, "Father, forgive them, for they don't know what they are doing."[13] This, of course, aligned perfectly with his earlier teaching to "love your enemy and pray for those who persecute you."[14] While no person is righteous enough to make the claim, "he who has seen me has seen Christ," can we not, at a minimum, strive to say, "The person who has seen me has seen an imperfect servant who strives to display Christ-like characteristics?"

INTERSECTION OF ACCOUNTING AND CHRISTIANITY

Accounting is defined as "an information system that measures, processes, and communicates financial information about a business."[15] Up until the

---

9. John 8:11 (NET).
10. Matt 16:23 (NET).
11. Garber, *Fabric of Faithfulness*, 57.
12. John 14:8–9 (NET).
13. Luke 23:34 (NET).
14. Matt 5:44 (NET).
15. Needles et al., *Principles of Accounting*, 48.

stock market crash of 1929, there were no uniform accounting standards throughout America. The crash and subsequent onset of the Great Depression were the catalysts necessary for a push towards uniform standards. The process of setting such standards began in earnest at that time and is ongoing to this day as new standards are published periodically.

While uniform accounting standards are themselves a modern phenomenon, many tasks that are thought of today as elements of accounting have existed for millennia and related economic issues and practices appear throughout the Bible. For example, a historical accounting of funds that were collected for repairing the temple in Jerusalem is recorded in 2 Kgs in a process that would be considered "payroll" in modern accounting parlance:

> When they saw the chest was full of silver, the royal secretary and the high priest counted the silver that had been brought to the Lord's temple and bagged it up. They would then hand over the silver that had been weighed to the construction foremen assigned to the Lord's temple. They hired carpenters and builders to work on the Lord's temple, as well as masons and stonecutters. They brought wood and chiseled stone to repair the damage to the Lord's temple and also paid for all the other expenses. The silver brought to the Lord's temple was not used for silver bowls, trimming shears, basins, trumpets, or any kind of gold or silver implements. It was handed over to the foremen who used it to repair the Lord's temple. They did not audit the treasurers who disbursed the funds to the foremen, for they were honest.[16]

At the end of this passage, it is emphasized that because of the honesty of the treasurers an audit of the process was unnecessary. If every business were conducted with such integrity there would be no demand for the modern profession of auditing. Sadly, auditing is a thriving segment of the accounting profession simply because integrity and honesty cannot be assumed.

In the New Testament, Jesus also mentioned the process of accounting, specifically the importance of accurately budgeting and estimating the costs of construction:

> For which of you, wanting to build a tower, doesn't sit down first and compute the cost to see if he has enough money to complete it? Otherwise, when he has laid a foundation and is not

---

16. 2 Kgs 12:10–15 (NET).

able to finish the tower, all who see it will begin to make fun of him. They will say, this man began to build and was not able to finish.[17]

Likewise, taxation, another function that today is categorized within the realm of accounting, is encountered frequently in both the Gospels and the writings of Paul. The apostle Matthew was a hated publican, or tax collector, before being called by Jesus into his ministry. As the apostle himself describes, "As Jesus went on from there, he saw a man named Matthew sitting at the tax booth."[18]

An accounting instructor, therefore, teaches the modern techniques of an ancient vocation. These techniques are now defined by what are known as "accounting principles," "auditing standards," or "IRS regulations," among other names. These guidelines are written in language that is typical of the dominant modern/postmodern philosophies and worldview of the era in which they have been written. In *Living at the Crossroads: An Introduction to Christian Worldview*, the authors describes the modern mindset as "a narrative of progress that says we are moving toward ever-greater freedom and material prosperity, and that we are doing so by human effort alone, especially through science embodied in technology, and in the application of scientific principles to our social life, in economics, in politics, and in education."[19] It is no wonder, then, that spiritual matters are not given recognition in any contemporary secular accounting standards or manuals. Nor is accountability to God ever considered.

Yet, the standards themselves reveal a biblical infrastructure, which, to an individual who has a Christian worldview should come as no surprise. Indeed, a mature Christian worldview leads an individual to readily recognize biblical precepts embedded into the fabric of society. Psalm 127:1 reads, "[I]f the Lord does not build a house, then those who build it work in vain."[20] Modern accounting standards are no exception. These standards are in place to build a solid foundation for the process of accounting. A person with a Christian worldview should thus be aware that for the accounting profession at large to be perceived as dependable, the profession itself must model its principles after biblical precepts. Not

17. Luke 14:28–29 (NET).
18. Matt 9:9 (NET).
19. Bartholomew and Goheen, *Living at the Crossroads*, 7.
20. Ps 127:1 (NET).

surprisingly it does, although the biblical origins of these precepts are not often acknowledged. In the section that follows, I will be exploring several examples of the ways in which a biblical worldview must underly a coherent approach to accounting.

CODE OF PROFESSIONAL CONDUCT

The American Institute of Certified Public Accountants (AICPA) adopted their widely referenced "Code of Professional Conduct" in 1988 and has subsequently amended it as necessary. Found in it are broad definitions of acceptable conduct, as well as the prescribed handling of specific situations. Below are some of the specifics of the code along with comments as to how the code parallels biblical precepts.

Section 1.100.001 of the code states, "In the performance of any professional service, a member shall maintain objectivity and integrity, shall be free of conflicts of interest, and shall not knowingly misrepresent facts or subordinate his or her judgment to others."[21] The foundation of this section of the code was spelled out thousands of years ago on Mt. Sanai as recorded in Lev 19:11, " . . . you must not tell lies, and you must not deal falsely with your fellow citizen."[22] Obviously, the Bible did not borrow this principle from the AICPA Code of Professional Conduct. Rather, the AICPA, in an attempt to provide a foundation for the profession of accounting, borrowed this biblical precept, without giving credit, of course.

Section 0.300.050 reads, "Integrity is measured in terms of what is right and just. In the absence of specific rules, standards, or guidance, or in the face of conflicting opinions, a member should test decisions and deeds by asking: Am I doing what a person of integrity would do?"[23] The Code of Professional Conduct here recognizes what King Solomon knew and recorded about the importance of integrity around three thousand years ago in Prov 10:9, "the one who conducts himself in integrity will live securely, but the one who behaves perversely will be found out."[24]

Section 0.300.050 speaks to the importance of an accountant's objectivity: "Objectivity is a state of mind, a quality that lends value to

21. AICPA Code of Professional Conduct, 2021.
22. Lev 19:11 (NET).
23. AICPA Code of Professional Conduct, 2021.
24. Prov 10:9 (NET).

a member's services. It is a distinguishing feature of the profession. The principle of objectivity imposes the obligation to be impartial, intellectually honest, and free of conflicts of interest."[25] Indeed, if an accountant is supposed to report honest information, then the accountant must be objective. For as much as an accountant may want his company to be profitable, if it in fact is not, he must still report the facts. God is likewise an impartial judge of facts as recorded in Rom 2:11, "For there is no partiality with God."[26] The code unwittingly instructs accountants to take on God's characteristic of judging situations objectively.

Section 0.300.020 reads, "In carrying out their responsibilities as professionals, members should exercise sensitive professional and moral judgments in all their activities."[27] The AICPA recognizes the importance of making "moral judgments." In John 7:24, Jesus admonished his followers to "judge according to proper judgement."[28] The AICPA here is merely paraphrasing the words of Jesus in this section. However, nowhere does the AICPA define the source for their system of morality. Christians, on the other hand, know and understand that what is moral and just is defined in scripture. So, while the AICPA standards testify to the importance of "moral judgement," they fall short of admitting the source of those morals.

CONCEPTUAL FRAMEWORK

Besides the "Code of Professional Conduct," there are other areas of accounting standards which bear witness to biblical principles. One such area is the "conceptual framework." This framework is essentially a broad set of philosophies that serves as the background for a detailed set of accounting rules, known as generally accepted accounting principles (GAAP). GAAP has been described as "an accounting constitution."[29] Within the conceptual framework is the concept that accounting information must reflect the quality of "faithful representation." This basically means that the financial information must fairly represent the truth. As an example, if inventory valued on the balance sheet was purchased for

---

25. AICPA Code of Professional Conduct, 2021.
26. Rom 2:11 (NET).
27. AICPA Code of Professional Conduct, 2021.
28. John 7:24 (NET).
29. Spiceland et al., *Intermediate Accounting*, 19.

$100,000, but can only be sold for $10,000 because of obsolescence, then its value must be written down to reflect the decline in value. The write down of inventory is typically undesirable to management because it negatively affects reported profits, which in turn affect bonuses, thereby creating an ethical dilemma for management. Exod 20:16 reads, "you shall not give false testimony against your neighbor."[30] Fraudulent profit essentially is false testimony, which is communicated to investors and creditors through financial statements. Thus, this important biblical precept is embedded within accounting's "conceptual framework."

GENERALLY ACCEPTED AUDITING STANDARDS

Generally Accepted Auditing Standards (GAAS) also reflect a biblical foundation. One of the most important aspects of auditing is the evaluation of a company's "internal control." Internal controls are the policies and procedures that companies put in place to safeguard their assets and to ensure compliance with company policies. Separation of duties is one such internal control. Generally speaking, the more separated certain duties are, such as record keeping and custodianship of a company's assets, the less likely there will be any theft, embezzlement, or inaccurate reporting. Internal controls and even auditing itself are largely necessary due to the sinful nature of mankind. As quoted previously from 2 Kgs, "they did not audit the treasurers who disbursed the funds to the foremen, for they were honest."[31] If everyone were honest, there would be little need for auditors. The only role auditors would have would be to detect honest mistakes. As it is, however, auditors and companies also use internal controls to prevent fraud and theft. Exod 20:15 reads, "you shall not steal."[32] Unwittingly, internal control procedures are written to enforce a fundamental biblical principle.

It is doubtful that the accounting profession will ever acknowledge that it has appropriated biblical principles as its own. Therefore, it is the responsibility of Christian accounting educators to ensure that students recognize the source of the foundations of accounting standards. As Fant writes in his book *The Liberal Arts: A Student's Guide*, "Part of the task of Christian scholars in our culture is the recovery of these co-opted ideas,

30. Exod 20:16 (NET).
31. 2 Kgs 12:15 (NET).
32. Exod 20:15 (NET).

which affirm the legitimate place of Christianity at the table of the intellectual discourse."[33]

Over the course of the last century there have been numerous accounting scandals, all of which testify to the fact that neither GAAP, nor GAAS, nor any ethical code is sufficient to restrain the dishonest intentions of mankind. The accounting profession as well as governmental oversight bodies have attempted to legislate their moral code into the hearts of practitioners of accounting, while ignoring God at the same time. Their effort has consisted of writing an ever-expanding register of rules and standards, all with the intention of upholding an honest and fair profession. When each new scandal arises, the solution is always more rules.

There is perhaps no greater of example of this phenomenon than the aftermath of the financial collapse of 2008. Ferguson, in his book, *The Ascent of Money*, characterizes the crisis as "a spasm in the credit system precipitated by mounting defaults on a species of debt known euphemistically as subprime mortgages"[34] The calamity was years in the making and was the result of a multitude of questionable loans, which later turned into bad debts. In other words, if banks would not have loaned money to individuals unable to pay their mortgages, the crisis never would have occurred. To prevent a similar future crisis, the solution seems rather obvious. However, the United States Congress failed to grasp the heart of the problem it seems and instead passed the eight hundred and forty-eight page Wall Street Reform and Consumer Protection Act, which was signed into law in July of 2010. The law proved to be a "near-perfect example of excessive complexity in regulation. The Act required that regulators create 243 rules, conduct 67 studies and issue 22 periodic reports"[35] With so much red tape and bureaucracy, it is hard to say with confidence that a future crisis will be avoided, which sadly was received as welcome news in some circles. For instance, the AICPA in its preliminary guidance to CPAs released a statement touting the new opportunities created due to the complexity of the law, stating, "The many complexities and uncertainties of the new legislation create myriad

33. Fant, *Liberal Arts*, 40.
34. Ferguson, *Ascent of Money* (2008), 8.
35. Ferguson, *Ascent of Money* (2018), 383.

opportunities for CPAs to become indispensable partners in helping clients and employers understand and comply with new regulations."[36]

The truth is that internal restraint within a person that comes from a proper fear of God is the best deterrent to dishonesty. The beginning of wisdom is to fear the Lord.[37] A person that develops a mature Christian worldview will readily recognize that no accounting scandal of the last century would have taken place if those involved would have had a proper fear of God. Further, without godly fear future accounting scandals are certain to occur, even if the volume of accounting rules and regulations increase substantially. If every person were to become committed to upholding biblical principles, then all the rules put in place to prevent fraud and theft would be useless because they would prevent nothing.

CONCLUSION

There is nothing in God's world that is not subject to his truths. The Christian faith is more than a moral code or warm-hearted devotional practices, for the Christian faith influences not only how we act but also what we believe, how we think, how we write, how we teach, how we lead, how we govern, and how we treat one another.[38] Yet, providing a "Christian education" is an art, not a science. The art involves using a Christian worldview to apply the truths of Scripture to modern settings, including the field of accounting. Steven Garber, in his book *The Fabric of Faithfulness*, writes of former Nazi, Albert Speer, who thrived as an architect during the rule of Adolf Hitler. Speer was not a supporter of Hitler's policies, but he reasoned within himself that he was only providing architectural expertise, and thus disconnected his personal life and belief system from his business enterprises. The book describes him as "a type which is becoming increasingly important in all belligerent countries: the pure technician, the classless bright young man without background."[39] Truly, if accounting students from Christian colleges only learn the technicalities of accounting, then we have failed them. Amen!

---

36. AICPA Financial Reform.
37. Prov 9:10.
38. Dockery and George, *Great Tradition of Christian Thinking*, 79.
39. Garber, *Fabric of Faithfulness*, 111.

BIBLIOGRAPHY

AICPA Code of Professional Conduct, 2021. https://pub.aicpa.org/codeofconduct/ethicsresources/et-cod.pdf.

AICPA Financial Reform—What It Means for CPAs. https://www.aicpa.org/research/studiesandpapers/whatfinancialreformmeansforcpas.html.

Bartholomew, Craig and Michael Goheen. *Living at the Crossroads: An Introduction to Christian Worldview*. Grand Rapids: Baker, 2008.

Dockery, David S. and Timothy, George. *The Great Tradition of Christian Thinking: A Student's Guide*. Wheaton, IL: Crossway, 2012.

Fant, Gene. *The Liberal Arts: A Student's Guide*. Wheaton, IL: Crossway, 2012.

Ferguson, Niall. *The Ascent of Money: A Financial History of the World*. New York: Penguin, 2008.

———. *The Ascent of Money: A Financial History of the World*. New York: Penguin, 2018.

Garber, Steven. *The Fabric of Faithfulness*. Downers Grove, IL: InterVarsity, 1996.

Needles, Belverd, et al. *Principles of Accounting*. 12th ed. Boston: Cengage, 2013.

Spiceland, David, et al. *Intermediate Accounting*. 7th ed. New York: McGraw-Hill, 2013.

Faithful Education in Mathematics and the Natural Sciences

12

Faithful Education in the Discipline of Human Biology

GABRIELA GALEY

INTRODUCTION

IN HIS BOOK, *THE Fabric of Faithfulness,* Steven Garber observes that *convictions, character,* and *community* are the three major influences on how to weave together our belief and behavior into a fabric of faithfulness. Believers who manage to do so are the ones who will find their purpose and place in this world and who are able to serve God with integrity of heart and mind. Or as Garber says,

> Men and women who sustain visions of faith over a lifetime learn to take into their hearts the disappointments and sorrows that come to them, finding a deeper, truer faith as they do so. Rather than being shipwrecked by the brokenness of the world, they learn to navigate their way through, holding onto the integrity of their vocations through life. Indeed, they have *woven together belief and behavior into a fabric of faithfulness* and that has kept their hearts alive in the face of evils and injustice, grief and pain.[1]

I have found these same observations to be so true in my own life.

1. Garber, *Fabric of Faithfulness*, 18.

Convictions

Looking back, I remember when God called me to do mission work. It was a clear call, and I was already in medical school at the time. Although I had in mind a distinct picture of working among children in rural Africa, God made it very clear to me that it would be up to him *where*, *when*, *with whom*, and *in what capacity* I would go. Halfway through medical school, God put my "vision" and passion to the test. He led me to quit medical school, get married, and attend seminary. In retrospect, I can see how God has used these seminary years to shape a solid Christian worldview in me and to lay an even deeper foundation of faith, which he would test and solidify over the years.

Character

During my seminary years, one of my professors, Dr. Mary Wilder, became a close friend and my spiritual mentor. Dr. Mary had been a missionary doctor to Pakistan for seventeen years before returning home to Portland to take care of her aging mother and teach at the seminary. Many of our meetings took place in her office, where we both unpacked our lunch and enjoyed our time together. She had such spiritual wisdom, and because of our common medical background, I was drawn to her even more. After we found out that I was pregnant while still attending seminary, she was the first person I told. Dr. Mary taught me by example how to stay true to your convictions and beliefs on this winding road of life, which is often filled with obstacles and turns we do not expect, much less know how to handle. She was the person who consistently encouraged and exhorted me to seek God first, no matter what.

Community

After graduating from seminary, my husband and I moved to Germany where God opened doors for us to be involved in missions—and for me to finish medical school. From early on in my life, God had sparked in me a fascination about the wonders and workings of the human body, and this spark has not diminished over the years. Furthermore, through regular Bible reading and study, God revealed to me the importance of understanding the human body as body, soul, and spirit. Through different circumstances, God has also led me to study nutrition, which so beautifully complements maintaining a healthy human body, fit for serving our Lord. Last, but not least, God also gave me a great desire and passion to share the knowledge I have acquired during my life. Over the years I developed relationships, both in the United States and Germany, with many equally committed Christians, who provide a network of stimulation and support for me to live out my worldview and beliefs in whatever position God has placed me.

When I think about how I can faithfully educate students in the discipline of human biology, I know that this is a calling much greater than merely imparting knowledge about the human body. It is a quest to help students understand that man is not simply a biological organism, but rather a being with a body, soul, and spirit, who is created in the image of the living God. It is a quest to spark in my students the same fascination about the human body that gripped me so many years ago. And most importantly, it is a quest to equip students during their college years to stand strong in their faith and find their purpose and place in this world as servants of God within their various vocations. Just as these major influences (*conviction*, *character*, and *community*) have helped me to weave together belief and behavior into a fabric of faithfulness, allowing me to serve God unswervingly in many different capacities, we should strive to create a college environment that provides students with the same three avenues of influence. We should empower them to establish and weave together their own belief and behavior into a fabric of faithfulness, without having to choose between faith and vocation—between serving God and earning a living.

WORLDVIEWS (CONVICTIONS)

Even though many people could not verbalize an answer to the question of what worldview they hold, every human being develops a system of beliefs and values as he grows up and interacts with his family and culture. Donald K. Smith defines a worldview as "an overall term embracing values and beliefs. It includes the culture's ideas about the nature of reality, the nature of God, of humankind, of the universe, and of the relationships between God, the universe, and human beings."[2] Paul G. Hiebert adds another insight: "At the core of each culture, there seem

2. Smith, *Creating Understanding*, 257.

to be certain basic assumptions about the nature of reality and morality. Many are implicit, because they are taken for granted and never questioned. Together, they form a more or less consistent worldview that orders people's experiences and gives meaning to their lives."[3]

The importance of worldviews is that they "become ways of life, always and everywhere."[4] We live according to our beliefs and values. Or as Bartholomew and Goheen describe it, "Our worldview, the story we accept as true of which our lives are part, will give meaning to our lives and influence our behavior."[5] In other words, we try to make sense of our life. Every person will be pressed at some point in their lives to ask the question, "What is this life all about?"[6]

A distinctively Christian worldview will have the following marks: The Bible is the authoritative source of knowledge which answers the fundamental questions of existence, origins, God, the nature of man, his purpose and destiny, and the nature of evil. All things were created by an eternal, trinitarian God. Man was created in the image of this God and his purpose is to glorify him and to spend eternity in the joy and pleasure of his presence. Through the fall, sin and death, and thereby separation from God, entered the world. God remedied the problem of sin by sending his eternal Son in the person of Jesus Christ to accomplish redemption for mankind by destroying the works of Satan through his death on the cross. Man can now be restored to eternal fellowship with God by placing his faith in the finished work of Christ on the cross.

The Christian worldview is only one of many other worldviews. The Enlightenment philosophy of the seventeenth and eighteenth centuries has strongly shaped western European and North American thought with its emphasis on human reason and autonomy. Bartholomew and Goheen see it like this:

> The story that has shaped Western culture for several centuries is a narrative of progress that says we are moving toward ever-greater freedom and material prosperity, and that we are doing so by human effort alone, especially through science embodied in technology, and in the application of scientific principles to our social life, in economics, in politics, and in education.[7]

3. Hiebert, *Cultural Anthropology*, 369.
4. Garber, *Fabric of Faithfulness*, 188.
5. Bartholomew and Goheen, *Living at the Crossroads*, 5.
6. Garber, *Fabric of Faithfulness*, 179.
7. Bartholomew and Goheen, *Living at the Crossroads*, 7.

They further argue that for us as believers, it is of critical importance that we develop a solid Christian or biblical worldview, or else our surrounding culture will press us into its mold of thinking:

> Thus at both the academic and practical levels, serious Christian engagement with life and culture—that is, Christian mission—requires the development of a Christian worldview. Since we live and think out of our worldviews, it not a question of whether we have one worldview or not. The question instead is this: Out of which worldview will we think, live, and work? If we refuse to develop and indwell a Christian worldview, we will merely leave ourselves vulnerable to the influence of the worldviews present in the culture that surrounds us.[8]

To what drastic extent our worldviews and thinking have been influenced by our culture is well addressed in Mary Poplin's book, *Is Reality Secular? Testing the Assumptions of Four Global Worldviews*. In this book, she thoroughly discusses the assumptions of four major worldviews: material naturalism, secular humanism, pantheism, and monotheism (referred to as Judeo-Christianity), where she opens with the profound observation that "truth has become an idea rather than a description of reality, and it can be set aside even though seeking truth is or once was the sole reason for the university."[9]

In order for us to successfully hold on to our Christian worldview while engaging in the culture around us, it is imperative that we realize that there will be a conflict within us. This conflict arises from the fact that "each culture tells and lives out a world-story that is to some degree incompatible with the gospel."[10] If the worldview of our society is radically different than a Christian worldview, this conflict has the potential to break us and disable us from living lives successfully in service to God. The challenge is to learn to live at the crossroads, as Bartholomew and Goheen describe it, the intersection of two stories, which both claim to be true and comprehensive:

> As those who have embraced the gospel, we are members of a community that believes the Bible to be the true story of the world. But as participating and living members of the cultural community, we are also part of the other story that has been

---

8. Bartholomew and Goheen, *Living at the Crossroads*, 29.
9. Poplin, *Is Reality Secular?*, 13–14.
10. Bartholomew and Goheen, *Living at the Crossroads*, 6–7.

shaping Western culture for a very long time. We cannot simply opt out of the surrounding culture: our lives are woven into its institutions, customs, language, relationships, and social patterns. Our embodying of the kingdom of God must take cultural shape in our own particular time and place. So we find ourselves at the crossroads, where we live as part of two communities, in two stories each largely incompatible with the other, but both of which claim to be true—and claim the whole of our lives.[11]

Recognizing this conflict is one of the key elements to our success in learning to live at the crossroads. We need to make our students aware of the realities that govern their thinking and therefore their lives. Studying worldviews, as Bartholomew and Goheen expound, "can make us more fully aware not only of the comprehensive scope of the gospel and of our mission, of the religious power and all-embracing reach of our own culture's secular 'faith,' but also of the unbearable tension that comes with living at the crossroads where these two stories intersect."[12] Steven Garber looks at this from yet a different angle and puts forth the following thesis, "what we believe about the most important things in life affects the way that we live in the world; but the reverse is also true: the way that we live and the world in which we live affect what we believe."[13] The task is not an easy one. And just as in soccer "a good offense is often the best defense," I would like to apply this principle to our lives and strongly agree with Bartholomew and Goheen:

> If we are to live faithfully in the biblical story, we must become critical participants in the cultures that surround us . . . As critical participants in culture, however, we will often find ourselves standing in opposition to it, reflecting and challenging the idolatry that twists, and distorts its development. There are thus two sides to this faithful engagement: affirmation and rejection, participation and opposition, solidarity and separation. This has often been expressed as being "in the world" but not "of the world" (John 17:13–18).[14]

---

11. Bartholomew and Goheen, *Living at the Crossroads*, 8.
12. Bartholomew and Goheen, *Living at the Crossroads*, 174.
13. Garber, *Fabric of Faithfulness*, 194–95.
14. Bartholomew and Goheen, *Living at the Crossroads*, 132–33.

HIGHER EDUCATION (CHARACTER AND COMMUNITY)

Higher education can have all kinds of shapes and forms. Growing up in Germany and having attended three different medical universities has given me insights into an education that is very much aimed at producing highly trained medical doctors. General education in Germany takes place in high school, a school system much more rigorous than what I have seen in the United States. Once someone attends university, however, all subjects the student takes relate directly to his specific discipline. The student-professor ratio is very high and there are no personal relationships between professors and students, at least not in the early university years. I hardly remember any names or faces of any of my professors over these six years. Attending seminary in Portland, Oregon, on the other hand, turned my whole view of higher education upside down. The professors did everything they could to help me with my studies; they befriended me and were available outside of class; some even invited my husband and I to their homes to share a meal with them and their family. I remember every professor I had during those years—their names, their faces, and their character. We are still in contact with a lot of them, even though it has been over thirty years. These professors had a tremendous influence in my life that changed me forever.

Christian Liberal Arts

How does all this apply to higher education on an undergraduate level? What does it mean to be educated in the liberal arts, in particular the Christian liberal arts? Gene C. Fant shows the origin of liberal learning from the ancient Greek perspective: "Liberal learning, sometimes called the liberal arts (as distinct from the practical arts), aimed at the breadth of knowledge that included a wide range of subjects that trained the mind to analyze challenges and formulate solutions or to anticipate future opportunities and strategies."[15] He states that formerly the liberal arts "sought to prepare morally wholesome persons according to the appropriate culture's standards,"[16] And also that "traditional liberal learning, then,

---

15. Fant, *Liberal Arts*, 24–25.
16. Fant, *Liberal Arts*, 29.

always connects the individual with a larger purpose beyond the self."[17] Steven Garber quotes Edward Long, whose book, *Higher Education as a Moral Enterprise*, contains the following statement that beautifully sums up this concept:

> Higher education dares not become merely the avenue to success; it must be the gateway for responsibility. It should not be concerned with competence alone, but with commitment to civic responsibility. An academic degree should not be a hunting license only for self-advancement, but an indication of abilities to seek, cultivate and sustain a richer common weal. It is not enough to achieve cultural literacy; we must engender social concern. It is not enough merely to open the mind; it is necessary to cultivate moral intentionality in a total selfhood.[18]

If Christianity is added to the purpose of liberal learning, then, according to Fant, "education in the liberal Christian context has the chance to redirect the individual's impulses away from unworthy thoughts and futile actions into a higher vision of what may be possible in service to God and his people."[19] This is an incredible aspect of education, which has a magnitude way beyond teaching students a vocation or profession. Garber concluded well with his statement, "Education must be oriented to the preparation of a calling and not just training for a career."[20]

How do we give liberal learning a Christian context? It certainly is not simply an addendum, and definitely not an easy undertaking. Christian higher education has to aim at helping students to develop a Christian worldview and teaching every subject through the lens of Scripture. Dockery and George say it well:

> As Christians ... we are not free to view the Bible as though we had it at our disposal, as though we ourselves were not claimed by its story, as though we had already mastered this ancient document and could now move on to other bodies of knowledge without the discernment we have learned from Scripture ... Divorced from the biblical narrative, a purely abstract knowledge becomes not only self-referential but also self-defeating, fatuous, and sterile.[21]

17. Fant, *Liberal Arts*, 45.
18. Garber, *Fabric of Faithfulness*, 92–93.
19. Fant, *Liberal Arts*, 48–49.
20. Garber, *Fabric of Faithfulness*, 89.
21. Dockery and George, *Great Tradition of Christian Thinking*, 61–62.

Teaching through the lens of Scripture, however, will always leave us on a battlefield, as Bartholomew and Goheen keenly observed:

> Faithful Christian scholarship will be characterized by both an acknowledgement of the insights of the Western cultural tradition of scholarship and a critique of the ideological settings in which those insights are embedded. Since all academic work is an accounting of the order of creation, and since God has upheld that order and upheld the image of God in humanity, scholarship will always give insight into God's world. And since human sin and idolatry affect all cultural endeavors, academic insights into God's creation order will always be distorted to some degree . . . Scholarship, like all other aspects of human life, is on the field of battle between the kingdom of God and the kingdom of darkness. Both powers vie to shape and direct scholarship for their own ends. This is a vital place for Christians to be involved in culture.[22]

Without a Christian worldview that addresses the "deepest human questions—those of meaning and morality," education becomes an end in itself.[23] We might produce qualified men and women, but we miss the whole point of training responsible servants for God. If we fail to address the deepest human questions and help our students develop a solid Christian worldview, and if we fail to teach them all disciplines through the lens of Scripture, we will cripple our students' ability to connect their beliefs with their behavior.

The Importance of the College Years

I love the quote from Jacques Ellul that Steven Garber used for the introduction to his first chapter, entitled "Learning to Care":

> Remember your Creator during your youth: when all possibilities lie open before you and you can offer all your strength intact for his service. The time to remember is not after you become senile and paralyzed! Then it is not too late for your salvation, but too late for you to serve as the presence of God in the midst of the world and the creation. You must take sides earlier—when you can actually make choices, when you have

---

22. Bartholomew and Goheen, *Living at the Crossroads*, 164–65.
23. Garber, *Fabric of Faithfulness*, 82.

many paths opening at your feet, before the weight of necessity overwhelms you.[24]

These words carry such weight and truth. For many of us, the years between adolescence and adulthood are spent in college. These are critical years that shape our lives. Garber calls them the "years of deciding how one will make sense of life over the course of life."[25] All of a sudden, these young adults are on their own. Their beliefs and values will be challenged. Many will ask themselves, "Is what mom and dad believe really what I believe?" Worldviews are not necessarily being formed from scratch, since, according to Smith, two-thirds of an individual's basic knowledge about the nature of reality, God, humankind, and the world have been formed, mostly nonverbally, by the time a child is seven years old.[26] But worldviews are certainly being challenged and developed during college, and depending on the influence during these years, the outcome of the students' worldview at the end can be quite different from the worldview they had at the beginning of their college education. The question is the direction of this change: will it be more toward a Christian worldview or not?

Over many years, Steven Garber had been studying questions like: What happens during the university years to students who come through with habits and mind so in place that they move on into the responsibilities and privileges of adulthood without compromising their basic integrity and faith? "How does a person decide which cares and commitments will give shape and substance to life, for life? How do students learn to consciously connect what they believe about the world with how they live in the world?"[27] He concludes his studies with the following thesis:

> During the critical years in which moral meaning is being formed in ways that last, students need to be people who: [1] Develop a worldview that can make sense of life, facing the challenge of truth and coherence in an increasingly pluralist world; [2] Pursue a relationship with a teacher whose life incarnates the worldview the student is learning to embrace; [3] Commit themselves to others who have chosen to live their lives imbedded in that same worldview, journeying together in truth after the vision of a coherent and meaningful life. Is this a guarantee

24. Garber, *Fabric of Faithfulness*, 37.
25. Garber, *Fabric of Faithfulness*, 95.
26. Smith, *Creating Understanding*, 260–1.
27. Garber, *Fabric of Faithfulness*, 33–34.

of the good life? We can never engineer human happiness, of course. And yet we can listen and learn, doing our best to understand the world that God has made and our place in it. But when the day is done, every truly good life is always, first and last, a story of grace.[28]

I have spent much time demonstrating the importance for us as faculty to help our students develop a Christian worldview; however, Garber's second point clearly goes beyond that. First, we as Christians need to incarnate our own worldview. Second, if students see that we are true and real to our convictions on and off campus and pursue a relationship with us, we need to be available to them as mentors. According to Garber, the combination of living out our own worldview and being available to our students can have a tremendous outcome: "Again and again, it is that dynamic relationship of a faculty member opening his life up to a student which enables young people to understand that their worldview can also become a way of life."[29] There is no greater joy for me as a professor at a Christian college than to have students coming to me asking for guidance in certain personal decisions or for prayer about issues in their lives. Some of my students have even asked me to mentor them in how to walk in intimate fellowship with God on a daily basis and how to more thoroughly study and know the Bible, even though I am their biology instructor. My husband and I have always tried to be available to our students; some we have mentored weekly (sometimes for years), with some we have conducted pre-marital counseling, and many of them have been to our home to share a meal or spend personal time with us. Over the years, I have been privileged to witness the impact this can have in the lives of students.

Garber goes on, however, to say that the role of a mentor is limited:

> But our study also shows that teachers and mentors, on their own, are insufficient models. As crucial as they are, their role is to act as a bridge into a larger, more communal embodiment of the convictions the student is learning to live with. For those who take their university-framed ideas about what is real and true and right and deepen rather than discard them as they move into the responsibilities of adulthood, they have seen a social construction of their beliefs in the life of communities along the way. Often more stumbling than strategic, they have

---

28. Garber, *Fabric of Faithfulness*, 185.
29. Garber, *Fabric of Faithfulness*, 143.

time and again found themselves among like-minded people whose own deepest beliefs are incarnated in a common life.[30]

The students will have to forge friendships with people whose common life is embedded in the same worldview as theirs. These friends usually become friends for life and help them to live their lives with integrity of heart and mind and to remain true to their convictions. All human beings in every generation and every culture long for a belief system that is coherent; for Christians that would be a faith that is coherent.[31]

My hope and prayer is that students at our college will actually develop a biblical worldview, find a mentor that incarnates these convictions, and form friendships with those who hold the same beliefs and values. I want to be a professor whose name and face students will remember because I was available for them and because of the godly influence I had on their lives.

THE DISCIPLINE OF HUMAN BIOLOGY

Educating students faithfully in the discipline of human biology is a quest with its own beauty and challenges. As Christians we have certain beliefs (convictions) in our understanding of the natural world and the human body. Scripture clearly teaches that the human body is not merely a clump of cells which function together as a living organism, but rather a being with a body, soul, and spirit, created in the image of the living God. But even within a Christian worldview, we will find differences in beliefs and values concerning biology, which leads to some questions that must be addressed.

There is the question of origins, a topic that has caused much debate among Christian scientists. Some hold to the creation account as we read it in Genesis. These scientists will be forced to interpret scientific data found in the last decades differently than commonly interpreted by most of the scientific community. Creationist groups often lack credibility with the vast majority of scientists and are therefore under tremendous pressure while maintaining their convictions.

Others hold the view that God is the Creator, but evolution is the mechanism used by God in the creation process. As Bible-believing Christians, they run into problems as well. Some of the questions they

---

30. Garber, *Fabric of Faithfulness*, 187.
31. Garber, *Fabric of Faithfulness*, 191.

will have to answer are: Was there a historical Adam and Eve? At what point did God decide that the species had advanced enough to be called "human," to "have been created in the image of God?" If there was no historical Adam and Eve, when did sin enter the world? If there was no historical Adam and Eve, how much of the rest of the Bible can be trusted as historically accurate? If God took millions of years to create the earth, will he also take millions of years to create a new heavens and earth as described in Revelation?

Yet another approach arose in the mid-1990s, that of the "Intelligent Design" movement, which sits in opposition to both young-earth-creationism and theistic evolution. The main argument for ID is, briefly stated, that certain features of the universe and some biological systems exist that cannot be accounted for by naturalistic mechanisms and are better explained with an intelligent cause. Some of the arguments include the irreducible complexity of certain biological structures, the complex and specific information content in DNA, the life-sustaining physical architecture of the universe, and the geologically rapid origin of biological diversity in the fossil record.[32] According to Venema and Paulton, the idea of intelligent design was strongly critiqued by many scientists, because it would require a redefinition of the term science to include the supernatural.[33]

The question about origins is certainly a significant topic among Christians, but most biologists do not consider it as *the* most important one. I believe that students need to be made aware of the conflicts each view holds, but there is no need to press them into believing the same way as their professors do. Moreover, it should be noted that the scientific method is limited to the realm of natural phenomena, and therefore cannot prove or disprove the existence of a supernatural being (e.g., the God of the Bible). Agreeing with Bartholomew and Goheen, students as well as professors must be aware that a Christian worldview and western scholarship will have conflicts with which we have to deal, but not necessarily to be afraid of, since all truth is God's truth:

> This twofold cultural stance means two things when it comes to dealing with scholarship that is shaped by other religious commitments. On the one hand, since God is faithful to his creation, much true insight into God's world will come to us

32. Center for Science and Culture, "What is intelligent design?"

33. Venema and Paulton, "Christian Perspective on Biology," in Downey and Porter, *Christian Worldview and the Academic Disciplines*, 112–15.

from the non-Christian academic community; on the other hand, the idolatry that underlies Western scholarship will be at work to distort that insight. The task of the Christian scholar is to embrace and to celebrate true insights into the world from whatever source they come, but also to uncover the idolatry that has twisted them.[34]

Another subject that must be addressed in teaching biology through the lens of Scripture is the limits of our research. I watched a DVD with my class about "cracking the code," i.e., finding the sequence of the human genome. This great advancement in science, as well as other achievements of the last century, comes with numerous ethical issues and a tremendous responsibility (character) Christians must wrestle with. Are there moral limits to scientific development? How far are we allowed to go in our research and intervene in God's creation, even under the pretense of healing diseases? Is it okay for parents or a single mother to decide that a child with Down syndrome is too much of a burden and therefore should not be allowed to live? What about more severe diseases or anomalies that will cause a child to die within hours, days, or a few years after birth? Is it okay to abort those? What if the mother's life is endangered by continuing a pregnancy? If we choose "in vitro fertilization," what will happen to the rest of the fertilized eggs which were not implanted? Do we donate them to stem cell research? Do we opt to have them all implanted, even if that would mean to possibly bear quadruplets and quintuplets and might endanger the mother's well-being? Do we have them destroyed or frozen for later usage? Does a fertilized egg already have a soul? What kind of contraception should a married couple use? Is contraception even okay in God's eyes? Can we ethically choose a method of contraception that does not hinder ovulation, but rather the implantation of an already fertilized egg? What if we were ignorant of the fact that this is how certain contraceptives work?

These are tough, tough questions. My attempt is to address as many thought-provoking questions as possible while I teach students about the human body. And even though, more often than not, there is not one right answer, our students will have to be made aware of the technological advances and their ethical problems. To simply give them answers to these questions would not benefit them in their character formation. Rather, we must teach them critical thinking, because by the time they graduate,

---

34. Bartholomew and Goheen, *Living at the Crossroads*, 163.

science will already have leaped into new spheres. We must train them to go back to the Bible with their questions and see what God says, for example, about discrimination (choosing only healthy embryos), human beings (created in the image of God), and so forth. Not all answers will be clearly stated in the Bible, but we can always look for principles. One day these students might find themselves in a position where they will have to make one of these tough decisions. They will have to be prepared to think critically and biblically, for exactly this situation. Ultimately, they will be accountable to God for their actions. Knowledge is not enough; we want them to become responsible Christians and American citizens. This responsibility goes beyond their personal lives. Their participation, or lack thereof, in politics and their surrounding culture will influence what will or will not be allowed in this country. Dockery and George conclude the following:

> Disconnected from the biblical story, such disciplines can tell us how things work but not what they are for; how to clone a human baby but not whether this should be done; how to construct an atomic bomb but not whether it should be used; how to build a maximum security prison but not how to treat the prisoners. Without some teleology, there is no flourishing and no future for the human community.[35]

Our knowledge that humans are created in God's image and that they have a body, soul, and spirit must have implications for human biology and medicine. To omit this fact from our approach in dealing with people or to find treatments for diseases is an enormous mistake. We have known for a long time that an aching, sick soul can manifest itself in bodily sicknesses. The worldview that has been shaping our Western culture in the last decades does not encourage us to think about humans as physical and spiritual beings. The beauty of teaching at College of the Ozarks is that I can incorporate all these aspects into my teaching. I have the freedom to tell the students that ultimate healing will not take place in this world, no matter how good of a nurse, physical therapist, doctor, or dietician they may become. I can comfort my Christian students with physical disabilities or illnesses that one day their bodies will be healed—for eternity. Our life here on earth is only temporary; our knowledge, despite how far we have come, only limited.

---

35. Dockery and George, *Great Tradition of Christian Thinking*, 62.

CONCLUSION

Writing this chapter has been an amazing journey. It has changed my view and approach of teaching anatomy and physiology at a Christian liberal arts college. It has clarified in my mind which factors contributed to my own journey of navigating through life while holding on to my faith. Finally, it has convicted me that, as a Christian college educator, I should strive for nothing less than equipping my students to stand strong in their faith and find their purpose and place in this world as servants of God within their various vocations.

BIBLIOGRAPHY

Center for Science and Culture. "What is intelligent design?" http://www.intelligentdesign.org/whatisid.php.

Dockery, David S., and Timothy George, eds. *The Great Tradition of Christian Thinking: A Student's Guide*. Wheaton, IL: Crossway, 2012.

Downey, Deane and Stanley Porter, eds. *Christian Worldview and the Academic Disciplines: Crossing the Academy*. Eugene, OR: Pickwick, 2009.

Fant, Gene C. *The Liberal Arts: A Student's Guide*. Wheaton, IL: Crossway, 2012.

Garber, Steven. *The Fabric of Faithfulness: Weaving Together Belief and Behavior*. Downers Grove, IL: IVP, 2007.

Bartholomew, Craig and Michael Goheen. *Living at the Crossroads: An Introduction to Christian Worldview*. Grand Rapids: Baker Academic, 2008.

Hiebert, Paul G. *Cultural Anthropology*, 2nd ed. New York: Baker Academic, 1990.

Holmes, Arthur F. *The Idea of a Christian College*. Grand Rapids: Eerdmans, 1987.

McGrath, Alister E. *Theology: The Basics*, 2nd ed. Malden, MA: Wiley-Blackwell, 2008.

Poplin, Mary. *Is Reality Secular? Testing the Assumptions of Four Global Worldviews*. Downers Grove, IL: IVP, 2014.

Rapinchuk, Kyle D. and Dusty Deevers. "King, Kingdom, and Kingdom People: A Biblical, Theological, and Worldview Approach to Scripture." https://theclassicalthistle.files.wordpress.com/2017/08/king-kingdom-and-kingdom-people-a-theology-of-the-hebrew-bible.pdf.

Smith, Donald K. *Creating Understanding: A Handbook for Christian Communication Across Cultural Landscapes*. Grand Rapids: Zondervan, 1992.

13

Faithful Education in Mathematics

Craig L. Haile

"It is the heart which experiences God, and not the reason."

—Blaise Pascal[1]

"You know, I don't think math is a science. I think it is a religion."

—Calvin, from the comic strip *Calvin and Hobbes*, by Bill Watterson[2]

Hanging on the wall of my office is a simple black and white framed poster which shows my academic "family tree," produced as part of the Mathematics Genealogy Project.[3] The early scholars in my academic genealogy studied theology, languages, philosophy, medicine, physics and mathematics as intertwined fields.[4] By contrast today, while mathematics is still considered the "queen and servant of science," it is generally

---

1. Pascal, *Pensees*, 95. Blaise Pascal was a French mathematician and physicist, who lived from 1623–62.
2. Watterson, *Calvin and Hobbes*. In the comic strip, the villainous teacher who causes Calvin much misery is Miss Wormwood, a reference to *The Screwtape Letters* (1942) by C.S. Lewis.
3. "Mathematics Genealogy Project."
4. At the top of my academic tree is Gregory Palamas, "a prominent theologian and ecclesiastical figure of the late Byzantine period" ("Mathematics Genealogy Project").

perceived (with Calvin's opinion above an exception) to be neutral to and disconnected from theology, worldview, and Christian faith.[5]

I believe the reason for this common view is that when most people (including mathematicians) think of mathematics, they are thinking strictly of the content of mathematics, the straightforward question of how to do it. But to faithfully educate our students, it is also important to consider questions of why we choose to do mathematics, and what degree of trust we place in mathematical "truths." How we arrive at our mathematical philosophy can have implications for how we arrive at our worldview, which in turn can impact how we understand, teach, and apply mathematics. In this chapter, I plan to step out of my comfort zone (the content of mathematics) and consider carefully this whole view of the mathematical field and what I believe are key tenets of a faithful education in mathematics.

A LOOK BACK

"Do nothing from selfish ambition or conceit, but in humility count others more significant than yourselves. Let each of you look not only to his own interests, but also to the interests of others."

—PHILIPPIANS 2:3–4[6]

"So if you asked me: why do mathematics? I would say: mathematics helps people flourish."

FRANCIS SU[7]

I wish I could say I chose to pursue mathematics at the outset because I was concerned with the interests of others and wanted to help people flourish, but my actual reasons are a lot more self-centered. Math didn't have the dirt, heat, and cold of farming, the smells of biology, the potential

---

5. See Bell, *Mathematics*.
6. Phil 2:3–4 (ESV).
7. Su, "Mathematics for Human Flourishing," in Pitici, *Best Writing on Mathematics*, 118. Francis Su is an American mathematician, former president of the Mathematical Association of America, and former board member of the Association of Christians in the Mathematical Sciences.

explosions of chemistry, the dress code of business, or (so I thought) the pages of writing of the humanities and social sciences.

Also, although I did well in most subjects, I stood out from my peers in mathematics. This was not because I was exceptional in talent. Rather, while I found mathematics interesting, most everyone else seemed to really dislike it. Even my friends who were good students tended to see math as just a means to an end, a subject to be tolerated in order to have the tools necessary for the discipline they were really interested in. I was probably most attracted to math just by the fact that I could do it any time, any place, with at most the requirement of pencil and paper. As an added bonus, many other academic studies were perceived by me at the time to be in conflict and tension with the Christian faith, and mathematics didn't seem to have that baggage. Although I know the majority of people who taught me mathematics K-16 were Christian, and many served as mentors and encouragers over my life, the content they taught seemed no different than what I might encounter with a non-Christian mathematics teacher. I did not see this as a drawback; in fact, it encouraged me that I could go as far as I wanted in mathematics without a potential challenge or compromise to my faith. This has always caused me to ponder, what (if anything) makes a Christian mathematician different in the mathematics field, and what (if anything) can a Christian mathematician contribute to the body of Christ outside of the field of mathematics. This leads to the current question: how could I faithfully educate my students any differently than any other mathematician?

WHAT MAKES A MATHEMATICIAN?

"A mathematician is a device for turning coffee into theorems."

—Alfréd Rényi[8]

Almost every college or university student must study mathematics at some level, as quantitative literacy and problem solving are essential skills. But why would someone choose the study of mathematics as their vocation, and could this choice be influenced by or influence their Christian faith? I would say that one of the primary qualities of a mathematician is that they are very bothered by a lack of understanding, and have a certain

---

8. Quoted in Suzuki, *History of Mathematics*, 731. Alfréd Rényi was a Hungarian mathematician, who lived from 1921–70. This quote is often ascribed to Paul Erdös, another well-known Hungarian mathematician, who lived from 1913–96.

tenaciousness that drives them to seek answers that satisfy them not just in an emotional sense but also in a rigorous rational and logical way. Of course, people in other fields have this drive as well.[9] What distinguishes a mathematician is that they usually care the most about problems that are not limited to the context of any discipline or application. The same theory or technique can apply to music, engineering, or psychology, and mathematics provides a vehicle for abstraction that allows all these problems to be considered under one umbrella.

Most mathematicians will not fully accept an argument that they cannot reason out for themselves. This requires a very careful consideration of definitions, assumptions, and what is already known. This drives the mathematics educator as well, for they want their students to know not just the results and formulas that work, but just as importantly why they work. I have found that many times tension in a mathematics classroom is present because students desire the former but not the latter.

Thus, an oversimplified summary would be to say that those who choose to be mathematicians are driven to solve problems in their most abstract form and are convinced by only the most rigorous of arguments. From a Christian faith perspective, this can make an unbelieving mathematician a tough evangelistic nut to crack, as we tend to be a skeptical, stubborn, and often arrogant lot, too impressed with our own intellectual abilities to accept any conclusions that we have not derived ourselves. On the flip side, once convinced of the Christian faith, we tend to hold tenaciously and steadfastly to the truth and determined that others should be inculcated in that same truth.

WHAT IS A FAITHFUL EDUCATION IN MATHEMATICS?

"Indeed, the study of mathematics promotes important thinking habits of all sorts: analyzing carefully the implications of one's statements, being careful with the meanings of words, imagining alternative interpretations or possibilities of action, and recognizing that the mere declaration of your opinion on an issue does not render it true."

—Bradley and Howell[10]

9. It took me a while to see this (typical arrogance of a mathematician), but my many colleagues at C of O, and especially my wife, have shown me that academic rigor, logic, and depth abound in many areas.

10. Bradley and Howell, *Mathematics Through the Eyes of Faith*, 248.

FAITHFUL EDUCATION IN MATHEMATICS

A faithful education in mathematics has Christian content by having correct content. The content of mathematics, the "doing" of mathematics, is the bread and butter of any mathematics program or class. We derive the theorems, techniques, and formulas of our discipline that allow us to "do" mathematics, whether it be solving an equation, manipulating a function, proving a result, conducting a statistical test, etc. We model problem solving and proof and strive to build up the abilities and understanding of our students. In the sense of the equations, theorems, and techniques that form the "doing" of mathematics, it is reasonable to think of math as independent of worldview. Russell Howell of Westmont College writes:

> If one agrees to play the game of mathematics, then one implicitly agrees to follow the rules of the game. Different people following these rules will—Christian or not—agree with the conclusions obtained in the same way that different people will agree that, at a particular stage in a game of chess, white can force checkmate in two moves. In this sense mathematical practice is 'world-viewishly' neutral.[11]

Likewise, Calvin Jongsma of Dordt College says:

> Is there a Christian way to add 5 + 7 or to apply the quadratic formula or to prove the Pythagorean Theorem? Sure. In the way it was meant to be done! In a way that contributes to a larger pattern of obedient living. Is there only one way to do it, stipulated by the Bible or our theological doctrines? No; but some ways may be more in tune with how God structured this aspect of creation or may be more appropriate in one context or time than another. Will the ways these things are done clearly demonstrate a religious core or a worldview foundation or a philosophical outlook? Possibly not. For one thing, it is not the role of religious commitment or worldview or philosophy to prescribe the content of our knowledge.[12]

Finally, in the same vein Holmes states:

> If I were teaching symbolic logic, which is as close as a philosopher comes to mathematics, my Christianity would come

---

11. Howell, "Matter of Mathematics," 74.
12. Jongsma, "Mathematics: Always Important, Never Enough."

through in my attitude and my intellectual integrity far more than in the actual content of my course.[13]

A faithful education in mathematics should enable students to flourish. So, considering the above statement, how does my attitude matter in teaching mathematics? Broadly, a faithful educator will encourage, not discourage. I have come to the realization after many years that I was not hired to teach at College of the Ozarks because of my mathematical content knowledge or ability to transmit that content knowledge. Those qualities were necessary but far from sufficient. I was hired to help students appreciate, understand, engage, and do mathematics. Math is hard for most college students, even at what most mathematicians would consider an elementary level. It is easy to be condescending, to signal the fixed mindset that mathematical ability is inborn and set and not something a student can do much about. If I throw cold water on a student's belief that they can be successful in mathematics, I set up an obstacle not just in the class, but in their ability to grow as a problem solver and critical thinker, and I discourage them from pursuing a field that requires mathematical thinking. In his retiring presidential address, Francis Su of the Mathematical Association of America noted this potential problem. He asked, "Why should anyone persist in doing math or seeing herself as a mathematical person when others are telling her in subtle and not so subtle ways she doesn't belong?"[14]

It is easy to teach the "A" student who always reads the material before class, understands everything on the first try, and asks the insightful questions unprompted. Probably the best thing I can do is not get in their way. Much harder, but more valuable in that I can have influence, is to work with the student who struggles, and who may be tempted to think their value lies in their mathematical ability. As an undergraduate at Southwest Baptist, I sensed the care of the mathematics faculty, even when they were correcting me. I see the same in my colleagues in the department here at College of the Ozarks. I have also been in classrooms, conferences, seminars, and talks where it seemed the primary purpose of those present was to belittle those around them. It was those experiences that convinced me I did not want to be a research mathematician, even though that is what I was trained to be. The best decision I made in graduate school was to choose a dissertation committee that was kind and

13. Holmes, *Idea of a Christian College*, 47.
14. Su, "Mathematics for Human Flourishing," 18.

who showed grace to me despite my many mistakes, despite the four-foot stack of papers that represented ideas for proofs in my dissertation that didn't work. My hollow sense of failure, blunted by their encouragement, is something I try to remember in my interactions with my students. I have seen many former students who I tended to see as "weak" in my classroom go on to have tremendous success in their career and life, and I often wonder and worry if they saw me as help or hindrance to their path. As I strive to faithfully educate, I struggle to balance rigor, content, and high standards with grace, understanding, and encouragement.

A faithful education in mathematics should connect logic, reason, and faith. Most books and articles about the integration of mathematics and faith are actually about the philosophy of mathematics, even though this is not the realm in which most of my students or myself primarily interact with mathematics.[15] However, I think there are some important points that should be made as it is in this realm that one most often encounters worldviews that are potentially in opposition to the Christian faith. I will call these worldviews broadly "naturalist" and "humanist," although there are perhaps a countably infinite number of ways these views could be named. First, in the "naturalist" view of mathematics, parallel to the worldview of scientism, mathematics is elevated to being equal with God, positing that everything can be explained in terms of mathematical notions. This view would believe that math and its application in the sciences is the ultimate source of truth and knowledge and eliminates the need for God. Referring to the worldview of scientism, Mary Poplin says that for its adherents, "Science is the only thing that is objective, real, and true."[16] A newer and almost polar opposite view is that of "humanist" mathematics. This treats mathematics strictly as a human endeavor, where we create our own rules (like a game of chess) that we can change at any time. Thus, despite the great applicability of mathematics, a humanist mathematician would have us believe everything is ultimately meaningless, that there is no real truth or reality in anything done in mathematics.

A biblical worldview should help us realize that math is grounded in reality, for we see even the "purest" of mathematics seems to show up in everything from physics to finance, music to e-commerce. We should not be surprised by its effectiveness as it models and reflects the created

---

15. See, for example, Bradley and Howell, *Mathematics Through the Eyes of Faith*.
16. Poplin, *Is Reality Secular?*, 47.

order. God created the world with a distinctly mathematical structure. There is certainly a creative and inventive element in mathematics in the notation we use, the way we structure and argue our proofs, the way that we choose the most effective algorithms, but our activities are bounded because ultimately we do want our results to have meaning. We can and do form our own definitions, rules, and axioms, but if we start with a set of rules that lead to outcomes like "1 + 1 = 3", our mathematics is likely to not get very far or be of much interest to anyone.

It is worth considering what "rules" or axioms mathematicians do agree upon that have led to its effectiveness, and whether that has implications for our faith. I think perhaps the most important thing to note is that math does in fact have axioms, ideas so foundational as to be considered true *without proof*. Even a simple result like "1 + 1 = 2" is dependent on an understanding of the context of addition in base 10 arithmetic and the Peano Axioms.[17] Thus, we cannot say that this result (or any other result in mathematics) is unquestionably true; it is only true in that it follows logically from our presuppositions. I must *believe*, dare I say, I must have *faith*, that these presuppositions are true, in order to *prove* that 1 + 1 = 2.[18]

Does that mean I should not believe 1 + 1 = 2 or other mathematical results? I don't think so (although six-year-old Calvin from the comics would obviously disagree). There is a lot of evidence that mathematics "works," that it reflects real life, and that it is useful and effective. Therefore, it is not irrational or illogical to make use of mathematical results, even though they are grounded in belief. Likewise, when I say that I believe the Bible, or summary theological statements like the Apostles Creed and Nicene Creed or the *Baptist Faith and Message*, I do so based on the presupposition that God is trustworthy, and so his Word is true.[19] This is not an irrational faith like "1 + 1 = 3", rather it is an informed faith like "1 + 1 = 2" that is grounded in the reality of Jesus Christ, his life, death, and resurrection, and has been borne out and evidenced in my life and

---

17. Wikipedia, "Peano axioms."

18. Think about what you need to know in order to prove this simple result. For a start, you have to agree on the definition of terms like "1", "2", "+", and "=". Arithmetic seems obvious until you try to formalize it. In Alfred North Whitehead and Bertrand Russell's *Principia Mathematica* (1925–27), which attempted to establish mathematical foundations, the proposition 1+1=2 wasn't mentioned until late in Volume I, and not proved until Volume II, accompanied by the statement, "The above proposition is occasionally useful."

19. Southern Baptist Convention, *Baptist Faith and Message*.

the life of many generations of fellow believers. I am not blind or illogical to have the faith that I have, but I do acknowledge, like Ronald Nash, that "an acceptance of the presuppositions of the Christian Worldview will lead a person to conclusions very different from those that would follow a commitment, say, to the presuppositions of naturalism. One's axioms determines one's theorems."[20] It is perhaps futile to argue with someone from a divergent worldview, as their axioms aren't the same.

I tend to think that a mathematician struggling to find the "right" axioms is similar to the work of theologians who wrestle with the correct way of framing and expressing a Christian worldview, trying to be precise and careful while most mathematicians and Christians use a "working" worldview almost unconsciously.

In mathematics there are axioms that are not always obvious, and even controversial, like Euclid's fifth postulate or the Axiom of Choice.[21] It might be tempting to do away with these "problematic" axioms altogether to avoid controversy, just as some would do away with sections of God's word they see as inconvenient. But without them we are stuck at a more shallow understanding, and limited in the theorems that we can derive.

In mathematics, our presuppositions often lead to ideas that seem paradoxical or counterintuitive. For instance, the set of integers has the same "size" of infinite as the set of rational numbers even though it is a proper subset of the rational numbers, while the irrational numbers are an altogether "larger" infinity. "Gabriel's Horn" is a surface of revolution that has a finite volume but infinite surface area (thus, you could easily find enough paint to fill the horn up but never enough to paint the surface of the horn). Gödel was the first to show the limitations inherent in any axiomatic system, but of course this has not led to the rejection of mathematics or the idea that mathematics is somehow false or irrational.[22]

Similarly, the Bible also has ideas that may seem paradoxical. For example, Jesus says in Matt 10:39 (and this theme is repeated many times

20. Nash, *Worldviews in Conflict*, 23.

21. Euclid's fifth postulate is often known as the Parallel Postulate, although in original form it says nothing about parallel lines. However, when combined with the first four axioms, it is equivalent to saying that in a plane, given a line and a point not on it, at most one line parallel to the given line can be drawn through the point. It is controversial because (compared to the others) it is non-obvious ("Parallel postulate," *Wikipedia*). Together with the Zermelo-Fraenkel Axioms, the Axiom of Choice forms the set-theory axiomatic system ZFC ("Zermelo-Fraenkel set theory," *Wikipedia*).

22. Gödel and Feferman, *Kurt Gödel*.

in the New Testament), "For whoever would save his life will lose it, but whoever loses his life for my sake will find it."[23] Russell Moore also talks about seeing paradoxes such as "the deity of Christ and the humanity of Christ, or the sovereignty of God and the responsibility of human beings."[24] The Bible and mathematics both contain ideas that are difficult to understand, counterintuitive, seemingly paradoxical, and yet absolutely true. To reject one as invalid and accept the other is inconsistent.

One final note on axioms. Most mathematicians don't dwell on axioms on a regular basis. I certainly don't as an applied mathematician. I didn't explicitly know the Peano Axioms or ZFC when I started my study of college mathematics, and we don't emphasize them to undergraduate students. The results that stem from them have always seemed "right" without a formal declaration of the presuppositions. Likewise, when I responded to the tug of the Holy Spirit to accept Christ as a nine-year-old at FBC Lamar, Missouri, my biblical knowledge and understanding were pretty thin, and I had never read the *Baptist Faith and Message*, let alone the Apostles or Nicene Creed.[25] We should be grateful that development in mathematics and the Christian faith doesn't always depend on formal training in every particular area.

A faithful education in mathematics should value both utility and beauty. As I have said before, I consider myself an applied mathematician. My interest has always been what math can model, approximate, and predict, especially in other areas of science. To paraphrase the mathematician and statistician John Tukey, the best thing about being a statistician (or mathematician) is you get to play in everyone's back yard. I have been able to play in many back yards over the years, from Naval Intelligence to Nursing. The subjects that I consistently teach (probability, statistics, differential equations, numerical analysis, linear algebra) are primarily concerned with mathematics that is applied in the "real world." They determine how we model and approximate physical processes, interpret and make decisions using data. They are almost always dependent upon assumptions and prone to error, and thus also prone to bias and misuse. In the field where I did my PhD (Differential

---

23. Matt 10:39 (ESV).

24. Baptist Press, "Moore examines paradoxes in scripture & ministry."

25. As a Southern Baptist, I was brought up to be suspicious of creeds, lest they be considered as authoritative as Scripture itself. However, I do appreciate how they allow Christians to have a defined common ground across denominations. The *Baptist Faith and Message* is, to my understanding, technically a "confession."

Equations), we study mechanical, biological, and physical models where even the slightest change in parameters or initial conditions can lead to drastically different long-term predictions of behavior. Another field I work in (Probability and Statistics), repeatedly shows the uncertainty in estimating these parameters and conditions. But at the end of the day in the "real world" decisions have to be made, hopefully taking into account these limitations.

This (making decisions while recognizing uncertainty, evaluating the limits of assumptions and possible bias) is where I hope students can see that their academic pursuit is spiritual, and that their Christian worldview should motivate them to acquire the knowledge to make the best decisions possible, even when it involves disciplines they may not particularly enjoy pursuing. For instance, if a medical professional can't understand the results of a statistical hypothesis test so that they misinterpret the dosage, effectiveness, or side effects of a drug, then no matter how well-meaning they are, they have done harm. On the flip side, an engineer who correctly applies mathematical and statistical techniques to reduce waste or make a product more efficiently may not just save a company money, but may in turn save jobs or encourage expansion, benefiting many people. Likewise, incorrect application can lead to bridges failing and planes crashing. At that point math is "real," not just an exercise to try to get a good grade. Even the most abstract mathematics can have real consequences, and real benefits for our lives (GPS, Google search algorithms, RSA encryption, mp3 and jpeg compression, weather forecasts, retirement portfolio risk analysis, etc.).

I have in my life and work encountered people that have said that they are "not a math person" or never really cared for or about mathematics, and yet in their work they must make decisions that require the application of logic and are based on numerical information. It saddens me that some are protective of their decision-making authority and power and yet willfully ignorant of even basic quantitative skills. In contrast, even when not doing mathematics I still think as a mathematician. When I mow the yard, attend a Bible study, or serve on an academic committee, I bring a distinct mathematical perspective to the activity, one that I hope at least occasionally adds value. I hope I am also humble enough to be grateful for and recognize the value of other modes of thinking and reasoning.

Finally, I should say that just because I deal with math that mostly has utility in other areas, that doesn't mean that I don't see beauty and elegance as valuable and desirable. Sometimes I see beauty in a different way. There is an old apocryphal story of one of the greatest mathematicians of all time, Johann Carl Friedrich Gauss, who, when he was young, was given "busy work" by a teacher because he became a nuisance when he was bored.[26] Gauss was tasked with adding up the numbers 1 to 100.

$$1 + 2 + 3 + \ldots + 100$$

Of course, there is a very straightforward but tedious way to do this, by adding the terms in order from left to right: 1+2 = 3, 3+3 = 6, 6+4 = 10 etc. But Gauss saw a different way. He noticed that if you add the first and last term (1 + 100), the second and second to last (2 + 99), the third and third to last (3 + 98), and so on, you always get 101. He then noticed that there would be fifty of these pairs (100/2). Thus, to get the sum you could add 50 identical terms of 101, or 50(101) = 5050.

What's more, he realized this idea could be readily generalized to the first n positive integers, with a slight tweak to take into account the possibility of an odd number of terms:

Proof.

$$S = 1 + 2 + 3 + \ldots + (n-2) + (n-1) + n$$

Reversing the terms:

$$S = n + (n-1) + (n-2) + \ldots + 3 + 2 + 1$$

Adding these two expressions together term-by-term we find:

$$2S = (1 + n) + (2 + (n-1)) + (3 + (n-2)) + \ldots + (n-2+3) + (n-1+2) + (n+1)$$

Note there are n terms of $(n + 1)$ so the sum is:

$$2S = n(n+1)$$
$$S = \frac{n(n+1)}{2}$$

For me, this is a prototypical elegant and beautiful result in mathematics. It turns a tedious computation into a relatively simple one, and the logic seems obvious (after the fact). Mathematicians favor, and even expect, such results. It is a compliment to be told "that is an elegant proof"

---

26. I have always liked this story because I think many of my elementary school teachers often viewed me as a nuisance. The best ones were always finding ways to challenge me (Gauss is an academic great x9 grandfather).

or "that is a simple proof," as opposed to a proof that is "technical" or "only accessible to experts." A joy I had the last time I taught Numerical Analysis (which sometimes involves rather tedious computer programming) was having a student turn a twenty-line program I had written into a five-line program that did the same thing. It wasn't "more correct," but it was definitely "better." I think it is a gift from God that we can appreciate elegance and beauty not just in art, literature, and music, but also in the brevity and utility of a mathematical statement.

CONCLUSION AND SUMMARY

"In mathematics you don't understand things. You just get used to them."

—JOHN VON NEUMANN[27]

"All these equations are like miracles. You take two numbers and when you add them, they magically become one new number! No one can say how it happens. You either believe it or you don't."

—CALVIN, FROM THE COMIC STRIP *CALVIN AND HOBBES*, BY BILL WATTERSON[28]

Most of the time, my content and methods will not be greatly different than those of a mathematician at a secular university who may or may not be a believer. As a matter of fact, many of the Christian mathematicians that I admire and respect the most, like my brother Brian, choose to be salt and light at secular, public institutions.[29] However, my experience has shown me that even small moments and illustrations that give students the opportunity to think more deeply and from a Christian perspective are valuable and can have lasting impact, and for the freedom and responsibility to engage in those moments at College of the Ozarks, I am grateful.

Mathematics has presuppositions that must be accepted without proof. One could argue (as Calvin does in the quote above) that mathematics must be taken on faith. I would argue (unlike Calvin) that that

27. Quoted in Zukav, *Dancing Wu Li Masters*, 208. John von Neumann was a Hungarian-American mathematician and physicist, who lived from 1903–57.

28. Watterson, *Calvin and Hobbes*.

29. Chair and Professor of Mathematics, Northwest Missouri State University.

doesn't make it wrong, as long as we put our faith in the correct axioms of mathematics. The axioms that we agree upon, although perhaps imperfect, produce math that positively impacts the world. A different choice of axioms might take us along a less productive path. I think this is a good analogy for worldviews. Everyone can have a different worldview, and different worldviews may sometimes lead to the same results ("murder is wrong," "cake is good"), but with the wrong worldview one misses out on the deeper and most meaningful conclusions about life and our relationship with God.

Mathematics is a worthwhile pursuit. It has connections and applications to so many fields: science, engineering, music, and business, just to name a few. One can learn to appreciate elegance and beauty in mathematics just as in the arts and literature. Although many may see mathematics as sterile, boring, and disconnected from the Christian faith, that view was not always prevalent, and it need not remain so. As I pointed out in the beginning, the earliest mathematicians were also theologians and natural philosophers who considered the practice of mathematics a daily part of the creation mandate and restoration of our relationship with God. The challenge to myself is to reconnect with that view and make it evident in my mathematical study and teaching.

BIBLIOGRAPHY

Baptist Press. "Moore examines paradoxes in scripture & ministry." http://bpnews.net/52522/moore-examines-paradoxes-in-scripture-amp-ministry.
Bell, Eric Temple. *Mathematics: Queen and Servant of Science.* Cambridge: Cambridge University Press, 1996.
Bradley, James and Russell Howell. *Mathematics Through the Eyes of Faith.* New York: Harper Collins, 2011.
Gödel, Kurt and Solomon Feferman. *Kurt Gödel: Collected Works.* Oxford: Oxford University Press, 1990.
Holmes, Arthur. *The Idea of a Christian College.* Grand Rapids: Eerdmans, 1987.
Howell, Russell W. "The Matter of Mathematics." *Perspectives of Science and Christian Faith* 67.2 (2015): 74–88.
Jongsma, Calvin. "Mathematics: Always Important, Never Enough: A Christian Perspective on Mathematics and Mathematics Education." https://digitalcollections.dordt.edu/pro_rege/vol35/iss4/3).
"Mathematics Genealogy Project." https://www.genealogy.math.ndsu.nodak.edu/.
Nash, Ronald H. *Worldviews in Conflict: Choosing Christianity in a World of Ideas.* Grand Rapids: Zondervan, 1992.
"Parallel postulate." *Wikipedia: the Free Encyclopedia.* https://en.wikipedia.org/w/index.php?title=Parallel_postulate&oldid=896838389. Accessed 20 June 2019.

Pascal, Blaise. *Pensees*, Translated by W.F. Trotter. New York: Random House, 1941.
"Peano axioms." *Wikipedia: The Free Encyclopedia.* https://en.wikipedia.org/w/index.php?title=Peano_axioms&oldid=902201641. Accessed 20 June 2019.
Pitici, Mircea, ed. *Best Writing on Mathematics 2018.* Princeton: Princeton University Press, 2018.
Poplin, Marry. *Is Reality Secular?: Testing the Assumptions of Four Global Worldviews.* Downers Grove, IL: InterVarsity, 2014.
Southern Baptist Convention. *Baptist Faith and Message.* http://www.sbc.net/bfm2000/.
Suzuki, Jeff. *A History of Mathematics.* Hoboken, NJ: Prentice Hall, 2002.
Watterson, Bill. *Calvin and Hobbes* (March 9, 2011). www.gocomics.com.
Whitehead, Alfred North and Bertrand Russell. *Principia Mathematica.* Cambridge: Cambridge University Press, 1925–27.
"Zermelo-Fraenkel set theory." *Wikipedia: The Free Encyclopedia.* https://en.wikipedia.org/w/index.php?title=Zermelo%E2%80%93Fraenkel_set_theory&oldid=899643937. Accessed 20 June 2019.
Zukav, Gary. *The Dancing Wu Li Masters: An Overview of the New Physics.* New York: HarperCollins, 2001.

14

FAITHFUL SCIENCE EDUCATION

BARBARA FENNELL

AS A CHRISTIAN WHO is a science educator, I have often been confronted by the general misconception of a great dichotomy between science and faith. I have endured more than one well-meaning sermon (or Sunday School lesson) that seeks to enlighten Christians about the evils of science. I have suffered through more than one conversation with colleagues (or lectures from professors) that relegated a belief in God to the realm of the unsophisticated and uneducated. However, in my struggle/journey of faith and education over the past years, I have found much less "either-or" and much more "both-and" when it comes to my personal understanding of faith and the principles of science.

MY JOURNEY (ABBREVIATED)

As a college student who was always seeking a challenge, I changed my major from computer science (I mean, where was that field going anyways, and besides, who wants to spend hours in front of a computer monitor each day?) to physics at the end of my freshman year of college. I think I actually surprised my physics professor as I was not the best in the class. At the same time, I saddened my computer science teacher since he liked my work ethic. During the same time period in my life, I was involved in a personal revolution of thought about what it meant to be a Christian. My parents were (and are!) good people, and we attended church regularly, but Christianity did not seem to permeate my life the way it did the lives of others whom I met. During my freshman year I came to a crisis of faith: had my experience with Christ only been an out-growth of my involvement with church, or did I have a relationship with Christ? So, since the beginning of my interest in physics, it and my faith have been intertwined.

Although some might believe that the choice of physics was a result of my aptitude, physics did not come easily for me. I started upper-level classes with a calculus deficit. I always seemed to be a step behind others, and one professor always commented that I did not do problems in the "conventional way"—he could not find fault in my method, but in a good-natured way he was sure it would catch up to me one day. I did not excel in math, but stuck with the rigorous coursework because I wanted to understand physics. I missed being an honor graduate by 0.01 points—a deficit I could have easily remedied by withdrawing from a field where I was faced with constant struggle.

I share my experience as a college student because it shaped my desire to be a college educator. Prior to graduate school, I never imagined myself in education in any capacity. However, through a teaching assistantship I discovered a desire to encourage students in their struggles and also a God-given ability to teach. I am a naturally shy, reserved person, but in the classroom I felt empowered in a way that no other activity had ever made me feel. I may not be a gifted instructor, but I do experience the giftedness of the Holy Spirit when I teach. This call has shaped the decisions and direction of my life and ultimately brought me to College of the Ozarks. So when I am asked about how my faith affects my teaching, it is difficult to separate the two as I feel that my teaching is a gift of God and also my calling. Without this calling I can assure you that I would not subject myself to standing in front of a group of students. Without this calling I would be unable to teach when students seem uninterested. Without this calling I would definitely look for another line of work!

MY "HOT BUTTON"

When people ask what I do, I tell them that I teach. Of course, the natural follow-up question is: "What do you teach?" My answer almost always elicits a grimace and/or confusion. Many people have a fear of physics, and many Christians assume that studying science is a non-Christian activity. I find myself having to explain that not all Christians feel that science is anti-biblical and that not all scientists are anti-God. I agree with Bartholomew and Goheen: "it [does] not have to be this way; religion and science are not in irreconcilable conflict."[1]

As I have thought about these encounters through the lens of "faithfully educating," I may have found a good countering scenario. Many (if not most) Christians want to distance themselves from actions of particular groups of extremists who claim a Christian worldview yet act in ways that do not represent Christ well (i.e., picketing the funerals of soldiers or children killed in tornados). However, many of these same people are perfectly willing to accept that the views of a few anti-Christian scientists represent the views of the entire scientific community and the scientific worldview.

I know that I cannot change every person's view of this "conflict," but I can enlighten my students as to the harm caused by an improper view. I want to equip my students with the best tools for exploring this divisive debate.

MY AIM

Life is less dichotomous than it may appear on the surface. God calls us to live lives of integrity and fullness, not of fragmentation. This idea of connectedness is not only taught in the Bible, but is also being discussed in the educational arena. Outside of the Christian college environment, there is a movement to whole-person integration in the classroom. As educators (and physics educators in particular) have begun looking at why American students do not seem to be internalizing learning, the education movement has made a plea for authentic, whole-person teaching and assessment.

Although the popular opinion that repetition of a skill leads to mastery of that skill still lurks in physics departments across the country, I try to steer my physics courses away from repetitious working of problems as the primary means of learning physics. Connectionism, as proposed by Edward Thorndike, debunked this popular idea and cautioned against teaching content devoid of context: "Students need to understand how to apply knowledge and skills they acquire. Uses

---

1. Bartholomew and Goheen, *Living at the Crossroads*, 90.

should be learned in conjunction with the content."[2] Physics is uniquely suited to connectionism. It is the science which fundamentally sets out to explain how and why things work the way they do. Most basic physical laws have been witnessed by every person on Earth long before they enter a college classroom. An abundance of context is available; it is up to me to take advantage of this by making the connections.

Students need to know that the purpose of their being in the physics classroom is not just to learn the facts of physics, but to gain a broader understanding of the world in which they live. In this type of setting, the purpose is to root out misconceptions in a non-threatening way and to provide support and resources to help establish the proper connections between observations of the world and the laws that govern the world. I must give up *some* measure of control in order to develop a learning environment that allows for mistakes to be made and correction to occur in non-emotionally charged ways. Knowing that fear is a prime motivator for student non-participation, Smith finds merit in Carl Rogers's methodology, which he calls "student-centered teaching," in which the "threat to the self of the learner is reduced to a minimum, and differentiated perception of the field of experience is facilitated."[3]

While the more traditional teacher-centered classroom and the more modern student-centered classroom each have some advantages, what can be lost in both of these classrooms is the focus on the subject. Palmer advocates neither a teacher-centered nor a student-centered classroom, but instead a subject-centered classroom:

> A subject-centered classroom is not one in which students are ignored. Such a classroom honors one of the most vital needs our students have: to be introduced to a world larger than their own experiences and egos, a world that expands their personal boundaries and enlarges their sense of community. This is why students often describe great teachers as people who "bring to life" things that the students had never heard of, offering them an encounter with otherness that brings the students to life as well.

A subject-centered classroom also honors one of your most vital needs as teachers: to invigorate those connections between our subjects, our students, and our souls that help make us whole again and again. By

---

2. Schunk, *Learning Theories*, 77.
3. Smith, "Carl Rogers."

putting the "Secret" that Frost wrote about at the center of the circle, we re-member the passion that brought us into this work in the first place—a re-membering that cannot happen when we and our students sit in that circle alone.[4]

This resonates with me. I do not want to control the classroom environment, but instead I want to manage it. I also do not want to turn the classroom (and the choice of content) over to the students; if they do not know anything about physics, how will they make good choices about the content? Instead, my aim is to connect science, physics specifically, with the experiences of my students—not just the "science-y" experiences, but experiences throughout their lives. For in searching to establish a subject-centered classroom, I do not want to fall victim to the error of "many Christian faculty members [when they] end up teaching their courses in ways that differ little from their secular counterparts at other universities; they do not teach in distinctively Christian ways that drip with theological content."[5] My aim is for my Christian worldview to inform and to permeate my views as a scientist and as an educator, as Byl sums up, "we construct and choose those theories that accord best with our basic worldview, our deepest convictions about the nature of the universe. Our worldview affects virtually all our thinking."[6]

MY (EVER-EVOLVING) PLAN

As a science educator, I see two reasons to address the dichotomy between science and Christianity: first, in my opinion, this dichotomy is greatly exaggerated by both sides and has caused much damage; second, teaching as a whole person is more beneficial to my students and to me, as well as being pleasing to God. Parker Palmer expresses it this way, "good teaching cannot be reduced to technique; good teaching comes from the identity and integrity of the teacher."[7] I believe integrity can be maintained in the science classroom by exploring the claims of the scientific worldview.

---

4. Palmer, *Courage to Teach*, 120.
5. Fant, *Liberal Arts*, 91–92.
6. Byl, "Christian Perspective on Physics," in Downey and Porter, *Christian Worldview and the Academic Disciplines*, 392.
7. Palmer, *Courage to Teach*, 10.

Science is—by its own definition—agnostic, not atheistic. In the words of Fant, "Rightly understood, science is a tool, not a philosophical system."[8] Science cannot prove the existence of God, but by its own bounds it cannot disprove the existence of God! I believe that an understanding of the nature of science helps remove the dichotomy of the "science verses religion" debate. Science looks for an explanation and a cause for the universe and its processes; Christians know the cause but do not always understand the processes. McGrath describes it this way, "It has become increasingly clear that many of the fundamental beliefs of western culture lie beyond proof. . . . Some things can indeed be proven; but some, by their very nature, lie beyond proof. God is one of these."[9]

In my opinion, if science could arrive at a definitive proof of God, then there would be no need for faith, for "without faith it is impossible to please God."[10] Faith is necessary for the Christian and for the scientist. God's ways are high above our ways, so science seeks to find understanding (God gave us a spirit of curiosity!), but there are mysteries which are too great for us to know. Intellectually honest scientists (believers or not) will readily admit that science is the process of attaining knowledge about the universe, but that all of the universe and its processes are not knowable. This thought is demonstrated in a statement comparing Christianity and the natural sciences: "Polkinghorne stresses that Christianity, like the natural sciences, is concerned about making sense out of the world on the basis of the evidence that is available."[11]

The scientific worldview assumes some basics premises. First, objective reality exists; that is, we do not live in our minds, but objects are real. Second, the universe is knowable. This is probably the point of departure for most people between science and Christianity. Science claims that all is knowable, while Christianity is willing to concede that there are things in the universe without explanation from a human perspective. The third premise is that the universe's operation is regular and predictable. This is why scientists strive to make accurate predictions and perform experiments to provide a body of knowledge. Without these presuppositions, scientific thinking cannot proceed. Scientists concede that these may not be valid, but without some basic principles, it is impossible to operate in

8. Fant, *Liberal Arts*, 70.
9. McGrath, *Theology*, 2.
10. Heb 11:6 (NIV).
11. McGrath, *Theology*, 8.

the realm of science. Our *experience* tells us that science works! We forge ahead with science based on our presuppositions.

Additionally, an understanding of the nature of science (NOS) is imperative not just to those pursuing scientific literacy, but also to every believer in Christ. Science does not claim to be truth—some scientist may claim this, but they are speaking from their own personal biases, not as ambassadors for science. The National Science Teachers Association (NSTA), as well as other science organizations, has begun to advocate for explicit NOS instruction. NSTA's official position includes the following statement: "Science, along with its methods, explanations and generalizations, must be the sole focus of instruction in science classes to the exclusion of all non-scientific or pseudoscientific methods, explanations, generalizations and products."[12] This and other statements of like kind are one of the reasons I choose not to teach in a high school setting. For fear of offending a few, the association has struck a hard blow on the wedge that exists between science and religion. Although there are many ideas about what constitutes NOS, there are several generally agreed upon ideas that will serve the believer well in evaluating scientific claims. These include tentativeness, subjectivity, and presuppositions.

Tentativeness

The concept of the tentativeness of science can lead to some epistemological conundrums. In the words of Clough, "Asking whether our ideas concerning the natural world are absolutely true is asking an unanswerable question. ... Science teachers should acknowledge that even though much scientific knowledge is quite durable, all scientific ideas are open to revision in light of new evidence and interpretations."[13] Take the oft-quoted example of a stationary Earth. Prior to the seventeenth century, observations of the sky, both during the day and during the night, backed up the idea that the Earth was fixed in space and stationary on its axis. However, upon collection of more data this idea has been revised; the Earth spins on its own axis and revolves around the Sun. Science can (and does) change. Christians need to know that although some scientists may advocate an eternal view of science, science is tentative—new information shapes and may ultimately overthrow the current theories.

12. National Science Teachers Association, "NSTA Position Statement."
13. Clough and Olson, "Nature of Science," 15.

Science does not make a claim for absolute truth. As Kuhn has argued, "To be accepted as a paradigm, a theory must seem better than its competitors, but it need not, and in fact never does, explain all the facts with which it can be confronted."[14] Chalmers puts it this way, "Although it can never be legitimately said of a theory that it is true, it can hopefully be said that it is the best available; that it is better than anything that has come before."[15] Every scientific theory seeks to be the best explanation possible, but when evidence contradicts or offers refinement, the theory will be adapted. This does not mean that science is not durable, just that it can and does change. The phenomenon that is being explained does not change, but the *explanation* does. Consider Newtonian mechanics, which was the prevailing theory for more than two hundred years, "yet today most physicists would consider it to be false; it has been replaced by Einstein's theory of relativity."[16] I do not believe that the idea of tentativeness is taught appropriately in most science classrooms. The majority of students are left with the impression that scientific knowledge is absolute. Emphasizing the tentative nature of science when teaching physics allows students to be discerning in their acceptance of scientific theory. Students can realize that the scientific evidence supports a particular view, but when better information is available, scientists will revise the theory. This will continue to happen—science is durable, but it is also tentative.

To be fair, the interpretation of Scripture has also changed. As better, older, and more complete manuscripts become available, exegetes improve the translations of Scripture that are available. The interpretation of Scripture may be modified, but the message of Scripture is unchanged.

Subjectivity

Scientists are generally regarded as objective, and Christians as subjective. However, no human being can be completely objective—his opinion, culture, and knowledge will impact any information that comes to him. These biases are often overlooked, leading to sweeping descriptions of scientific thought that might be tainted by subjectivity. "Too often, science instruction suggests that scientists make unproblematic

---

14. Kuhn, *Structure of Scientific Revolutions*, 17–18.
15. Chalmers, *What Is This Thing Called Science?*, 60.
16. Byl, "Christian Perspective on Physics," in Downey and Porter, *Christian Worldview and the Academic Disciplines*, 392.

observations, that interpretations of data are fairly straightforward, and that the methodology of science results in objective knowledge about the natural world."[17] Intellectually honest people (both scientists and Christians) are aware of their biases and realize that these may lead them to faulty assumptions. "The notion of scientific neutrality and objectivity is largely a myth."[18] Bias is inevitable, but it is not evil—it just needs to be acknowledged.

Just as Christians must study the entirety of Scripture to hope to glean meaning from individual passages, the scientist must look at the theory and the facts and interpret new data in light of what is known. Fant explains, "The data themselves do not drive the interpretation; the interpreter's understanding of the world generates the interpretation. Much of the perceived conflict between faith and science is really an issue of data hermeneutics."[19] Biblical interpretation also falls victim to subjectivity on at least two levels: first, as readers of an English translation, some interpretation has already been done for us, and, second, we bring our own views (either knowingly or unknowingly) into our reading of the Scripture.[20]

Experimentation is a hallmark of science. When students perform a physics lab exercise, they are exploring the subjectivity of science. Although these students have been given some structure and have a general idea of what *should* happen, the experiment does not always go as planned. Students then must use their knowledge of the theory and their own interpretations of data to make conclusions. I have had more than one student become frustrated and ask what the answer is supposed to be, but I have to tell them that I do not know—I may be able to guide them, but they must interpret their own data. The idea that there is one true answer is a fallacy in physics. There are "best" approximations, but there is always error. At this point I try to make students aware that while any interpretation will be subjective, the phenomenon is not. Chalmers acknowledges this in his statement, "It is well appreciated that all observations are subject to some degree of error, as reflected in the practice of

---

17. Clough, "Nature of Science," 14.

18. Byl, "Christian Perspective on Physics," in Downey and Porter, *Christian Worldview and the Academic Disciplines*, 393.

19. Fant, *Liberal Arts*, 78.

20. Fee and Stuart, *How to Read the Bible*, 14–15.

scientists when they write the results of a particular measurements as $x \pm dx$, where dx represents the estimated margin of error."[21]

When scientists experiment, they also manipulate. As Chalmers writes, "To acquire facts relevant for the identification and specification of the various processes at work in nature, it is, in general, necessary to practically intervene to try to isolate the process under investigation and eliminate the effects of others."[22] Subjectivity always enters into interpretation. If this were not so, why are there a multitude of denominations of Protestants all claiming to follow the Scriptures?

Presuppositions

Christians are routinely viewed as having presuppositions to support their worldview; while, on the other hand, scientists (and the general population) are generally less likely to admit that science also rests on presuppositions. In fact, *all* worldviews are built upon presuppositions. Acknowledging these can help the Christian have an appropriate view of science and can help the scientist have an appropriate view of Christianity. Chalmers explains, "We are bound to run into trouble if we seek rational justifications of every principle we use, for we cannot provide a rational argument for rational argument itself without assuming what we are arguing for."[23] In other words, we have to have some basis for a belief system—be that Christianity or science—to be able to build the belief system.

"Since scientific theorizing is heavily dependent on our philosophical and religious presuppositions, the critical question is: What do we choose as our starting point?"[24] As Christians, "we presuppose that God made the world, we end up with a way of making sense of the world that makes a lot of sense of things ... the existence of God resonates well with what can be observed of the world. It is thus a confirmation, but not a proof, of God's existence."[25] Science has had a harder time choosing a starting point, which is why there are so many views of science. Physics

---

21. Chalmers, *What Is This Thing Called Science?*, 50.
22. Chalmers, *What Is This Thing Called Science?*, 28.
23. Chalmers, *What Is This Thing Called Science?*, 53.
24. Byl, "Christian Perspective on Physics," in Downey and Porter, *Christian Worldview and the Academic Disciplines*, 393.
25. McGrath, *Theology*, 6.

and its prevailing paradigms have led to various worldviews. Newton's mechanics lead to a clockmaker view of God and quantum mechanics has led to a view of relativism in *all* aspects of life.[26]

In addition to presuppositions about the underpinnings of a worldview, Chalmers points out experimental results require effort to obtain and the results of experimentation depend heavily on the knowledge used to interpret them.[27] For example, physicists up until the mid 1900s went back and forth on the nature of light. Experiments were done to prove the wave nature of light; since these were set up with this intent then the success of the experiment was in proving the wave nature. However, other equally valid experiments were designed to prove the particle nature of light; these were also successful. At the time, these scientists were unaware that the experimental set up was determining the outcome and that light could not be categorized as wave-only or as particle-only. Light has properties of both and is therefore something that neither theory can completely explain. There was no interpretation error, but there was a problem that resulted from the presuppositions held by the scientists.

One of the premier examples of an overt presupposition is one of Bohr's postulates. In the realm of classical mechanics, a body needs to be constantly supplied with energy to maintain a stable orbit around another body. In describing the nature of the atom, Bohr made the assumption that electrons in stable orbits do not radiate. Although this was the observed phenomenon, it did not fit with Newtonian mechanics—a presupposition had to be made to align the observation with the theory. Without this "rule" the planetary model of the atom could not work. What Bohr did not know at the time was that he need not have forced the postulate as the non-radiating orbit of the electron is perfectly acceptable in quantum mechanics.

Isaac Newton was faced with these same challenges: he could not derive an approximation for the period of a pendulum without assuming that the bob was a point mass; he needed to ignore air resistance to create his general ideas for motion; he chose to gloss over the gravitational effects of planet-on-planet when describing celestial mechanics because

---

26. Byl, "Christian Perspective on Physics," in Downey and Porter, *Christian Worldview and the Academic Disciplines*, 397.

27. Chalmers, *What Is This Thing Called Science?*, 30–31.

the sun overwhelmed those forces.[28] Presuppositions had to be made in order to advance science.

Some scientists will dismiss Christian teachings because of the emphasis on faith; however, the basis of science is assumption, which is not far removed from the "faith" which is used to condemn the Christian. When both sides approach the schism with intellectual integrity, the schism narrows significantly.

THE (NEVER-ENDING) STRUGGLE

Because of the deep-rooted nature of the "science versus religion" debate, there are many Christian students who believe that accepting certain physical science ideas (such as The Big Bang Theory) is tantamount to rejecting salvation. While I agree with Bartholomew and Goheen that "In the Christian story, the belief in creation is of foundational importance," I find their proclamation that "Such a belief means that Christians view the world in a way wholly different from the sort of scientific worldview . . . within [which] the cosmos is a random product of time and chance" to be dismissive.[29] In my opinion, the Christian worldview encompasses the meaning of the origin while the scientific worldview only seeks the process of the origin. Although some of my students may ascribe to this idea, Christians (as well as scientists!) can admit that there are limitations to the scientific worldview without rejecting it outright. Far too many students reject ideas without investigating because that is what they have been told to do. Holmes addresses this shallow learning in reference to some Christian colleges with an insular view; he writes that "the student who is simply conditioned to respond in certain ways to certain stimuli is at a loss when he confronts novel situations."[30] Palmer further reminds the teacher that "good education is always more process than product. If a student has received no more than a packet of information at the end of an educational transaction, that student has been duped. Good education teaches students to become both producers of knowledge and discerning consumers of what other people claim to know."[31]

28. Kuhn, *Structure of Scientific Revolutions*, 31–32.
29. Bartholomew and Goheen, *Living at the Crossroads*, 25.
30. Holmes, *Idea of a Christian College*, 5.
31. Palmer, *Courage to Teach*, 94.

Many physicists (Newton, Einstein, Faraday, Kelvin, Maxwell) have expressed religious views. However, the religious context of their statements and ideas does not often accompany the description of their scientific discoveries. Fant describes two reasons for this removal: "Sometimes this is because of legitimate ignorance of the Christian intellectual tradition or even basic biblical literacy, and sometimes it is due to outright hostility toward all things religious or more pointedly toward Christianity."[32] I believe the reintroduction of the Christian context for physicists and their ideas is the minimum of integration for an educator who is Christian and is a scientist.

Even science educators at universities without a Christian mission have begun to explore the link between a student's religious views and that student's view of science. Southerland and Scharmann found that some secondary teachers avoid teaching controversial subjects if they or their students have objections based on religious beliefs; this "prevents students with religious beliefs counter to mainstream science from receiving a robust science education."[33] At College of the Ozarks, which has a distinctive Christian mission and accepts students based on this mission, I have to realize that my students may not have been taught a proper view of science *because* of their conservative Christian values. The science course(s) taken at College of the Ozarks may be the last chance for these believers to encounter the scientific worldview in a non-contentious manner.

MY "CONCLUSION"

Science is not a body of knowledge, but a process. As such, it faces limitations that are not always dwelt upon. Clough and Olson strongly recommend that science teachers "explicitly raise questions and ideas that help students understand the creative side of science, that data does not speak for itself and must be interpreted in light of other knowledge, the impossibility of absolute objectivity, the implausibility of a universal step-by-step method, and other important ideas about how science works."[34] Explicitly addressing some of these limitations and the hermeneutics

---

32. Fant, *Liberal Arts*, 39.

33. Southerland and Scharmann, "Acknowledging the Religious Beliefs Students Bring," 61.

34. Clough and Olson, "Nature of Science," 2.

of science gives my students the best opportunity for understanding and application. Psychologist Laura E. Berk agrees: "Adolescents also benefit from exposure to increasingly complex problems and to teaching that highlights critical features of scientific reasoning."[35] This kind of opportunity asks students to employ higher reasoning skills—not just regurgitate memorized facts. Likewise, German physics instructor Heinz Meyling surveyed hundreds of students and recorded all of his lessons, and, in 1997, he published the results: he found that infusing the curriculum with NOS ideas helped over three-quarters of his students develop more sophisticated conceptions. In addition to the advance in understanding, Meyling found that "at the end of the four semesters 86% of the students expressed their approval of epistemological discussions in physics courses."[36] His students enjoyed the infusion of NOS ideas!

By nature, I am not a confrontational person and I always desire for people to like me. So I struggle with the results of teaching students that science does not contradict the Christian worldview. Students may experience a deep dissatisfaction: "at least for a while. . . . students who have been well served by good teachers may walk away angry—angry that their prejudices have been challenged and their sense of self shaken. That sort of dissatisfaction may be a sign that real education has happened."[37] If this is the case, then I must trust that the Holy Spirit can continue to work in that student's life even when I am not longer directly involved. Education is not an instant gratification vocation.

A Christian worldview can explain the supernatural and science seeks to explain the natural. Science cannot explain God (and I for one am glad of that fact!), but God is the basis for science. To me, rejecting outright evidence that science has gathered is dismissing the opportunity to grasp at the hem of the robe of God. Scientists will never explain God, but God loves the scientist and instilled in her the curious and creativity nature.

---

35. Berk, *Development through the Lifespan*, 386.
36. Meyling, "Change Students' Conceptions," 412.
37. Palmer, *Courage to Teach*, 94.

BIBLIOGRAPHY

Bartholomew, Craig and Michael Goheen. *Living at the Crossroads: An Introduction to Christian Worldview*. Grand Rapids: Baker, 2008.

Berk, Laura E. *Development through the Lifespan*, 5th ed. Boston: Allyn & Bacon, 2010.

Chalmers, Alan. *What Is This Thing Called Science?*, 3rd ed. Indianapolis: Hackett, 1999.

Clough, Michael. "The Nature of Science: Understanding How the Game of Science is Played." *The Clearing House* 74.1 (2000): 13–17.

Clough, Michael and Joanne Olson. "The Nature of Science: Always Part of the Science Story." *The Science Teacher* 71.9 (2004): 28–31.

Downey, Deane and Stanley Porter, eds. *Christian Worldview and the Academic Disciplines: Crossing the Academy*. Eugene: Pickwick, 2009.

Fant, Gene C. *The Liberal Arts: A Student's Guide*. Wheaton: Crossway, 2012.

Fee, Gordon and Douglas Stuart. *How to Read the Bible for All Its Worth*, 2nd ed. Grand Rapids: Zondervan, 1993.

Garber, Steven. *The Fabric of Faithfulness*. Downers Grove, IL: InterVarsity, 1996.

Holmes, Arthur. *The Idea of a Christian College*. Grand Rapids: Eerdmans, 1987.

Kuhn, Thomas. *The Structure of Scientific Revolutions*, 3rd ed. Chicago: University of Chicago Press, 1996.

McGrath, Alister. E. *Theology: The Basics*, 3rd ed. Chichester: Wiley-Blackwell, 2012.

Meyling, Heinz. "How to Change Students' Conceptions of the Epistemology of Science." *Science and Education* 6 (1997): 397–416.

National Science Teachers Association. "NSTA Position Statement: The Nature of Science." http://www.nsta.org/about/positions/natureofscience.aspx.

Palmer, Parker J. *The Courage to Teach: Exploring the Inner Landscape of a Teacher's Life*. San Francisco: John Wiley & Sons, 1998.

Schunk, Dale. *Learning Theories: An Educational Perspective*, 6th ed. Boston: Allyn & Bacon, 2012.

Smith, Mark. "Carl Rogers, Core Conditions and Education." https://infed.org/mobi/carl-rogers-core-conditions-and-education/.

Southerland, Sherry and Lawrence Scharmann. "Acknowledging the Religious Beliefs Students Bring into the Science Classroom: Using the Bounded Nature of Science." *Theory into Practice* 52.1 (2013): 59–65.

Faithful Education in the Creative Arts

15

LIVING WORSHIP
How God's Revealed Story of Humanity Informs an Approach to Teaching in the Academic Disciplines

RICHARD W. CUMMINGS

INTRODUCTION

THIS CHAPTER, THOUGH FOCUSED on human creativity and oriented towards visual art, provides a particular approach to faithful education that can be modified to fit any number of disciplines. The arguments in this chapter proceed out of the belief that God's relationship with humanity as revealed in Scripture can inform an effective approach to faithful education. It is only necessary for the educator to possess a basic theological understanding of Christianity and a basic understanding of the Bible to place a particular discipline within the story of God's past, present and future intentions for humanity.

Traditionally, the biblical story has been broken down into four periods: creation, fall, redemption, and restoration. This established structure is where I situate my biblical and theological exploration of God's mandate and blessing of human creativity. Though my particular focus is on visual art, every discipline involves some form of human creativity and inquiry. Human creativity flows out of our God-given capacity to experience and respond to the created universe. Human creativity is an inherent part of life and an essential facet of human flourishing. Our gifted creativity is a key component of who we are as image bearers of our triune Creator.

I pray that this brief discourse on human creativity might inspire educators to discover how their disciplines flow out of God's revealed story, and knowledge of the story of God begins with the Bible. So, what does the Bible offer the faithful educator? Does the Bible reveal truth for a particular discipline? Can biblical principles in one academic area be applied to another? How do the creation, fall, redemption, and restoration narratives apply to course content? How does biblical revelation relate to ethical situations that arise in particular areas of study? How do I know that my interpretation of the Bible is valid? Also, will I really be stoned if I don't keep the Sabbath?[1]

CREATION

Luckily for me, a visual artist and professor of art, God's self-revelation in Scripture begins with an act of creation: "In the beginning, God created the heavens and the earth."[2] This introductory verse provides a wonderful entry into the story of God and his intentions for humans and their creativity. There are certainly important implications for human creativity found in the first verse of the Bible, but a more complete understanding of what the Bible reveals about human creativity requires a more complete understanding of the revealed story. In the first few verses of Genesis, however, the basic context for how human creativity fits into the revealed story of God becomes clear—humans are made in the image and likeness of the triune God and are entrusted to steward and creatively shape the creation.

Humanity is fashioned in the image of the triune God. This truth is reflected in the holistic nature of the human person—the physical, spiritual, and intellectual components, as well as humanity's expressive capacities. Two narratives are essential to a proper biblical understanding of human creativity. The first narrative is the creation account found in Genesis, and the second (in Exodus) is the account of the planning and fabrication of the Israelite tabernacle. Several questions related to human

---

1. Exod 31:14. For a well-informed approach to engaging the more difficult Old Testament biblical interpretation issues, refer to Todd, *Sinai and the Saints*.
2. Gen 1:1 (ESV).

creativity and visual art are simultaneously raised and answered in these two biblical accounts. These questions include: What does it mean to be created in the image of God? Is human creativity part of the image of God in humanity?[3] And, does God accept the creative works of humans, even those made by fallen, sinful hands?[4]

In the beginning the triune God created. This opening flourish to Scripture, expressed in Gen 1:1, is an accepted, theological tenet. It is important to note that, though the texts referring to God in Gen 1 do not explicitly express his triune nature, Christian theologians have proclaimed that it was the triune God who was present and active in creation. At creation the Spirit of God hovered over the waters,[5] and New Testament texts repeatedly identify Christ's active role in creation (and also its sustaining).[6]

Still, God's creative nature expressed in Gen 1:1 contributes nothing to a biblical exploration of human creativity if it cannot be demonstrated that humans share in God's creative nature. Fortunately, Scripture clearly states that humans are made in the "image" and "likeness" of God.[7] How the image and likeness of God manifests itself in humanity has been a matter of debate. Being created in the image of God is a mystery beyond simple definition or human speculation. Augustine argued that humanity was made in the image of the Trinity as an unequal likeness through a sort of imitation.[8] The authors of Genesis felt no need to elaborate upon what was meant by their ambiguous statement about the image of God in humanity.[9] They simply portrayed a God who deliberated in plurality and fashioned a creature in his own singular-in-plurality image.

The biblical commentator Victor Hamilton presents a conception of the image of God in humanity that is sensitive to the Genesis text but is also sensitive to the totality of Scripture. Hamilton concludes that, when delving into the nature of the image of God in humanity, it is important that:

---

3. Gen 1:1—2:19.
4. Gen 1:1—2:19; Exod 31:1–11, 37:7–9.
5. Gen 1:2; Hamilton, *Book of Genesis*, 11–14.
6. John 1:1–3; Col 1:15–17; Heb 1:3.
7. Gen 1:26–27 (ESV).
8. Louth, *Ancient Christian Commentary*, 30.
9. McKeown, *Genesis*, 281.

> Any approach that focuses on one aspect of man—be that physical, spiritual, or intellectual—to the neglect of the rest of man's constituent features seems doomed to failure . . . to be human is to bear the image of God. This understanding emphasizes man as a unity. No part of man, no function of man is subordinated to some other, higher part or activity.[10]

Hamilton's conclusion, that no part or function of humanity is subordinate to any other, is a guiding principle for my educational practice. Hamilton's picture of the image of God in humanity portrays a holistic, human creature; a unity of mental, physical, emotional, sensual and spiritual capacities. Maintaining that humans are made in the image of God neither suggests that we are divine copies of God, as Augustine points out, nor does maintaining that humans are made in the image of God suggest that the entire image of the limitless God can be contained within the limited faculties of the human creature.

In Gen 1, the narrative that surrounds and encompasses verse 26 describes the actions of God in unmistakably anthropomorphic terms. Like humans, God speaks (vv. 3, 6, 9, 11, 14, 20, 24, 26, 28, 29), God sees (vv. 4, 10, 12, 18, 21, 25, 31), God makes (vv. 4, 7, 12, 16, 21, 25, 27), God names (vv. 5, 8, 10), and God blesses (vv. 22, 28). In Gen 2, the anthropomorphic acts of God continue as he rests at the conclusion of his creative work (vv. 2, 3). These continuities by no means exhaust the concept of the divine image in humanity, but they do suggest clear areas of similarity and points of connection between mankind and God.

For a Christian educator teaching in a creative discipline, the accounts of God naming various aspects of his creation are of particular interest. Genesis 2 contains two events surrounding the creation of humans that illuminate the relationship between the image of God in humanity and humanity's creative capacity. The first event is God's *ex creatis* forming of the first human out of the dust of the earth. The second event is the biblical account of Adam naming the animals.

Found in Gen 2, the account of God forming Adam out of dust is significant for a biblical understanding of human creativity. Commentator Gordon Wenham characterizes the verb "shaped" as being related to the work of a potter.[11] Like Wenham, when translating the word "built" used in the creation of Eve, Robert Alter describes the Hebrew verb used

---

10. Hamilton, *Book of Genesis*, 137.
11. Gen 2:7; Wenham, *Genesis*, 59.

in the fashioning of Adam as a potter's term.[12] The "forming" of the first human from the dust of the earth and the "building" of the first woman out of man is significant because God is expressing himself in Scripture as the first sculptor—the first culture maker and creative shaper of new forms out of the raw materials of his *ex nihilo* creation.[13] Here we witness God the Creator modeling the *ex creatis* creative process to humanity. God is creating in the way that humans create. But this *ex creatis* act of God is not merely an act of neutral formation. Instead, it is an act of divine love.

God's process of forming Adam out of dust displays the love and intimacy with which God formed the man and breathed life into him. God got his hands dirty. Like a potter, he formed the first human from dust and clay. Throughout Scripture, biblical writers poetically adopt this image of God. Writers repeatedly reference the intimate touch of God's hand in the forming of humanity.[14] To touch is to be, quite literally, connected to the object receiving the touch. The skillful, knowledgeable hand of the artist lovingly forms potentials into realities. To God, humanity did not just remain a good idea; instead, humanity became an actualized material reality; brought into being out of his self-giving love.

It was also out of love that God mandated and blessed the creativity of his newly formed humans. This mandate and blessing are clearly demonstrated in the account of Adam naming the animals:

> Now out of the ground the Lord God had formed every beast of the field and every bird of the heavens and brought them to the man to see what he would call them. And whatever the man called every living creature, that was its name.[15]

The biblical account of Adam naming the animals is a neglected but significant passage of Scripture. The brief account illuminates two essential points regarding human creativity. The first point is that God mandated for Adam to be creative. The second point is that God blessed Adam's creativity. In mandating and blessing the creativity of the first human, God, by extension, mandates and blesses the creative capacity found in all humans.

---

12. Gen 2:22; Gen 2:7; Alter, *Genesis*, 9.

13. Crouch, "Gospel," in Taylor, *Beauty of the Church*, 32.

14. See, for example, Job 10:8; Ps 119:73; Isa 64:8. Cassuto, *Commentary on the Book of Genesis*, 105.

15. Gen 2:19 (ESV).

Scripture relates that God "brought" the animals before Adam to "see what he would call them." God gave Adam a task that he had equipped the man to accomplish. God also gave Adam freedom to respond out of his individual creativity. Adam appropriately forms something new in response to the creation—names for the animals.

Genesis 2:19 clearly relates that it was God who brings the animals to Adam. Adam did not initiate the event. In the wholeness of God's image in humanity, God intends for his human creature to do exactly what he is designed for. Adam did not name the animals solely out of the capacity of his discernment or even his authority, as many biblical commentators limitedly attest.[16] Instead, Adam names the animals out of the totality of his holistic being, which includes the ability to engage creatively with the creation and shape it into a new reality. Adam appropriately responded to God's revealed will by exercising his creative freedom. This freedom is a gift that God has given to all humanity.

By connecting the actions of the imaged human to the revealed actions of God, Scripture directly connects humanity's image to its prototype, and by relating that it was God who initiated the bringing of the animals before Adam to name, Scripture also reveals God's mandate for humanity to be creative. The mandate for human creativity is strengthened further when God blesses the creativity of Adam by accepting the names that he had provided for "every living creature." The acceptance of the animals' names by God is treated matter-of-factually: "Whatever the man called every living creature, that was its name."[17] By accepting the names that Adam, the first human, had creatively formed, God blessed not only the creative nature in Adam but also the creative nature in all of humanity.

Though the evidence from the first two chapters of Genesis provides some insight into the image of God in humanity and into God's mandate and blessing of human creativity in general, the ensuing exploration of Exodus will demonstrate that God's mandate and blessing of human creativity (when exercised appropriately) persisted after humanity had fallen into sin. Fallen hands would form the materials of this world into the tabernacle; the singular place where the glory of God would immanently dwell among his chosen people.

---

16. See, for example, Mathews, *Genesis*, 215.
17. Gen 2:19 (ESV).

THE FALL

Humanity's sinful disobedience in the Garden altered the context in which humans enacted their creativity. Humans, instead of creating new things in the way that God had intended, could now fashion abominations; idols that expressed the lusts and depravities of humanity's rebellion against God. To explore God's continued mandate and blessing of human creativity after the fall, we turn to Exodus and the account of the building of the tabernacle. Towards the end of Exodus, God details his plan for the tabernacle to Moses. The construction of the tabernacle, however, was left to the fallen hands of humans to construct. The use by God of human artisans for the construction of the tabernacle demonstrates the continued mandate and blessing of God for human creativity, even after the fall. The account also demonstrates that God continues to allow creative freedom in the artistic process, even when he gives particular guidelines.

The fall of humanity in the Garden of Eden did not prevent God from blessing fallen humans with the task of preparing his dwelling place amongst his chosen people. The Bible relates that Bezalel was filled with the Spirit of God and was equipped, as was Oholiab, to undertake and supervise the many creative tasks associated with the construction of the tabernacle.[18] In Exod 31:3, we see the phrase *ruach elohim*, "Spirit of God," used for the first time since the creation account in Genesis 1:2.[19] In Genesis, the phrase described the Spirit of God hovering over the waters of creation. In Exodus, God fills Bezalel with, "the Spirit of God, with ability and intelligence, with knowledge and all craftsmanship, to devise artistic designs, to work in gold, silver, and bronze, in cutting stones for setting, and in carving wood, to work in every craft."[20] The biblical text clearly shows that fallen humans were mandated to execute God's plan for the tabernacle, and those humans were going to have to utilize their individual creativity and artistic vision in order to do so.

I have at times heard preachers and teachers of the Bible highlight the "strict" instructions that God gave to Moses for the construction of the tabernacle. Scripture tells us that God showed Moses some form of pattern,[21] but the "instructions" that made their way into the text of Exodus are actually quite vague upon examination. The directions for

---

18. Exod 31:1–11; 35:30–39:31.
19. Hamilton, *Book of Genesis*, 111.
20. Exod 31:3–4, (ESV).
21. See Exod 25:9, 40; 26:30.

the priestly robes demonstrate the lack of specific guidance contained in the text:

> You shall make the robe of the ephod all of blue. It shall have an opening for the head in the middle of it, with a woven binding around the opening, like the opening in a garment, so that it may not tear. On its hem you shall make pomegranates of blue and purple and scarlet yarns, around its hem, with bells of gold between them, a golden bell and a pomegranate, a golden bell and a pomegranate, around the hem of the robe.[22]

To the person who was to fabricate the priestly robes, these directions may have provided more questions than answers. For instance, how large were the embroidered pomegranates on the hem of the robes supposed to be? What was to be the shape of the golden bells? How many pairs of alternating pomegranates and bells were to go around the hem? The text only specifically mentions two pair. It seems that two pair would be insufficient to go "around" the robe. The lack of precision in the directions reveals that God still desires that his humans enact their creative freedom, as Adam did when naming the animals. The presence of the Spirit of God ensures that even fallen humans are capable of appropriately exercising their creative freedom.

In the ESV, the Hebrew word *chashab* in Exod 31:4 is translated as "to devise." When placed within the verse, the translation reads, "to devise artistic designs." The translation confirms the autonomy that tabernacle artists enjoyed as they appropriately exercised their creative freedom in the Spirit. Consequently, any characterization that portrays Bezalel or any artist of the tabernacle as just some form of divine medium is contrary to the evidence found in Scripture. Bezalel and the artisans of the tabernacle were free to appropriately respond within God's expressed guidelines. God certainly could have fabricated the tabernacle himself and caused it to descend from heaven upon a fluffy cloud, but he chose instead to bless human artists by intimately involving them in the tabernacle's design and construction.

The tabernacle, like Adam's naming of the animals, was actualized through human creativity by artists made in the image of God. Both accounts of biblical creativity—one pre-fall, one post-fall—follow the same pattern. God mandates the creativity of his human creation; humans in their creative freedom respond appropriately by exercising

---

22. Exod 28:31–34 (ESV).

their creativity.[23] God then blesses the creative, particularized acts of his beloved humans by accepting their creations. God restrained his majesty and superior creative nature to allow his creaturely humans to act creatively. God provided the framework and the objectives. Humans executed the details in partnership with the Holy Spirit, and we know that as God blessed Adam's creativity by accepting the names of the animals, God also accepted and blessed the creativity of the fallen artists of the tabernacle by filling it with his presence.[24]

REDEMPTION

When Christ came to earth to redeem creation, the context of appropriate human response shifted once again. Because of Christ's redemptive work on earth, we live in a period of God's revelation through his indwelling Holy Spirit.[25] Today, the artist of Christian faith is empowered by the Holy Spirit to appropriately respond to God and to creatively communicate the love that God has for his creation.

The Holy Spirit opens God's revelation to us through Scripture, but the Holy Spirit also shares God's self-revelation to us through the material forms of creation, which necessarily include material forms shaped by human hands. Human formations are part of God's dynamic, living creation. Artwork then, which is appropriately created in response to the Holy Spirit, is a valid human activity and a proper form of worship.

Our imperfect acts of creativity, generated appropriately in partnership with the Holy Spirit, are made holy to the Father through the Son, who sits at the right hand of the Father and intercedes for us. We as followers of Jesus are adopted into Christ as co-heirs with him. Christ takes our unworthy acts of worship and, through his person, cleanses them and makes them holy to the Father. For Christians, the primary means of mediation between God and humanity is Christ, and we are united to Christ by the Spirit.

---

23. The ability to act creatively is a general grace given to all humanity. In the case of the construction of the tabernacle, appropriate creative freedom is safeguarded by the gifting of the Spirit of God to Bezalel and the other artisans. The role of the Holy Spirit in the appropriate creative response to the creation will be discussed further in the next section.

24. Exod 40:34–38.

25. Gal 5:18.

Steven Guthrie, in his book, *Creator Spirit*, offers a view of the human imagination as it is engaged in relationship and partnership with the Holy Spirit:

> The work of the Holy Spirit is to restore sight: to allow humans to see truly, no longer blinded by ideology... The work of the Spirit is to restore speech: to allow human beings to speak truly and creatively... The work of the Spirit is to restore freedom: to empower human beings to not only receive creation but also to become givers who add to the world.[26]

When the artist is in partnership and relation with the Holy Spirit, confusion is removed from our ideology. The re-humanizing power of the Holy Spirit allows us to see the creation properly. Through the Holy Spirit's power and guidance, Christians may add to the world's transformation. Indeed, the Spirit restores our original vocation to discern the truth and to remake the world in light of that truth.[27] The responsibility and freedom to envisage, shape, and remake the world has always been our human vocation.[28] We were designed in the triune image of God to discern creation appropriately and to transform it creatively. God's desire for humans and their creativity was applicable before the fall; it was applicable for humanity after the fall, and it is applicable in our current, redeemed age as we await the resolution of God's story in the world.

When discussing the capacity and expression of human creativity after Christ's redemptive work, we must first realize that all human artistic expression still remains under the curse of the fall. How then can artistic objects, created by fallen hands, be made acceptable to God? The answer to this question is simple—through worship.

Gerald Borchert describes worship as, "one's entire life of responding to God and divine mystery."[29] As the triune God created humanity in his image, so must humanity's worship of the triune God be out of the totality of being. Francis Schaeffer rightly quips, "There are no platonic areas in Christianity."[30] God made the whole person; the whole person is redeemed in Christ. Christ is Lord of the whole person, and the whole person will have a bodily resurrection and wholly completed

---

26. Guthrie, *Creator Spirit*, 153.
27. Guthrie, *Creator Spirit*, 153.
28. Wolterstorff, *Art in Action*, 74.
29. Borchert, *Worship in the New Testament*, 5.
30. Schaeffer, *Art and the Bible*, 14.

redemption.[31] The worship of God must be genuine and, reflecting the outpouring of the love of the triune God, must be self-giving and flow from the totality of our lives.[32]

Human creativity and visual art must be viewed under the broader category of worship. Worship is not limited to liturgical action in a building. But in our own fallen efforts, our worship is unworthy and unacceptable to the Father. There is only one true, acceptable offering to the Father. There is only one mediator between humanity and God—the incarnate Son.

James Torrance defines worship as, "the gift of participating through the Spirit in the incarnate Son's communion with the Father."[33] Through the Holy Spirit, God draws humanity into relationship with the Son and into his life of communion with the Father.[34] Torrance continues by describing the triune relationship of God as, "one of mutual love, mutual self-giving, mutual testifying, [and] mutual glorifying."[35] This love is incomprehensible, not because the triune God is completely "other," but rather for the complete opposite reason. Hans Urs von Balthasar's view is that God's triune love is incomprehensible precisely because we can experience it. We can share in the overwhelming and self-giving love of the triune God, who has expressed himself in the self-emptying love of Christ through the incarnation and through creation.[36]

In Christ's presenting himself as the one true offering to the Father, we are caught up by the Spirit and joined to Christ as he worships the Father. In the person of Christ and in his acceptable worship, our unworthy offerings are cleansed through our unity with Christ through our faith and by the Spirit. As we responsively offer ourselves in the totality of our bodies, minds, and spirits (and I would argue, creativity),[37] our self-giving offerings are mystically joined by the Spirit into Christ's perpetual offering. Through the person of Christ and his atoning sacrifice on the cross, our human creativity, offered in appropriate response to

---

31. Schaeffer, *Art and the Bible*, 14.
32. Borchert, *Worship in the New Testament*, 6.
33. Torrance, *Worship*, 21.
34. Torrance, *Worship*, 30.
35. Torrance, *Worship*, 31.
36. Nichols, *Key to Balthasar*, 30.
37. Torrance, *Worship*, 15.

God, is made holy to the Father. Christ's worship becomes our worship,[38] and through the Spirit, our worship becomes Christ's worship. Torrance writes, "we are graciously given the gift of worshiping the Father, in and through the Son, in the communion of the Holy Spirit."[39] Consequently, any artistic offering made by fallen hands through the Spirit in response to the truth of God's revelation is acceptable, regardless of its content. The Holy Spirit restores our capacity to respond appropriately in our reshaping of creation and allows us to see how we are presently situated within the story of God as it unfolds around us. But, if there is a future yet to come in the story of God, how might this future inform the work of creative humans of Christian faith who are made in the image of their Creator?

RESTORATION

Makoto Fujimura in his book, *Culture Care*, provides a vision of flourishing for the artist of Christian faith that is worked out in the present but keeps a view to our future restoration. Fujimura's vision keeps at its forefront God's victory over Satan and the ultimate restoration of both humanity and the creation in the new heaven and the new earth as culminated in the New Jerusalem. Fujimura calls this vision "Culture Care," and he expresses culture care as being composed of three parts: genesis moments, generosity, and generational thinking.[40]

A "genesis moment" is any life-giving interaction that leads to a more complete understanding of our humanity as intended by God at our creation. Through genesis moments we are nurtured in the present and transformed by the Holy Spirit into our future selves until our final restoration, when all things will be renewed. "Generosity" refers to living life as a gift and gifting life to others out of an abundance of love for the creation and for others. Generosity works "against a mindset that has survival and utility in the foreground. [Generosity reminds] us that life always overflows our attempts to reduce it to a commodity or a transaction—because it is a gift."[41] This world, even in its fallen state, is a gift, and as humans we need to think of the care of our culture not in terms of

---

38. Torrance, *Worship*, 15.
39. Torrance, *Worship*, 15.
40. Fujimura, *Culture Care*, 3.
41. Fujimura, *Culture Care*, 4.

just today, but in terms of human flourishing for the time that remains to humanity in this age. For Fujimura, this long view concept of culture care is "generational thinking."

During my own personal journey as an artist of Christian faith, I began (as do many of my art students) with the question: What kind of artwork am I as a Christian artist supposed to make? A related question might be: What is Christian art supposed to look like? I now realize that questions like these are problematic because they are simply the wrong types of questions to ask. These questions look externally to a mythical formulaic paradigm, where one may safely and unoffensively conform one's work into an acceptable pattern. Fujimura perfectly isolates the position from which artists of Christian faith pose these questions as he reflects: "I am not a Christian artist. I am a Christian, yes, and an artist. I dare not treat the powerful presence of Christ in my life as an *adjective* [emphasis added]. I want Christ to be my whole being."[42]

The fear of creating something "un-Christian" is often the fear that drives questions surrounding what "Christian" artists should make. These types of questions imply that there is some specific imagery or form of "Christian" art to do. "Christian" here is being used as an adjective to describe the artist, but using Christ in the form of an adjective fails to proclaim the weight and glory of the truth, which is Christ's supreme power and presence in our lives. The artistic expressions that seek to answer questions like, "What is Christian art supposed to look like?" tend to be populated with ubiquitous crosses and unambiguous Christian imagery.

The goal of the artist of Christian faith shouldn't be to make the most "Christian-looking" art. The artist of Christian faith should instead strive to make art that flows out of relationship and response to our triune Creator. Through this relationship, we are transformed from the inside out into the unique image of Christ in us. As we are transformed by the power of the Holy Spirit, we realize that the goal of our lives lived in worship isn't morality, but divine relationship. The triune God exists in relationship, and through Christ's redemption we are invited into this divine relationship by the power of the Holy Spirit. Through the Spirit, we are renewed to respond appropriately to God and his creation.

---

42. Fujimura, *Culture Care*, 63–64.

In *Culture Care*, Fujimura states, "the care and cultivation of culture begins with the care and cultivation of the soul."[43] If "the care and cultivation of culture" is understood as an individual's interaction with the whole of the created order, then the care and cultivation of the soul begins with the care and cultivation of our relationships, especially our relationship with our triune Creator. Cultivation of the soul by answering God's invitation into the divine relationship is the essence and beginning of a flourishing practice of human creativity. Joining the perichoretic dance of the Trinity puts us into direct relationship with our Creator, who fills us with his Holy Spirit so that we may know the power and presence of Christ in us; so that we are continually transforming into the image of Christ that his image might become our whole being.

The strength of the approach that Fujimura puts forth is that it embraces God's revealed story for humanity and all of creation. "Generative," "generous," and "generational" all conspicuously begin with "g–e–n," a not-so-subtle reference to Genesis. In Fujimura's conception, these three "gens" are part of our original purpose and design before the fall, but they are also a proclamation of our future restoration. In his model, Fujimura's first step acknowledges the fall, where brokenness is identified and articulated. This is an important step if Christians are to establish authentic relationships in a fallen world. Fujimura then proposes an attitude of hospitality, where "truth-telling" can be offered out of love. It is in this second stage that we Christians might offer a vision of truth and reality that is counter to the myriad false truths that engulf the contemporary individual. It is not that people in this relativistic, postmodern age are unbelievers, it is just that they believe "otherwise."[44] Christianity is only one of many worldviews vying for the attention of the disenchanted.

The final step of Fujimura's vision, where artists of Christian faith invite the world through their art into a vision of beauty, wholeness, and healing, is nothing more than an invitation into the story and presence of God. As our artwork flows out of response to our deepening relationship with the triune God, we anticipate the final restoration promised in Scripture and present a vision of reality that the Holy Spirit may use to draw those who are lost back into relationship with their source and sustaining.

---

43. Fujimura, *Culture Care*, 25.
44. Smith, *How (Not) to be Secular*, 47.

CONCLUSION

In a trinitarian view of human creativity as worship, we worship the Father by our creative actions offered in appropriate response to his self-revelation. In our fallen state, Christ takes our human creativity as worship to the Father in the singularly acceptable offering of himself. Through the Spirit, we are joined to Christ and invited to be remade into the renewed image of God in humanity, and we proclaim the future restoration of humanity and all of creation by acknowledging the fall and inviting others into the vision of our future wholeness; the model and goal of our remade humanity being Christ, who is the perfect image of God.[45] Finally, it is the Holy Spirit who is the vehicle by which our human creativity-as-worship is made acceptable to the Father through the person of his Son.

The model I have attempted to present in this chapter (that of placing my discipline into the revealed story of God) is one, I hope, others may utilize in their own disciplines. This integrated approach will require a basic knowledge of the revealed structure of human history from creation, to fall, to redemption, and to our ultimate restoration. It will also require a basic understanding of fundamental Christian theology. Finally, it will require some effort on the academic's part to research writers of Christian faith in their own disciplines.

As I advise my students about what kind of art a "Christian" artist is supposed to make, so too, I also advise you, don't begin with the question: What am I as a faithful Christian educator supposed to teach? Instead, I encourage you to answer the invitation to the dance. Dance in the transforming unity of our triune God, our source of life. Trust that the Spirit will mature you spiritually and transform the product of your teaching through the process of being remade into the image of Christ. And may the totality of our holistic humanness be forever offered as praise to the Father, through the Son, and in the power of the Holy Spirit, Amen.

---

45. 2 Cor 4:4.

BIBLIOGRAPHY

Alter, Robert. *Genesis*. New York: W.W. Norton, 1996.

Borchert, Gerald R. *Worship in the New Testament: Divine Mystery and Human Response*. St. Louis: Chalice, 2008.

Cassuto, Umberto. *A Commentary on the Book of Genesis: from Adam to Noah*. Vol. 1. Translated by Israel Abrahams. Jerusalem: Magnes, 1978.

Fujimura, Makoto. *Culture Care*. New York: Fujimura Institute and International Arts Movement, 2015.

Guthrie, Steven R. *Creator Spirit: The Holy Spirit and the Art of Becoming Human*. Grand Rapids: Baker Academic, 2001.

Hamilton, Victor P. *The Book of Genesis 1–17*. Vol. 1. *New International Commentary on the Old Testament*. Nashville: Eerdmans, 1990.

Louth, Andrew. ed. *Genesis I–II*. Vol. 1. *Ancient Christian Commentary on Scripture: Old Testament*. Chicago: Fitzroy Dearborn, 2001.

Mathews, K A. *Genesis*. Vol. 1A. *The New American Commentary*. Nashville: Broadman & Holman, 2002.

McKeown, James. *Genesis*. Grand Rapids: Eerdmans, 2008.

Nichols, Aidan. *A Key to Balthasar: Hans Urs von Balthasar On Beauty, Goodness, and Truth*. Grand Rapids: Baker Academic, 2011.

Schaeffer, Francis A. *Art and the Bible*. Downers Grove, IL: InterVarsity, 1973.

Smith, James K. A. *How (Not) to be Secular: Reading Charles Taylor*. Grand Rapids: Eerdmans, 2014.

Tasker, R. V. G. *The Gospel According to St. Matthew: An Introduction and Commentary*. Tyndale New Testament Commentaries. 2 Vols. Grand Rapids: Eerdmans, 1983.

Taylor, W. David O. ed. *For the Beauty of the Church: Casting a Vision for the Arts*. Grand Rapids: Baker, 2010.

Todd, James. M. *Sinai and the Saints: Reading Old Covenant Laws for the New Covenant Community*. Downers Grove, IL: IVP Academic, 2017.

Torrance, James B. *Worship, Community, and the Triune God of Grace*. Downers Grove, IL: IVP Academic, 1997.

Wenham, Gordon J. *Genesis 1–15*. Vol. 1. *Word Biblical Commentary*. Edited by John D. W. Watts. Waco, TX: Word, 1987.

Wolterstorff, Nicholas. *Art in Action: Toward a Christian Aesthetic*. Grand Rapids: Eerdmans, 1980.

16

Assuming a Posture of Care
The Role of Composition in Christian Formation

Paige A. Ray

If rhetoric does what we traditionally define as communicating the rhetor's view of reality (at least some of it) through symbol, then what follows are manifold and complex implications about the rhetor's influence—the power, however broad or narrow, of the one who wields language. Fittingly, implications also follow regarding my responsibility as a composition teacher: my responsibility to the minds of college writers whose goals and vocations, regardless of exact career or discipline, will ask them to function as meaningful rhetors. And, necessarily, our Christian calling deepens this obligation further both for instructors and students beyond ethics and morality, toward a fullness that integrates language, self, other, and worldview. As the key thrust of this volume, articulated by my colleagues in the introduction and elsewhere, is to thoughtfully respond to trends that have fragmented the soul of the university by working towards the life-giving reintegration of faith and academia, then courses that specialize in the craft of writing and the currency of words are paramount. Language is the currency of our learning, thinking, sharing, and a major contribution to our identity formation—thus, writing has incredible power to integrate the self, as well as the community of intentional writers and communicators that constitute the Christian college.

This chapter is the result of my own exploration of how my faith meets my work in the comp classroom, which began with the observation that many students are not aware of their potential power as writers, nor the implicit responsibility and (what I call) the *ethic of care* that accompanies such power. Specifically, I have observed that many first-year composition students lack awareness of the reader. When writing, they function as if in monologue, assuming that writing is always and only a mode of self-expression. This approach hinders students in that they are unable to pattern the development of their ideas in a way that anticipates the needs of the reader and gauges a hypothetical response.

Having instructed students for the past fifteen years in English and writing, I see an interesting link between students' tendencies toward monological self-expression and the heavy influence of an era of hyper-individualism. Under this influence, students learn to effectively brand and cultivate their own identity. However, they lack a sense of reciprocity toward the very communities that have formed their sense of identity. Christian students might perceive and link themselves to the larger Christian narrative, finding their identity within the body of Christ. But many young Christians have not entirely escaped the effects of a culture that prizes the self. This poses a particular challenge for the Christian college as it seeks to form students of Christian character who are other-centered, living in God's design for us to be relational. Ultimately, we want students to move away from a monological approach to life that prizes self-expression, and into a dialogical approach that engages with and attends to the needs of surrounding communities.

I find that college composition can play a key role in developing in students an awareness of our relational design as beings created to participate in dialogue. In composition courses, student writers inevitably encounter the dialogical implications of language, and hopefully become more sensitive to the person at the receiving end of that dialogue. This shift away from a focus on self-expression toward an ethic of care for others prepares students to respond well as Christians in the necessary dialogues of their everyday lives, whatever the mode or medium.

THE PROBLEM OF HYPER-INDIVIDUALISM

In my experience, if freshmen composition students gravitate toward a particular genre of writing, they tend to gravitate toward the personal narrative. This is both encouraging and fitting. Encouraging because they like to write about *something*. And fitting because, as Robert Jenson articulates in "How the World Lost its Story," it is the human tendency to orient oneself by means of narrative, to find identity, purpose, and coherence in the context of a larger story, a narrative identity. Before the current era of postmodernism, the supposition of the modern West, as Jenson puts it, was "that an omniscient historian could write a *universal* history, and . . . this is so because the universe with inclusion of our lives is in fact a story written by a sort of omnipotent novelist."[1] However, postmodernism rejects the supposition that the "world somehow 'has' its own true story, antecedent to, and enabling of, the stories we tell about ourselves in it."[2] Thus, the human compulsion to orient the self in the context of a narrative is in conflict with the postmodern loss of the concept Jenson identifies as "the narratable world."[3] Young students exist in a culture that rejects the concept of a coherent narrative, yet they still seek narrative identity.

The implicit danger in this tension is that as individuals seek narrative identity in a culture that rejects a common sense of meaning, they develop an inward focus solely on the self: who am I, how does this or that occurrence affect *me*? It is a development that pushes us further into the dangers of hyper-individualism. And in such a self-centered environment, young minds often fail to connect and engage meaningfully with a community, to be other-centered. This phenomenon is quite visible through the growing presence of social media in an era which lauds authenticity, but excels in the production of the manufactured "selfie," an ultimate irony. In fact, some young voices, and some not so young, attempt to create their own personal stories and realities via the digital realm, proclaiming "what's right for me" and casting off the attempts of any community that tries to offer truth and accountability. While social media can offer platforms for emerging communities and for sharing life in meaningful ways, many young participants fail to engage with those communities. When my sweet, fourteen-year-old niece posts many, varied, and often contrived images of herself on Instagram, she *does* receive and process feedback from her peer community. However, she feverishly searches these responses only for affirmation and a sense of

---

1. Jenson, "How the World Lost its Story."
2. Jenson, "How the World Lost its Story."
3. Jenson, "How the World Lost its Story."

self-worth. Does this exchange constitute a dialogue, or at least a meaningful dialogue? Does she, and do we live simply and fatally in a one-way narrative of self? If so, then we are experiencing dysfunction, for we are designed to live in relationship and called to engage with community.

In her commencement address to the 2015 graduating class at the University of Rochester, education strategist Deborah Bial also speaks to the pattern of hyper-individualism. She shares, "I feel like we are living in a time that's all about self-obsession. [You] have an opportunity out there to promote your own 'brand.'"[4] She mourns the current trend for people to sell themselves as a product, to market themselves, because this trend reiterates focus on the self and often leads to deception and distortion. Bial exhorts the graduates of Rochester University, "We've got to be mindful about how we represent ourselves, not just for the sake of our personal integrity, but for the dignity of our society. While we all want to build a good life for ourselves, we also have a responsibility to contribute to a world with moral character. Our world depends on it."[5] Bial is calling her young audience to a virtuous representation of the self, to authenticity. This is good, but she misses something; her appeal falls short. Bial's exhortation does not call students from the monologue of self into responsible and responsive dialogue.

DIALOGUE, COMMUNITY, AND THE NEED FOR RECIPROCITY

The question follows, what are students missing if they fail to engage in dialogue? I would argue that because we are designed to live in relationship and community, failure to engage in dialogue hinders the individual from living in the fullness of human experience, including what Steven Garber calls the "coherent life." In *The Fabric of Faithfulness*, Garber suggests that a coherent life, one that integrates belief with behavior, necessarily stems from and engages with community.[6] The relationship between the individual and his community should be reciprocal. Garber cites Alasdair MacIntyre's observation about the loss of this reciprocity:

> With the loss of a sense of being 'on a journey with set goals ... toward a given end'—a narratable world—the modern

4. Bial, "Don't Just Be A Brand," 243.
5. Bial, "Don't Just Be A Brand," 243.
6. Garber, *Fabric of Faithfulness*, 157.

person has also lost the sense of 'an interlocking set of social relationships . . . that define [his] obligations and [his] duties.' The consequence? A fraying social fabric that gnaws away at our feeling of responsibility to and for each other, and that nurtures cynicism about anyone and everything at the highest levels of public responsibility.[7]

Even though Christian students embrace a common journey toward Christ-likeness, as products of a "fraying social fabric," it is likely that they still struggle to navigate the larger social environment; thus, they feel a disconnect. Garber cites *Habits of the Heart: Individualism and Commitment in American Life*, which identifies "the language of the isolated self" as endemic to this generation. This is problematic because "there are truths we do not see when we adopt the language of radical individualism. [For] we find ourselves not independently of other people and institutions but through them. We never get to the bottom of ourselves on our own. We discover who we are face to face and side by side with others in work, love, and learning."[8] We hope that students recognize the formative nature of community and appreciate the communities that have taught them to work, love, and learn. But the bigger challenge is to revive in students a sense of responsibility toward others.

What we do in higher education must not stop at forming authentic and honest individuals. The Christian liberal arts institution cannot leave students focused inwardly. It is not enough to say to our students, be good, be redeemed, live in the freedom of Christ, surround yourself with a great community that pours into your cultivation. We must discuss the implications of being good, redeemed, and free that reach outward. As an institution, we help students ground themselves in the truth of the living God; we coach them to think carefully through philosophy, theology, and other disciplines. But we hope, above all, that those students will not exist as insular beings, holding the truth passively within themselves, for relationship with community is indeed reciprocal and is inherent to a holistic Christian worldview. There is a problem if our students' journeys end in knowing God, in finding personal relationship and a sense of personal identity in their Christian experience. Though it is at a disadvantage in an era of hyper-individualism, the Christian college can teach students that Christ, as the living God, the Son of God, the Word, was, in his earthly

---

7. Garber, *Fabric of Faithfulness*, 158.
8. Garber, *Fabric of Faithfulness*, 159.

life, in constant dialogue both with his heavenly Father and with those around him. In fact, if students come to know God fully and live accordingly, this knowledge will compel students to serve and interact with the people he has created.

In *Is Reality Secular?*, Mary Poplin reflects on her experience observing the works of Mother Theresa and the Missionaries of Charity in Calcutta: "I could explain what they did but not how or why they did it. I could only tell half the story with secular language; I could not adequately describe their core motivations and had no way to explain the peace and power that accompanied their works."[9] She expresses her astonishment that "when they tended the most desperate and unlovable person, they believed they were tending Jesus in the distressing disguise of the poor?"[10] It is their very knowledge and love for the living God, the Word incarnate, that compelled these missionaries to be aware of human need, human community, and to assume a posture of care towards others. Thus, relationship with God calls us to assume that posture of care toward the larger community, both the body of Christ, and the whole of humanity.

TOWARDS A POSTURE OF CARE

How then, do we call students out of themselves, and cultivate in them an awareness of others and a compulsion to participate in community in meaningful ways? How do we call them out of monologue and into dialogue, and compel them to find their own "Calcutta" as Poplin found hers? The curriculum and assignments of a composition course will not cure the predicament of Western society's hyper-individualism. And likely, most teachers do not claim that those who pass their entry-level writing courses have learned to perfectly understand their place in the cosmos and are now engaging in ideal and responsible dialogue with their respective communities. However, the hope is that learning to write challenges each student to be conscious of the power of language, the necessity of dialogue, and the existence of the reader, and furthermore, that the student will eventually move beyond awareness and assume a posture of care towards others: the presumed reader, listener, and community. This

---

9. Poplin, *Is Reality Secular?*, 24.
10. Poplin, *Is Reality Secular?*, 24.

awareness and eventual posture of care provide an ultimate coherence in the life of the individual.

THE DIALOGICAL NATURE OF LANGUAGE

The process of coaching students in this direction begins with an understanding of language, its function and design. In *The Message in the Bottle*, Walker Percy identifies the essential nature of man with man's capacity for language. He affectionately recognizes man as "*Homo loquens, Homo symbolificus*, man the speaking animal, man the symbol-monger."[11] Similarly, Charles Taylor, philosopher and professor emeritus at McGill University, refers to man simply as the "language animal."[12]

It is doubtful that many freshman composition students understand language as the phenomenon that enables them to conceive of being, and to relate their being to the rest of the world. In fact, because language, speech, writing, and texting are the necessary currency of our daily interactions, we seldom pause to investigate them. As Percy notes, "Man's capacity for symbol-mongering in general and language in particular is so intimately part and parcel of his being human, of his perceiving and knowing, of his very consciousness itself, that it is all but impossible for him to focus on the magic prism through which he sees everything else."[13] Pausing to consider the function of language, we might conclude that it is a means, an instrument for expression, for communicating information, for directing imperatives. But Charles Taylor argues that language is not simply an instrument; rather, it is constitutive of our ability to understand our own existence, and to articulate and share our human experience.[14] Walker Percy explains the significance of this human capacity, setting man apart from all other animals:

> Each being is in the world, acting upon the world and itself being acted upon by the world. But when a man appears and names a thing, when he says this is water and water is cool, something unprecedented takes place. What the third term, man, does is not merely enter into interaction with the others—though he does this too—but stand apart from two of the terms

11. Percy, *Message in the Bottle*, 30.
12. Taylor, *Language Animal*.
13. Percy, *Message in the Bottle*, 13.
14. Taylor, *Language Animal*, 332.

and say that one 'is' the other. The two things which he pairs or identifies are the word he speaks or hears and the thing he sees before him. This is not only an unprecedented happening; it is also, as the semanticists have noted, scandalous. A [the liquid substance] is clearly not B [the phonological word]. But were it not for this cosmic blunder, man would not be man; he would never be capable of folly and he would never be capable of truth. Unless he says that A is B, [assigning meaning through the use of symbol], he will never know A or B; he will only respond to them. A bee is not as foolish as man, but it also cannot tell the truth. All it can do is respond to its environment . . . Man is not merely a higher organism responding to and controlling his environment. He is, in Heidegger's words, that being in the world whose calling it is to find a name for Being, to give testimony to it, and to provide for it a clearing.[15]

Percy's point here is that we are not merely responders to the world in which we live. Through language, through the use of symbol, we "build ourselves landscapes of meaning" by which we orient ourselves in the world and establish footings for relationships and dialogue with others.[16]

These landscapes of meaning are complex, for the naming power of language does not end in a two-year-old's ability to point at an item on the floor and identify it as "book." As she acquires language, a toddler can conceive of experiences like fear, affection, delight, and surprise, identify their sources, and successfully communicate these complexities. Moreover, my students can conceivably (and hopefully) articulate a careful analysis of a text by choosing nuanced and precise words. The end result, namely dialogue, though often taken for granted, is miraculous. Percy addresses the dialogical phenomenon directly: "How does it happen that you can talk and I can understand you? Or, how does it happen that you can write a book and I can read it?"[17] Essentially, and according to Port-Royal *Grammar*: "[Human language is a] marvelous invention by which we construct from twenty-five or thirty sounds an infinity of expressions which, having no resemblance in themselves to what takes place in our minds, still enable us to let others know the secret of what we conceive and of all the various mental activities that we carry out."[18]

15. Percy, *Message in the Bottle*, 157–8.
16. Taylor, *Language Animal*, 332.
17. Percy, *Message in the Bottle*, 33.
18. Taylor, "Origin of Language," 79.

In his investigation of the function of language, Percy discusses the profound experience of Helen Keller who was trapped inside of herself until, at age eight, she experienced a breakthrough discovery, and shifted "from [a mere] responding animal" to a "name-giving and sentence-uttering" human being. Helen Keller recounts this critical experience with her care-giver, Miss Sullivan:

> We walked down the path to the well-house, attracted by the fragrance of the honeysuckle with which it was covered. Someone was drawing water and my teacher placed my hand under the spout. As the cool stream gushed over one hand, she spelled into the other the word *water*, first slowly then rapidly. I stood still, my whole attention fixed upon the motion of her fingers. Suddenly I felt a misty consciousness as of something forgotten—a thrill of returning thought, and somehow the mystery of language was revealed to me. I knew then that 'w-a-t-e-r' meant the wonderful cool something that was flowing over my hand. That living word awakened my soul, gave it light, hope, joy, set it free! There were barriers still, it is true, but barriers that could in time be swept away.
>
> I left the well-house eager to learn. Everything had a name, and each name gave birth to a new thought. As we returned to the house every object which I touched seemed to quiver with life.[19]

John Sykes summarizes the crucial shift in Helen's discovery: "In Percy's account, the eight-year-old Helen enters the well-house as a responding animal, capable of using hand signals to satisfy biological needs, but she leaves it a full-fledged Homo symbolificus, who wants not water, but the name of water. Percy finds in this description nothing less than testimony to the birth of human consciousness and the establishment of a world, in contrast to a mere environment."[20]

Humans, by God's design, are meant to be awake and aware, able to make sense and meaning of experience. In fact, after this discovery, Helen recounts being able to make sense of events and experiences that before eluded her and left her in the darkness of ignorance. John Sykes explains the transformation:

> Once [Helen] becomes a symbol-user, a new set of joys and sorrows are open to her as she becomes a creature capable of

19. Percy, *Message in the Bottle*, 34–35.
20. Sykes, *Flannery O'Connor, Walker Percy*, 90–91.

[assigning meaning]. Her own account speaks of 'light, hope, joy' she had not previously known. She later speaks of tears of repentance she shed for a doll she had previously broken in a fit of temper, her awakening to words having given her a new purchase on what we might almost call her preconscious life. The world established by words seems to bring with it the possibility of good and evil as well as joy and sorrow.[21]

So then, language gives us, like Helen, the ability to recognize our selves apart from the environment, orient our selves within that environment, and begin to identify the common ground of meaning from which we can communicate with others. Helen enters what Charles Taylor identifies as the "linguistic dimension" which "not only enables a new kind of awareness of the things which surround us, but also a more refined sense of human meanings, and hence a more complex gamut of emotions."[22] Furthermore, according to Taylor, this dimension also renders "human agents capable of new kinds of relations, of new sorts of footings that they can stand on with each other, of intimacy and distance, hierarchy and equality."[23] Suddenly, within the linguistic dimension, Helen experiences the fullness of human consciousness: she is able to make meaning, naming the elements of her environment and the elements of her own internal experience. This ability becomes available to her only when she finds the most essential common ground of her culture, language. She experiences what Charles Taylor calls the "shared consciousness of the world."[24]

I wonder whether students new to the study and practice of composition are aware of this "shared consciousness" created by and through language. I suspect that some consider certain forms of language and writing simply a means of self-expression. In fact, some composition students seem to perceive the assigned essay as monological: "This is what I have to say; this is what I have to offer on the subject." They construe their thoughts and reflections as best they can, feeding their final copies into the machine of the institution and hoping for a particular grade. However, students, and perhaps many individuals forget that by our very presence and use of language, we have a voice in the "shared consciousness of the world." Taylor clarifies that "the linguistic capacity is

21. Sykes, *Flannery O'Connor, Walker Percy*, 91.
22. Taylor, *Language Animal*, 28.
23. Taylor, *Language Animal*, 28.
24. Taylor, *Language Animal*, 333.

essentially shared: it sustains a shared consciousness of the world, within which individuals differentiate themselves by becoming particular voices in an ongoing conversation. This shared understanding develops a place for monological speech and writing, but this option is available for us only because we are inducted into speech as conversation."[25] The student's ability to communicate at all points to their place in and participation with the larger cosmos. Furthermore, Taylor's discussion proposes that language gives testament to the relational and social nature of human existence. And we see evidence of this. As instructors hoping to communicate truth to our students, we must first establish a footing, a common ideological ground where we can meet them. As members of families, friendships, and various structures of society, we rely on a common plane of understanding. Within the body of Christ, the church community, we find our shared space in the biblical narrative.

In *Speech and Reality*, Eugen Rosenstock-Huessy offers the summation of language's power to connect the individual, through mere vocables, to common history and the cosmos:

> Man offers his respiratory system, his ears, his gestures, and his body as a whole for the purpose of functioning in this cosmic mail service. Nothing remains undiscussed that man does experience. A never-ending stream of communication connects the first man to all of us as is shown by the fact that we speak the same language after six thousand years. And this cosmic service is to overcome the limitations in time and space of any cosmic event. We, all the time, spread the good and the bad news. And to spread news is the function of homo sapiens . . . When man began to speak, the existing universe began to be reflected a thousand times in the prism of human language.[26]

Acknowledging its power and function, how do we as Christians better understand God's purpose in giving us the gift of language, the ability to engage with him and others?

THE GOD OF LANGUAGE

Presuming we agree on a narratable world and, as Christians, a universal story with a universal story teller; the nature of language by which we

---

25. Taylor, *Language Animal*, 333.
26. Rosenstock-Huessy, *Speech and Reality*, 121.

orient ourselves in God's narrative reflects his perfect design and intention. In an effort to understand language and its ideal usage and in an effort to use it well in the image of the God, we look to his revealed Word in the Scriptures. For, as Eugene H. Peterson explains in *Tell it Slant*, "Our interaction with God begins with God speaking the first word. Before it ever occurs to us to speak to or even think of God, God speaks to us."[27] In *Eat this Book*, Peterson addresses this approach directly:

> We begin at the beginning. We call [the Bible] 'revelation,' God revealing himself and his ways to us, not so much telling us something, but *showing* himself. Books have authors. However we conceive the words to have gotten written on the pages of our Bibles, the Christian church has always held that God is somehow or other responsible for this book in a revelatory way, in contrast to a merely informational way. The authority of the Bible is immediately derived from the authorial presence of God. In other words, this is not an impersonal authority, an assemblage of facts or truths ... This is revelation, personally revealed—letting us in on something, telling us person to person what it means to live our lives as men and women created in the image of God.[28]

God expresses himself through the use of language, but of course, it is not and must not be seen as monological. Revelation is not a one-way event. As James Gerard McEvoy explains in "Dialogue: Drawn into the Life of the Trinity," "Revelatory texts offer a possible world and invite us to envisage ourselves in terms of the world they embody."[29] Through his Word to us, God invites us into his world, invites us to understand our existence and role in the context of his universal narrative. Through the use of language, God meets us on common ground in order to affect us. It is amazing that God gave us language, and then condescended to speak of his infinite self within those "twenty-five or thirty sounds," to let us "know the secret of what [he] conceive[s]."[30] Peterson candidly comments on God's choice to share with us through language: "I sometimes marvel that God chose to risk his revelation in the ambiguities of language. If he had wanted to make sure that the truth was absolutely clear, without any possibility of misunderstanding, he should have revealed his truth by

---

27. Peterson, *Tell it Slant*, 149.
28. Peterson, *Eat This Book*, 24.
29. McEvoy, "Dialogue," 246.
30. Taylor, "Origin of Language," 79.

means of mathematics. Mathematics is the most precise, unambiguous language that we have. But then, of course, you can't say 'I love you' in algebra."[31]

God chose the linguistic dimension with purpose and with love, in the ultimate posture of care. And because of that love and care, God's Word and revelation is not cold, hard, informational fact. It creates relationship, invites response, and works in us. Peterson defines the formative nature of God's word and of language in general:

> In our readings of [the Bible] we come to realize that what we need is not primarily informational, telling us things about God and ourselves, but formational, shaping us into our true being. It is the very nature of language to form rather than inform. When language is personal, which it is at its best, it reveals; and revelation is always formative—we don't know more, we become more. Our best users of language, poets and lovers and children and saints, use words to *make*—make intimacies, make character, make beauty, make goodness, make truth.[32]

God uses language to refine us and form in us beauty, goodness, and truth. And undoubtedly, we use language best when we use it to reveal these elements and help form them in others.

Certainly, this focus was key to Christ's work while living among humanity. God's most pointed and poignant revelation to us was in the physical presence of his Holy Son.[33] And in turning to study Christ, who used language perfectly and operated perfectly within the context of dialogue, we encounter and are compelled to investigate his identity as the Word of God. In *The Promise of Narrative Theology*, George W. Stroup notes that, "Revelation, for Christians, is always the revelation of God's Word and that Word can never be separated from the narrative history of Jesus Christ, because it is only in relation to Christian narrative that the Word has its power to engraft the identities of individuals and communities into Jesus Christ."[34] So, how did and does Christ, through the revelation of his earthly life, engraft individuals and communities into God's truth?

---

31. Peterson, *Eat This Book*, 93.
32. Peterson, *Eat This Book*, 23–24.
33. McGrath, *Theology*, 71.
34. Stroup, *Promise of Narrative Theology*, 244.

Both Peterson and McEvoy give particular attention to the scope of Christ's language. McEvoy identifies parables as "language events" and "a profoundly dialogical mode of preaching."[35] He explains that, "While appealing to hearers' concrete circumstances, parables both attempt to reorient them to the Reign of God and call them to find their lives in that place—to conceive their lives anew in relationship to the Kingdom."[36] Peterson affirms the idea that Jesus' teaching, whether through story or direct proclamation, calls his listeners to active engagement and appropriate response. He claims, "Preaching is language that involves us personally with God's action in the present . . . The listener is not permitted to suppose that the preached words are for anyone other than himself or herself . . . Preaching reveals God in action here and now—for *me*."[37] Here again, God's use of language is intentional, formative, and dialogical, inviting the hearer or reader to experience the paradigm shift, to perceive daily experience and circumstances through the ultimate reality and truth of God's narrative, and to live accordingly. Peterson also offers notable commentary on the important function of teaching in the Christian tradition, specifically in the "church's life." He explains: "Teaching also continues in the church's life as our pastors and theologians train us in cultivating an intelligent and faithful obedience while dealing with politics, business affairs, family matters, personal failures and sufferings, living whole and integrated lives. Teaching resurrects dead words so they live again. It occupies a large field in the way we use language in this life of following Jesus."[38] Peterson's observations here certainly apply to instructors in the Christian college where we seek to offer students coherence.

Beyond teaching and preaching, Peterson isolates and emphasizes a third category of Christ's language: informal conversation. Peterson draws particular attention to these moments of conversation because it speaks to the most common interactions of our daily lives. Whether our students become preachers or teachers, they (and we) are prolific conversationalists in all sorts of mediums. And Christ models language in that arena as well. The following passage stresses the significance of our countless interactions, in dialogue of all sorts, with others, both within the body of believers, and outside of that environment:

35. McEvoy, "Dialogue," 247.
36. McEvoy, "Dialogue," 247–8.
37. Peterson, *Tell it Slant*, 11.
38. Peterson, *Tell it Slant*, 13.

When Jesus wasn't preaching and when he wasn't teaching, he talked with the men and women with whom he lived in terms of what was going on at the moment—people, events, questions, whatever—using the circumstances of their lives as his text. Much as we do. Preaching begins with God: God's word, God's action, God's presence. Teaching expands on what is proclaimed, instructing us in the implications of the text, the reverberations of the truth in the world, the specific ways in which God's word shapes in detail the way we live our daily lives between birth and death. But unstructured, informal conversations arise from incidents and encounters with one another that take place in the normal course of going about our lives in families and workplaces, on playgrounds and while shopping for groceries, in airport terminals waiting for a flight and walking with binoculars in a field with friends watching birds. Many of the words that Jesus spoke are of this nature. Most of us are not preachers or teachers, or at least not designated as such. Most of the words that we speak are spoken in the quotidian contexts of eating and drinking, shopping and traveling, making what we sometimes dismiss as 'small talk.'[39]

These conversational encounters comprise Luke's ten-chapter travel narrative, Jesus' journey through Samaria. But Peterson notes that, "What began as a 'Travel Narrative' has developed in the telling into a metaphor, a metaphor for the way Jesus uses language between Sundays, between the holy synagogues of Galilee and the holy temple in Jerusalem."[40] In passage after passage, we hear the voices of those who encounter Jesus on this journey. The man who proclaims, "I will follow you wherever you go."[41] The expert in the law who challenges Jesus, "And who is my neighbor?"[42] The woman in the crowd who calls out, "Blessed is the womb that bore you, and the breasts at which you nursed."[43] The ten lepers who cried out in chorus, "Jesus, Master, have mercy on us."[44] The crippled woman to whom Jesus spoke first, "When Jesus saw her, he called her over and said to her, 'Woman, you are freed from your disability.' And he laid his hands

---

39. Peterson, *Tell it Slant*, 13–14.
40. Peterson, *Tell it Slant*, 18.
41. Luke 9:57 (ESV).
42. Luke 10:29 (ESV).
43. Luke 11:27 (ESV).
44. Luke 17:13 (ESV).

on her and immediately she was made straight, and she glorified God."[45] Jesus always responds "using the circumstances of their lives as his text."[46]

Through the intentional use of language, Jesus assumes a posture of care and enters into the narratives of the lives of individuals. Of course, as the perfect, knowing interlocutor, his responses are sometimes soft, gentle, and full of mercy, and at other times they are hard, forceful, and full of rebuke. But always, they are wholly restorative to those who will meet him on the redemptive ground of God's ultimate revelation: the life, death, and resurrection of Jesus Christ, the living Word of God.

As Christians, it is valuable to pause and conduct this study in Christ's use of language. He lived in dialogue. Certainly, he was in constant dialogue and communion with the heavenly Father and the Holy Spirit. We see this in Scriptural texts that depict his prayer life, and even in his responses in human conversation. When, in John 14, Phillip asks to see the Father, Jesus replies, "Don't you believe that I am in the Father, and the Father is in me? The words that I say to you I do not speak on my own authority. But the Father who dwells in me does his works. Believe me that I am in the Father and the Father is in me."[47] Jesus Christ is the very revealed Word of his Father. And, in *Realism and Christian Faith*, Andrew Moore proposes that as the fulfillment of God's covenantal promise, Christ incarnate is also God's ultimate speech-act, for "Word and action have always been one in the teleological enactment of God's promises."[48]

In considering God's interaction with humanity through this revelatory event, the sending of his Word, we see that he performed this great "speech-act" in a particular way, through particular means, and at a particular time in human history. As George W. Stroup observes, "Revelation in Christian faith refers . . . to an event of disclosure. What is disclosed is not primarily a piece of information, a proposition, or an idea, but the Word of God as it appears in Jesus of Nazareth."[49] God's revelation in Christ came to us at a precise time, in a specific way, and as a message of redeeming truth. These are key characteristics of God's

---

45. Luke 13:12–13 (ESV).
46. Peterson, *Tell it Slant*, 18.
47. John 14:10–11 (ESV).
48. Moore, *Realism and Christian Faith*, 213.
49. Stroup, *Promise of Narrative Theology*, 239.

revelatory speech-act. Yet, the truth and resonance of the revealed Word is not contained, it is not merely a time/space event. Stroup explains:

> Revelation is not merely a historical artifact that lives only in the distant past, but also an event that occurs in the contemporary experience of individuals and communities . . . It has a content, an object, something (or in this case 'someone') which can be known, talked about, and proclaimed, which Christians refer to as the Word of God and which they insist is both a reality in the narrative history of Jesus of Nazareth and something that is heard in the midst of the human words of contemporary Christian communities.[50]

God's word and revelation to humanity resounds with an infinite truth through all the ages, in every context. It lays waste to any finitely constructed narrative, but invites all humanity into the absolute, infinite narrative. It establishes worth and meaning, exacts justice and offers redemption. It is evidence of his awareness of us, and his desire to be in dialogue and relationship with us.

IMPLICATIONS FOR INSTRUCTION AND FORMATION

In summary, because God is the God of language, and because he has designed us to exist in the linguistic dimension, engaging in dialogue with him and the people of his creation, we study how God uses language. We find that God intentionally engages us in dialogue that reveals truth, restores us, and redeems us. Understanding God's use of language has great implications for the work of the Christian college, for we are ushering each student into the history of ideas. Every discipline calls students to see and walk the varying topography of the landscape of meaning, meaning that has been constructed, and sometimes deconstructed, through humanity's long conversation. And, as we help them gain sure footing, grounded in the Christian narrative and worldview, we invite them to realize their own voices and contribute to the dialogue. It is important to acknowledge that our students can enter this dialogue and contribute to the history of ideas most effectively if they understand the power of language and can wield it as responsible speakers and writers, using language to reveal truth, restore others, and participate in God's redemptive work. Essentially, we are ushering them out of habits of

---

50. Stroup, *Promise of Narrative Theology*, 239–40.

self-interest and allowing them to view the world through the broader lens of the Christian narrative so they may be compelled to see and respond to others.

Because this formative process necessarily occurs in the linguistic dimension, teaching students to use language well is key. On several occasions in composition class, I have explained to my students that as writers, and as human beings operating in the currency of words, we are living in the image of God, the God who spoke us into creation and sent his Word to live among us. Through the work of the Spirit, he renders his Word alive and active in us. Alister McGrath asserts that our existence as image-bearers is "above all an affirmation of *responsibility* and *accountability* towards the world in which we live."[51] For, as Andrew Moore articulates, the church "participates in bringing to present effect that conforming of the world to God's word that Christ has already achieved. And for this task it needs to find its identity as Jesus did: in being sent."[52] This is a formidable mission. We operate constantly in the currency of words. How do we use language, God's gift, in alignment with his truth and revelation, and in a posture of care, in each and every occasion? In *Tell it Slant*, Eugene Peterson articulates the challenge to "use God's gift of language in consonance with the God who speaks."[53] He continues:

> Language, all of it—every vowel, every consonant—is a gift of God. God uses language to create and command us; we use language to confess our sins and sing praises to God. We use this very same language getting to know one another, buying and selling, writing letters and reading books. We use the same words in talking to one another that we use when we're talking to God: same nouns and verbs, same adverbs and adjectives, same conjunctions and interjections, same prepositions and pronouns. There is no 'Holy Ghost' language used for matters of God and salvation and then a separate secular language for buying cabbages and cars . . . Every time we open our mouths, whether in conversation with one another or in prayer to our Lord, Christian truth and community are on the line. And so, high on the agenda of the Christian community in every generation is that we diligently develop a voice that speaks in consonance with the God who speaks, that we speak in such a way that truth is told and community is formed . . . I want to nurture

---

51. McGrath, *Theology*, 49.
52. Moore, *Realism and Christian Faith*, 234.
53. Peterson, *Tell it Slant*, 1.

an awareness of the sanctity of words, the holy gift of language, regardless of whether it is directed vertically or horizontally. Just as Jesus did.[54]

Of course, this is a difficult, and for those who are not yet redeemed, impossible charge. Fortunately, despite our fallen nature, God continually conforms our behavior to Christ's likeness.[55] This sanctifying, redemptive process restores the possibility of meaningful human discourse, enabling the church to represent him and to re-present him to the world.[56] As Christian teachers then, we want to disciple our students in the careful use of language and intentional dialogue within our disciplines, and in every context.

COMPOSITION AND COHERENCE

So, in the composition classroom of a Christian college, students encounter an interesting tension. They have grown up in an era of hyper-individualism and self-importance (no doubt, stumbling blocks for many generations in various forms). Yet, as Christians they are called to use language to speak and write meaningfully in response to their communities and society. I want to acknowledge that some young Christians, despite hyper-individualism, are conscious and careful of their behavior in the linguistic dimension. And some students do live a patterned posture of care toward those they encounter on a daily basis, even on social media. But students are also called to effectively contribute to urgent conversations of political and cultural concern and to engage in relevant and often secularized conversations within their chosen professions. For students to have an effective voice requires training toward a mastery of language, writing, and communication across the curriculum so that they can speak as Christians with authority into a variety of contexts.

This authority sounds lofty, and for first-year composition students in the throes of literary analysis, it might sound unattainable. However, even the small and tedious discipline of the five-paragraph essay can begin the necessary training, calling students out of themselves and away from common misconceptions of the value of writing.

54. Peterson, *Tell it Slant*, 2–4.
55. McGrath, *Theology*, 100.
56. Moore, *Realism and Christian Faith*, 230.

In his discussion of college writing, Chris Kearns identifies the typical student approaches toward writing: the belief that the end of writing is mere self-expression, that it is simply a means to a grade or degree, or that it is valuable only as an "instrumental tool" with which to embellish portfolios and resumes.[57] He identifies these approaches as problematic in that they are "fundamentally monological."[58] This monological perception of writing is arguably most evident in college students who view "writing as an extension and declaration of the self"; such students "exemplify what Charles Taylor calls 'expressivist youth culture.'"[59] Kearns summarizes Taylor's premise:

> The rise of this culture is rooted in Romantic ideals regarding the primacy of the private individual, the value of authenticity, and the quasi-moral imperative of self-discovery ... In college composition classes, expressivist undergraduates tend to regard writing as an organic process to be evaluated on the basis of its sincerity or intrinsic beauty rather than according to *external* criteria such as coherence or cogency.[60]

This undergraduate perspective fails to recognize the dialogue implicit in college writing. The writer must be aware of his own consciousness as well as that of the reader. Though his analysis of college writing is not necessarily rooted in a Christian worldview, Kearns does address the ethic of care in writing, declaring that care for the reader is the necessary "intellectual virtue" that allows a writer to "break free of the bewitchment of self-concern"[61]:

> The desire to be understood requires us to find ourselves in relation to the purposes and needs of the reader, who must serve as a partner in shaping our language ... The essential feature of composition confronting all thoughtful undergraduates is that it establishes a real human relationship. In this sense, all writing is inescapably social.[62]

In the effective teaching of composition, we hold students accountable to the dialogical relationship. We require students to assume the role

---

57. Kearns, "Recursive Character of College Writing."
58. Kearns, "Recursive Character of College Writing."
59. Kearns, "Recursive Character of College Writing."
60. Kearns, "Recursive Character of College Writing."
61. Kearns, "Recursive Character of College Writing."
62. Kearns, "Recursive Character of College Writing."

of both writer and reader. Ideally, as students revisit their writing again and again, they begin to perceive, in consideration of another's consciousness, any inaccuracies, imprecisions, or inconsistencies in their prose.

Through the recursive nature of writing, students can begin to master the use of language and grammar for great purposes. Kearns examines the recursive nature of writing and its significance:

> The recursivity of undergraduate prose, its complex form of self-generating reflexivity provides the essential tools necessary to understand and take greater responsibility for the ways our relationship to language maps the surrounding world and orients our attention prior to any conscious decisions on our part. College writing, in other words, provides an opportunity to form the contents of our consciousness and the effectiveness of our communication and also to shape the constitution of our character.[63]

In this passage, Kearns claims that learning to write plays an important role in forming coherence in the life of the student. He identifies writing as the reflective act that forces us to connect "the contents of our consciousness," "the effectiveness of our communication," and "the constitution of our character."[64]

As a Christian college, this is the coherence that we want to form in our students, helping them to integrate the Christian narrative that informs their consciousness, the Christian purposes of communication, and the Christian constitution of their character. Educating students toward such an integrated life will enable them to offer, as God does, words that speak to the circumstances of precise moments in time and space, and that speak into the larger cosmic narrative. The recursive nature of writing can form in college students a coherence that comes through in their essays as well as in their approach to dialogue in general, a coherence that reflects their sanctification as they seek to reveal truth, restore others, and participate in God's redemptive work.

BIBLIOGRAPHY

Bial, Deborah. "Don't Just Be A Brand. Be a Person." *Vital Speeches of The Day* 8.18 (2015) 243.

Garber, Steven. *The Fabric of Faithfulness*. Downers Grove, IL: InterVarsity, 1996.

63. Kearns, "Recursive Character of College Writing."
64. Kearns, "Recursive Character of College Writing."

Jenson, Robert W. "How the World Lost its Story." *First Things* (2010). https://www.firstthings.com/article/2010/03/how-the-world-lost-its-story.

Kearns, Chris. "The Recursive Character of College Writing." https://wac.colostate.edu/docs/books/collegelevel/chapter23.pdf.

McEvoy, James Gerard. "Dialogue: Drawn into the Life of The Trinity." *Pacifica* 25.3 (2012): 239–57.

McGrath, Alister. *Theology: The Basics*, 2nd ed. Oxford: Blackwell, 2008.

Moore, Andrew. *Realism and Christian Faith: God, Grammar, and Meaning*. Cambridge: Cambridge University Press, 2003.

Percy, Walker. *The Message in the Bottle: How Queer Man Is, How Queer Language Is, and What One Has to Do with the Other*. New York: Farrar, Straus and Giroux, 1954.

Peterson, Eugene H. *Eat This Book: A Conversation in the Art of Spiritual Reading*. Grand Rapids: Eerdmans, 2006.

———. *Tell it Slant: A Conversation on the Language of Jesus in His Stories and Prayers*. Grand Rapids: Eerdmans, 2008.

Poplin, Mary. *Is Reality Secular?: Testing the Assumptions of Four Global Worldviews*. Downers Grove, IL: InterVarsity, 2014.

Rosenstock-Huessy, Eugen. *Speech and Reality*. Norwich: Argo, 1970.

Stroup, George W. *The Promise of Narrative Theology: Recovering the Gospel in the Church*. Atlanta: John Knox, 1944.

Sykes, John. *Flannery O'Connor, Walker Percy, and the Aesthetic of Revelation*. Columbia: University of Missouri Press, 2007.

Taylor, Charles. *The Language Animal: The Full Shape of the Human Linguistic Capacity*. Cambridge, MA: Belknap, 2016.

———. "The Origin of Language." *Journal of Creation*. 11.1 (1997): 76–81.

17

THE STUDY OF MUSIC AND THE FAITHFUL EDUCATOR

CLARA CHRISTIAN

How does a music career look different for a Christian? Christian professional musicians and music students face many challenges; how do we handle marketing, competition, self-image, self-expression, and hours of practicing and rehearsal as a Christian? Arthur Holmes in *The Idea of a Christian College* claims, "Especially in performance areas and in the disciplined development of skills . . . the attitude of the teacher or student is the initial and perhaps most salient point of contact with the Christian faith."[1] A Christian educator has the opportunity to equip students with a heart for truth, excellence, and service. To understand what this means, I will look at three different topics: the purpose of a liberal arts education as a whole, the study of music, and then using our musical skills as part of our vocation.

THE CHRISTIAN AND THE LIBERAL ARTS EDUCATION

I remember years ago listening to a radio talk show in which a Christian writer talked about Christians as being some of the greatest literary critics and analytical writers, and he attributed this to the fact that Christians

---

1. Holmes, *Idea of a Christian College*, 47.

read! They read their Bible, carefully analyzing each and every word, and they listen to sermons where they carefully critique the message they are hearing. Unfortunately, while this is the ideal, it is not always true—many times worship services or personal devotions do not delve into Scripture with the highest level of detail possible.

But the idea that the Christian must always be thinking, evaluating, and learning is incredibly vital to the furthering of Christ's kingdom on this earth. So many Christians either err by avoiding the world, or by being swept up into contemporary culture and either consciously or unconsciously embracing it, barely able to hold onto their faith, much less impact the lives of others. Young people are more likely to do the latter, and this is where the Christian liberal arts education comes into play. Christians should never fear education as inherently contradicting their faith or endangering their relationship with God. Nor should they look down on it, as if Bible study is all we need, and our vocations and "worldly" callings are secondary. Scripture provides many role models in both the Old and New Testament of Christians who were knowledgeable about their own faith, but also studied the laws and cultures of the pagan world around them: Moses in Egypt, Daniel in Babylon, and Paul in the Roman Empire.

There are at least three reasons why a liberal arts education is important, and why a Christian liberal arts education becomes a double-edged sword: God's creation mandate in Gen 1, God's command to preach the gospel to all nations, and the Bible's directive to Christians to live in service of others.

God commanded Adam and Eve in the Garden of Eden not only to be fruitful and multiply, but also to subdue the earth. Genesis declares, "So God created man in his own image, in the image of God he created him; male and female he created them. Then God blessed them, and God said to them, 'Be fruitful and multiply and fill the earth and subdue it, and have dominion over the fish of the sea and over the birds of the heavens and over every living thing that moves on the earth.'"[2] God's command to subdue the earth encompasses both the practical and the aesthetic: to plant seeds and hunt game to fulfill their daily needs, but also to *understand* the earth—to bring it under dominion, just as Adam gave names to all the animals, and to pursue a deeper knowledge of what God has created for us to enjoy or to better others or ourselves. God made us

---

2. Gen 1:27–28 (NKJV).

in his image, which means we have the desire to be creative and then to see that what we create is "good." It is only because sin has crept in that Christians must fight laziness, discouragement, anxiety, and sometimes factors beyond our control, which make education a challenge for us. But learning should be a lifelong pursuit and should be both a joy for the Christian, and something we feel a responsibility to pursue.

The fact that God created the world and then said that it was good also shows he is invested in the earth, he has a comprehensive view of the earth, and he preserves the earth. In studying any aspect of the created world, including art or music created by humans made in God's image, students are given the opportunity to learn more about God himself. "The pursuit of the Greater glory of God remains rooted in a Christian worldview in which God can be encountered in the search for truth in every discipline,"[3] say Dockery and George in *The Great Tradition of Christian Thinking*. Cornelius Plantinga states, "the original goodness of creation implies that all of it . . . is potentially redeemable . . . everything made by God retains at least some part of its goodness and promise."[4]

A second very important reason for a Christian to be liberally educated, and why a Christian education empowers the graduate in every area of their lives, is God's call to evangelize and to further his kingdom. Matthew 28:19–20, now known as the "Great Commission," contains Jesus' parting commands to his disciples: "Go therefore and make disciples of all nations, baptizing them in the name of the Father and of the Son and of the Holy Spirit, teaching them to observe all that I have commanded you. And behold, I am with you always, to the end of the age."[5] Christians should not be driven to evangelize because of their fear of hell, because they are afraid there is only limited room in heaven, or because they are looking for a special reward. Though we often fail in our Christian lives, we should be driven by thankfulness and gratitude as unworthy recipients of God's love and grace.

Dockery and George describe the relationship between reason and a Christian education this way, "The great tradition of Christian thinking helps us all better see the relationship between the Christian faith and the role of reason, while encouraging Christ followers to seek truth and engage the culture with a view toward strengthening the church and

---

3. Dockery and George, *Great Tradition of Christian Thinking*, 92.
4. Plantinga, *Engaging God's World*, 41.
5. Matt 28:19–20 (ESV).

extending the kingdom of God."[6] Plantinga points out that we will never fully succeed in creating a Christian world on this earth, a particularly poignant reminder as we live in an age of increased ungodliness and secularism in the United States. But no matter which period of time, which epoch in the history of the church, the Christian is commanded to spread the gospel and be light in this dark world. Plantinga argues, "On the one hand, we need to avoid triumphalism, the prideful view that we Christians will fully succeed in transforming all or much of culture . . . (but) on the other hand we also need to avoid the despairing tendency to write the world off, to abandon it as a lost cause."[7] Later, I will discuss the particulars of being a musician in the secular world and how "being a person with a responsible dominion in the world"[8] applies to having a career in music.

Gene C. Fant. brings up the biblical examples of Moses, Daniel, and Paul in an effort to defend the liberal arts education for the Christian. A liberal arts education gives students a knowledge of culture, a knowledge of history, and the ability to reason and defend their faith without being ignorant about the beliefs of non-Christians, both past and present. Some church leaders as far back as Tertullian (c. AD 155–240) already wanted nothing to do with secular culture and the evil found therein. Fant says, "Tertullian summarized his broad concerns with what became a famous statement 'What indeed has Athens to do with Jerusalem?' These critics, however, seemed to turn a blind eye to the effects of liberal learning that enabled Moses and Daniel to serve as particularly effective shapers of culture and, especially to Paul's later usage of classical pagan thought."[9] Augustine of Hippo is a later example of a highly educated, learned scholar who practiced his faith and communicated that faith to others. Arthur Holmes states, "unless we understand the thought and value patterns of our day . . . unless we speak fluently the language of our contemporaries, we tragically limit our effectiveness."[10]

A third, very important role of the Christian liberal arts education is that it enables young Christians to better serve others: in their church, in their families, and in their workplace. A student who has a

6. Dockery and George, *Great Tradition of Christian Thinking*, 92.
7. Plantinga, *Engaging God's World*, 119.
8. Plantinga, *Engaging God's World*, 126.
9. Fant, *Liberal Arts*, 35.
10. Holmes, *Idea of a Christian College*, 47.

broad understanding of various disciplines and various ways of thinking is better equipped for service and better able to understand others in different jobs, with different backgrounds, and with different worldviews. Fant says, "Liberal Arts learners in a Christian context are able to build connections between people as well as viewing education as a relational objective not found in other approaches. This human connection is always important to Christians in particular, because of the gospel focused nature of our lives and callings."[11] Dockery states, "A love for learning encourages a life of worship and service,"[12] and Holmes calls work "a stewardship of God's creation in service to others."[13]

Cornelius Plantinga says that "Christians (as images of God) therefore reject both the materialist reduction of our status and (the) humanist exaggeration of it."[14] The Christian's career and calling will always differ from the non-believer's, for the Christian's focus is not self, but God. This does not mean that the Christian cannot be competitive, or that they cannot excel in their work. But their purpose is to "glorify God and fully to enjoy him forever,"[15] and glorifying God means serving him and serving others *with excellence*. Holmes points out that "if a person is at heart a religious being, then all her activities are animated and informed by her faith, be they intellectual or artistic, political or commercial."[16] The student must be aware that every individual is operating under the direction and guidance of their worldview, that everyone's worldview impacts their lives and work, and it is necessary to intentionally base our lives on the service of God.

Service is not just thought, it is also action—it is the practical working out of our faith. We can have a worldview that is God-centered, and we can even have the correct answers when faith comes up in conversation. But just as with lifestyle evangelism, students must ask themselves if their everyday lives exhibit the knowledge, worldview, and understanding they may be receiving at a Christian liberal arts college. How do our beliefs make us stand out? Steven Garber, in *The Fabric of Faithfulness*, quotes a Christian in a secular workplace, "I have always been impressed

---

11. Fant, *Liberal Arts*, 35.
12. Dockery and George, *Great Tradition of Christian Thinking*, 92.
13. Holmes, *Idea of a Christian College*, 38.
14. Plantinga, *Engaging God's World*, 41.
15. Vos, *Westminster Larger Catechism: A Commentary*, 3.
16. Holmes, *Idea of a Christian College*, 16.

by people who live integrated lives; the epitome of that comes in seeing the life of Christ in someone. Living a life of glory to God is living a life of integrity, a life that speaks louder than words."[17] He goes on to say, "I believe that the issue of integrity will be the key in the next decade, and we will come at it from every direction, including the sciences. Other qualities are honesty, trustworthiness, respect of others. Integrity, though, is the bridge between word and deed—the only valid theory of action."[18] True service is defined by integrity—one who sustains his or her commitments, both to God, and to others.

THE CHRISTIAN AND THE STUDY OF MUSIC

The challenges faced by musicians in the workplace, as well as student musicians in an educational setting, are many. A music professor teaching at a Christian liberal arts college has a huge responsibility because we are equipping music students for a variety of vocations, be it church musician, music educator, or performer. The church musician must learn to dig deeper and seek to offer God the best they possibly can, leading other Christians in offering worship which represents a high level of musical achievement and honors God with mind, talent, and ability. Psalm 33 says the musician is not only to worship with the right attitude, but they must also play skillfully: "Praise the Lord with the harp; Make melody to Him with an instrument of ten strings. Sing to Him a new song; Play skillfully with a shout of joy."[19] The music educator has the opportunity to provide leadership and inspiration for young students for whom a good foundation can create an impact that lasts a lifetime. And the performer has perhaps the greatest challenge of all, tying together the highest possible level of achievement (God's creation mandate) with service for others, and the unique opportunity to evangelize in many secular environments.

First, let's examine the impact of the cultural mandate provided in the Garden of Eden and how this affects the education of a music student in a Christian liberal arts setting. Sacred vocal music represents a long tradition of excellence, including the first notation of music and the earliest organization of chamber singers dating back to the 1100s, when the

17. Garber, *Fabric of Faithfulness*, 126.
18. Garber, *Fabric of Faithfulness*, 126.
19. Ps 33:2–3 (NKJV).

monks in the Roman Catholic Church devoted themselves to preserving and creating music along with visual art. Through the centuries, sacred choral music has brought Scripture and biblical truth into secular performance spaces, all the way through the present day. Classical composers, who may or may not have been true believers, wrote and continue to write music with words taken from Scripture or from Christian literature or poetry. This is one of the ways we see God's truth emerging in secular culture; even an agnostic or an atheist cannot help being moved by a Bach cantata or Brahms' *A German Requiem*. A.N. Whitehead suggests that early modern science developed because of the encouragement given to it in the religious atmosphere of the Middle Ages.[20] Similarly, the early development of music notation, counterpoint, and harmony occurred in the Roman Catholic Church and then was expanded further during the Protestant Reformation and the Catholic Counter Reformation. Augustine says, "it takes reverence and love for God to motivate us adequately toward aesthetic values like beauty and creativity" and certainly there is evidence of this mindset in the years between AD 800 and 1600.[21]

Aside from the genres of church music and large-scale sacred choral works, the bulk of the compositional output within the classical or "art music" tradition is instrumental or secular vocal music, and many classical composers and performers are not believers. At the same time as linking artistic inspiration and devotion to God, St. Augustine also said, "all human discovery should be viewed in the light of the incarnation and biblical revelation, not merely those discoveries that were produced by believers."[22] While certain composers from the classical tradition, such as J.S. Bach, Felix Mendelssohn, or Johannes Brahms, were intentional about honoring God with their music, they are not the only composers to whom God endowed talent, ability, and opportunity. It is here that the liberal arts student and the music student becomes challenged to expand his or her horizons and be engaged on an intellectual level, examining the nature of beauty and aesthetics. Elton Trueblood, in *The Idea of a College*, said, "the Christian faith is the sworn enemy of all intellectual dishonesty and shoddiness."[23] "The Christian believes that in all that she does intel-

---

20. Holmes, *Idea of a Christian College*, 47.
21. Holmes, *Idea of a Christian College*, 48.
22. Fant, *Liberal Arts*, 36.
23. Holmes, *Idea of a Christian College*, 48.

lectually, socially, or artistically, she is handling God's creation and that is sacred," says Arthur Holmes.[24]

The Christian music student, whether listening to a concert, taking a class, or studying music with a professional goal in mind, must be ready to challenge himself with the truth about what excellence is. This pursuit of truth and excellence takes several forms; it means studying the great composers of the past and present (music history), understanding more about how to listen (which often falls under music theory or appreciation), and being prepared to reach a higher level of performance (applied music). Music is often considered merely a means of therapy, emotional release, or social connection, whether in churches, schools, or most mainstream secular environments; but the Christian music student must pursue the truth found in music at a much deeper level, even when it's not easy. Howard Best, in *Music Through the Eyes of Faith*, describes what he believes is a God-honoring approach to music making: "Because God does all things well, we should likewise do well. While we strive to be truthful, we will strive to state truth beautifully. And in proceeding in this way, I (we) honor God by trying to work as God does."[25]

Cornelius Plantinga points out with great insight into our modern culture, "Superficiality is the curse of our age. The doctrine of instant satisfaction is a primary spiritual problem. The desperate need today is not for a greater number of intelligent people, or gifted people, but for deep people."[26] David W. Rushton says it comes down to learning to listen. He writes, "we need to contemplate (i.e., think about) what we see and hear if we are to more fully grasp the essence of a musical work. Also, a more active and thoughtful approach to listening will eventually help us become more discriminating, enabling us to distinguish varying levels of quality and make more informed value judgments about the worth of a particular piece."[27] This thoughtful approach to listening represents seeking excellence, and as a listener must make value judgements, a performer and composer must make even fuller and more continual evaluation and self-evaluation.

What drives non-Christians to study and perform music at such a high level, with so much detail? Why do non-Christians frequently excel

---

24. Holmes, *Idea of a Christian College*, 48.
25. Best, *Music Through the Eyes of Faith*, 44.
26. Plantinga, *Engaging God's World*, 41.
27. Downey and Porter, *Christian Worldview and the Academic Disciplines*, 327.

at music more than Christians? Why is music in the church often at such a low level? For the unbelieving professional musician or artist, music is so deep, so fascinating, so endless with possibilities, it becomes their god. They are curious, they are competitive, and they are often very much in touch with themselves and their own need to fill a spiritual or emotional void—and they fill it with music. Yet, "Even when these thinkers reject God, they recognize that the world is out of joint and that human beings, too, are "alienated," or "divided."[28] They are searching for the Truth, but even as they achieve such a high level of excellence, fame, and success, there still come the questions: Where does beauty originate? Why does it have value? And why does it matter to us? Douglas Yeo, bass trombonist with the Boston symphony orchestra, believes beauty and the desire for pursuing beauty originate from God: "It is God alone who bestows on composers the mysterious gift of composition and on performers the unspeakable gift of interpretation."[29]

In addition to facing the challenging fact that most of the world's greatest achievements and highest level of excellence is found among professional musicians that scoff at God, the study of music presents a second difficult question for Christian liberal arts students: What is truth in music? Are certain styles of music ungodly? Philippians 4:8 contains the well-known directive from Paul about what we should study, what our minds should dwell on: "Finally, brethren, whatever things are true, whatever things *are* noble, whatever things *are* just, whatever things *are* pure, whatever things *are* lovely, whatever things *are* of good report, if *there is* any virtue and if *there is* anything praiseworthy—meditate on these things."[30] How do Christian students apply this to music in which they like the style, but the music may have questionable lyrics (such as hip-hop, rap, or other pop music). On the other hand, how does the Christian student respond to contemporary classical music, which may not have any images, lyrics, or vulgar associations, but on an aesthetic level, sounds ugly to him?

At College of the Ozarks, I frequently face this question of aesthetics from the outset, as most of my students come from backgrounds where they have been exposed to very little classical music, and what they have been exposed to did not include twentieth-century or twenty-first-century

---

28. Plantinga, *Engaging God's World*, 48.
29. Downey and Porter, *Christian Worldview and the Academic Disciplines*, 328.
30. Phil 4:8 (NKJV).

composers. During a recent visit to Strasbourg, France, for the international SaxOpen Conference, I did listen to one performance that to me was not truthful because it did not represent excellence, and was aesthetically offensive; but one of the performers had sat next to me in church the previous Sunday and was performing in the event. Howard Best, who served as Dean of the Wheaton College Conservatory of Music for twenty-seven years, says that truth and beauty should not be equated:

> We need a new paradigm that separates truth and beauty yet allows each its proper place. I call this *revelation and creation*. According to this paradigm, the maker and what is made are not interchangeable or equitable, and beauty can apply to everything made and said. Thus truth can be beautifully stated and lived out; things can be beautifully made—even though it might be extremely unpleasant—can be dealt with simply as a lapse in aesthetic judgement.[31]

In this particular performance I attended in Strasbourg, it was not merely strange sounds, harmonic dissonances or extended techniques which I found overbearing; it was the visual component, which included blinding flashes of light and disturbing images, and the aural component, an extremely loud beat projected through speakers.

The distinction between "beauty" and "ugliness" becomes a fine line when acoustic (non-amplified) classical music with more dissonance than a student is accustomed to becomes something the student disrespects, refuses to consider music, or simply writes off as not "Christian" or not worthy of study. It becomes especially difficult to expose students to the history of classical music through the twentieth century, or to current composers, when a student doesn't understand it and then labels it as lacking truth, excellence, or beauty. A professional musician or a listener who has learned the advanced harmonic language (through listening to hundreds of new music performances) may hear beauty and even enjoy atonal music such as the serialist compositions of Schoenberg, Webern, or Berg. In such cases, the student's perception should not be the guiding factor in deciding what is "good" or "truthful." He must recognize that there is a larger framework than merely his own aesthetic values.

Plantinga says "created things," whether composers, compositions, or performers, are sometimes mysterious, but that does not mean they lack aesthetic value. He argues, "Created things—and their parts and

---

31. Best, *Music Through the Eyes of Faith*, 44.

processes—are unique and sometimes mysterious, but because they have come from the wisdom of God, they are also purposive and, in principle, intelligible."[32] Rushton talks about the fact that we can distort the arts if we "attempt to use a work of art rather than recognize that its beauty (even its abstraction) and craftsmanship are their own reason for being."[33] He quotes another author who suggests that "the more abstract the art, the more it takes its reason for being from the innate creativity which infects every human being."[34] Holmes points out that "aesthetics and other areas of value" are "not a simple case of black and white."[35] What better time to learn, than while in college, how to engage all parts of culture; to be able to identify with more than merely the familiar or the known?

The faithful educator must consistently point students towards discovering truth. Holmes points out, "truth . . . is a liberating experience that enlarges horizons, deepens insight, sharpens the mind, exposes new areas of inquiry, and sensitizes our ability to appreciate the good and the beautiful as well as the true."[36] For a student, this means listening to music which is accepted as reputable and of high value (it has stood the test of time and is respected by performers and academics the world over), even when that music may not be immediately "likeable." It also means taking the extra time to practice and perfect music which a student may enjoy playing, but doesn't want to have to spend too much time developing. Recognizing that there is always another level to achieve when studying classical music can be discouraging at first, but it is truly thrilling that even a lifetime of study still doesn't reach the limit of what can be discovered, even within the literature for a single instrument, such as piano.

THE CHRISTIAN AND A VOCATION IN MUSIC

For the Christian educator, searching for excellence, expanding students' horizons, and exposing them to a deeper, fuller, and more detailed

---

32. Plantinga, *Engaging God's World*, 35.

33. Rushton, "Christian Perspective on Music," in Downey and Porter, *Christian Worldview and the Academic Disciplines*, 328.

34. Rushton, "Christian Perspective on Music," in Downey and Porter, *Christian Worldview and the Academic Disciplines*, 328.

35. Holmes, *Idea of a Christian College*, 32.

36. Holmes, *Idea of a Christian College*, 19.

musical world, is only the start. A Christian liberal arts education is preparing a student for evangelism and for service—the truth a student learns is needed in order to more effectively evangelize and serve to a fuller capacity. Holmes points out, "God's grace has restored us as Christians . . . to understand Creation and with heart and mind to join in the cultural undertaking of the human race."[37] What a great responsibility we have as Christians to represent music in the proper light, whether as teachers or performers; and not only to understand it, but to continue creating it. Fant says, "Imagination is a deeply human trait that derives its abilities from the mind of God,"[38] and Rushton writes, "artistic productivity is . . . a human response to God's creativity."[39]

At College of the Ozarks, there is an especially clear focus on vocation in addition to education, and truly the two go hand in hand. If I look back on my education, it was full of various experiences, and my experiences have been an education. I have seen too many students (mostly not at College of the Ozarks) who have knowledge and education, but don't know how to apply it in their vocations, or if they do, they may not know how to apply it in a holistic, spiritual sense. I concur with Holmes that the curiosity and love for learning fostered by a liberal arts education should help a student continually try to achieve more in their vocation, taking it to the next level. And while experience is crucial, the role of an educator brings that experience to the next level, as a teacher is devoted to helping their student along, literally serving the student and providing an example of how to serve.

In applied music, experience is perhaps even more crucial than in many other disciplines. Practicing the piano is active; it involves the experience of feeling the topography of the keys and keeping your eyes moving on the page at the right speed, and through it all, training the ear. Performing must also be practiced, as it is a different skill from what is developed in a practice room; it involves knowing how to deal with nerves, how to connect with audience members, and how to take the skills honed while alone and use them to serve others. This is part of the reason why as a teacher I must keep performing, as it reminds me of how to face the challenges of daily practice and performance stress, and it

---

37. Holmes, *Idea of a Christian College*, 23.
38. Fant, *Liberal Arts*, 83.
39. Downey and Porter, *Christian Worldview and the Academic Disciplines*, 325.

also allows me to lead by example. Howard Best describes the connection between the Christian performer and audience member this way:

> If musicians assume themselves to be above the community, they end up denying the very reality that has made their way of creating possible . . . they can drink in from as many sources as possible, giving thanks for the rich world of musical creativity, drawing people in and serving them. Then, linked to the body of Christ and obligated to the world community, they fling themselves out as servants, shepherds, helpers, teachers, bards, and prophets.[40]

I must work regularly with my students on how to handle performance anxiety, which is often linked to an inaccurate view of self, of competition, or of the music being performed. Having an attitude of service towards God and others and a proper view of self does not make performance anxiety disappear, but it does aid in putting it in perspective and gradually minimizing it. Providing students with practical experience playing in environments where they are not competing or showing off, but humbly providing a service, is part of the process. And, like expanding listening skills and working to understand new harmonic language, it takes repetition.

Ultimately, my role as a faithful educator is to expose students to the imprint of God throughout music; perhaps a particularly exciting and fulfilling field for the Christian. My greatest passion and most extensive background is as a classical performer, specializing in piano music that is not overtly Christian, and could be labeled "secular;" but is such a varied, rich world of beauty and aesthetic value, and provides many opportunities to serve. Holmes breaks down the boundaries between the words "secular" and "sacred" with his statement, "For all human sin has done to distort the scene, this world is still God's creation, of value to both God and human beings . . . the secular is not itself evil; in fact, in God's world, it too is sacred."[41] My goal for my students studying piano performance is that they will make a practice of continuing to learn on their own throughout their lives, practicing new music and always finding opportunities to perform, no matter how small the setting.

Students who have the opportunity to study music history and literature learn to expand their base of knowledge and become better

---

40. Best, *Music Through the Eyes of Faith*, 36.
41. Holmes, *Idea of a Christian College*, 1.

equipped to engage their culture and evangelize to others. I've presented to them hard questions like, "Is this bad music because I don't like it, or should I appeal to a different mode of value than my personal aesthetic judgements?" I also explain to both my music history students and my applied students that they cannot truthfully serve God with their gifts if they don't work to develop, change, and grow. The process of pushing themselves toward excellence means that they are honoring God, and by serving God, they serve other people, even though other people may not always recognize or even welcome musical excellence. In a sense, each one of us becomes a teacher, and whether a student or graduate is fulfilling a role as an educator, a worship leader, or a performer, they are part of a much greater purpose than they may feel in the moment, and for their work they will be blessed.

> Psalm 1:1–3: "Blessed *is* the man
> Who walks not in the counsel of the ungodly,
> Nor stands in the path of sinners,
> Nor sits in the seat of the scornful;
> But his delight *is* in the law of the Lord,
> And on His law he meditates day and night.
> He shall be like a tree
> Planted by the rivers of water,
> That brings forth its fruit in its season,
> Whose leaf also shall not wither;
> And whatever he does shall prosper."[42]

---

42. Ps 1:1–3 (NKJV).

BIBLIOGRAPHY

Best, Howard M. *Music Through the Eyes of Faith*. New York: HarperCollins, 1993.

Best, Howard M. *Unceasing Worship: Biblical Perspectives on Worship and the Arts*. Downers Grove, IL: InterVarsity, 2003.

Dockery, David S. and Timothy, George. *The Great Tradition of Christian Thinking: A Student's Guide*. Wheaton, IL: Crossway, 2012.

Downey, Deane E.D. and Stanley E. Porter. *Christian Worldview and the Academic Disciplines: Crossing the Academy*. Eugene, OR: Wipf and Stock, 2009.

Fant, Gene C. *The Liberal Arts: A Student's Guide*. Wheaton, IL: Crossway, 2012.

Garber, Steven. *The Fabric of Faithfulness*. Downers Grove, IL: InterVarsity, 1996.

Holmes, Arthur F. *The Idea of a Christian College*. Grand Rapids: Eerdmans, 1987.

Plantinga, Cornelius. *Engaging God's World: A Christian Vision of Faith, Learning, and Living*. Grand Rapids: Eerdmans, 2002.

Schaeffer, Francis A. *How Should We Then Live? The Rise and Decline of Western Thought and Culture*. Wheaton, IL: Crossway, 1976.

Seerveld, Calvin. *Human Responses to Art*. Sioux Center, IA: Dordt College Press, 1983.

Turner, Steve. *Imagine: A Vision for Christians in the Arts*. Downers Grove, IL: InterVarsity, 2016.

Vos, Johannes G. *The Westminster Larger Catechism: A Commentary*. Phillipsburg, NJ: P&R, 2002.

*Faithful Education
in the Professional Disciplines*

18

The Teleology of Argument

Gary C. Hiebsch

EVERY SEMESTER I ASK my public speaking classes to tell me why the college requires speech in the general education curriculum. Invariably, students will come up with a justification which mixes pragmatism with utilitarianism. "I will need it at my job someday," or "everybody has to speak at some point to get a good job," reply the students. Unlike in a history or literature class, nobody asks, "when will I ever use this?" Furthermore, most of my students profess Christianity. However, the students never respond, "the college wants me to learn to speak well so I can defend the truth," or "the ability to contribute to our society by advocating the truth is part of our responsibility as citizens." The students see their education as a way to serve their career goals. In the words of Steven Garber, education can be viewed as a "passport to privilege."[1]

Nancy Pearcey has urged Christians to "find the idol" and "test the idol against the real world."[2] J.P. Moreland and William Lane Craig have urged Christians to pay more attention to philosophy. Moreland and Craig assert many of the ideas taught in our universities have philosophical underpinnings. The Christian college professor could unwittingly teach models or theories based upon atheistic underpinnings. The professor could then undermine the very faith the institution tries

---

1. Garber, *Fabric of Faithfulness*, 83–87.
2. Olasky, "Nancy Pearcey: Idol Inspection."

to inculcate.³ Thus, professors at a Christian college need to examine the models and theories in their disciplines, identify their philosophical underpinnings, and then figure out ways to appropriately teach their discipline. In so doing, they may discover idols they have unwittingly encouraged students to worship.

This chapter attempts to do this in the communication discipline. First, this essay will examine the model of argument advanced by Stephen Toulmin. Taught in numerous communication departments, Toulmin's model has become a standard part of curriculums across the country. Yet, scholars rarely discuss the philosophical foundations of the model. This chapter will examine those philosophical foundations. Next, this chapter will review how Augustine and the early Christians approached rhetoric. We will see the wisdom the early church provided us with regarding how to integrate pagan learning into a Christian curriculum remains relevant for us today. In this discussion, this chapter suggests an alternative to the approach advocated by Toulmin. Overall, this chapter argues philosophical pragmatism lies at the heart of Toulmin's model. This philosophical pragmatism serves the idol of the self. A Christian professor can teach the model, yet, the focus of a communication classroom ought to be our service to the Lord and to our neighbor.

TOULMIN AND THE MODEL OF ARGUMENT

Stephen Toulmin published *The Uses of Argument* in 1958. Toulmin, a British philosopher at the University of Leeds, wanted to challenge the exclusive use of the rules of logic in argumentation. Toulmin outlined a model of argument which is now known as the Toulmin model. While his book had little impact in his native England, Wayne Brockriede and Douglas Ehninger introduced the model to America in 1960.⁴ Ehninger published the most influential public speaking book of the day, *The Principles of Public Speaking*, and incorporated Toulmin's model into his textbook. Since then, Toulmin's model has become a standard in Public Speaking and Argumentation and Debate textbooks. It is also included in many Persuasion, Business and Professional, and Small Group textbooks.

Toulmin's model contains the following elements:

---

3. Moreland and Craig, *Philosophical Foundations*, 11–27.
4. Brockriede and Ehninger, "Toulmin on Argument."

THE TELEOLOGY OF ARGUMENT

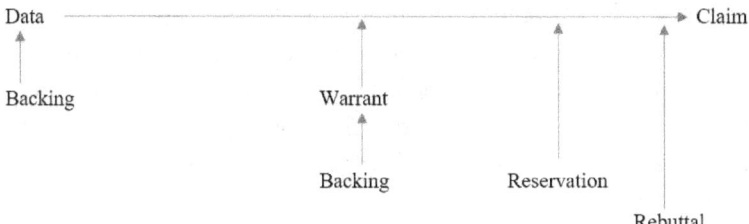

The elements interact in the following manner:

Claim: This is the proposition the speaker wants believed or acted upon. (A prosecuting attorney may claim the defendant murdered the victim.)

Data: This is the evidence for the claim.
(The police found the defendant's fingerprints on the murder weapon: a knife.)

Warrant: This is the reason to believe the data supports the claim.
(Only the killer would have handled the knife.)

Backing: The backing provides support for the reasonableness of the data or warrant.
(Scientific evidence shows each person has a unique set of fingerprints.)

Reservation: This indicates the force of the argument. Words such as "every time," "most of the time," and "possibly," are examples.
(The defendant almost certainly murdered the victim.)

Rebuttal: This is phrase indicating the presence of a counter argument and how it might be refuted.
(Despite having only ten minutes to commit the crime, the defendant almost certainly murdered the victim.)[5]

As noted above, Toulmin wanted to escape the close tie between logic and argumentation. Throughout his works, Aristotle recommended the use of the categorical syllogism:

All men are mortal.
John is a man.

5. Toulmin, *Uses of Argument*, 87–100.

John is mortal.

In Aristotle's conception of an argument, the speaker would use syllogisms and enthymemes to persuade an audience. An enthymeme is a syllogism with a premise removed. The audience supplies the missing premise, thus becoming involved in their own persuasion. The audience judges the validity of the speaker's arguments by how closely they adhere to the rules of logic.[6]

Toulmin noted two problems with Aristotle's position. First, Aristotle's conception of evidence and proof differed greatly from modern conceptions. Aristotle divided proof into artistic and inartistic categories. A speaker using reasoning to develop an argument used artistic proof. A speaker who pointed to evidence in the modern sense used inartistic proof (the presence of fingerprints on a murder weapon would be an inartistic proof). Aristotle minimized the value of inartistic proofs. The development of empirical science elevated inartistic proofs above artistic proofs. Toulmin's model attempted to acknowledge this change in the value of types of proof.

Furthermore, the categorical syllogism searches for certain truth. Argumentation occurs in a realm of uncertainty. Deliberation and debate occur when, in the words of rhetorical theorist Lloyd Bitzer, an exigence, "an imperfection marked by urgency" occurs.[7] People simply do not know the future or the full consequences of their actions. Yet they know they must mobilize the collective will of the community to address the problem. Thus a "positive modification" of the exigence "can be assisted by discourse."[8] The community must make decisions without all the data. Thus, the use of the syllogism creates the search for a certainty which does not exist.[9]

Toulmin created his model as part of a larger intellectual project. Toulmin located his thinking within the pragmatism of William James and John Dewey, the neo pragmatism of Richard Rorty, and the language analysis of Ludwig Wittgenstein. The thinking of these men opened the possibility of questioning the search for certainty. Toulmin offered his model as middle ground between the extremes of relativism and absolutism.

---

6. Aristotle, *Art of Rhetoric*, 2.22–23.
7. Bitzer, "Rhetorical Situation," 6–7.
8. Bitzer, "Rhetorical Situation," 6–7.
9. Toulmin, *Uses of Argument*, 110–25.

Toulmin believed Western philosophy had taken a wrong turn with René Descartes in the seventeenth century. Descartes distrusted human experience and wanted to place philosophy on a sounder footing. Descartes searched for undeniably true premises from which to start arguments. The most famous of these was, "I think therefore I am." Descartes also developed and used the ontological argument for God's existence.[10] Descartes separated the mind from the body and hoped to find mental first principles upon which to start philosophical arguments. Ultimately, Descartes sought to find a way to unify philosophy and society around certain conclusions derived from these principles. Toulmin asserted this project had run its course. The quest for absolute certain principles had failed and it was time to turn in a different direction.[11]

The direction Toulmin advocated used the pragmatic philosophy of William James and John Dewey. James advocated an approach to truth which considered something true to the extent to which it produced a useful conclusion. James asked, "what, in short, is the truth's cash-value in experiential terms?"[12] James made human experience, goals, and aspirations central to truth. A person could not assume something to be true simply from logical principles. Humans needed to test ideas to see if the ideas could be verified. Unverifiable ideas were valueless. Thus, no inherent truths exist. Something is made true by the continual process of testing and verification. Something true today might become less relevant and less useful as time progresses. Truth "becomes true, it is made true by events."[13]

Such a view of truth had important implications. Truth could become tied to a field of study. A truth in religion might be different than a truth in psychology. Second, such an approach to truth became time bound. The truths of a prior generation might not work for a future generation. Finally, truth became culturally bound. One culture's truth might not be that of another culture. Such an approach opened the door to relativism. James acknowledged this but offered no answer. However, Toulmin hoped his model would provide some help.

John Dewey added to James's pragmatism. Dewey agreed with James on the value of experience. Yet Dewey, operating from an explicit atheism,

---

10. Skirry, "René Descartes."
11. Toulmin, *Cosmopolis*.
12. James, *Pragmatism*, 97.
13. James, *Pragmatism*, 97.

insisted no external sources of knowledge exist. Philosophers had hoped to find universal and absolute first principles. Dewey viewed such a quest as futile. Instead, Dewey advocated experimental empiricism. If one had an idea, one should put the idea into practice, see what happened, and then judge the results. Such a view put all matters into flux. Dewey challenged the idea "that the institutions of marriage and family developed in medieval Europe are the last and unchanging word."[14] Furthermore, Dewey believed our society should experiment with different economic and educational arrangements.

Much of this thinking developed out of Dewey's regard for Darwinian evolution. For Dewey, Darwin had shown human life, like all life, existed in a state of flux. Along these lines humans could develop new systems which would better serve their interests.[15] Of course, just as animals had adapted to different environments, so too different groups of humans might need to adapt to different environments. Furthermore, as time progressed, and humans changed, so too could their systems of meaning. Dewey asserted, "there is no need of deciding between no meaning at all and one single, all embracing meaning. There are many meanings and many purposes in the situations by which we are confronted."[16] Dewey viewed humans as free to experiment with different social, familial, and economic relationships.

Ludwig Wittgenstein's philosophy of language fit well into this emerging pragmatism. A common-sense understanding of language focuses upon its representational quality. A word represents an underlying reality. For example, the word "knife" represents a long metal object used to cut. However, Wittgenstein viewed language differently. Language derives its meaning from the way it is used. Wittgenstein used the example of construction workers and the word "slab." The word could refer to a piece of concrete. However, the word could be an inquiry, a point of clarification, or a command. Wittgenstein coined the term "language games." By game Wittgenstein did not minimize the seriousness of language use. Instead, to derive meaning from a word a person needed to understand the language game being played and its rules. Wittgenstein viewed this as a larger phenomenon. Various groups within society played different language games. According to Wittgenstein, "to imagine a language

---

14. Dewey, "What I believe," in Hickman and Alexander, *Essential Dewey*, 24.
15. Bernstein, *John Dewey*.
16. Dewey, "What I believe," in Hickman and Alexander, *Essential Dewey*, 25.

means to imagine a form of life."[17] Thus, language did not simply represent reality. Different people, using different language games, would have different forms of life. If somebody wanted to change the world, then they needed to change the language game being played. A new set of rules would engender a new reality.[18] Humans could choose what world they wanted to inhabit by the language games they chose to play.

Finally, the neopragmatism of Richard Rorty requires mentioning. Rorty published his writings after Toulmin's publication of *The Uses of Arguments*. However, Toulmin would cite Rorty's work approvingly.[19] Rorty rejected both foundationalism and representationalism. Our language games make it impossible to describe the world objectively. Thus, our minds can't become a mirror of nature. Instead, our arguments are conversations. We can form communities with people who agree with our ideas. One can judge an idea, not upon how closely it conforms to the truth, but upon its usefulness to how we live our lives.[20] We should not even search for the truth as a foundation for society. Thus, Rorty's thought encourages the development of multiculturalism.

Of course, a possible implication of these ideas is relativism. Each person could decide upon the way of life most beneficial to the individual. Such a society would eventually tear itself apart. While most of these thinkers rejected relativism, their thought opened its possibility. As we have seen with William James, some had no answer for this problem.

More importantly, scholars have noted the close connection between pragmatism and the thought of the ancient sophists. The most famous of the ancient sophists, Protagoras, developed a skepticism of the existence of the gods and appealing to them for knowledge.[21] Furthermore, Protagoras declared, "Man is the measure of all things."[22] Plato accused the sophists of a reliance upon individual perception for knowledge. Of course, perception can vary with the perceiver. Once again, the twin issues of subjectivism and individualism raise their heads. Logically, politics becomes critical, since only governmental action can provide unity in the absence of an agreed upon foundation. The sophists put a great

---

17. Wittgenstein, *Philosophical Investigations*, I19, 8.
18. For a further explanation of this, see Grayling, *Wittgenstein*, 82–99.
19. Toulmin, *Cosmopolis*.
20. Rorty, *Philosophy and the Mirror of Nature*, 315–94.
21. Diogenes Laertius, *Lives of the Eminent Philosophers*, 9.8.
22. See Plato, *Theaetetus*.

deal of emphasis on politics, and Dewey believed his work could enliven democracy. Both sophistry and pragmatism call for dialogue, negotiation, and interpretation of public policy.[23]

Thus, one can now place Toulmin's model within its intellectual context. Toulmin rejected absolutism and relativism. He wanted to create a model to serve as a guideline for the judgment of arguments. One could not accept an argument from simple personal preference. An argument needed publicly accessible warrants and backing with which one could test it. The community formed around an argument would judge its merits. At the same time, a community could not appeal to a fixed and settled truth. Future generations and future individuals could advance other arguments. A person could expect revisions to lifestyles and expectations as revised understandings emerged. Since contingency lies at the bottom of all arguments, Toulmin's model pictures endless conversation. The only teleology to the model is the ever-increasing improvement of life. Toulmin hoped his model would provide the middle ground between absolutism and relativism.

Toulmin's model illustrates well what Mary Poplin has termed secular humanism.[24] The pragmatism of James, Dewey, and Rorty does not admit of any outside influence. This permits us to create ourselves and the world we want to inhabit. As scholar Louis Menand has observed, "everything James and Dewey wrote as pragmatists boils down to a single claim: people are the agents of their own destinies."[25] Yet, how would one mediate between various incompatible claims? For James and the early pragmatists, absolute claims of being in the right, made by the abolitionists, produced the Civil War.[26] Toulmin believed the acceptance of Descartes and the search for foundations and certainty occurred because of the political instability of the Thirty Years War.[27] Yet, both James and Toulmin rejected foundationalism. Subsequently, as rhetorical scholar Robert Danisch has observed, "Toulmin's model of argument provides a mechanism for grounding decisions not on absolute, universal principles

---

23. Mailloux, "Sophistry and Rhetorical Pragmatism," in Mailloux, *Rhetoric, Sophistry, and Pragmatism*, 22.
24. Poplin, *Is Reality Secular?*, 105–64.
25. Menand, *Metaphysical Club*, 371.
26. Menand, *Metaphysical Club*, 49–83.
27. Toulmin, *Cosmopolis*, 45–87.

but on contextual claims made on the basis of probability and the uniqueness of a situation."[28]

A CHRISTIAN RESPONSE TO TOULMIN

The easiest thing for a Christian professor to do would be to reject Toulmin's model outright. Given the model's rejection of any eternal fixed truth, it would appear the teaching of this model would potentially harm the spiritual development of students. Yet such a response would betray a lack of knowledge of church history and the history of rhetoric. This is not the first time the Christian church, and a Christian teacher of rhetoric, has faced the issue of how to integrate a secular work into a Christian classroom.

As author George Kennedy has noted, several of the early church fathers, including Tertullian, Cyprian, Arnobius, Lactantius, and Augustine, taught rhetoric. Several others, such as Ambrose, Hilary, and Jerome, had training in classical rhetoric.[29] These Latin fathers struggled with what to do regarding the incorporation of pagan rhetoric into the church. Frequently their struggle revolved around how to deal with the works of the Roman statesman and orator Cicero.

Cicero's work presented the church with a problem. Most of the Latin fathers had learned the Ciceronian categories of rhetoric. In Cicero, they found much to admire. Cicero saw the proper application of rhetoric as a useful civic art. The well-educated and well-trained public speaker could defend the civil rights of Roman citizens against attack. Furthermore, such an individual could contribute wisdom to the decision-making process of the society. For Cicero, the ideal speaker was a well-educated, civic minded individual who sought to improve the society.[30] When one adds to this Cicero's defense of the Roman Republic, his refusal to participate in its destruction, and his eventual murder at the hands of Antony, one of those who seized power, one can see how many would come to idolize him.[31]

Yet, idolatry concerned the church. Cicero and all the Latin and Greek philosophers dedicated their works to pagan gods. Thus, Christians

---

28. Danish, *Pragmatism, Democracy, and the Necessity of Rhetoric*, 157.
29. Kennedy, *Classical Rhetoric*, 146.
30. Cicero, *De Oratore Books I & II*.
31. Clayton, "Cicero."

could view their works as being contaminated by adherence to pagan standards. Furthermore, some of the church fathers viewed their own devotion to Cicero as a form of idolatry. Jerome loved Cicero. Yet he became so concerned he even dreamt of being rebuked by God at the final judgement with the words, "Thou dost lie—thou are not a Christian, but a Ciceronian."[32] Others suggested the church should discard the use of pagan rhetoric.

Augustine rejected the idea of discarding rhetoric. Augustine had been a teacher of rhetoric. He realized his teaching gave students the "tricks" they needed to convince people.[33] Yet, he also admired Cicero and realized the importance of rhetoric. Christianity, with its stress upon teaching and preaching the Word, had a great interest in an art which sought to persuade. Furthermore, first against the Manicheans, then against the Donatists, and finally against Pelagius, Augustine spent his life teaching orthodoxy and refuting heresy. Finally, as a bishop who occasionally faced heckling in the churches in which he preached, Augustine desired ways to persuade his audience more effectively.[34] Unlike the pragmatists, Augustine saw argumentation serving the cause of truth against falsehood. Augustine feared a situation in which rhetorically savvy heretics pleading a false cause knew "from the beginning how to make their audience well-disposed, attentive, and docile." The orthodox opponent would "state the truth in a way that is wearisome to listen to, not clear to understand, and finally, not pleasant to believe."[35] Augustine embraced rhetoric, not for its ability to create a useful argument, but from its ability to advance the truth.

Augustine changed the teleology of argument. Perhaps, Augustine's personal experience with Ambrose, the Archbishop of Milan whose preaching helped to convert him, played a role. Augustine confessed his love of listening to Ambrose, not due to Ambrose's preaching the truth, but because "my pleasure was in the charm of his language."[36] Eventually, Augustine listened to the content of Ambrose's sermons. He believed this content led him to Christ. Furthermore, as the Bishop of Hippo,

32. Murphy, "St. Augustine and the Debate about a Christian Rhetoric," in Enos and Thompson, *Rhetoric of St. Augustine*, 211.

33. Augustine, *Confessions*, 4.2.

34. Brown, *Through the Eye of a Needle*, 291–368.

35. Augustine, *De Doctrina Christiana*, in Enos and Thompson, *Rhetoric of St. Augustine*, 2.3.

36. Augustine, *Confessions*, 5.8.

Augustine utilized Cicero's rhetorical style. He urged the citizens of Caesarea in Mauritania to cease their custom of having a town brawl once a year. The brawl regularly produced deaths. Augustine used what Cicero termed the grand style. The eloquence Augustine used moved the people to tears and they gave up the brawl.[37]

Thus, Augustine viewed rhetoric as a tool: morally neutral. A person could use rhetoric to advance their selfish interests. Or, a person could use rhetoric to advance the truth. Thus, Augustine adopted Cicero's rhetoric. Augustine saw Cicero as part of the gold of the Egyptians. Just as the children of Israel plundered the Egyptians when they left, so too, the church could use the learning of the pagans to advance its agenda.[38] Augustine encouraged his readers to adopt the eloquence advocated by Cicero to educate, please, and move their audiences. Augustine refused to participate in a genetic fallacy. Cicero served pagan gods, but if a Christian could use the tool he left, then the Christian ought to employ it.

AUGUSTINE, TOULMIN, AND THE TEACHING OF RHETORIC

The question now becomes, can one separate the gold of Toulmin's model from the dross of pragmatism? This chapter will answer this question with a qualified yes. Pragmatism has many noteworthy features. Certainly, the philosophy of Descartes took skepticism of human experience to an extreme. The Christian can assert the fact of God's creation of the world. Furthermore, human beings can experience the world and testify about their experiences. The Christian faith rests upon the testimony of the apostles who witnessed the resurrected Jesus. At the same time, our knowledge is limited. The apostle Paul tells us we "see through a glass darkly."[39] While a Christian will always assert there is truth, our ability to know the truth has limits. The pragmatic approach to experimentation and revision can serve to usefully help us test ideas and increase our knowledge of the world.

---

37. Augustine, *De Doctrina Christiana*, in Enos and Thompson, *Rhetoric of St. Augustine*, 24.53.

38. Augustine, *De Doctrina Christiana*, in Enos and Thompson, *Rhetoric of St. Augustine*, 40.60.

39. 1 Cor 13:12 (ESV).

The use of Toulmin's model helps students to understand the elements of an argument. Toulmin's model has a descriptive as well as a prescriptive purpose. All arguments start as claims. Usually, those claims require evidence and reasoning for support. Frequently, claims in a contingent area have reservations or a rebuttal attached. A student who understands Toulmin's model can more ably discern the nature of an argument and its potential weaknesses. Such discernment is of great value to any person. It can help with decision making and critical thinking.

Nevertheless, in refuting Descartes's pessimism regarding human experience, pragmatism makes a mistake in the other direction. In the pragmatic universe envisioned by James, Dewey, and Rorty there is no sin. There is no evil and no devil trying to undermine human existence. A person will judge arguments based upon their usefulness, not their truth. Such a position raises the possibility of idolatry. The pragmatist makes his or her goals the central focus of their life. Furthermore, the pragmatist does not consider the possibility of deception. The writer of Proverbs tells us, "There is a way that seems right to a man, but its end is the way to death."[40] By excluding any external standards, the pragmatist deceives herself and the world. The professor at a Christian institution needs to challenge students with the notions of mission, calling, and wisdom.

As Alister McGrath points out, the Christian believes in a creator God who is separate from creation yet speaks to people and acts within creation.[41] God speaks throughout the scriptures using calling. God called Abram to leave Ur and go to the land to which he calls him. God called Gideon, Samson, Saul, and David to lead his people. God called Isaiah and Jeremiah to prophesy. Jesus called the disciples to follow him. These examples point to the fact that God calls people to follow and serve him. Martin Luther understood calling as applying to all Christians. God calls us to serve him in our jobs, as citizens, in our families, and in our churches.[42] God has "made from one man every nation of mankind to live on all the face of the earth, having determined allotted periods and the boundaries of their dwelling place."[43] Thus, we find ourselves living in twenty-first-century America, not due to random chance, but to the design of God. The excellence of our service can be a witness to the world

40. Prov 16:25 (ESV).
41. McGrath, *Theology*.
42. Veith, *God at Work*.
43. Acts 17:26 (ESV).

about God. We love our neighbors by fulfilling our vocation. A Christian college professor should operate from the assumption God has called each student to himself. Furthermore, each student should realize God has called them to serve in these areas. One can think of argumentation as a form of service. Businesses, churches, families, and our communities need people committed to the truth. The advancing of arguments designed to encourage the best interests of the groups to which God has called us serves them. Thus, a Christian does not view something as merely useful, the Christian views life as service.

Calling implies mission. In the post-modern world, skepticism abounds regarding metanarratives. A metanarrative is a grand narrative by which one could organize one's life. Marxism serves as an example of this. The Marxists believe the cycles of history in which there is thesis, antithesis, and new thesis, will end with the arrival of communism and the workers' paradise. It has proven impossible to come to an agreement regarding a governing metanarrative. Furthermore, those who have given allegiance to metanarratives have committed numerous atrocities in their name. Thus, one ought to abandon such metanarratives.[44] Instead, as Rorty envisioned, numerous groups in the society could live by their own narratives.

Yet, as Christopher Wright has shown, one can read the Bible as a grand narrative. God has the purpose of encouraging people from all nations to worship him.[45] The Bible relates the stories of Abraham, Moses, David, and Daniel amongst others. Jesus sent out his disciples to make disciples of all nations. God uses each individual to advance the mission of establishing and promoting his worship. As John Piper has pointed out, "missions exist because worship doesn't."[46] Traditionally, many people confine missions to the task of evangelism amongst unreached peoples. Such an approach unnecessarily limits mission. If one accepts Luther's understanding of calling, then a Christian could be called to any legitimate profession. The Christian could contribute to the mission of God's people by the excellence of their fulfilling of God's calling. Many will discover public speaking and the making of arguments to be part of their calling. If they use those arguments to fulfill God's mission, even

---

44. Lyotard, *Postmodern Condition*.
45. Wright, *Mission of God*.
46. Piper, *Let the Nations be Glad!*, 15.

when those arguments do not directly contribute to God's kingdom, then they will live as part of the mission of God.

Another important aspect of rhetoric involves the exercise of wisdom. The Proverbs repeatedly commend wisdom to us. The author tells us "get wisdom; get insight; do not forget, and do not turn away from the words of my mouth."[47] It would be possible for God to enlighten us with direct wisdom. However, God commands us to get wisdom. This implies actions on the part of humans. Furthermore, argumentation exists in an area of uncertainty. At times, God has told his people about the future. Yet, most of the time God has not made such knowledge available, and people need to make decisions about the future.

The scriptures point out that "the fear of the LORD is the beginning of wisdom, and the knowledge of the Holy One is insight."[48] For the arguments of God's children to make an impact, they need to express wisdom. Of course, wisdom begins by doing those things God's word commands. The Christian should always seek to tie their arguments to the scripture. However, scripture does not address all issues. Situations will arise which require Christians to demonstrate wisdom. Yet, just as no scriptural passage told Solomon how to decide which prostitute was truly the mother of the baby,[49] situations in the Christian's life will require wisdom regarding issues which scripture does not address. As John Piper noted in commenting on this passage, "the wisdom which follows God's Word and the wisdom which discerns the way to act when there is no clear word from God are not separate."[50] Piper urges Christians to saturate their minds with God's Word "that we gain the spiritual wisdom to guide us in all situations."[51] This wisdom becomes the basis of argumentation.

The Bible provides examples of individuals who functioned in secular contexts at the highest levels of power: Joseph and Daniel. Both men found themselves taken captive to a foreign land. Both men refused to compromise their integrity and obeyed God's instructions. Both men suffered for this at times. Eventually, the rulers of their lands recognized their wisdom and promoted them to the highest levels of government. In these positions, both men did something interesting.

47. Prov 4:5 (ESV).
48. Prov 9:10 (ESV).
49. 1 Kgs 3:16–28.
50. Piper, "Get Wisdom."
51. Piper, "Get Wisdom."

Joseph saved the land of Egypt and the children of Israel from starvation. Indeed, his actions eventually ended up strengthening the power of Pharaoh. While the Pharaoh of Joseph's day respected God, Egypt remained an idolatrous nation. As the administrator of Egypt's granaries, and as the deputy ruler of Egypt, God called Joseph to govern Egypt. Undoubtedly, Joseph faced may practical day-to-day issues not recorded in scripture. These issues would have required him to judge the arguments of others, and advance arguments of his own. Joseph feared the Lord and gained wisdom. This wisdom he applied to the practical affairs of governing Egypt.

Daniel also provides an example of wisdom. He served the king of the empire which had destroyed his homeland and deported him to Babylon. As such, he helped to govern and rule the land. His abilities caused his position to be virtually unchanged despite the Persian Empire succeeding Babylon. He held himself to the highest standards of personal integrity; so much so, his enemies had to outlaw his actions to find any guilt in him. As John Lennox has noted, "this level of personal integrity is very impressive indeed, and sadly extremely rare."[52] Such personal integrity fits well into the classical rhetorical category of ethos. Ethos refers to the personal integrity of the speaker. Augustine urged the aspiring speaker to live a life "beyond reproach." The same speaker should "forecast what is good before God and man, in as far as possible, by fearing God and by caring for man."[53] Again, just as with Joseph, Daniel would have had to assess and make arguments. His fear of the Lord, and the wisdom he derived from it, permitted Daniel to function at the highest levels of a pagan society.

IMPLICATION AND CONCLUSION

Christian Smith identified "moralistic, therapeutic deism" as the de facto religion of the American teenagers he surveyed. Smith stated American teenagers viewed religion as something which gave them rules to live by. Thus, it was moralistic. God wanted people to be happy. Thus, religion was therapeutic. Finally, God pretty much left humanity alone to figure out how to achieve these goals. Thus, the God pictured here was deistic.

---

52. Lennox, *Against the Flow*, 200.

53. Augustine, *De Doctrina Christiana*," in Enos and Thompson, *Rhetoric of St. Augustine*, 28.61.

Smith conceded no teenager would state, "I am a moralistic, therapeutic deist." Instead, Smith argued, teenagers had absorbed this view from the larger culture.[54] This chapter has argued something similar has happened with pragmatism.

The pragmatic thought presented in this chapter does not contradict, but instead complements the moralistic, therapeutic deism discovered by Smith. Pragmatism promises to make it possible to create a world of our own choosing. To answer Nancy Pearcey's challenge to find the idol, the idol of pragmatism becomes ourselves: our desires, our aspirations, our goals. A deistic God would leave us alone to figure out how to make ourselves feel better. As long as we could claim to be good as we pursued our goals, then all would be fine.

For a professor of communication, confronting this idol remains difficult. A committed pragmatist can use the subject matter presented in a communication classroom to further their aims. Furthermore, students have learned to think pragmatically from the surrounding culture. Many see no contradiction between it and their Christian lives. Indeed, the Christianity presented in many contemporary churches relies heavily upon pragmatic principles. For example, the church growth movement suggests people will find Christianity attractive when they see its relevance to their lives.[55] Thus, pastors give sermons on how to rear children, have a satisfying marriage, and manage money. The concerns of our lives become the primary concerns of the church with little room for an outside calling.[56] Such a vision inevitably deemphasizes theological considerations that fail to contribute to the church's growth. The church becomes increasingly hollow with little call for submissive discipleship.[57] Such developments fit the pragmatic worldview well, minimizing the conflict between pragmatism and Christianity. Thus, it would be easy to shut up, pray prior to class, and call my efforts at faithful education good. Yet, I have become convinced an unconfronted pragmatism remains one of the idols of our day. The major challenge has become awareness of the problem.

I wrote the bulk of what would become this chapter in the summer of 2017. During the 2017–2018 academic year, I attempted to bring

---

54. Smith and Denton, *Soul Searching*, 118–71.
55. Warren, *Purpose Driven Church*.
56. Horton, *Christless Christianity*, 101–58.
57. Abraham, *Logic of Evangelism*, 70–91.

discussions of pragmatism into my teaching of the Toulmin model. In my opinion, such discussions yielded little fruit. Pragmatic thinking has become so engrained that students simply remain unaware of it. As of this writing, it would appear I will need to change the presentation of courses and materials to give the students enough background to assess the nature and possible benefits of the Toulmin model. Such a revamping needs to focus on a change in the teleology of the course. My courses will need to more closely mirror the teleology Augustine gave to the study of rhetoric.

However, this chapter points to the issue of the teleology of education. Most students come to College of the Ozarks looking to improve themselves and their lot in life. Undeniably, education increases the amount a person can earn. Putting myself into their shoes, I would approach education with the same attitude. Yet, the Word of God confronts people with the calling God places upon their lives. God has a purpose and agenda for the life of each person. Yet, that purpose comes from outside of the person. Our education needs to persuade students of the value of God's calling on their lives. Such a view is not pragmatic, but it is biblical.

BIBLIOGRAPHY

Abraham, William. *The Logic of Evangelism*. Grand Rapids: Eerdmans, 1989.
Aristotle. *The Art of Rhetoric*. Translated by J.H. Freese. Cambridge: Harvard University Press, 1982.
Augustine of Hippo. *Confessions*. Translated by Henry Chadwick. New York: Oxford University Press, 1991.
Bernstein, Richard J. *John Dewey*. New York: Washington Square, 1966.
Bitzer, Lloyd. "The Rhetorical Situation." *Philosophy and Rhetoric* 1.1 (1968): 114.
Brockriede, Wayne and Douglas Ehninger. "Toulmin on Argument: An Interpretation and Application." *Quarterly Journal of Speech* 46.1 (1960): 44–53.
Brown, Peter. *Through the Eye of a Needle: Wealth, the Fall of Rome, and the Making of Christianity in the West, 350–550 A.D.* Princeton: Princeton University Press, 2012.
Cicero. *De Oratore Books I & II*. Translated by E.W. Sutton and H. Rackham. Cambridge: Harvard University Press, 1942.
Clayton, Edward. "Cicero." *Internet Encyclopedia of Philosophy*. http://www.iep.utm.edu/cicero/.
Danish, Robert. *Pragmatism, Democracy, and the Necessity of Rhetoric*. Columbia: University of South Carolina Press, 2007.
Diogenes Laertius. *Lives of the Eminent Philosophers*. http://www.perseus.tufts.edu/hopper/text?doc=Perseus%3Atext%3A1999.01.0258.

Enos, Richard and Roger Thompson, eds. *The Rhetoric of St. Augustine of Hippo*. Waco, TX: Baylor University Press, 2008.
Garber, Steven. *The Fabric of Faithfulness*. Downers Grove, IL: InterVarsity, 2007.
Grayling, A.C. *Wittgenstein: A Very Short Introduction*. New York: Oxford University Press, 2001.
Hickman, Larry and Thomas Alexander, eds. *The Essential Dewey: Volume 1 Pragmatism, Education, Democracy*. Bloomington: Indiana University Press, 1998.
Horton, Michael. *Christless Christianity: The Alternative Gospel of the American Church*. Grand Rapids: Baker, 2008.
James, William. *Pragmatism*. Cambridge: Harvard University Press, 1975.
Kennedy, George. *Classical Rhetoric and its Christian and Secular Tradition from Ancient to Modern Times*. Chapel Hill: University of North Carolina Press, 1980.
Lennox, John. *Against the Flow: The Inspiration of Daniel in an Age of Relativism*. Grand Rapids: Monarch Books, 2015.
Lyotard, Jean-François. *The Postmodern Condition: A Report on Knowledge*. Minneapolis: University of Minnesota Press, 1984.
Mailloux, Stephen, ed. *Rhetoric, Sophistry, and Pragmatism*. New York: Cambridge University Press, 1995.
McGrath, Alistair. *Theology: The Basics*, 2nd ed. Malden, MA: Blackwell, 2008.
Menand, Louis. *The Metaphysical Club*. New York: Straus and Giroux, 2001.
Moreland, J.P. and William Lane Craig. *Philosophical Foundations for a Christian Worldview*. Downers Grove, IL: InterVarsity, 2003.
Olasky, Marvin. "Nancy Pearcey: Idol Inspection." *World Magazine Online* (April 4, 2015). https://world.wng.org/2015/03/nancy_pearcey_idol_inspection.
Piper, John. "*Get Wisdom.*" Sermon delivered on May 24, 1981. http://www.desiringgod.org/messages/get-wisdom.
———. *Let the Nations be Glad!: The Supremacy of God in Missions*, 3rd ed. Grand Rapids: Baker Academic, 2010.
Plato. *Theaetetus*. Edited by Bernard Williams. Indianapolis: Hackett, 1992.
Poplin, Mary. *Is Reality Secular?: Testing the Assumption of Four Global Worldviews*. Downers Grove, IL: InterVarsity, 2014.
Rorty, Richard. *Philosophy and the Mirror of Nature*. Princeton: Princeton University Press, 1979.
Skirry, Justin, "René Descartes." *The Internet Encyclopedia of Philosophy*. http://www.iep.utm.edu/descarte/.
Smith, Christian and Melinda Lundquist Denton. *Soul Searching: The Religious and Spiritual Lives of American Teenagers* New York: Oxford University Press, 2005.
Toulmin, Stephen. *Cosmopolis: The Hidden Agenda of Modernity*. Chicago: University of Chicago Press, 1990.
———. *The Uses of Argument*. Cambridge: Cambridge University Press, 1958.
Veith, Gene. *God at Work: Your Christian Vocation in All of Life*. Wheaton: Crossway, 2002.
Warren, Rick. *The Purpose Driven Church*. Grand Rapids: Zondervan, 1995.
Wittgenstein, Ludwig. *Philosophical Investigations*. Translated by G.E.M. Anscombe. Oxford: Basil Blackwell, 1953.
Wright, Christopher. *The Mission of God: Unlocking the Bible's Grand Narrative*. Downers Grove, IL: InterVarsity, 1986.

19

Faithful Education in Engineering

Geoff Akers

As a high school senior, I accepted an ROTC scholarship to become an electrical engineer and serve in the United States Air Force. One Sunday that spring, my family had lunch with a visiting minister who asked about my career plans. When I proudly told him my plans to be an engineer, he replied, "What a shame! We need more young men like you to be pastors." As a seventeen-year-old, I was convinced that being an engineer in the military was my calling, yet this godly man seemed to question whether I could effectively serve God as an engineer.

Nineteenth-century author Hannah Whitall Smith observed, "Is it not just as solemn to live our everyday lives as it is to preach, and ought we not to do the one to His glory just as much as the other?"[1] More than thirty years after that discussion with the visiting minister, I have the credentials and experience for my calling to teach engineering at a Christian institution.

Even after more than twenty years of secular education, followed by twenty years of government service, being transparent about my faith in Jesus Christ in a professional environment is both liberating and daunting. For about two thousand years, Christians have regarded the truths of the Christian faith to be indispensable for a right relationship with God, as well as to thrive in any human relationship or endeavor. In the last

---

1. Smith, *Christian's Secret to a Happy Life*, 226.

two hundred years, faith and knowledge have come to be treated as two separate spheres of activity in the modern university, and it has been true for the professional environments in general. As a result, the discovery, communication, and application of knowledge has become disconnected from the Christian faith.[2] In my experience, the Christian walk of faith supports and encourages rational inquiry and requires truth-seeking, and therefore enhances my education and work. Moreover, my faith has been challenged and strengthened by Christian colleagues as much as by any sermon I have heard.

In this chapter, I consider how to faithfully educate engineering students. The Christian faith, as described in the brief epistle of Jude and interpreted by Dockery and George, is, "the proclamation of Jesus Christ as Lord of lords and King of kings; the Way, the Truth, and the Life."[3] Therefore, to faithfully educate is to instruct in a way that is consistent with *the* faith. The motivation and challenges of faithfully educating engineers are discussed. The College of the Ozarks engineering program is also used as an example of one approach to integrate general education requirements, as well as cocurricular aspects of the institution.

MOTIVATION

Several years ago, while traveling for work in California, I had a late-night discussion on science instruction with Todd, an engineering colleague. Todd argued that no supernatural events should be included in a science class, while I claimed creation should be taught as a valid origins model. We agreed there could only be one correct answer and that neither of us was present at the beginning. When I suggested current scientific theory could be wrong, Todd responded with, "It doesn't matter what happened." His stance was that truth does not matter; the supernatural has no place in a natural science curriculum. The irony is he would not (or could not?) recognize his argument as faith-based, the faith in the absence of the supernatural. Our worldviews led to an impasse, and we eventually agreed to disagree. We could not understand each other's position, because we did not share the same fundamental beliefs.

As stated in the introduction of this book, "a worldview is not merely a set of philosophical bullet points. It is essentially a master narrative, a

---

2. Dockery and George, *Great Tradition of Christian Thinking*, 21.
3. Dockery and George, *Great Tradition of Christian Thinking*, 67–68.

fundamental story about (a) what human life in the world should be like, (b) what has knocked it off balance, and (c) what can be done to make it right."[4] Purpose and hope for the future, or lack thereof, are derived from a personal worldview. Strom relates that our worldview helps us (1) explain why the world is like it is, (2) evaluate things as good or bad, (3) provide mental and emotional peace in times of personal crises, (4) integrate things that seem inconsistent, and (5) adapt to change.[5]

Natural laws and mathematical relationships are not worldview dependent. However, the same mathematics may be used to describe the motion of a mass suspended on a spring, as well as the transient response of the voltage across a capacitor in circuit. The psalmist declared in Psalm 19, "The heavens declare the glory of God; the skies proclaim the work of his hands."[6] In the same way a faithful engineer is led to declare the glory of God through observing the interactions of mathematic and scientific principles used in engineering design. Faithfully educating engineering students attempts to lead students to the same declaration.

Theodore Von Kármán, awarded the 1962 Medal of Science, famously stated, "Scientists study the world as it is, engineers create the world that has never been."[7] VanderLeest further explains that engineering "uses math, science, economics, psychology, and other disciplines to refine the choice of problem, identify constraints, create alternative solutions, and objectively select the optimum solution in the face of trade-offs . . . It is a creative endeavor, a fusion of science and technique."[8] Byker defines a "compleat ingineer" as an engineer who "seeks to integrate all aspects of his or her life; . . . [and who has] made his avocation his vocation." She notes this route takes us past the foot of the cross and the empty tomb.[9]

Like an artist, an engineer emulates God's creative nature. Theologians, mathematicians, and scientists study God and his creation. Engineers seek to apply this knowledge to create solutions for the benefit of society. The engineering design process reflects the creativity of the One who created us in his image. Recognizing this relationship, Dovich uses structural design and materials found in nature to explore engineering

4. Keller and Alsdorf, *Every Good Endeavor*, 157.
5. Strom, "What is a Christian Worldview?," in Downey and Porter, *Christian Worldview and the Academic Disciplines*, 19.
6. Ps 19:1 (NIV).
7. National Science Foundation, "Theodore von Kármán."
8. VanderLeast, "Twenty-Five Years of Christian Engineering."
9. Byker, "Compleat Ingineer."

design principles and observes, "The book of nature gives instruction in physical design principles, economy, functionality, aesthetics, safety, recyclability, and a holistic approach to design. These principles, drawn from the Master Engineer's designs, should be engrained in engineering minds and reflected in every design."[10]

My personal worldview also includes the literal interpretation of the creation account as described in the first chapter of Genesis, a view commonly referred to as young-earth creationism. Based on my reading of Scripture and scientific inquiry, I believe this is a faithful and reasonable interpretation of Scripture and observable evidence. This view conflicts with conventional interpretations of the fossil record, which many scientists believe points to a greater timescale.

Biomimicry, bionics, and bio-inspired design are some of the names of the research area that has inspired an incredible amount of research and inventions based on designs found in nature. From Velcro to prosthetics to cargo aircraft flying in formation like geese, the lessons learned from nature are indisputable. Viewing the original designs as creations of an intelligent mind for purpose and beauty, rather than the product of random processes allows an engineer the freedom to seek the Designer's original intent. (It is interesting that a family of algorithms used in design optimization, machine learning, and signal processing is called "evolutionary algorithms." However, the algorithms depend on a guided process requiring an intelligent coder.)

Engineering leverages mathematics and science and inherits, but is not limited to, the presuppositions of those disciplines. Being an heir to science and mathematics has led to material naturalism as the predominant worldview in the engineering discipline, as evidenced by my colleague Todd's earlier argument. However, secular humanism has a firm foothold as well, and pantheism is insidiously represented by the gods of Technology, Power, and Money.

Material naturalism denies any supernatural intervention in the natural world. The most aggressive material naturalists have been Richard Dawkins and Daniel Dennett, who argue that "the natural sciences are an intellectual superhighway to disbelief in God."[11] Likewise, secular humanists take the lack of supernatural intervention to the logical conclusion that humans are only accountable to themselves. Secular humanists

---

10. Dovich, "Our Creator—The Master Engineer," 10.
11. McGrath, *Theology*, 34.

ground their beliefs "in the assumptions that human beings have evolved enough and are good enough . . . and that human reason and science alone are sufficient to guide appropriate ethical actions."[12]

Some believe reason and science are sufficient to preserve the human race. Elon Musk is an engineer and CEO of SpaceX and Tesla. A recent article discussed his motivation to inhabit Mars: "'The excitement factor' is one part of the reason Musk thinks multi-planetary life will be important in the future. The second reason, he said, is more defensive: 'The Mars thing is really important to the preservation to life as we know it and humanity. It's a life insurance policy.'"[13]

In her 1996 speech "The Compleat Ingineer," based on a seventeenth-century book entitled *The Compleat Angler*, Byker observes that society as consumers of technology, and engineers in particular, are effectively setting up Technology to be the god of this age.[14] She quotes Postman of NYU:

> What we are facing, then, is a series of interconnected delusions, beginning with the belief that technological innovation is the same thing as human progress—which is linked to the delusion that our sufferings and failures are caused by inadequate information—which is linked, in turn to the most serious delusion of all—that it is possible to live without a loom to weave our lives into fabric; that is to say without a transcendent narrative.[15]

In the light of Postman's insight, consider the conclusions of one of the most accomplished contemporary engineers, Ray Kurzweil, with regard to transhumanism:

> Kurzweil said there are 3 stages of the human response to new tech: 1) Wow!, 2) Uh oh!, and 3) What other choice do we have but to move forward? Dr. Kurzweil predicts by the 2030s, we will be cyborgs. Nanorobots the size of blood cells will heal our bodies from the inside—connecting us to a synthetic neo-cortex in the cloud, and to virtual & augmented reality. 'We'll be funnier, more musical, wiser,' he said.[16]

12. Poplin, *Is Reality Secular?*, 116.
13. Dowd, "Elon Musk's Billion Dollar Crusade."
14. Byker, "Compleat Ingineer."
15. Postman, "Making a Living, Making a Life."
16. Dowd, "Elon Musk's Billion Dollar Crusade."

Others (possibly Musk and Kurzweil, as well) are motivated by the age-old gods of Money and Power. A review of the book, *Irresistible: The Rise of Addictive Technology and the Business of Keeping Us Hooked*,[17] explores how artificial intelligence and virtual reality are being used by businesses to achieve "maximally effective addiction," and the "only business constraint may be the loss of a revenue generating consumer as a result."[18] Money and power also drive much of the "publish or perish" mentality of the academic world, as well as many other areas of the engineering discipline, and society in general.

Many, particularly Christian conservatives in the Ozarks, may think Musk and Kurzweil are a few bricks shy of a load. However, both of these engineers have made positive contributions to technology and arguably to society as a whole. Elon Musk's company, Tesla, has been at the forefront of commercializing electric vehicles and has greatly improved energy storage capacity. SpaceX has revolutionized lower-cost space launch for the United States.[19] Ray Kurzweil was ranked eighth among entrepreneurs in the U.S. and has been called the "rightful heir to Thomas Edison" by *Inc.* magazine. He invented the flat-bed scanner, the first synthesizer to accurately reproduce the sound of a grand piano, the first print-to-speech reading machine for the blind, and many other beneficial technologies.[20]

Mark Noll argues, "There is simply nothing humanly possible to study about the created realm that, in principle, leads us away from Jesus Christ."[21] By recognizing "All truth is God's truth," we can, as Saint Augustine stated, "redeem the gold of Egypt."[22] As Creator of all that is visible and invisible, the physical laws, mathematical principles, and scientific truths are part of God's general revelation and are available for all to observe and explore.[23] While engineers and technologists may be motivated by other than Christian worldviews, the engineering principles, theories, and technologies they develop are not inherently evil. Just as Paul rejoiced in Phil 1:15–18 that Christ is preached even by those

---

17. Alter, *Irresistible*.
18. Isaak, "Call Me Irresistible (Or Else)."
19. "Elon Musk," *Forbes*.
20. "Ray Kurzweil."
21. Noll, *Jesus Christ and the Life of the Mind*, 25.
22. Holmes, *Idea of a Christian College*, 63.
23. John 1:1–3.

with false motives, we can rejoice that we know more about our Creator and his marvelous creativity.[24]

THE COLLEGE OF THE OZARKS ENGINEER

Engineering educators' purpose is to engrain professional and technical skills expected of all engineering graduates, as well as other characteristics deemed necessary through discussions with stakeholders. The vision of the College of the Ozarks Engineering Program guides the content and delivery of the curriculum:

> College of the Ozarks engineering graduates will be well versed in engineering fundamentals and a broad range of applications with the abilities necessary to think critically and to see the problem-solving processes from beginning to end. The work-proven and team-oriented graduates will possess the ingenuity, courage, humility, fortitude, accountability and integrity to step up to challenges, adapt to needs, make use of available resources, and serve their company and community to produce results that make a difference.[25]

This vision lives in the shadow of the vision of College of Ozarks, which is "to develop citizens of Christ-like character who are well-educated, hard-working, and patriotic."[26] Together these statements provide the plumb line for faithfully educating engineering students at College of the Ozarks. The characteristics of the envisioned faithfully-educated engineer cannot be instilled solely within the engineering curriculum. The engineering courses, mathematics and science courses, general education courses, work program, and Christian ministries program all play key roles in developing our engineering graduates.

CONTRIBUTION OF THE LIBERAL ARTS

The College of the Ozarks is a liberal arts institution, and the liberal arts have often been unappreciated by engineers. Though I enjoyed some of my general education courses, I considered the time I spent in them as detracting from the time I should spend learning the skills for my future

---

24. Phil 1:15–18.
25. "Program Details," College of the Ozarks.
26. College of the Ozarks, *2021–2022 College Catalog*.

profession. Ironically, I valued my ROTC courses, which focused on leadership, communication, and military history, without realizing they were liberal arts courses that benefited me as an engineer. The liberal arts also facilitate an "ability to be gracious toward others, to demonstrate the personal skills necessary to set others at ease, and to succeed in many areas of life at once."[27] The importance of these qualities in an engineer have been repeatedly affirmed by regional employers we have visited.[28]

Like many Christian liberal arts institutions, the required general education classes at College of the Ozarks include courses in Christian worldview, history, communications, art, as well as patriotic responsibilities. College of the Ozarks is also a federally-recognized work college. The importance of a mature work ethic developed by the work program at the College is discussed by Nowack.[29] The Christian cocurricular program, with its required chapel and convocation attendance, provide dedicated times for students to learn about and reflect on a personal relationship with Jesus Christ and its many facets.

Fant contrasts the Christian use of the word "liberal," which focuses on emptying one's self, to the secular use, which emphasizes the self and his or her "rights."[30] Holmes extends the Christian use of "liberal" to the liberal arts and observes, "Liberal learning leads to the contemplation of God . . . The liberal arts develop the mind's ability to see nature's laws and so to enjoy its order and beauty."[31] Engineering educators recognize the importance of an education more rounded by general education requirements, including those in the liberal arts, as evidenced by the ABET curriculum criterion requirement to include "a broad education component that complements the technical content of the curriculum and is consistent with the program educational objectives."[32]

While a completely integrated educational experience is beyond our capability, our vision for the engineering program is to capitalize on the solid foundation of the existing college courses, as well as the learning and work environments. To help our engineering students recognize the value of people and ideas outside of the engineering discipline, we plan

---

27. Fant, *Liberal Arts*, 56.
28. Nowack and Akers, "An Engineering Program Built Around Work," 3.
29. Nowack and Akers, "An Engineering Program Built Around Work."
30. Fant, *Liberal Arts*, 41.
31. VanZanten, *Joining the Mission*, 18.
32. "Criteria for Accrediting Engineering Programs, 2020–2021," ABET.

to involve curricular material and faculty from other programs in our engineering courses.

As an example, one of the engineering student outcomes required of our program by ABET is "an ability to communicate effectively with a range of audiences."[33] The faculty in the English and Communication Arts programs are experts in communication, so we have incorporated rubrics from their courses to ensure we provide students with consistent expectations between the general education courses and communications assignments within the engineering courses.

The psychology department better understands societal impacts of technology, so we have approached their faculty about guest lecturing to our engineering students about moral and ethical considerations in engineering design. Technology created by engineers affects society and has associated value. Our goal is to help students recognize the value of psychology, beyond just lip service, add legitimacy and depth to the value-laden technology discussion, as well as extend the students' network of friends and mentors.

Just as in 1 Cor 12, Paul draws the analogy between the church and the human body, faithfully-educated engineers have something to offer the body of the College. One of our goals is to teach engineering students to be inquisitive and seek opportunities to improve designs and processes in their environment. Their environment includes the College, which will likely be the target of their ideas for innovative designs. We encourage the College administration, staff, and faculty to be open to engineering students' creativity. Not all of these ideas will get off the ground, but a few may positively impact the College or even the world.

TEACHING PHILOSOPHY

In *What the Best College Teachers Do*, Ken Bain lists six characteristics of outstanding teachers: (1) They know their subjects well; (2) they treat teaching as a serious intellectual endeavor; (3) They favor objectives that embody the kind of thinking and acting expected for life; (4) they create a "natural critical learning environment;" (5) they reflect a strong trust in students, display openness, and encourage their students to be similarly reflective and candid; and (6) assessment of students flows from primary

---

33. "Criteria for Accrediting Engineering Programs, 2020–2021," ABET.

learning objectives.³⁴ These qualities, especially the third and fifth, are even more effective when viewed from a Christian perspective. Regarding helping students form moral meaning in ways that last, Garber adds that students need to pursue "a relationship with a teacher whose life incarnates the worldview the student is learning to embrace."³⁵ As Paul wrote, "Whether, then, you eat or drink or whatever you do, do all to the glory of God."³⁶

In the conduct of our profession as Christian faculty, we find ourselves rapidly switching roles from salesman, to customer service agent, to concierge, to manufacturing process optimizer, to trainer, to quality inspector, to warden or judge, to mentor, to friend, to career/life coach, to make-shift pre-marital counselor, to poorly prepared emergency pastor, to collaborator, to friend, and to brother or sister in Christ. On the surface this is impossible, or at least unreasonable! Upon reflection this is no more than what our Lord and Savior Jesus Christ offered us in that he is our brother, Creator, teacher, judge, substitutional atonement, companion and friend. It is our call as Christian faculty to imitate Christ as we fulfill these diverse and manifold roles.³⁷

Given my calling and what I have gleaned reading about and learning from great teachers, as well as serving as a teacher, below are some practical steps I strive to incorporate in curriculum development and instruction. Some of these areas are outside my comfort zone or nearly impossible for me; however, "I am confident of this very thing, that He who began a good work in [me] will complete it by the day of Christ Jesus."³⁸

As faithful educators, we are to "sift all content through a biblical worldview . . . [o]ne shaped by the biblical narrative."³⁹ This is not to be "window dressing" but to keep the truth up-front and center. It is also beneficial for students to recognize that faculty enjoy reading and studying the Bible. It is "the model for literary and aesthetic enjoyment."⁴⁰

---

34. See Bain, *What the Best College Teachers Do*, particularly chapter 1.
35. Garber, *Fabric of Faithfulness*, 185.
36. 1 Cor 10:31 (NASB).
37. Anson, "Philosophy of Teaching."
38. Phil 1:6 (NASB).
39. Schuurman, "What Makes an Education Christian?"
40. Dockery and George, *Great Tradition of Christian Thinking*, 25.

It is important to foster a safe learning environment that encourages inquisitiveness and where students feel valued. In 2016, the *New York Times Magazine* published the results of a two-year Google study of one hundred and eighty teams. It concluded, "Google's data indicated that psychological safety, more than anything else, was critical to making a team work."[41]

Helping students turn brick walls into hurdles is important for this generation of students. They have access to an incredible amount of information but do not know how to determine what is important. Following the lead of Claude Shannon, the father of information theory, "Almost every problem that you come across is befuddled with all kinds of extraneous data of one sort or another," Shannon said, "and if you can bring this problem down into the main issues, you can see more clearly what you're trying to do."[42]

Engineers tackle projects with no "book answer." There will be failure, which provides rich mentoring opportunities. These failures can be valuable learning experiences if students are mentored through the process of identifying the gaps in theoretical understanding that precipitated the failure and then iterate through the design process. Johanne Kepler, a devout Christian and German scientist and astronomer in the seventeenth century, is best known for his laws of planetary motion. His original attempt at determining the orbit of Mars deviated from the observed data by eight minutes. His response to this perceived failure was, "it is fitting that we should with thankful mind both acknowledge and honor this benefit of God . . . Because they could not be ignored, these eight minutes alone have led the way to the entire reformation of astronomy."[43]

Students need to see spiritual disciplines modeled and discussed. For example, observe a Sabbath rest. VanZanten argues that a Sabbath rest is the "first and most essential means of keeping your life together."[44] God set the pattern for a Sabbath rest in the creation week: "For in six days the LORD made the heavens and the earth, the sea and everything that is in them, and He rested on the seventh day; for that reason the LORD

---

41. Duhigg, "What Google Learned."

42. Soni, "11 Life Lessons."

43. Gingerich, "Kepler," in Lawrence and McCartney, *Mathematicians and their Gods*, 84.

44. VanZanten, *Joining the Mission*, 194–95.

blessed the Sabbath day and made it holy."[45] In the same way God blesses the tithe, in that the remaining 90% goes further than the 100% could without our obedience. I expect the same is true of taking a Sabbath rest.

Similarly, casual discussions about marriage and family are common before class. For example, following a colleague's recommendation, I have told students not to expect responses from me on Friday nights, as Friday nights are reserved for date night with my wife. Many students have not experienced healthy family environments, and those that have may not fully appreciate how they have been blessed until they see it modeled in others' lives.

REFLECTION

In *A Christian's Secret to a Happy Life*, Smith reflects on the stories of how Ulysses and Orpheus respectively overcame the fatally enticing songs of the sirens in the ancient Greek poem, *The Odyssey*. To avoid the danger, Ulysses instructed his men to plug their ears with bee's wax, while he had himself tied to the mast. When he pleaded to be released to join the sirens, his men tightened the cords. Orpheus gained a better victory by enchanting his men with sweeter music than the songs of the sirens. As a result, Orpheus and his men sailed by with contempt for the sirens rather than fatal attraction.[46]

Education with a Christian worldview should be "sweeter music." The natural principles and application examples are richer and deeper, knowing the One who spoke the world into existence and created us in his image has hidden "Easter eggs" throughout creation and delights when we find them. In the words of Proverbs, "It is the glory of God to conceal a matter, but the glory of kings to search out a matter."[47]

BIBLIOGRAPHY

Alter, Adam. *Irresistible: The Rise of Addictive Technology and the Business of Keeping Us Hooked*. New York: Penguin, 2017.
Anson, Scott. "Philosophy of Teaching and Student and Peer Mentorship: A Christian Perspective." Presented at the Christian Engineering Conference (2017), Cedarville

---

45. Exod 20:11 (NASB).
46. Smith, *Christian's Secret to a Happy Life*, 205.
47. Prov 25:2 (NASB).

FAITHFUL EDUCATION IN ENGINEERING

University. https://digitalcommons.cedarville.edu/cgi/viewcontent.cgi?article=10 01&context=christian_engineering_conference&httpsredir=1&referer=.

Bain, Ken. *What the Best College Teachers Do*. Cambridge, MA: Harvard University Press, 2004.

Byker, Gaylen. "The Compleat Ingineer." Presented at the Christian Engineering Education Conference (1996), Messiah College. https://www.christianengineering.org/publications/cec-proceedings.

"Criteria for Accrediting Engineering Programs, 2020–2021." ABET. https://www.abet.org/accreditation/accreditation-criteria/criteria-for-accrediting-engineering-programs-2020-2021/.

Dockery, David S. and Timothy, George. *The Great Tradition of Christian Thinking: A Student's Guide*. Wheaton, IL: Crossway, 2012.

Dovich, Laurel. "Our Creator—The Master Engineer." Presented at the 30th International Seminar on the Integration of Faith and Learning (2002), Seoul, South Korea. http://circle.adventist.org/files/CD2008/CD1/ict/vol_30/30cc_035-054.pdf.

Dowd, Maureen. "Elon Musk's Billion Dollar Crusade to Stop the AI Apocalypse." *Vanity Fair* (April 2017). https://www.kurzweilai.net/vanity-fair-elon-musks-billion-dollar-crusade-to-stop-the-ai-apocalypse.

Downey, Deane E.D. and Stanley E. Porter. *Christian Worldview and the Academic Disciplines: Crossing the Academy*. Eugene, OR: Wipf and Stock, 2009.

Duhigg, Charles. "What Google Learned From Its Quest to Build the Perfect Team." *New York Times Magazine*. https://www.nytimes.com/2016/02/28/magazine/what-google-learned-from-its-quest-to-build-the-perfect-team.html.

"Elon Musk." *Forbes*. https://www.forbes.com/profile/elon-musk/?sh=5af6cf117999.

Fant, Gene C. *The Liberal Arts: A Student's Guide*. Wheaton, IL: Crossway, 2012.

Garber, Steven. *The Fabric of Faithfulness*. Downers Grove, IL: InterVarsity, 2007.

Holmes, Arthur F. *The Idea of a Christian College*. Grand Rapids: Eerdmans, 1987.

Isaak, Jim. "Call Me Irresistible (Or Else)." *Technology and Society*. https://technologyandsociety.org/call-me-irresistible-or-else/.

Keller, Timothy and Katherine Alsdorf. *Every Good Endeavor: Connecting Your Work to God's Work*. New York: Penguin, 2012.

Lawrence, Snezana and Mark McCartney. *Mathematicians and their Gods*. Oxford: Oxford University Press, 2015.

McGrath, Alistair. *Theology: The Basics*, 2nd ed. Malden: Blackwell, 2008.

National Science Foundation. "Theodore von Kármán (1881–1963)." https://www.nsf.gov/news/special_reports/medalofscience50/vonkarman.jsp.

Noll, Mark. *Jesus Christ and the Life of the Mind*. Grand Rapids: Eerdmans, 2013.

Nowack, Mark and Geoff Akers. "An Engineering Program Built Around Work." Presented at the Christian Engineering Conference (2017), Cedarville University.

Poplin, Mary. *Is Reality Secular?: Testing the Assumption of Four Global Worldviews*. Downers Grove, IL: InterVarsity, 2014.

Postman, Neil. "Making a Living, Making a Life: Technology Reconsidered." *The College Board Review* 176–77 (1995): 8–13.

"Program Details." College of the Ozarks, Engineering Program. https://www.cofo.edu/Academics/Majors-Minors/Engineering/Program-Details.

"Ray Kurzweil." https://www.kurzweilai.net/about-ray-kurzweil.

Schuurman, Derek. "What Makes an Education Christian?" http://www.mpk-indonesia.org/uncategorized/2682/.

Smith, Hannah Whitall. *A Christian's Secret of a Happy Life*. New Kensington: Whitaker House, 2005.

Soni, Jimmy. "11 Life Lessons From History's Most Underrated Genius." *Forge*. https://forge.medium.com/10-000-hours-with-claude-shannon-12-lessons-on-life-and-learning-from-a-genius-e8b9297bee8f.

VanderLeest, S.H. "Twenty-Five Years of Christian Engineering: A Literature Survey." Presented at the Christian Engineering Conference (2017), Cedarville University.

VanZanten, Susan. *Joining the Mission: A Guide for (Mainly) New College Faculty*. Grand Rapids: Eerdmans, 2011.

Afterword

SHOW ME
The Way We Learn Forms the Way We Live

STEVEN GARBER

I STILL REMEMBER THE WARM chocolate chip cookies, and yes, the glass of fresh, cold milk, a wonderful gift of unexpected hospitality at the beautifully-imagined hotel on the campus of the College of the Ozarks—and then, as now, I pondered "why"?

For a few days I was a guest of the college, speaking to the faculty at the annual August retreat, coming together as they were to consider again their calling as professors in a school that has carved out a unique sense of vocation as an institution, one that believes in a pedagogy that twines together head, heart, and hands, offering students a curricular vision formed by a more coherent understanding of the meaning of their lives and learning, and the labor that will be their work in the world.

Walking around, listening in, it is clear that this school has imagined into being a different way to teach, and to learn. Born as it was of a desire to serve southwestern Missouri, especially the population that had little access to higher education, and therefore for whom a "work-your-way-through" education made college possible, over time it has developed a pedagogical commitment to a way of learning that makes the College of the Ozarks almost unique, believing that the best learning, the truest learning is always over the shoulder and through the heart.

Animal science students learning in and out of the classroom, reading their texts and then working on the College's farms, milking cows and raising beef cattle; and the same principle is true for business students, who learn the meaning of the marketplace by managing the College's hotel and restaurant— and offering warm cookies and cold milk to guests! The examples go on and on, across the curriculum.

None of this should surprise anyone who knows that Missouri is the "Show Me" state, known for more than a century as the place where ideas must have legs. As Congressman Willard Duncan Vandiver said in an address in Philadelphia in 1899, "I come from a state that raises corn and cotton and cockleburs and Democrats, and frothy eloquence neither convinces nor satisfies me. I am from Missouri. You have got to show me."

While that history is Missouri's, and of course is more pugnacious and promotional, the truth is ancient and universal, threading its way through centuries and cultures. As sons of Adam and daughters of Eve, born of the biblical metanarrative, human beings as human beings have at the very heart of their reason-for-being a responsibility for knowledge. Written into our human vocation is a way of knowing that has moral and pedagogical implications, which is why the primordial temptation is both epistemological and moral, the tree of knowledge of good and evil, setting before Everyman and Everywoman this most perennial of all questions: what will you do with what you know? All day long, for every son of Adam and every daughter of Eve, that is the question of life.

In the Hebrew and Christian tradition, which is the world and worldview from which the College of the Ozarks comes into being, the words themselves are our teachers. From Genesis on, *yada* means to have knowledge of, means to have responsibility to, means to have care for— making sense of marriage and the marketplace, of justice and mercy, of the whole of life. If one knows, one must care; and if we do not care, we do not know. In the gospels, echoing across the years are these words of the first chapter of John, "The Word became flesh and dwelt among us." The incarnation is not only the heart of Christian theology, but pedagogically genius, the gift of the Rabbi of all rabbis to all with ears to hear. Words must become flesh for us to understand them. Simply said, we do not understand unless we see; we must see if the words mean something, if they can be and will be worked out in life. Yes, show me.

But if this embodied learning is a deep, profound truth, grounded and rooted in the most ancient vision of knowledge, then the best teachers of the church have given this to us in their own ways. Take Augustine of Hippo, a professor and a pastor, who understood that it is only when head and heart and hands meet that we become most fully human. We are always and everywhere people who look for love in all the wrong places; misdirected affections have consequences for the way we love, learn and labor, for the whole of life. And because our loves define us, they must be ordered rightly if we are to flourish. One of his greatest contributions was setting forth the moral meaning of "affections," i.e. what we care most about, the commitments that form who we are and why we are, and therefore what we do with our lives.

If it is implicit in *Confessions*, this becomes explicit in *On Christian Doctrine*, which is sometimes translated as "On Christian Teaching." In Book IV, he offers his own *paideia*, arguing that teaching is incarnational at its heart. Moving beyond Cicero, who had emphasized that the mere study of rules was insufficient for the education of the orator, Augustine went further, maintaining that the rules are not necessary at all. "For boys do not need the art of grammar which teaches correct speech if they have the opportunity to grow up and live among men who speak correctly."

A fascinating look into this truth comes in his letter, "To Dioscorus, a Student." A young Greek who had traveled to Carthage to be educated in Latin literature—in Cicero's *Tuscalan Disputations*—Dioscorus wrote Augustine about questions that had come up in his studies. Perhaps remembering his own student days in Carthage where he had also studied Cicero, being converted by him and to him, Augustine wrote a lengthy reply, taking the student very seriously, understanding that the student was making sense of life for life, that his definitions of meaning and morality were being formed, "his set dispositions to behave in one way rather than another" were being decided. Even while chiding Dioscorus for the complexity and number of his questions—"You must have intended to wall me in, or even bury me completely, with your countless multitude of questions ... the length of time would exhaust my attention and wear out my fingers"—Augustine asks, "What good has the reading of all these dialogues done if it hasn't helped you define and attain the goal of all your actions?"

The letter is longer, with surprising thoughtfulness the master teacher responding to a young student; but at the end, after pressing Dioscorus to deeper, truer reasons for life and learning, he finishes with this, "Attract them by your way of life." Simply, if profoundly, he is saying, "Words have to become flesh, if they are to be understood." At some point, my young friend, all that you are learning must be seen in the way you live. Show them.

Centuries later, Bernard of Clairvaux made the same argument for his time and place, seeing the integral relationship of knowledge to life, of love to learning as he formed communities of Christ-followers throughout Europe.

> There are those who seek knowledge for the sake of knowledge; that is Curiosity.
> There are those who seek knowledge to be known by others; that is Vanity.
> There are those who seek knowledge in order to serve; that is Love.

Most of a millennia later, Michael Polanyi, the scientist who became a philosopher, chose to leave his research laboratory because he had become persuaded that "ideas have legs," for blessing and for curse, and was certain that a deeply-flawed way of knowing was at the heart of the modern world, and the implosion of European culture with its two wars that ravaged the first half of the twentieth century. The disembodied knowledge at the heart of the Enlightenment, severing facts from values, was a million miles from the "personal knowledge" that he believed was central to human being. And this truer knowing, a "tacit knowledge" that is behind and before the scientific-become-scientistic knowing born of the fragmenting "objective" and "subjective" Cartesian dualism, had not served the world well, being untrue to the way knowing honestly is and is supposed to be. And so he argued for a kind of knowing that is formed by "indwelling," by the very human work of living into what we know, most fully understood through a master-to-apprentice learning, teaching what is to be known and how it is be lived. As his literary executor, the theologian Thomas Torrance argued that Polanyi's vision was deeply incarnational, seeing into who we are and how we learn with profoundly-formed insight.

Not so far from the College of the Ozarks, just under an hour by car, is an architectural wonder brought into being by this same vision of learning. Known as the Thorncrown Chapel in Eureka Springs, Arkansas, it is the work of the imaginative heart of Fay Jones, a native of the Ozarks who apprenticed himself to Frank Lloyd Wright, perhaps America's best-known architect who had earned fame and fortune in Chicago for his "Prairie School" of architecture, twining together human beings with their environment in remarkably new ways, an "organic architecture" he called it. After a lifetime of Lake Michigan winters, he wanted more sunshine, and moved to Arizona, bringing into being the Taliesin Fellowship as a way of teaching the next generation what he knew about the art of design-and-build. Not undergraduates, these were working architects who wanted more, and were willing to come and live with Wright for a time, literally learning over-his-shoulder, and through-his-heart. A famous photo captures this pedagogy, with Wright at his large table, pen and paper before him, and a group of practicing architects behind him, wanting to see the master at work.

Fay Jones was one of those students, returning to his beloved home in the Ozarks, to his people and his place, eventually becoming the dean of the University of Arkansas' School of Architecture, to imagine and design ways to live that remembered to remember where they were from, with its distinctive mountains and skies and trees. Having learned all he could, Jones made his teacher's vision his own through a lifetime of great work, in his own vocation "indwelling" Wright's vision. As one writer notes, "simplicity of construction, use of native materials, attention to crafted details, and seamless integration of building to site"—and the Thorncrown Chapel is a uniquely beautiful architectural embodiment of those principles, with its natural light in and through its glass structure, "seeing" the woods as one worshiped. Having apprenticed himself to a master, in his own work he lived into beliefs about the world of the built environment that were uniquely his. At the end of his career, Jones was honored by his peers in the Association of Collegiate Schools of Architecture who awarded him the title of ACSA Distinguished Professor, having become a master himself.

Why should we be surprised that the truest truths are actually written into the grain of the universe? *Show me. To know means to care. Words must become flesh. Ideas have legs. The truest learning is over-the-shoulder, and though the heart.*

We learn that way, all of us; at least if it is true learning we are engaged in. Books are books, and I have a house full of them; it is not too much to say that I love books, and love them more. But books only take us so far. As the novelist and essayist Walker Percy noted with a warning lurking around the corner of everyone's life, we can "get all A's and still flunk life." Those words seem so contemporary with words that make sense within the modern academy; but in reality, the observation is as old as old can be. The Hebrew world and worldview taught this, in fact it was based upon this; and the very first words of Jesus, what we call "the Sermon on the Mount," finish with this same conclusion. In sum, he says to the ages, "There will be two responses to what I have said to you today. Some of you will have listened, and will put what I have said into practice. When the rains come and the winds blow, because your houses are built on rock, they will stand. Others of you will have listened to me, but will not put what I have said into practice. And when the rains come and the winds blow, your houses, built on sand, will wash away." There is something written into what it means to be human and holy that is formed by the integral connection of belief to behavior, of knowing to doing, of learning to life.

The College of the Ozarks is its own experiment in education, getting some things right, and I am sure, other things not-so-right. But its choice to create a college with a curriculum where ideas must have legs, where what is learned in the classroom must be worked out in life, is rooted in a pedagogy which is grounded in the reality of the world that is really there, the only universe that we have, the one in which everyone everywhere lives and moves, the one in which we all are human beings, where "show me" is what we all want, and what we all need—if we are going to believe what we see and hear to be true, which is the reason for being for this college, formed as it is by the commitments and loves of Christian faith, hope and love.

Steven Garber is a husband and father and grandfather who has lived among his friends and flowers in his Virginia home for over thirty years. A teacher of many people in many places, he is the author of several books, his most recent, *The Seamless Life: A Tapestry of Love and Learning, Worship and Work*. In addition, he serves as Senior Fellow for Vocation and the Common Good for the M.J. Murdock Charitable Trust, and as a Senior Advisor to the Economics of Mutuality, a project of the Mars Corporation.

Appendix

Thrive Pathway

On the following pages is our *Thrive Pathway* booklet, which employs the developmental framework discussed in chapter 2 in our institutional context, guiding students through our character development program and enhancing their learning in the academic, work education, and co-curricular programs on campus. We hope this paradigm encourages you as you cultivate your own faithful education programs and that you are able to make use of what we have learned at our institution as we all pour into the lives of our students.

A PATHWAY TO
THRIVE

THE KEETER CENTER FOR CHARACTER EDUCATION
COLLEGE *of the* OZARKS®

OVERVIEW

WHAT IS THE KEETER CENTER FOR CHARACTER EDUCATION?

The purpose of The Keeter Center for Character Education (KCCE) is to provide opportunities for students to develop in leadership, character, and service as they consider their calling and direction in life.

THE KEETER CENTER FOR CHARACTER EDUCATION
COLLEGE *of the* OZARKS®

The key is a symbol identifying life-changing opportunities at the College which unlock new pathways. In the bit of the key you will see the shape of the cross. This reminds us of Paul's teaching that character and hope come through struggle and suffering. The bow of the key has three interlocking teardrops symbolizing the Trinity. One way students can unlock a pathway is participation in the THRIVE initiative.

WHAT IS THRIVE?

THRIVE offers a framework for everyone at the College to look at growth in four phases: TILL, ROOT, GROW, and FRUIT. This process echoes what the Apostle Paul describes in Romans 5:3-5.

Paul's description is helpful for several reasons. First, it helps us value struggle (TILL). It also helps us understand that God's growth never ends but continues in a cycle. Finally, Paul illustrates that the goal of all our growth is not just character but hope. Hope is the recognition of and response to God in all situations. As we work through these stages in our lives, we are able to enjoy the FRUIT of God's presence, which allows us to THRIVE.

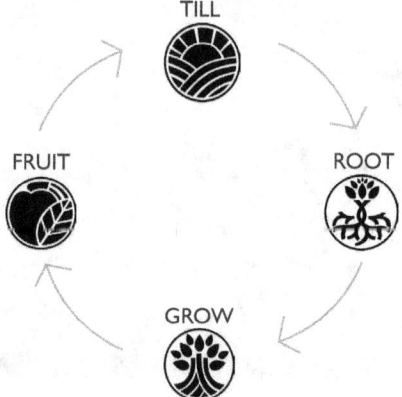

INITIATIVE

WHAT IS THE PATHWAY TO THRIVE?

Below, you will find a brief description of how these phases fit together and how the process works out while you are at the College:

Phase 1

TILL invites you to embrace challenging situations and be transformed by them, much like a plow turns over hard soil before planting. This phase challenges you to consider how your rigorous academic work and other experiences at the College will form you.

Phase 2

ROOT encourages you to reflect on your God-given identity, gifts, and abilities and to consider how the College's five-fold mission can support your growth. When you identify these qualities, you can ROOT more fully into your leadership and character and address places you would like to grow. Our goal for you during this phase is self-discovery, which allows you to push the ROOTS of your beliefs deeper.

Phase 3

GROW challenges you to consider how God uses struggle and community to help you GROW. During this phase, you may partner with a faculty or staff guide to consider how you've changed and what type of community you need in order to continue to GROW.

Phase 4

FRUIT empowers you to consider the character-based question that you have encountered throughout the THRIVE Pathway: "What do I have to offer society?" This question challenges you to identify the character, relationships, leadership, and learning you acquired at the College, while also encouraging you to recognize these qualities. The FRUIT of your College experience is meant to benefit other people in your family, workplace, community, and nation.

> **" WE REJOICE IN OUR SUFFERINGS, KNOWING THAT SUFFERING PRODUCES ENDURANCE, ENDURANCE PRODUCES CHARACTER, AND CHARACTER PRODUCES HOPE. "**
>
> Romans 5:3-5

CORE PROGRAM REQUIREMENTS

The THRIVE Pathway consists of eight CORE requirement programs and a variety of other EXPLORE opportunities that encourage you to invest in the five-fold mission of the College. This provides a clear direction for you to grow in leadership, character, and service, while also maturing in your calling.

START WITH THE CORE REQUIREMENT

 TILL
- ☐ 1   BASE CAMP / 1st YEAR EXPERIENCE
- ☐ 2   CHARACTER CAMP

 ROOT
- ☐ 3   THE CALL
- ☐ 4   MICRO-CONVOCATIONS

 GROW
- ☐ 5   BIG QUESTION COURSE
- ☐ 6   THE GIFT
- ☐ 7   FACULTY AND STAFF GUIDES

 FRUIT
- ☐ 8   CHRISTIAN WORLDVIEW II

FIVE-FOLD OPPORTUNITIES

Students who complete both the CORE requirements and EXPLORE opportunities in each area of the five-fold mission will be recognized as a Keeter Center for Character Education Leader in Society recipient for the investment they made in themselves.

CHOOSE TO EXPLORE OPPORTUNITIES

Five-Fold Mission — If you accomplish one in each category, you will have completed/accomplished the Thrive Pathway.

ACADEMIC
- ☐ Consistent Academic Excellence (Dean's or President's List)
- ☐ Present Original Research, Writing, or Creative Work at Academic Conference
- ☐ Publish Original Research or Creative Work in an Academic Journal
- ☐ Base Camp Leader
- ☐ Admission to Graduate School

CULTURAL
- ☐ Participation in the S. Truett Cathy Poverty Summit
- ☐ Participation in a Keeter Center for Character Education Spring Forum
- ☐ Participation in a Campus Musical or Play
- ☐ Character Camp Parent
- ☐ Club Leadership (President or Vice President)

VOCATIONAL
- ☐ Work Outcomes Growth that culminates in at least a 4.0 on the Work Outcomes Rubric
- ☐ Leadership in an On-Campus Work Station
- ☐ Participation in the HUNT Vocational Exploration Program
- ☐ Team Captain Athletics
- ☐ Major-based Internship

CHRISTIAN
- ☐ Night to Shine Participation
- ☐ Spring Break Service Trip Participation
- ☐ International Mission Trip Participation
- ☐ Small Group Training
- ☐ Club Leadership (BSU, Chi Alpha, CCM, LDT Council, or FCA)

PATRIOTIC
- ☐ Patriotic Education Travel Trip (Washington D.C. or Abroad)
- ☐ Participation in Bobcat GOLD
- ☐ Completing the Civil Rights Course
- ☐ Service Academy Leadership Conference
- ☐ Serve locally for at least 20 hours in one year

FRESHMAN

Each spring, farmers take plows into the fields to TILL the ground. Through the process of TILLING, plows loosen the soil, rejuvenate it, and prepare it for a new crop.

College of the Ozarks built its student programming to encourage students to experience a similar TILLING during their first year. Unlike many colleges, College of the Ozarks expects students to work, take rigorous academic courses, and participate in additional community activities, like Chapel and Convocations. Each of these programs cultivates Christ-like character in students as they build resilience, responsibility, and courage.

By submitting to this process, students transform in a way that allows the soil of their lives to be rich and ready to ROOT into their God-given identities and the five-fold mission of the College.

THRIVE PATHWAY

CORE REQUIREMENTS

- BASE CAMP / 1ST YEAR EXPERIENCE
- CHARACTER CAMP

EXPLORE OPPORTUNITIES

- 1st YEAR COMMUNITIES
- INTRAMURALS
- STUDENTS' U ACTIVITIES
- SERVICE PROJECTS
- CHRISTIAN CLUBS

What is THRIVE?

THRIVE is an initiative sponsored by The Keeter Center for Character Education that invests in opportunities that allow students to become citizens of Christ-like character. THRIVE is more than a program in that it provides a framework that allows students to be transformed in the process of TILLING, ROOTING, GROWING, and FRUITING.

Thrive Pathway

A series of programs the College offers, the THRIVE Pathway helps students navigate personal growth and enjoy the outcome of character: THRIVING. The purpose of this program is to encourage students to leverage their character growth to encourage themselves, their families, their communities, and our nation to THRIVE.

> **"** STRUGGLE PRODUCES ENDURANCE, ENDURANCE... CHARACTER, AND CHARACTER...HOPE. **"**
>
> Romans 5:4-5

ROOT

SOPHOMORE

ROOTS ground trees in their places, ground them during intense storms. ROOTS also allow trees to reach water deep in the soil that allows them to grow even in the midst of severe droughts.

Our hope for students during their second year at the College is that they ROOT more fully into their God-given identities and gifts as they benefit from the ROOTS of the College: the Academic, Christian, Cultural, Patriotic, and Vocational goals. As students consider their callings and how the College's mission can empower them, they ROOT and can withstand whatever storms and droughts they may face while also providing a refuge for those in need.

THRIVE PATHWAY

CORE REQUIREMENTS
- MICRO-CONVOS
- THE CALL

EXPLORE OPPORTUNITIES
- NIGHT TO SHINE SERVICE
- SMALL GROUP TRAINING
- MUSICAL/PLAY
- CLUB LEADERSHIP
- SERVE LOCALLY

Micro-Convocations

Micro-convocations are offered five times per semester. They help students grow ROOTS by considering different virtues that contribute to leadership and character growth. These convocations are hosted by faculty and staff members who share with students their own stories about the challenges of life, leadership, and character. To complete the THRIVE Pathway, students participate in five micro-convocations.

The CALL

Offered twice per year, the CALL Leadership Retreat, which is hosted by the Leadership Development Track, offers students the opportunity to ROOT into their God-given abilities, strengths, and identities. While at the overnight retreat, students consider their callings, learn practical ways to influence others, and serve in their communities.

> **"** CONTINUE TO LIVE YOUR LIVES IN HIM, ROOTED AND BUILT UP IN HIM, STRENGTHENED IN THE FAITH, AND OVERFLOWING WITH THANKFULNESS. **"**
>
> Colossians 2:6-7

JUNIOR

A THRIVING tree has deep ROOTS which allow it to GROW in times of drought and plenty. As a tree GROWS, it offers a sanctuary for all sorts of birds and animals by providing shelter, food, and protection for them. Out of the tree's ROOTEDNESS and GROWTH, others benefit.

Our hope for students during their third year parallels this process. Students' personal GROWTH is not simply for them. God's gift of GROWTH empowers students to consider how they can protect, nourish, and care for others. This applies in all contexts, but especially in their families, communities, and nation. As citizens of Christ-like character, students learn to pursue what is true, good, and just in themselves and others.

THRIVE PATHWAY

CORE REQUIREMENTS

- BIG Q COURSES*
- THE GIFT*

*These CORE opportunities are also available your fourth year.

EXPLORE OPPORTUNITIES

- S. TRUETT CATHY POVERTY SUMMIT
- CHARACTER FORUMS
- THE HUNT
- BASE CAMP LEADER
- INTERNSHIP
- PATRIOTIC TRIP

Big Question Courses

The Big Question courses challenge students to reflect on societal issues affecting the world. As students consider the reality and ramifications of these issues on society, they employ an ethical lens to discern how they, as citizens of Christ-like character, should respond. Although the subject matter for these courses changes, the goal remains the same: to empower students to ethically reason and faithfully address issues that impact our culture. To complete the THRIVE Pathway, students participate in one of these courses.

The Gift

The Gift, hosted by the Career Center, is a full-day retreat for upperclassmen that challenges students to consider their callings. Through a variety of workshops, students reflect on their work education program experiences as they develop personal mission statements, construct sets of core values, and build digital portfolios that they can share with potential employers.

> **AS EACH HAS RECEIVED A GIFT, USE IT TO SERVE ONE ANOTHER, AS GOOD STEWARDS OF GOD'S VARIED GRACE.**
> — 1 Peter 4:10

SENIOR

TILLING, ROOTING, and GROWING leads to one thing in a plant: its FRUIT. The FRUIT is the goal because FRUIT allows a plant to reproduce itself in other places.

Our hope for students, as they finish at the College, is that they take this transformative process of character development with them and bear FRUIT in the places God calls them to be. The College's investment in each of these women and men recognizes that they, as citizens of Christ-like character, will ultimately be the ones who lead our nation and world. Thus, as students make small choices in college to THRIVE, they embody Heraclitus' ancient maxim:

"The content of your character is your choice. Day by day, what you choose, what you think, and what you do is who you become."

THRIVE PATHWAY

CORE REQUIREMENTS
- WORLDVIEW II
- FACULTY AND STAFF GUIDES

EXPLORE OPPORTUNITIES
- CIVIL RIGHTS COURSE
- CHARACTER FORUM
- MISSION TRIP
- BASE CAMP LEADER
- CHARACTER CAMP PARENT
- THE HUNT

Worldview II

Facilitated by the Biblical and Theological Studies faculty, Worldview II provides a capstone experience that challenges students to consider how their academic majors intersect with their callings, work, and faith. In addition, students grapple with their responsibilities to live out their common Christian vocation — to pursue what is good, true, and beautiful — in the midst of a culture that is decaying.

Faculty and Staff Guides

Faculty and Staff Guides accompany upperclassmen as they complete the final steps of the THRIVE Pathway. As Guides engage with students, they help students consider what they have to offer the world by reflecting with the students about their work, character, leadership, and service growth through the College's programs.

> "REMAIN IN ME, AS I REMAIN IN YOU. NO BRANCH CAN BEAR FRUIT BY ITSELF; IT MUST REMAIN IN THE VINE. NEITHER CAN YOU BEAR FRUIT UNLESS YOU REMAIN IN ME."
> — John 15:4

13

THE KEETER CENTER FOR CHARACTER EDUCATION

THE FIVE GOALS OF THE KEETER CENTER FOR CHARACTER EDUCATION

The purpose is to provide programs and activities that enhance the development of character and good citizenship. In so doing, the Center reflects the principle upon which College of the Ozarks was established: character in young people is best developed from an education that includes the head, the heart, and the hands.

- To reflect the College's five-fold mission emphasizing academic, Christian, vocational, cultural, and patriotic growth, and to provide society with productive, responsible citizens.
- To promote basic Judeo-Christian values such as honesty, respect for and service to others, good citizenship, generosity, honor, courage, wise use of time and talents, and work ethic.
- To serve as a resource for administrators, teachers, and parents as they seek to fulfill their responsibilities as partners in the character-building process.
- To publicize information on character education.
- To serve as a model for those throughout the country who have the desire to establish similar centers or programs.

If you have any questions or would like information on the program, please reach out to Andrew Bolger, abolger@cofo.edu.

www.ingramcontent.com/pod-product-compliance
Lightning Source LLC
Chambersburg PA
CBHW071148300426
44113CB00009B/1126